XS 엑세스 Hybrid

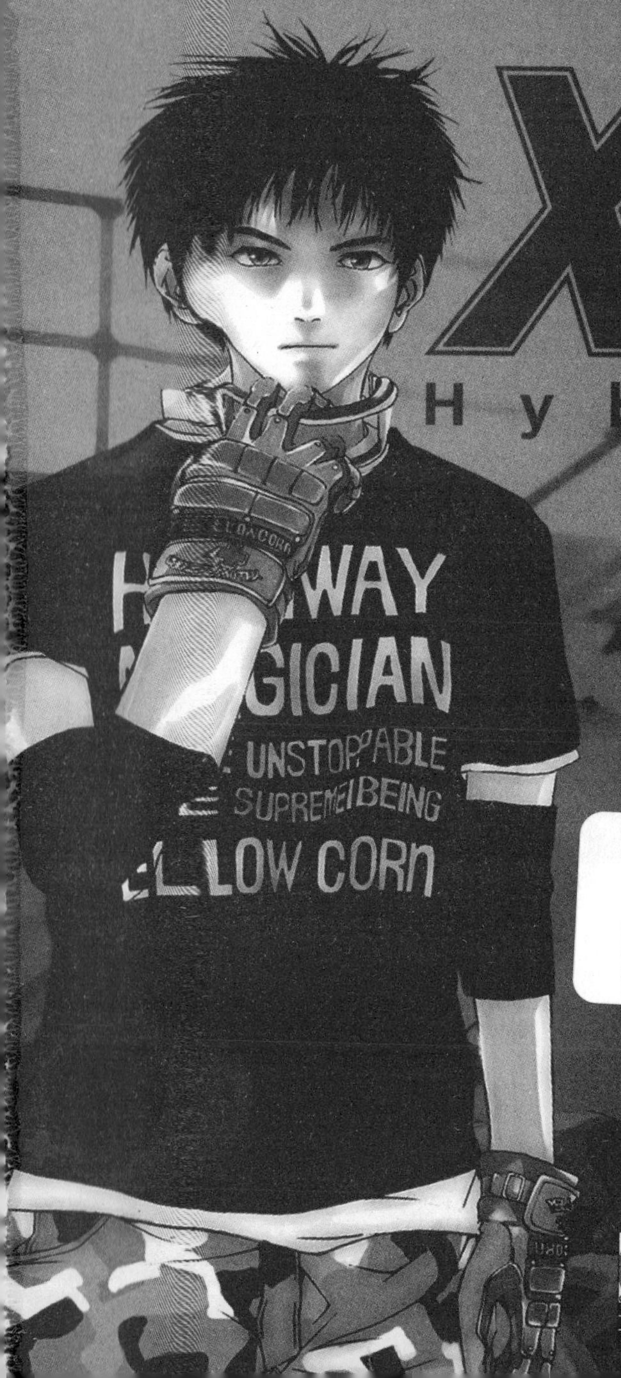

STORY AND ART
SONG JI-HYUNG

TRANSLATION
JAY SO

LETTERING
KATHRYN RENTA

DARK HORSE MANHWA

1st X Contents

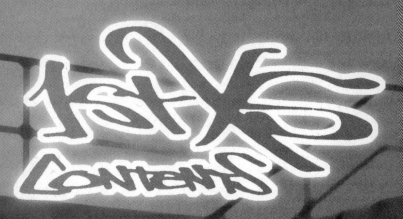

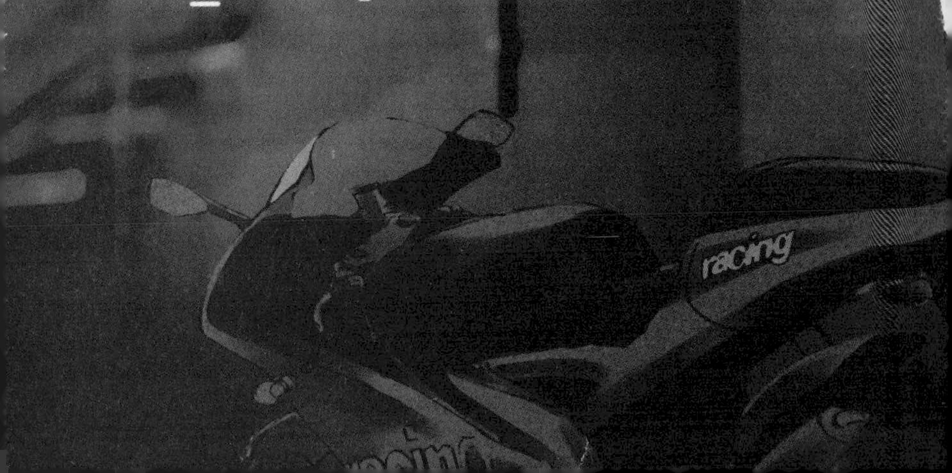
racing

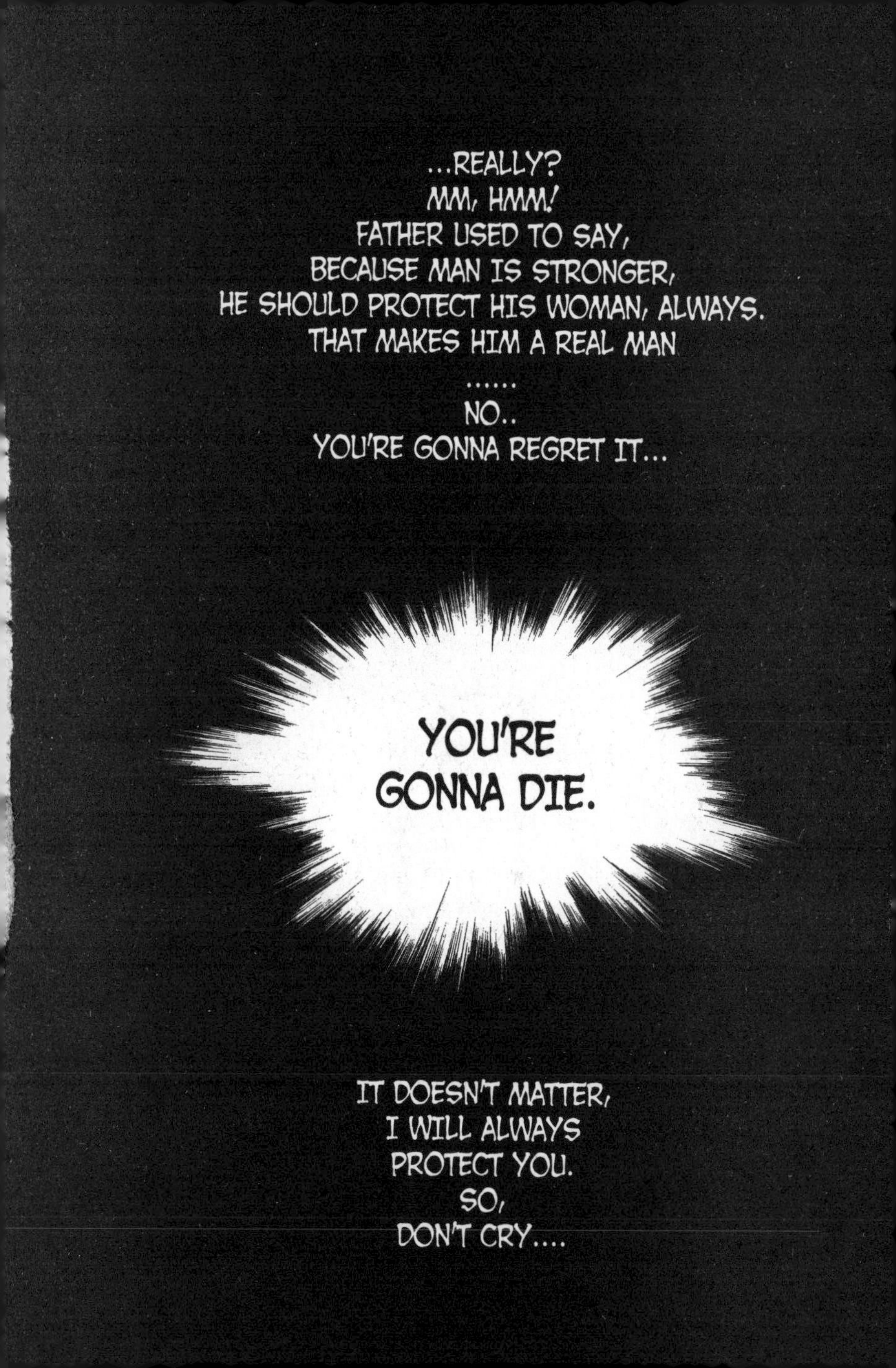
...REALLY?
MM, HMM!
FATHER USED TO SAY,
BECAUSE MAN IS STRONGER,
HE SHOULD PROTECT HIS WOMAN, ALWAYS.
THAT MAKES HIM A REAL MAN
......
NO..
YOU'RE GONNA REGRET IT...
YOU'RE GONNA DIE.
IT DOESN'T MATTER,
I WILL ALWAYS
PROTECT YOU.
SO,
DON'T CRY....

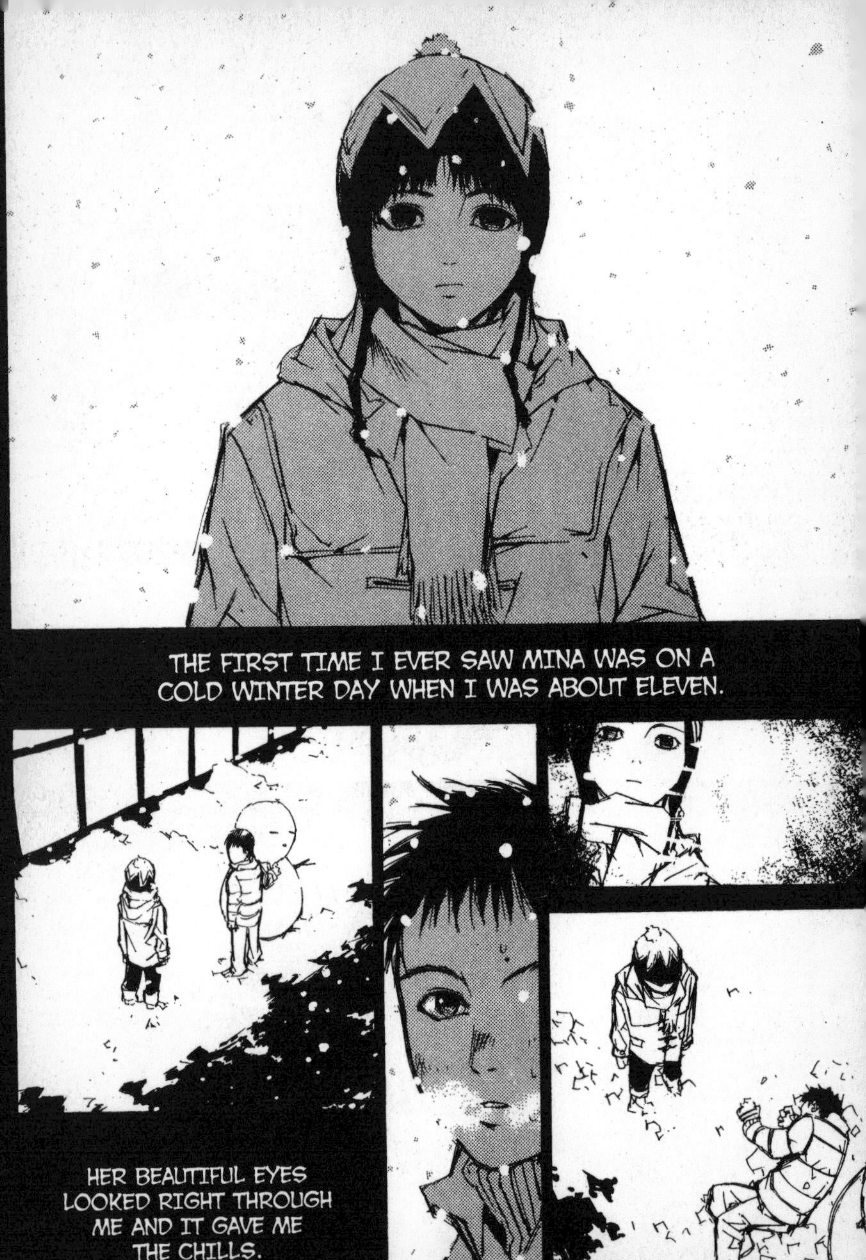
THE FIRST TIME I EVER SAW MINA WAS ON A COLD WINTER DAY WHEN I WAS ABOUT ELEVEN.
HER BEAUTIFUL EYES LOOKED RIGHT THROUGH ME AND IT GAVE ME THE CHILLS.

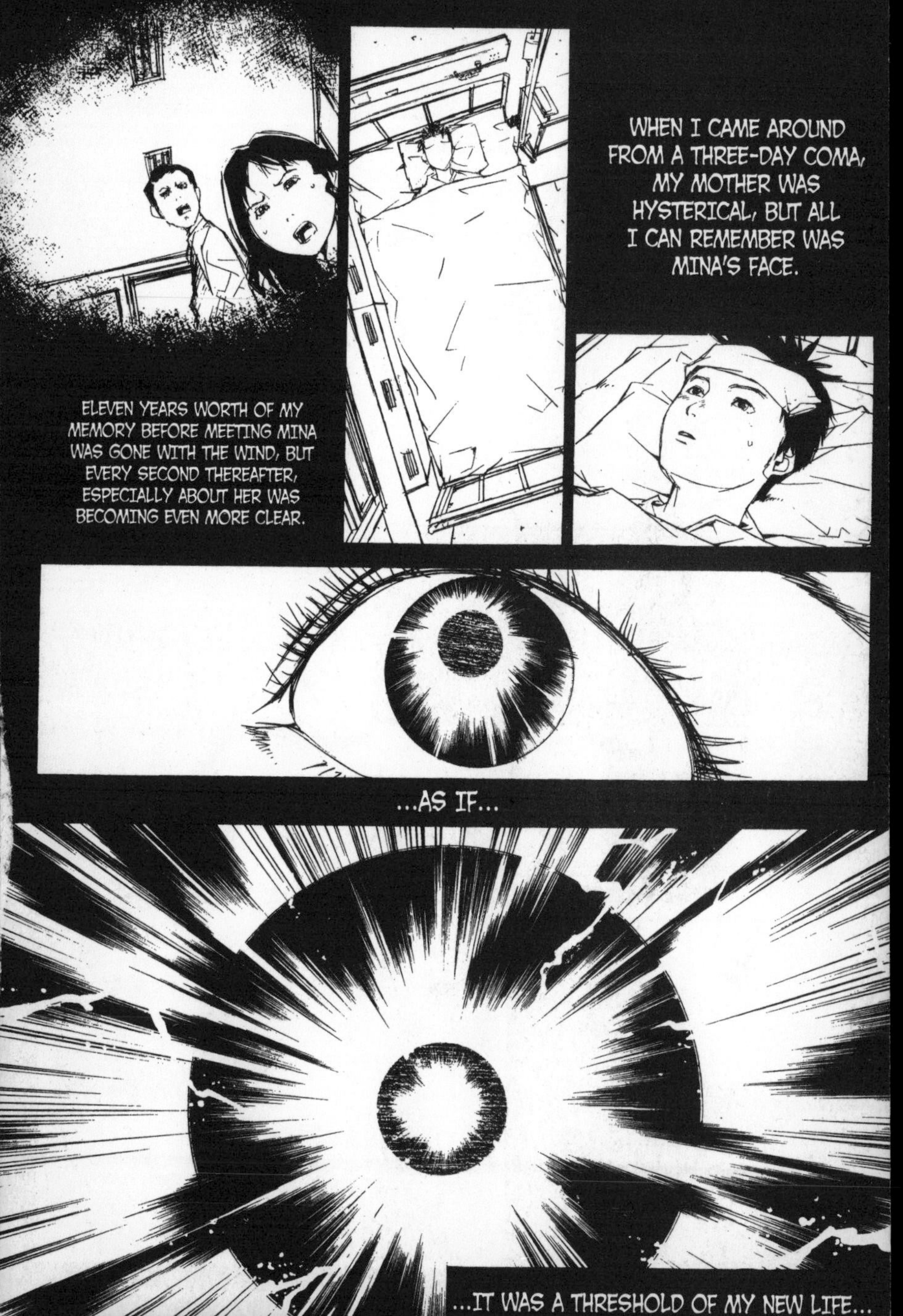
WHEN I CAME AROUND FROM A THREE-DAY COMA, MY MOTHER WAS HYSTERICAL, BUT ALL I CAN REMEMBER WAS MINA'S FACE.
ELEVEN YEARS WORTH OF MY MEMORY BEFORE MEETING MINA WAS GONE WITH THE WIND, BUT EVERY SECOND THEREAFTER, ESPECIALLY ABOUT HER WAS BECOMING EVEN MORE CLEAR.
...AS IF...
...IT WAS A THRESHOLD OF MY NEW LIFE...

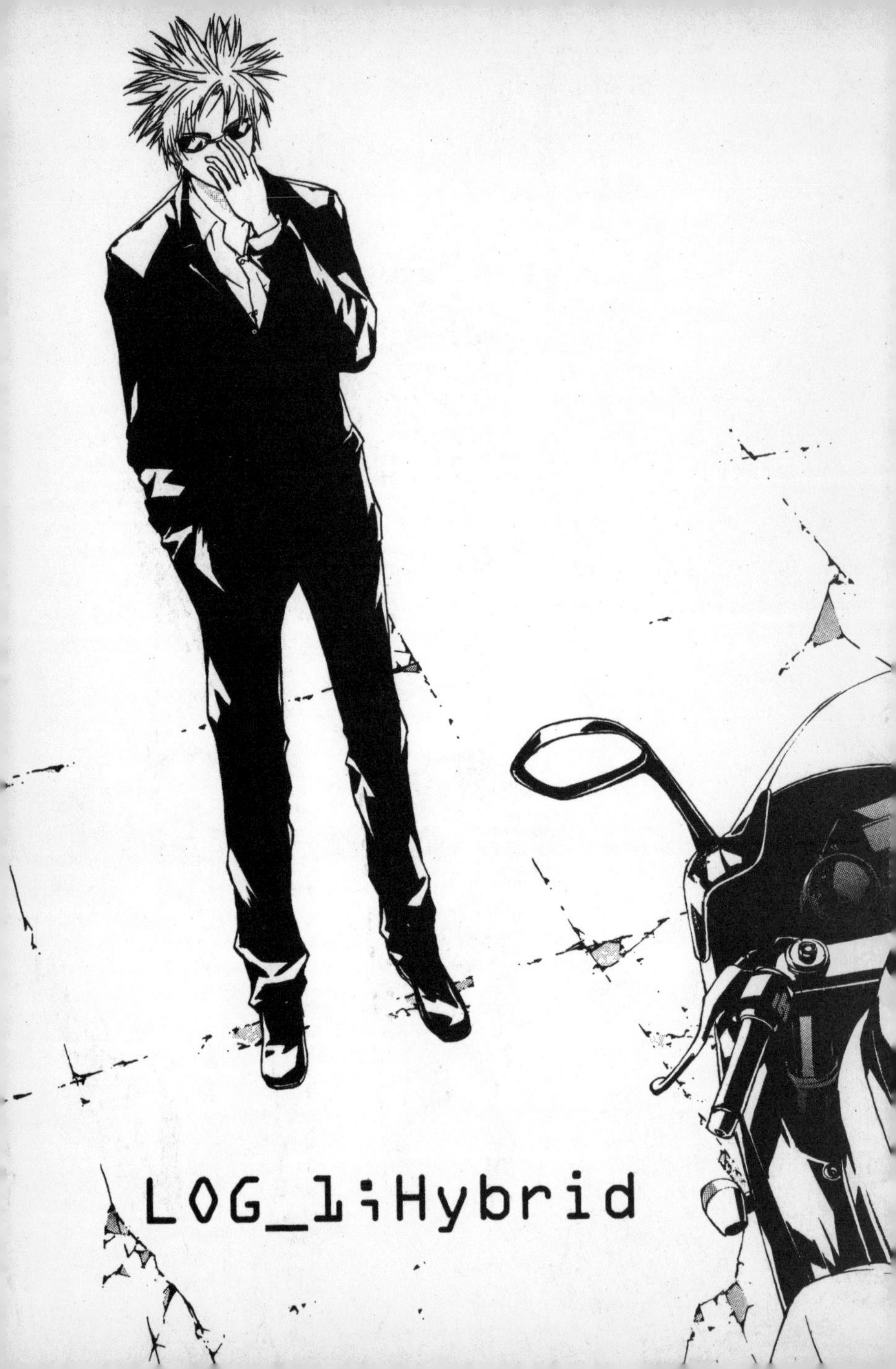

LOG_1;Hybrid

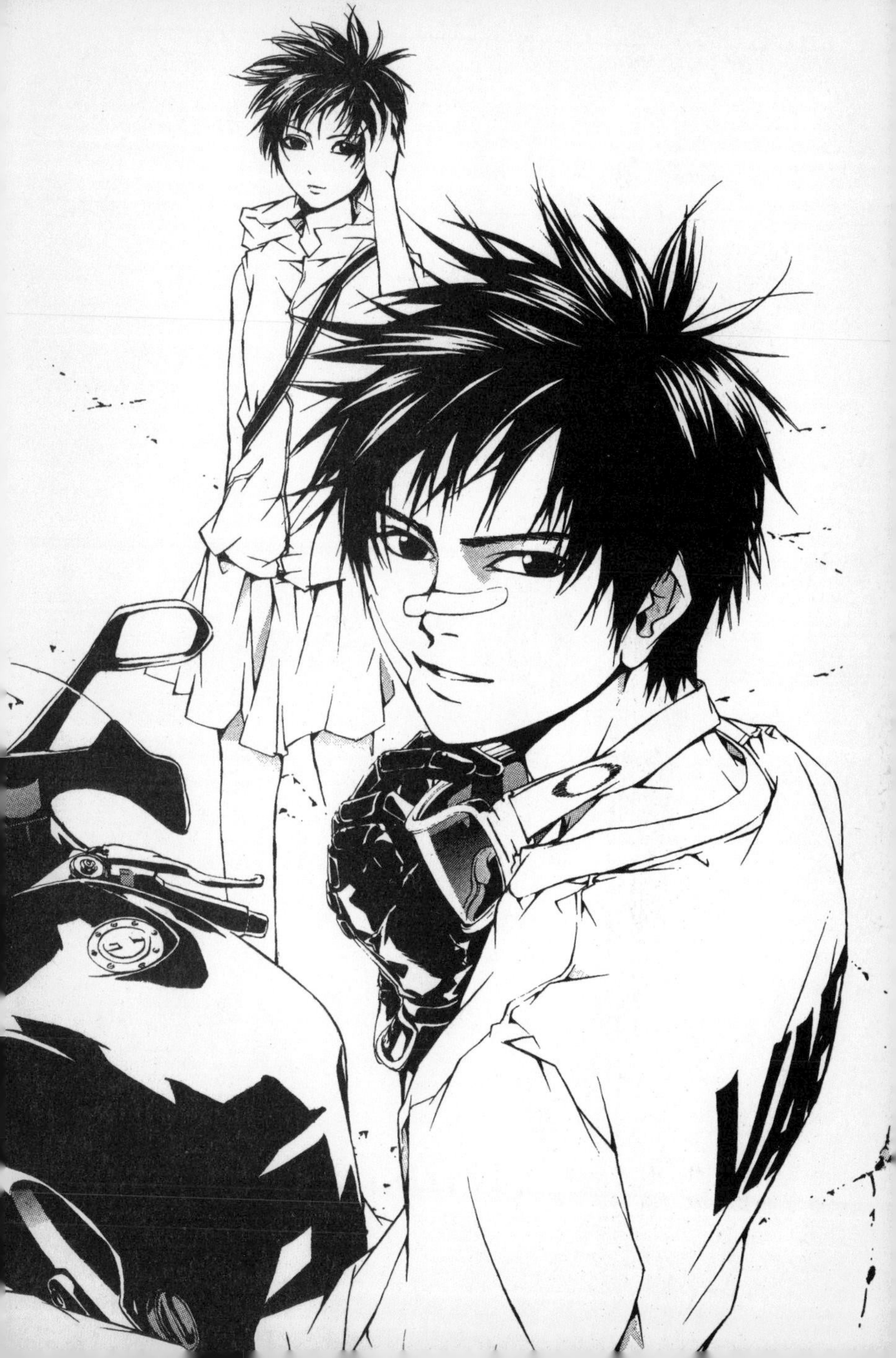

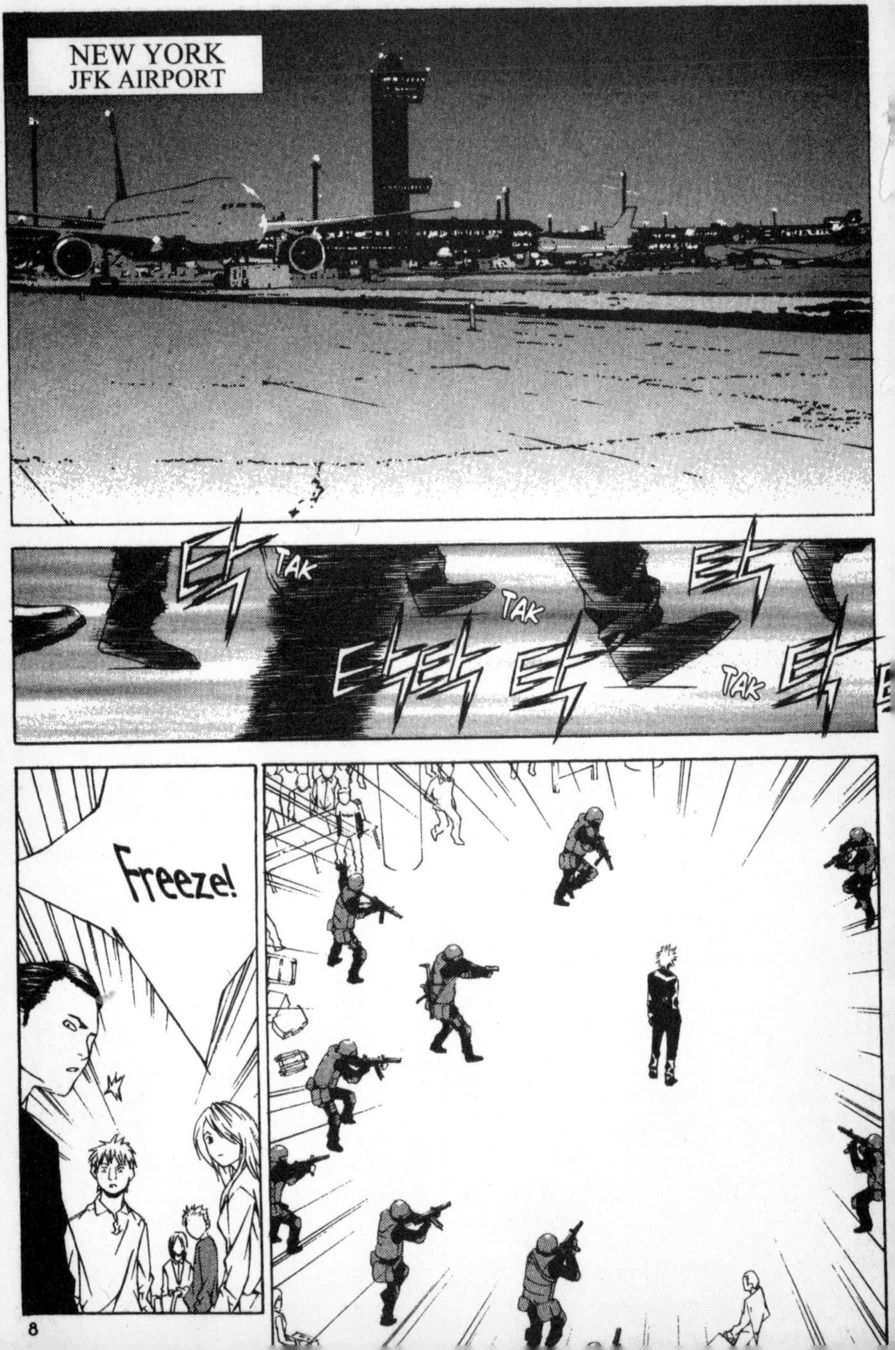
NEW YORK
JFK AIRPORT
탁
TAK
탁탁
TAK
탁
탁
TAK
탁
Freeze!

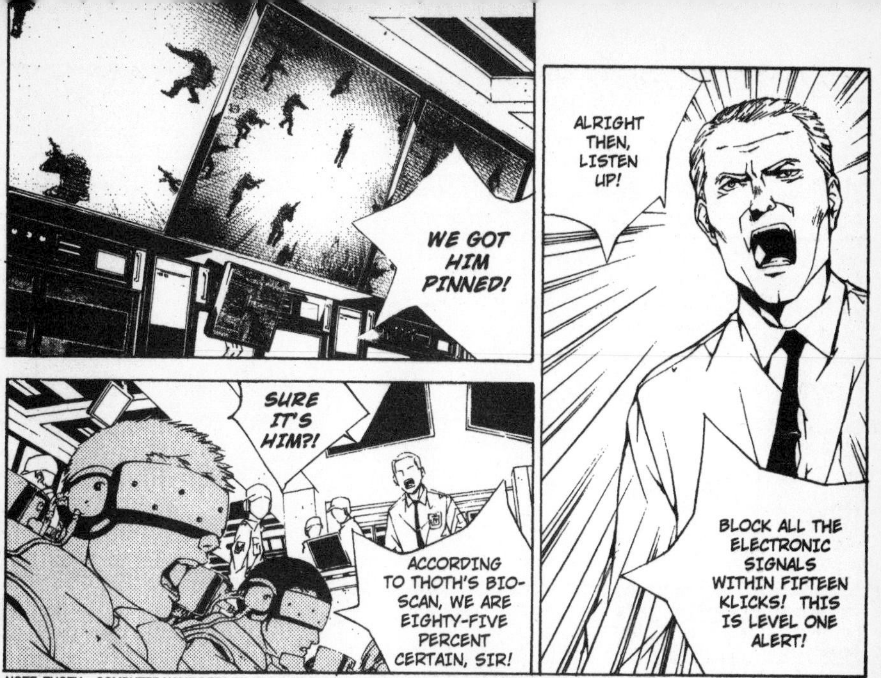
WE GOT HIM PINNED!
SURE IT'S HIM?!
ACCORDING TO THOTH'S BIO-SCAN, WE ARE EIGHTY-FIVE PERCENT CERTAIN, SIR!
ALRIGHT THEN, LISTEN UP!
BLOCK ALL THE ELECTRONIC SIGNALS WITHIN FIFTEEN KLICKS! THIS IS LEVEL ONE ALERT!

NOTE: THOTH – COMPUTER NAME DERIVED FROM ANCIENT EGYPT'S MYTHICAL GOD OF KNOWLEDGE.

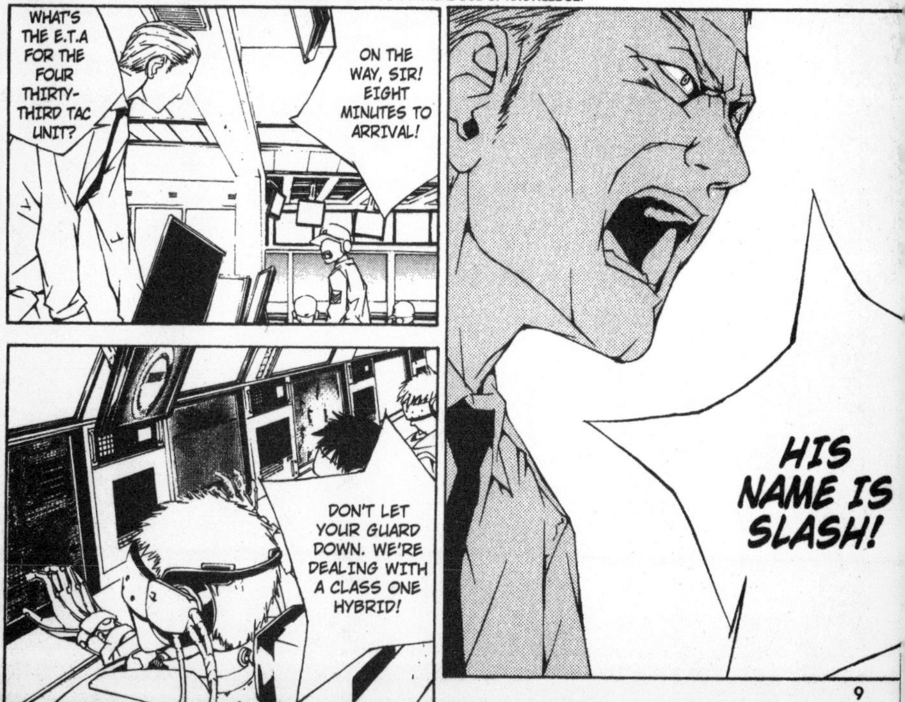
WHAT'S THE E.T.A FOR THE FOUR THIRTY-THIRD TAC UNIT?
ON THE WAY, SIR! EIGHT MINUTES TO ARRIVAL!
DON'T LET YOUR GUARD DOWN. WE'RE DEALING WITH A CLASS ONE HYBRID!
HIS NAME IS SLASH!

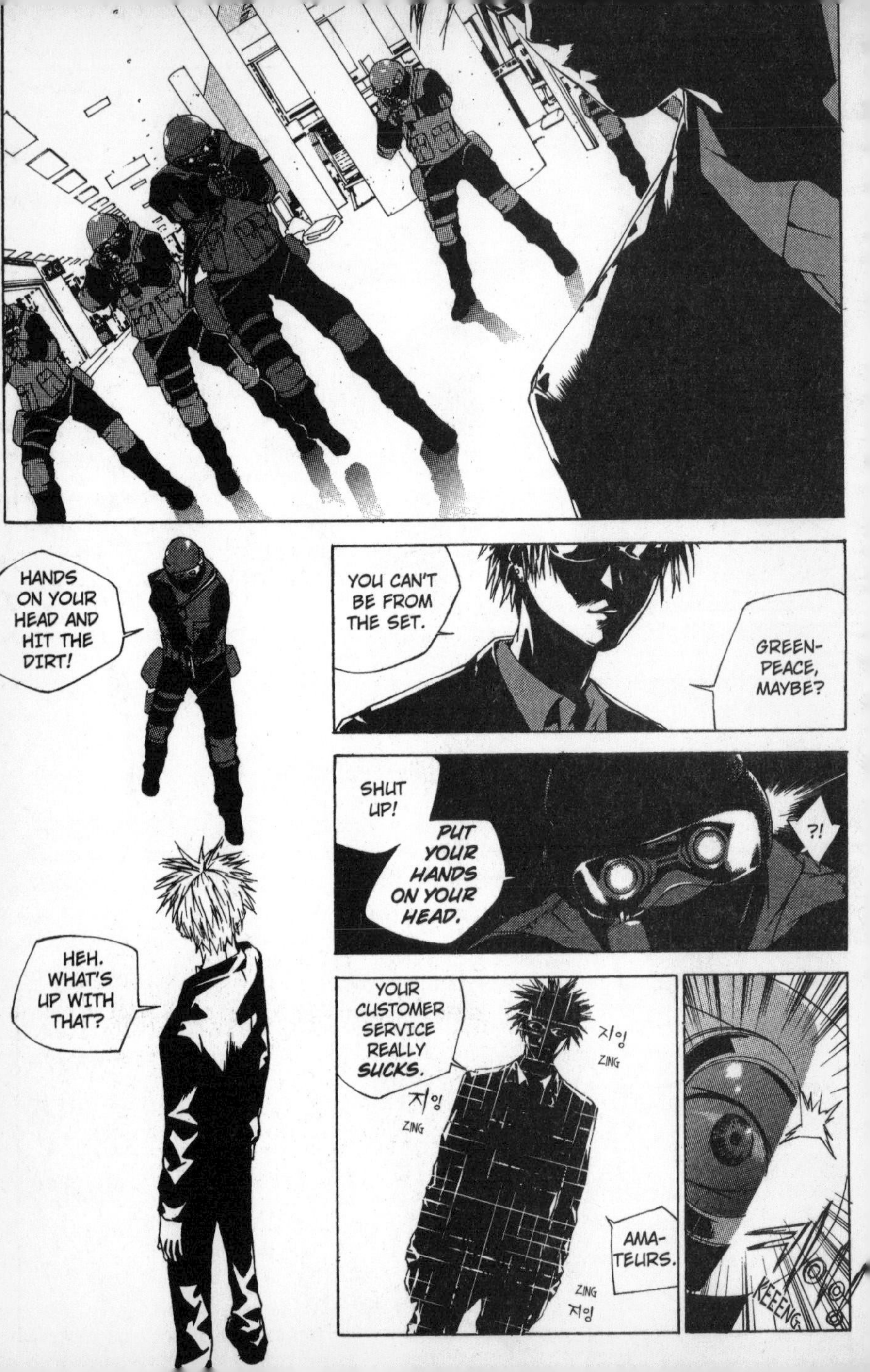
HANDS ON YOUR HEAD AND HIT THE DIRT!
HEH. WHAT'S UP WITH THAT?
YOU CAN'T BE FROM THE SET.
GREEN-PEACE, MAYBE?
SHUT UP!
PUT YOUR HANDS ON YOUR HEAD.
?!
YOUR CUSTOMER SERVICE REALLY SUCKS.
지잉
ZING
지잉
ZING
AMA-TEURS.
ZING
지잉
KEEENG

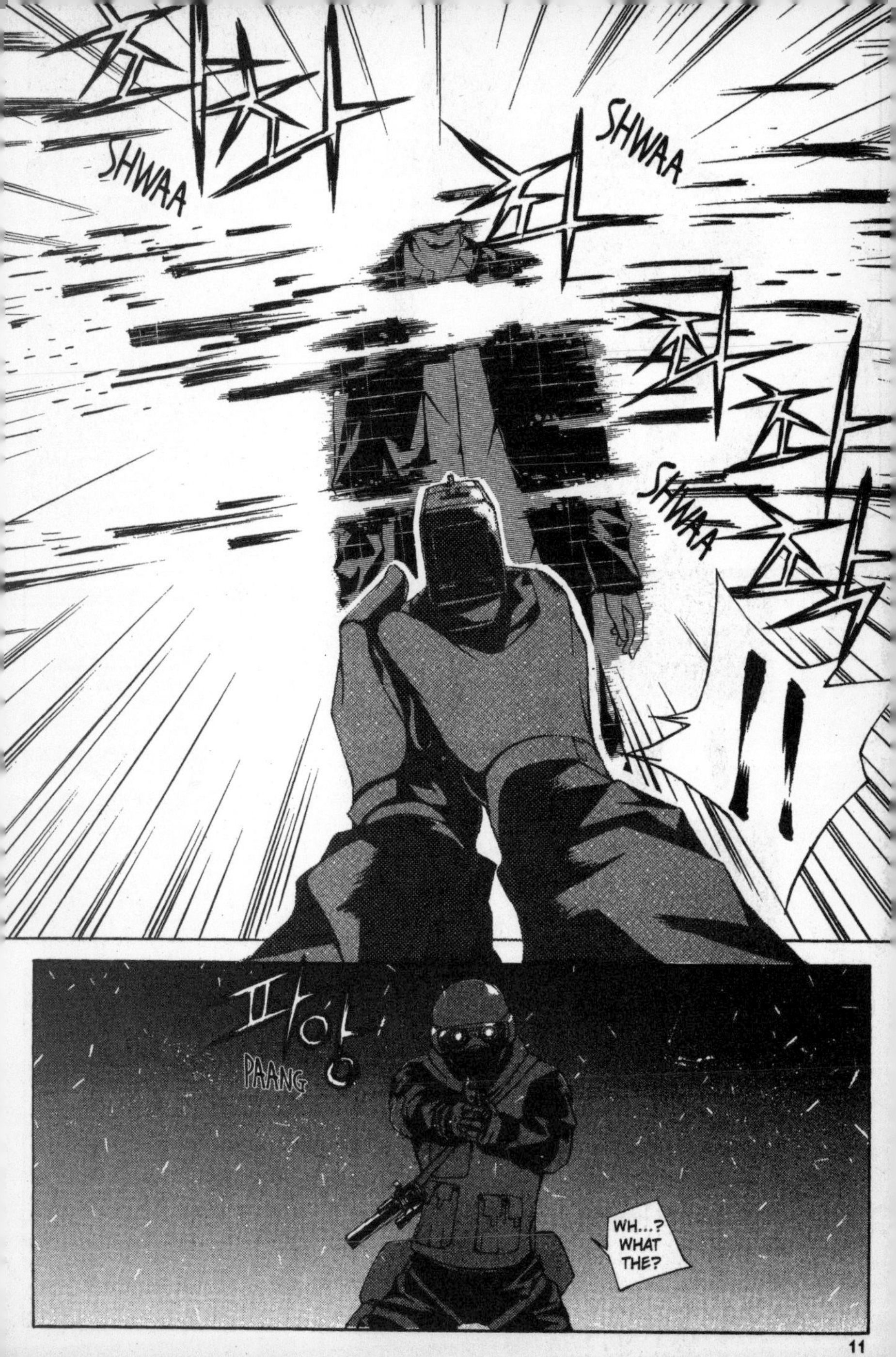
SHWAA
SHWAA
SHWAA
!!
PAANG
WH...? WHAT THE?

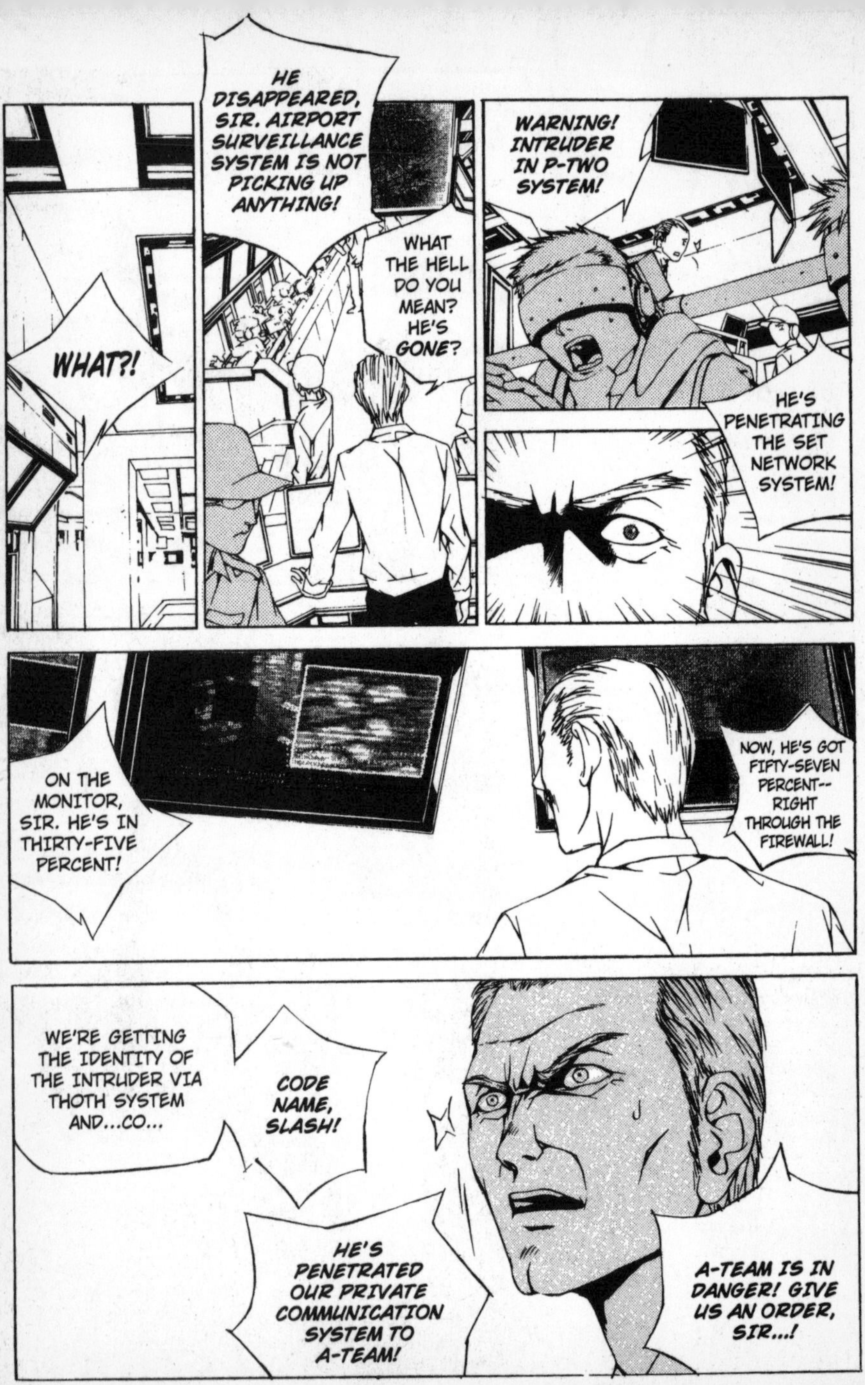
WHAT?!
HE DISAPPEARED, SIR. AIRPORT SURVEILLANCE SYSTEM IS NOT PICKING UP ANYTHING!
WHAT THE HELL DO YOU MEAN? HE'S GONE?
WARNING! INTRUDER IN P-TWO SYSTEM!
HE'S PENETRATING THE SET NETWORK SYSTEM!
ON THE MONITOR, SIR. HE'S IN THIRTY-FIVE PERCENT!
NOW, HE'S GOT FIFTY-SEVEN PERCENT--RIGHT THROUGH THE FIREWALL!
WE'RE GETTING THE IDENTITY OF THE INTRUDER VIA THOTH SYSTEM AND...CO...
CODE NAME, SLASH!
HE'S PENETRATED OUR PRIVATE COMMUNICATION SYSTEM TO A-TEAM!
A-TEAM IS IN DANGER! GIVE US AN ORDER, SIR...!

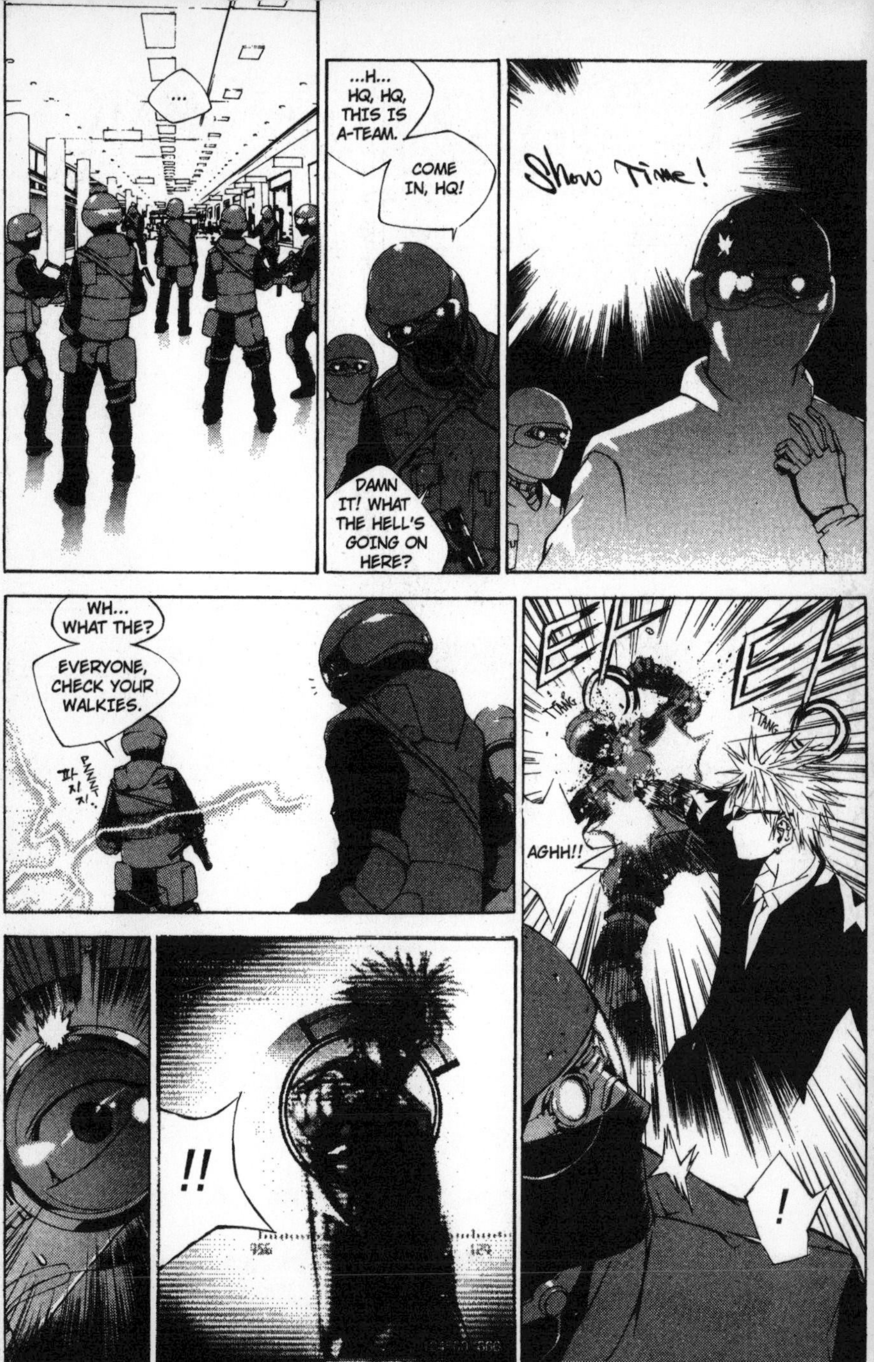
...
...H... HQ, HQ, THIS IS A-TEAM.
COME IN, HQ!
DAMN IT! WHAT THE HELL'S GOING ON HERE?
Show Time!
WH... WHAT THE?
EVERYONE, CHECK YOUR WALKIES.
PZZZT
파지지
!!
PTANG
PTANG
AGHH!!
!

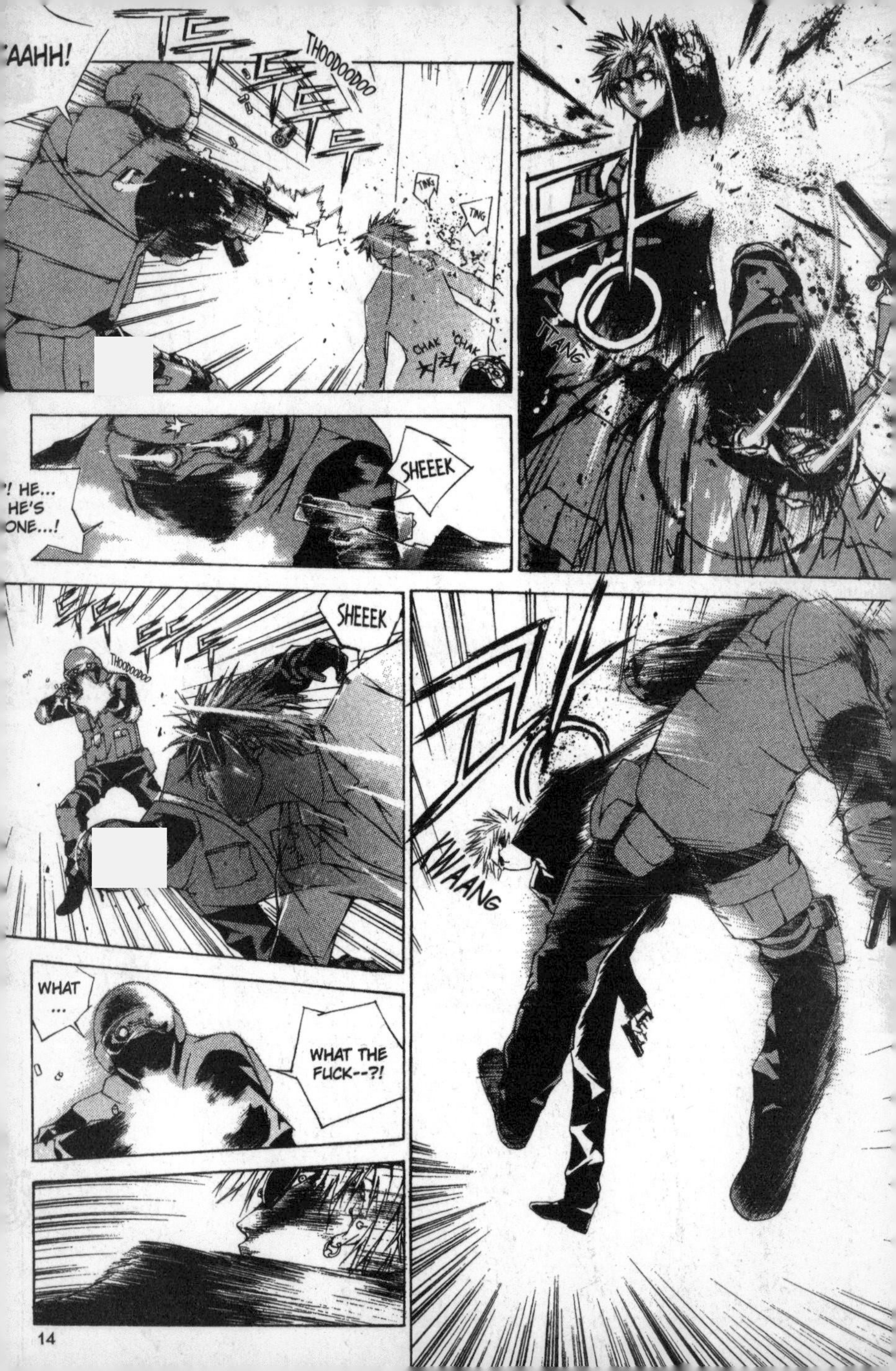

AAHH!
THOODOODOO
TING
TING
CHAK
CHAK
SHEEEK
?! HE...
HE'S
ONE...!
TTANG
THOODOODOO
SHEEEK
WHAT
...
WHAT THE
FUCK--?!
KWAANG

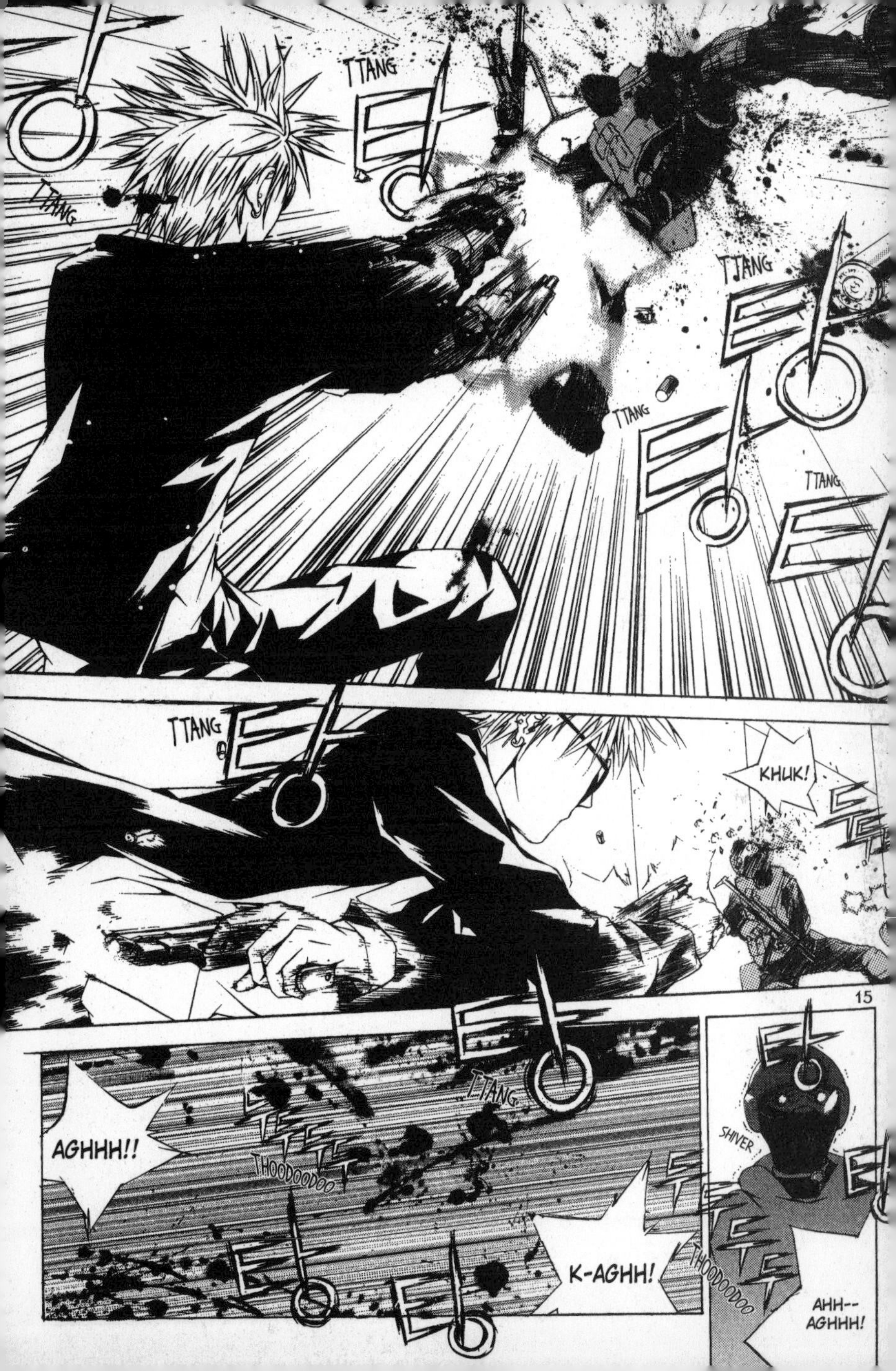
TTANG
TTANG
TTANG
TTANG
TTANG
TTANG
KHUK!
TTANG
AGHHH!!
THOODOODOO
K-AGHH!
SHIVER
THOODOODOO
AHH--
AGHHH!

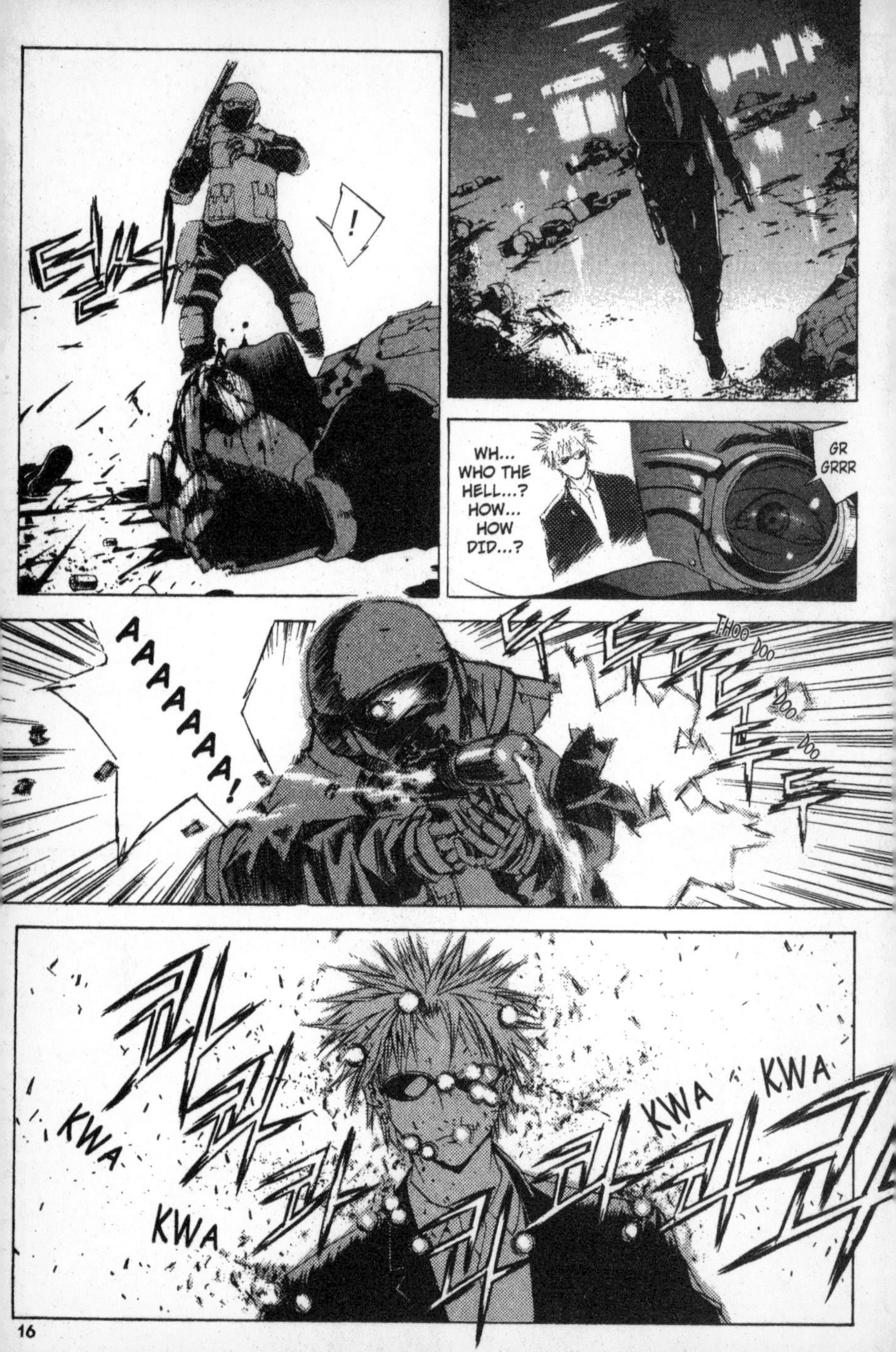
!
WH... WHO THE HELL...? HOW... HOW DID...?
GR GRRR
AAAAAAA!
THOO DOO DOO DOO
KWA
KWA
KWA
KWA

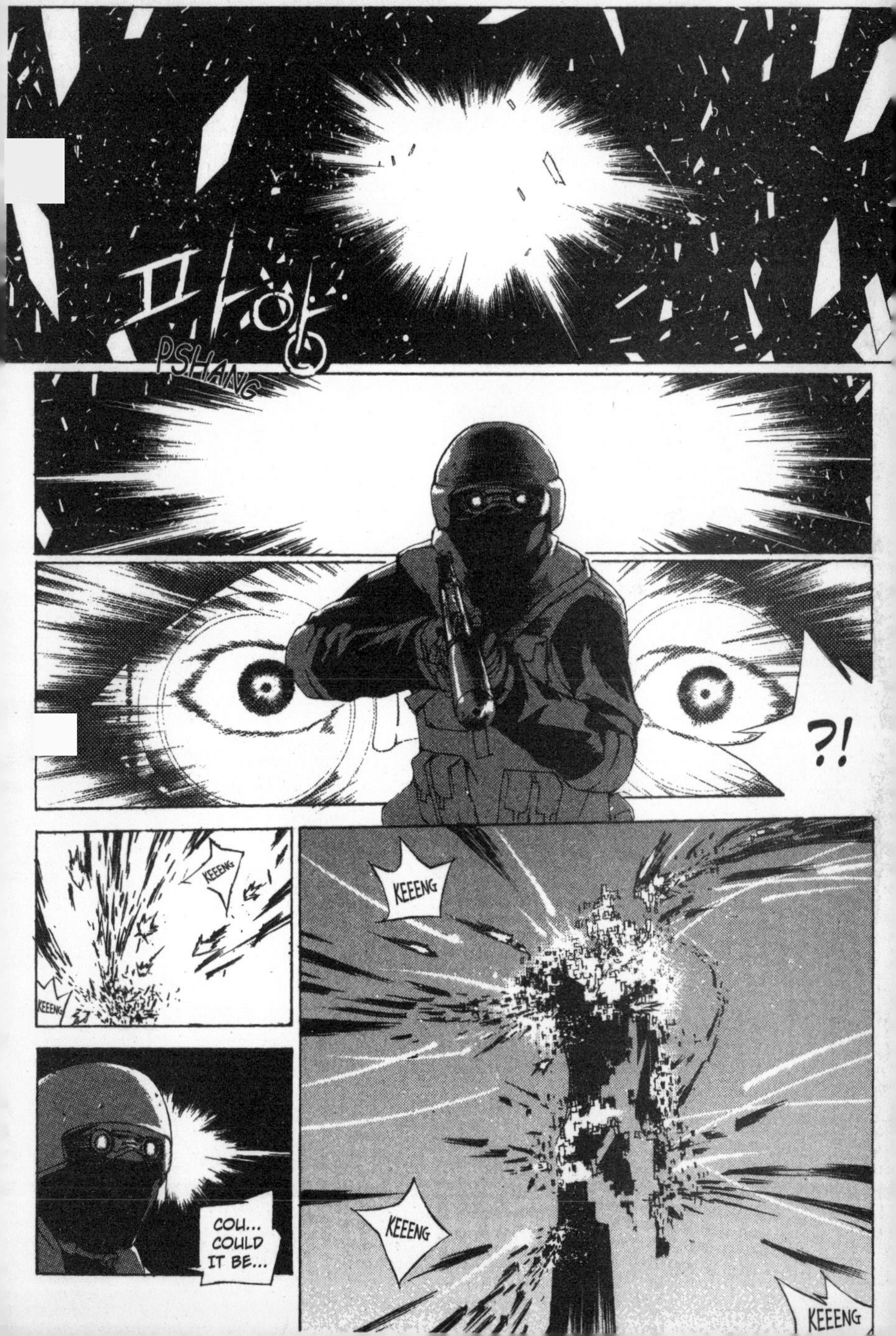
파샹
PSHANG
?!
KEEENG
KEEENG
KEEENG
COU... COULD IT BE...
KEEENG
KEEENG

... HA... HACKING?

DING-- DONG-- DANG!

HEEE

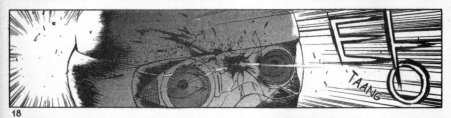

TAANG

18

KRNCH

...

DAMN YANKEES ...

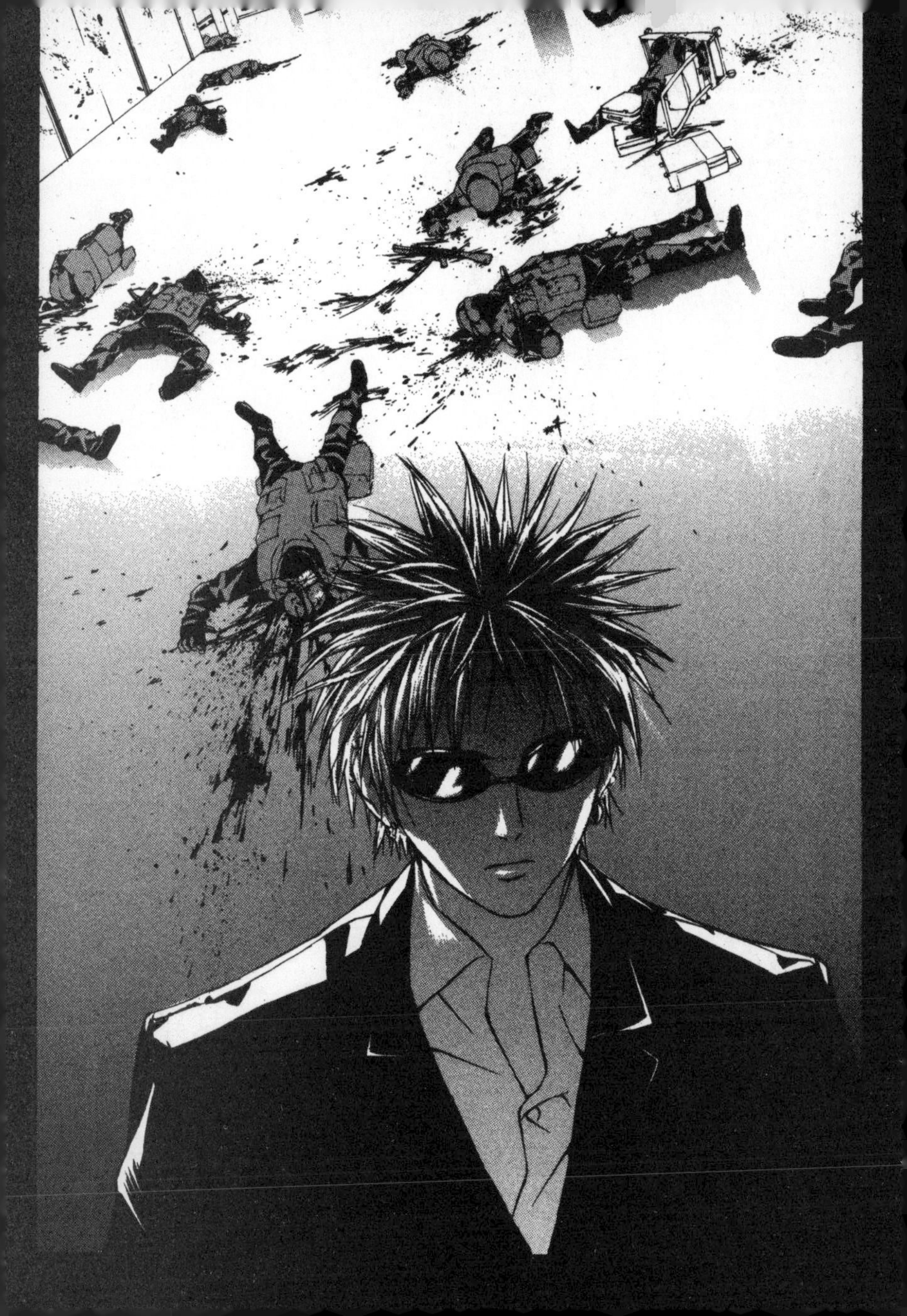

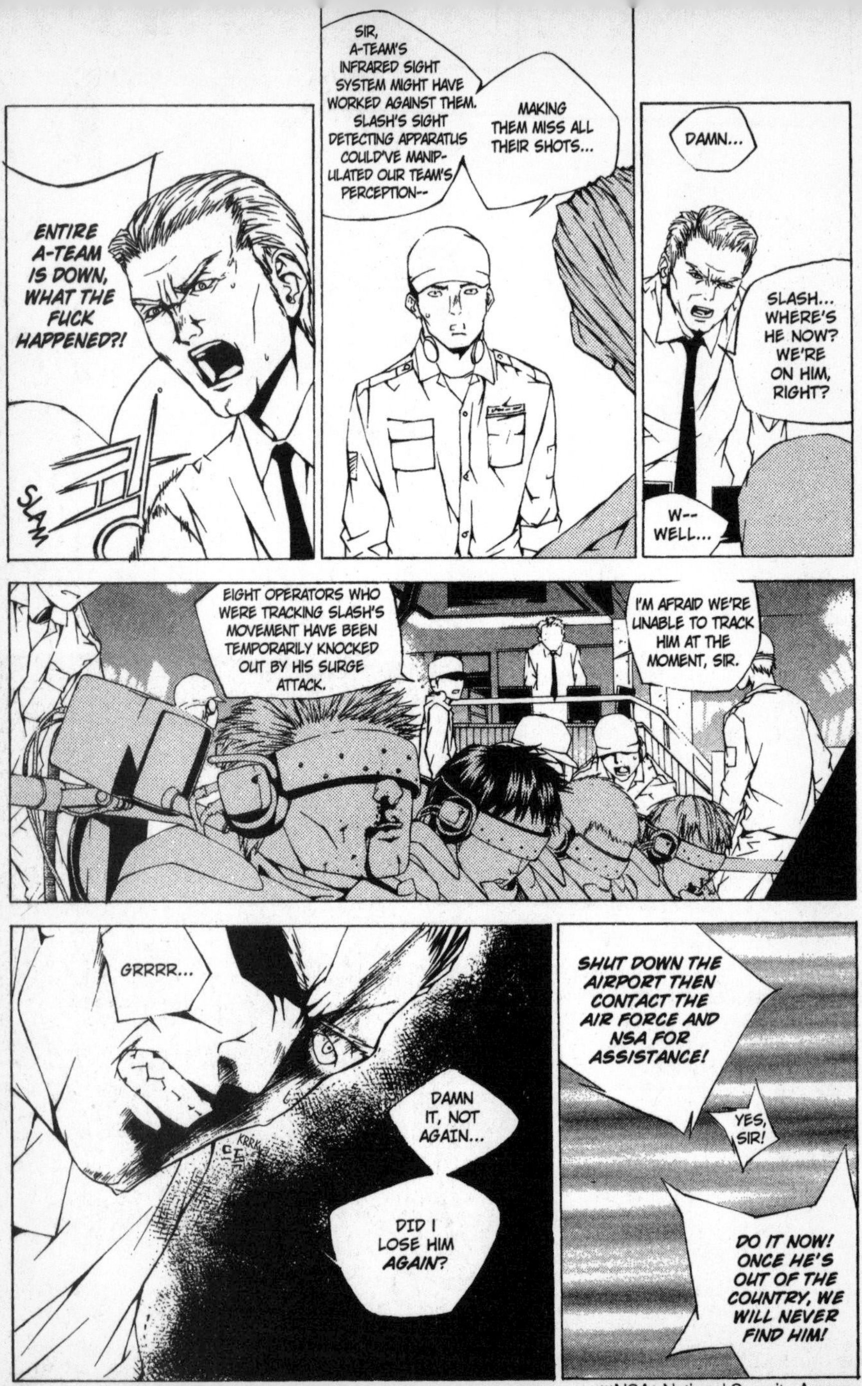
ENTIRE A-TEAM IS DOWN, WHAT THE FUCK HAPPENED?!
SLAM
SIR, A-TEAM'S INFRARED SIGHT SYSTEM MIGHT HAVE WORKED AGAINST THEM. SLASH'S SIGHT DETECTING APPARATUS COULD'VE MANIP-ULATED OUR TEAM'S PERCEPTION--
MAKING THEM MISS ALL THEIR SHOTS...
DAMN...
SLASH... WHERE'S HE NOW? WE'RE ON HIM, RIGHT?
W-- WELL...
EIGHT OPERATORS WHO WERE TRACKING SLASH'S MOVEMENT HAVE BEEN TEMPORARILY KNOCKED OUT BY HIS SURGE ATTACK.
I'M AFRAID WE'RE UNABLE TO TRACK HIM AT THE MOMENT, SIR.
GRRRR...
KRRK
DAMN IT, NOT AGAIN...
DID I LOSE HIM AGAIN?
SHUT DOWN THE AIRPORT THEN CONTACT THE AIR FORCE AND NSA FOR ASSISTANCE!
YES, SIR!
DO IT NOW! ONCE HE'S OUT OF THE COUNTRY, WE WILL NEVER FIND HIM!

※NSA: National Security Agency

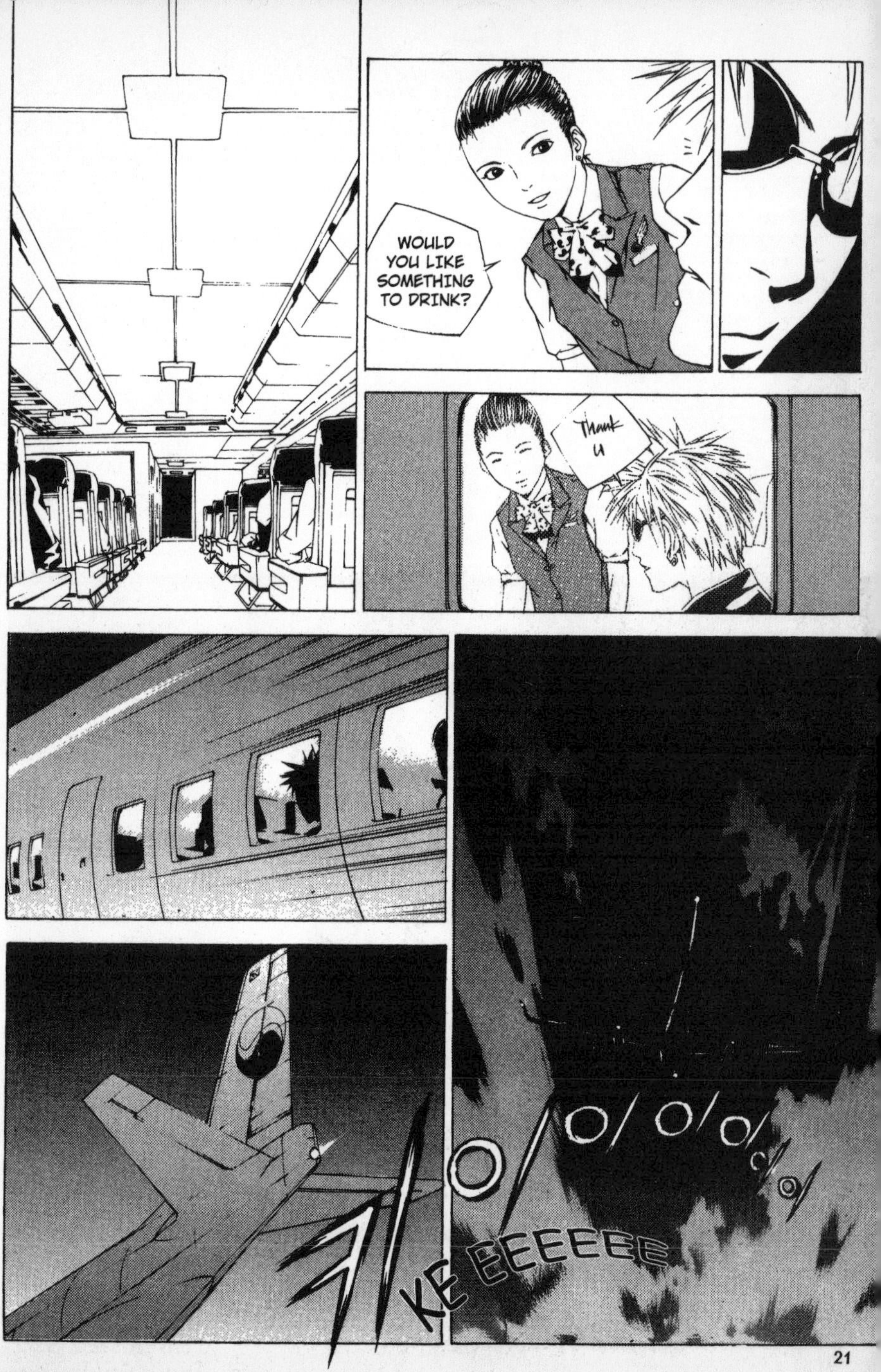
WOULD YOU LIKE SOMETHING TO DRINK?
Thank u
KEEEEEEE

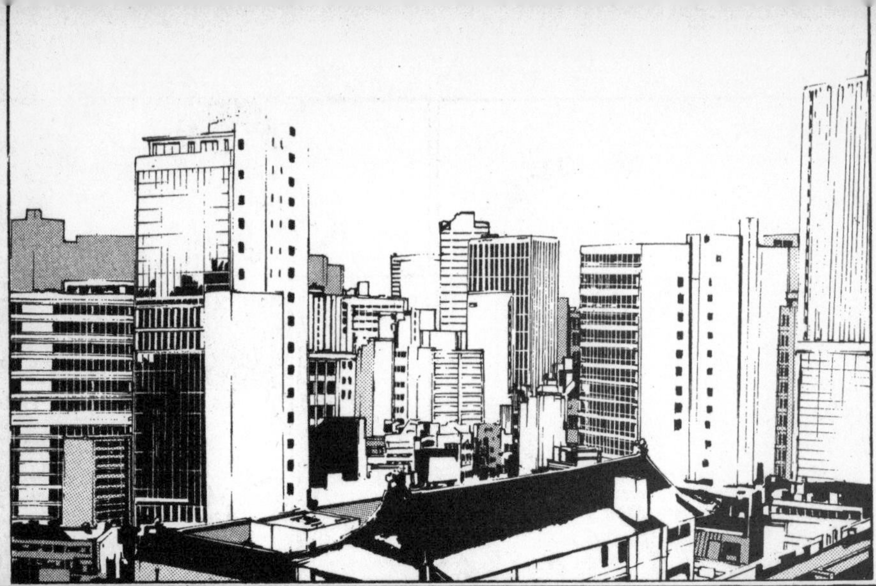

YOU'RE GOING TO DIE

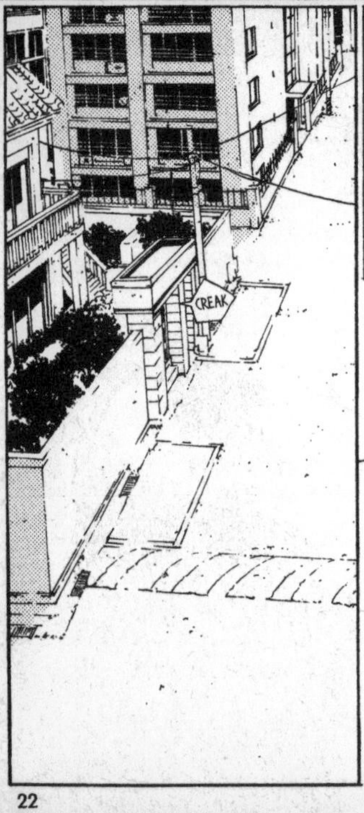
CREAK

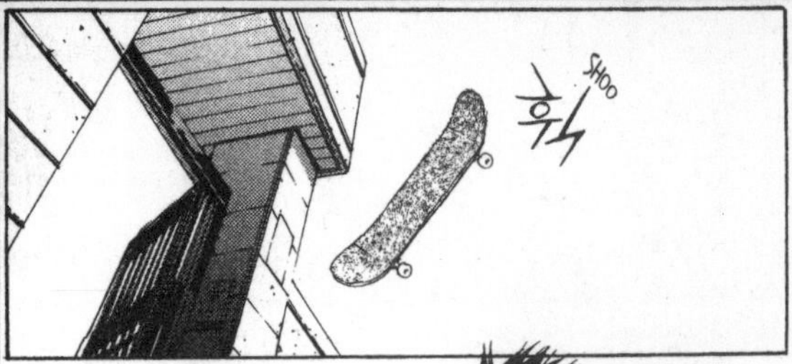
SHOO

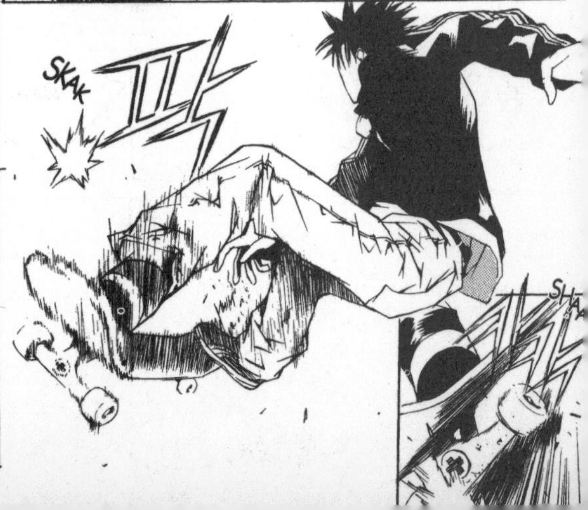
SKAK

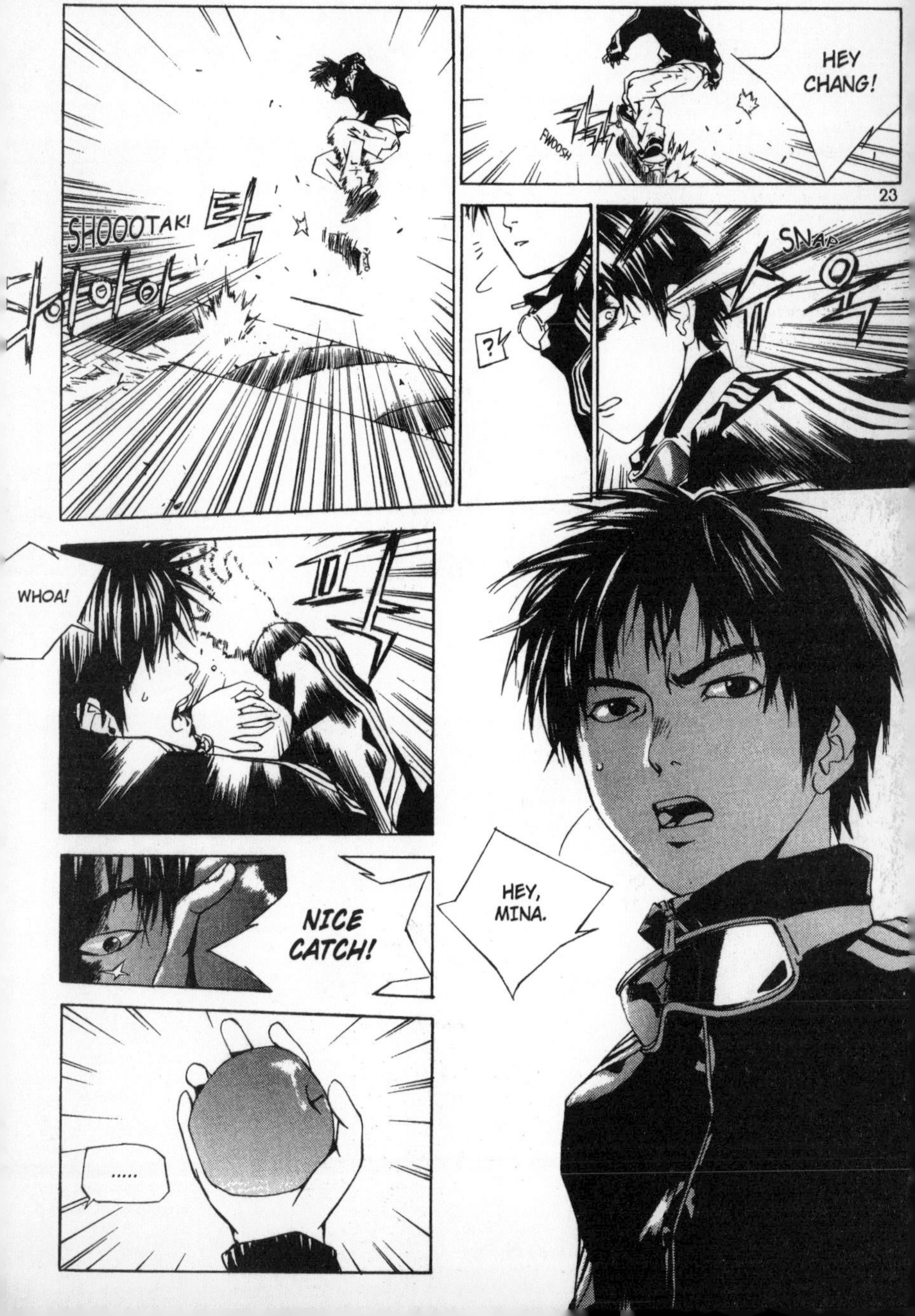
SHOOOTAK!
FWOOSH
HEY CHANG!
?
SNAP
WHOA!
NICE CATCH!
.....
HEY, MINA.

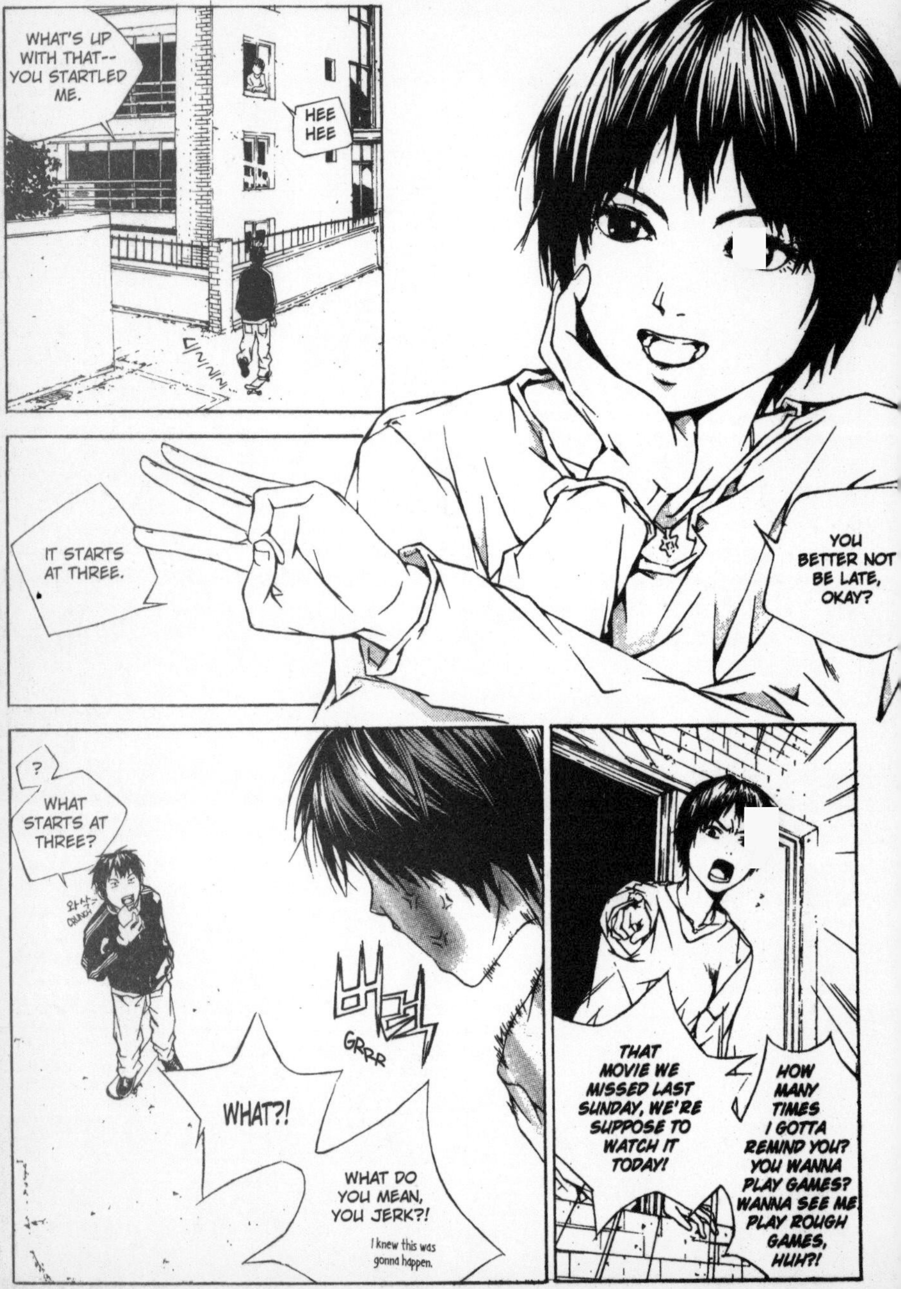
WHAT'S UP WITH THAT-- YOU STARTLED ME.
HEE HEE
IT STARTS AT THREE.
YOU BETTER NOT BE LATE, OKAY?
?
WHAT STARTS AT THREE?
CRUNCH
GRRR
WHAT?!
WHAT DO YOU MEAN, YOU JERK?!
I knew this was gonna happen.
THAT MOVIE WE MISSED LAST SUNDAY, WE'RE SUPPOSE TO WATCH IT TODAY!
HOW MANY TIMES I GOTTA REMIND YOU? YOU WANNA PLAY GAMES? WANNA SEE ME PLAY ROUGH GAMES, HUH?!

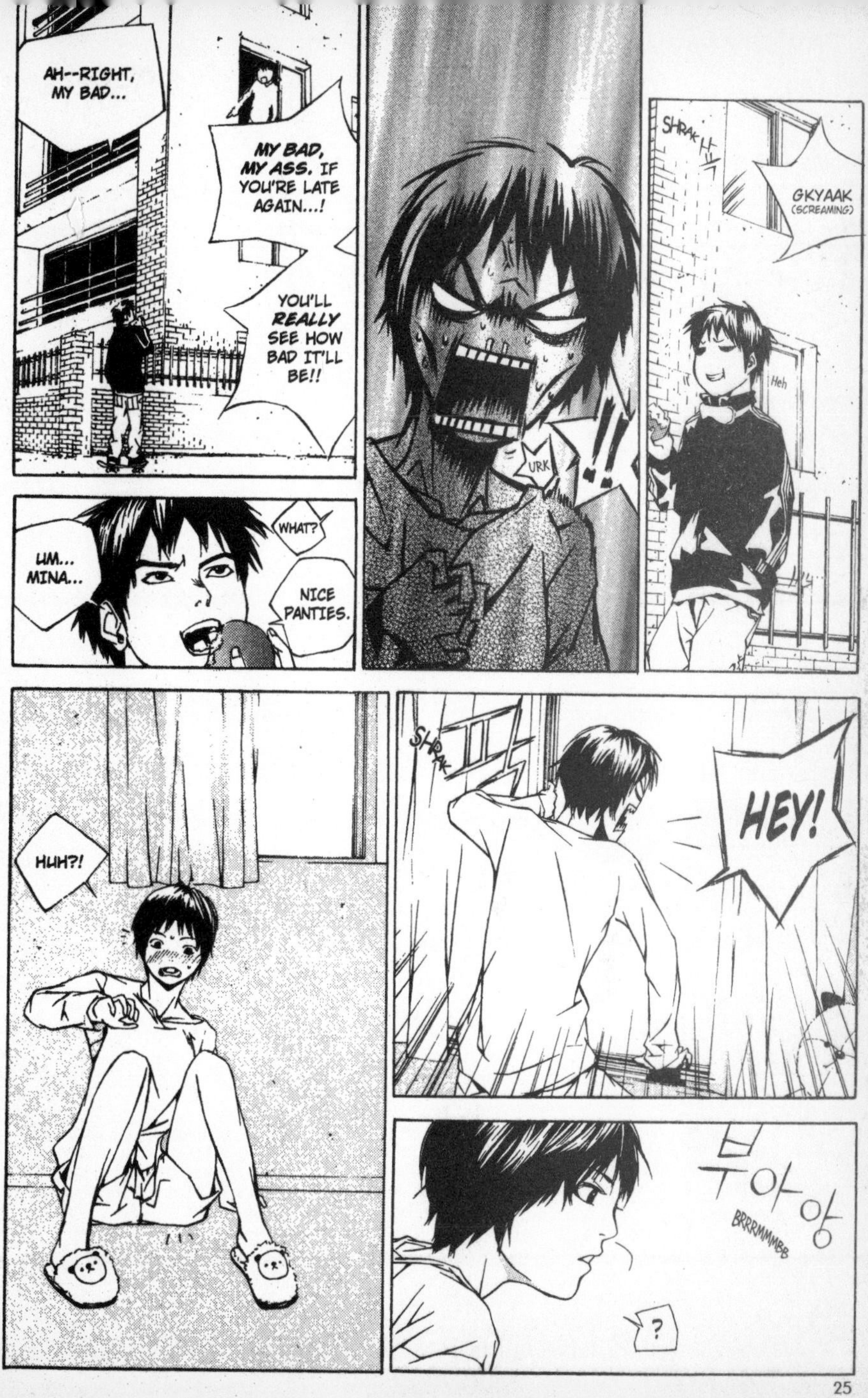
AH--RIGHT, MY BAD...
MY BAD, MY ASS. IF YOU'RE LATE AGAIN...!
YOU'LL REALLY SEE HOW BAD IT'LL BE!!
UM... MINA...
WHAT?
NICE PANTIES.
URK
!!
SHRAK
GKYAAK (SCREAMING)
Heh
HUH?!
SHRAK
HEY!
BRRRMMMBB
?

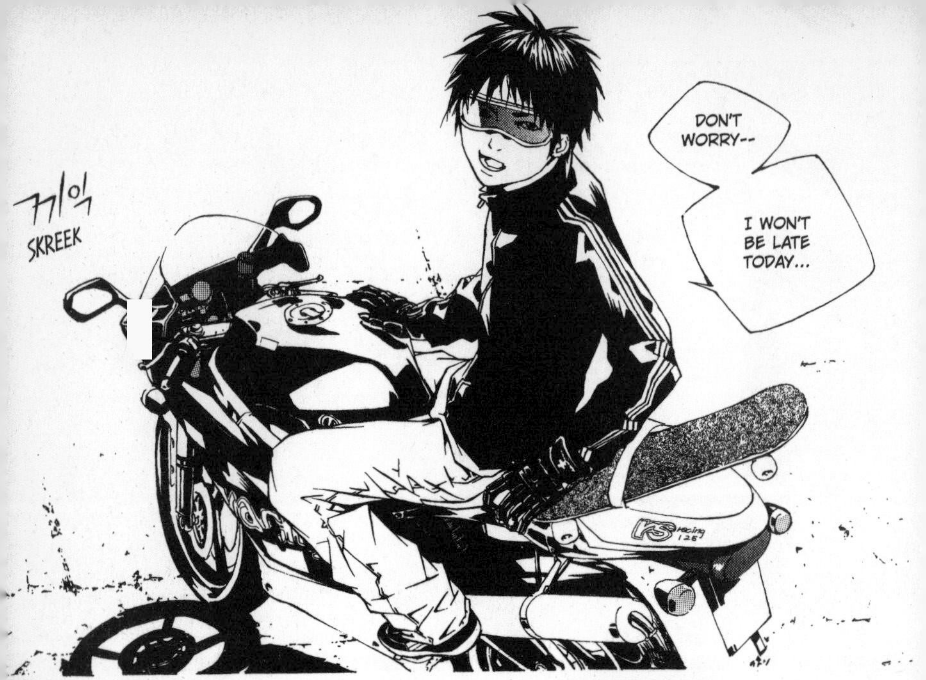
끼익
SKREEK
DON'T WORRY--
I WON'T BE LATE TODAY...

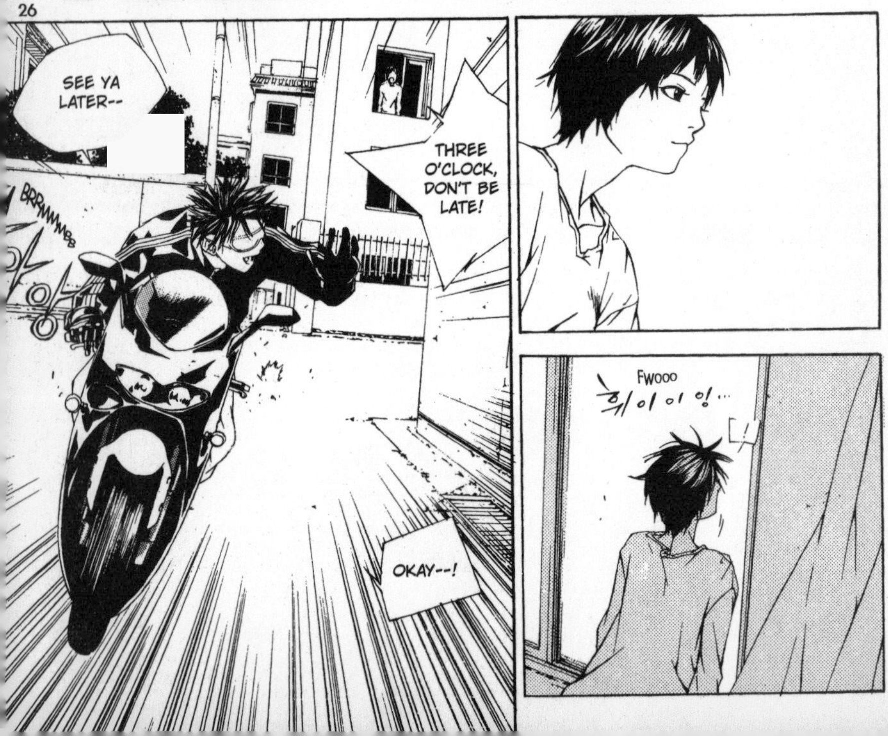
SEE YA LATER--
BRRMMMBB
THREE O'CLOCK, DON'T BE LATE!
OKAY--!
FWOOO
휘이이잉...

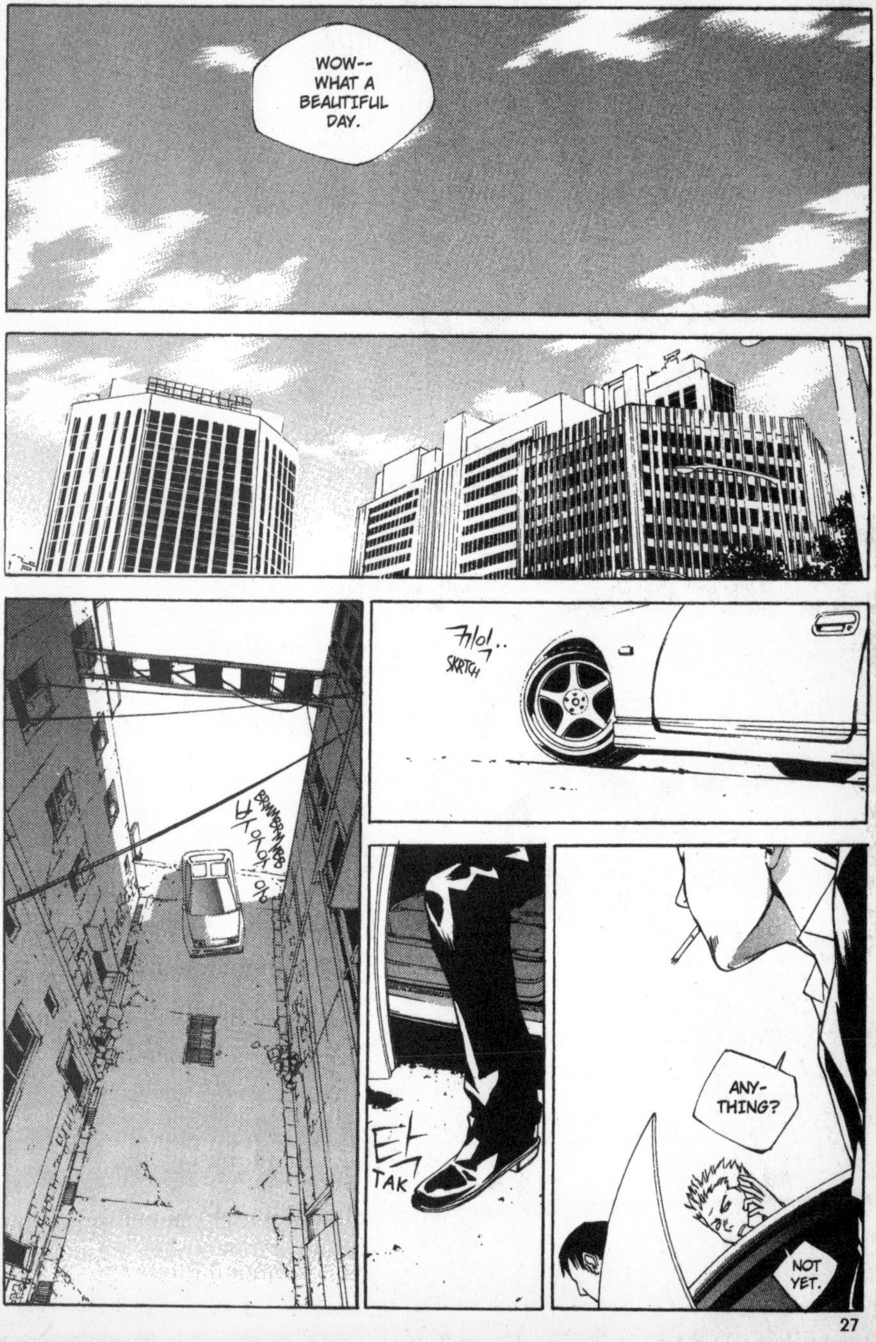
WOW--
WHAT A
BEAUTIFUL
DAY.
부아아아앙
BRMMBRMMBB
끼익..
SKRTCH
탁
TAK
ANY-
THING?
NOT
YET.

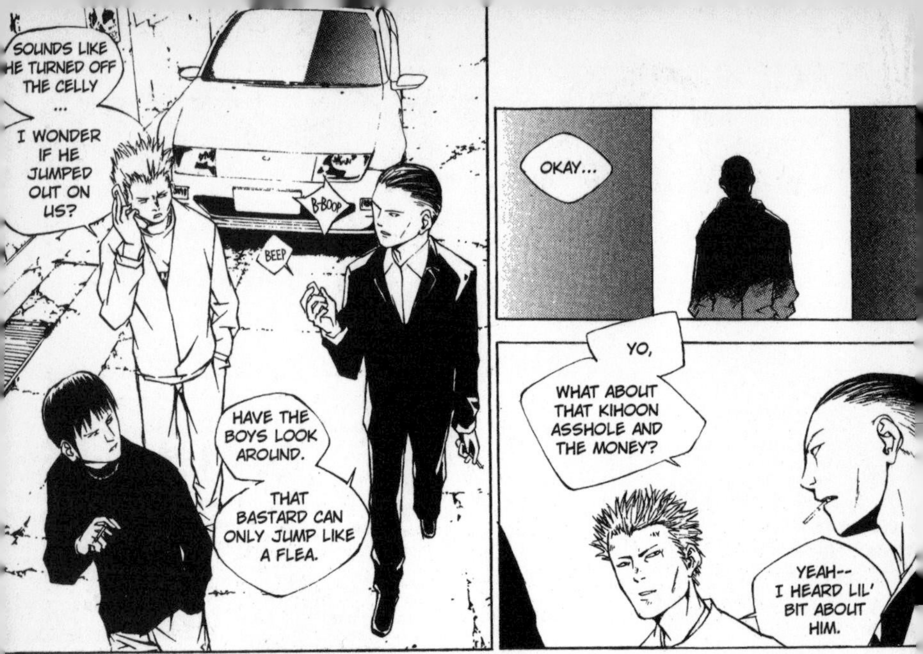
SOUNDS LIKE HE TURNED OFF THE CELLY
...
I WONDER IF HE JUMPED OUT ON US?
B-BOOP
BEEP
HAVE THE BOYS LOOK AROUND.
THAT BASTARD CAN ONLY JUMP LIKE A FLEA.
OKAY...
YO,
WHAT ABOUT THAT KIHOON ASSHOLE AND THE MONEY?
YEAH-- I HEARD LIL' BIT ABOUT HIM.

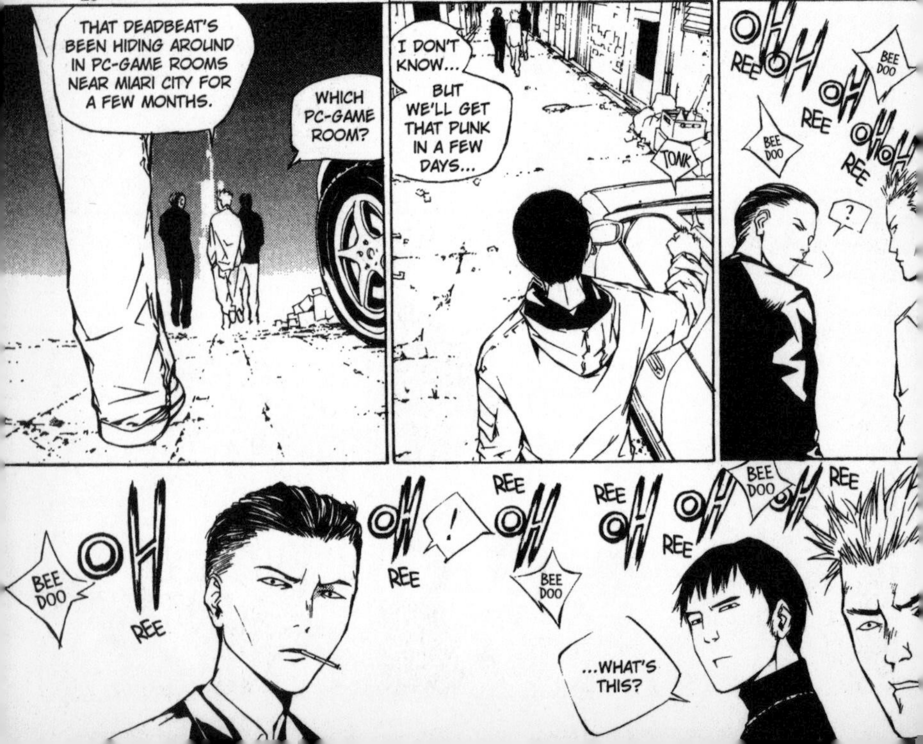
THAT DEADBEAT'S BEEN HIDING AROUND IN PC-GAME ROOMS NEAR MIARI CITY FOR A FEW MONTHS.
WHICH PC-GAME ROOM?
I DON'T KNOW...
BUT WE'LL GET THAT PUNK IN A FEW DAYS...
TONK
OHH REE OHH REE OHH REE OHH
BEE DOO
BEE DOO
?
BEE DOO
OH
REE
OH
REE
!
REE
OH
REE
OH
REE
BEE DOO
OH
BEE DOO
OH
REE
...WHAT'S THIS?

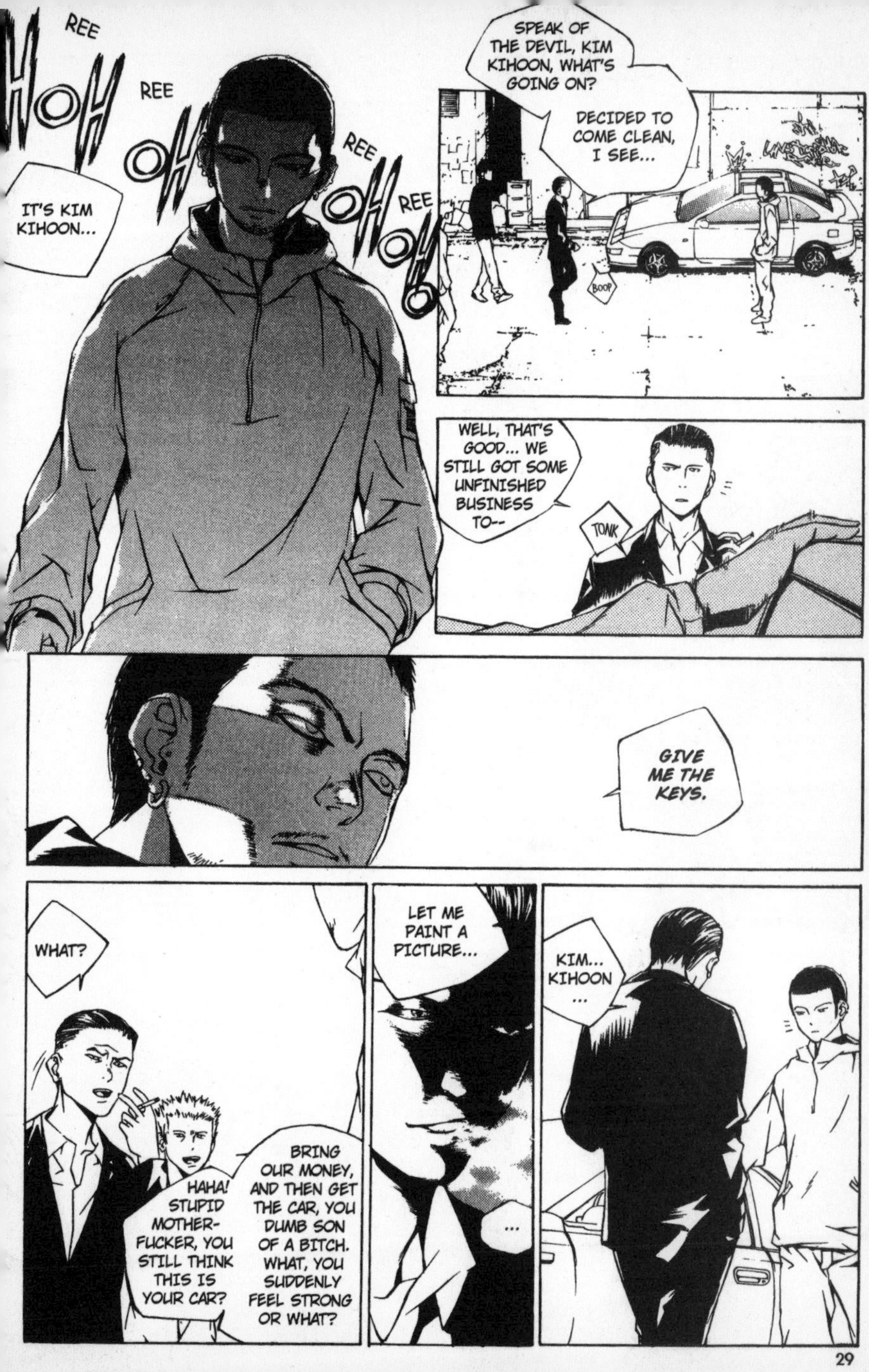
REE
HOH
REE
OH
REE
OHOH
REE
OHOH
IT'S KIM KIHOON...
SPEAK OF THE DEVIL, KIM KIHOON, WHAT'S GOING ON?
DECIDED TO COME CLEAN, I SEE...
BOOP
WELL, THAT'S GOOD... WE STILL GOT SOME UNFINISHED BUSINESS TO--
TONK
GIVE ME THE KEYS.
WHAT?
HAHA! STUPID MOTHER-FUCKER, YOU STILL THINK THIS IS YOUR CAR?
BRING OUR MONEY, AND THEN GET THE CAR, YOU DUMB SON OF A BITCH. WHAT, YOU SUDDENLY FEEL STRONG OR WHAT?
LET ME PAINT A PICTURE...
...
KIM... KIHOON ...

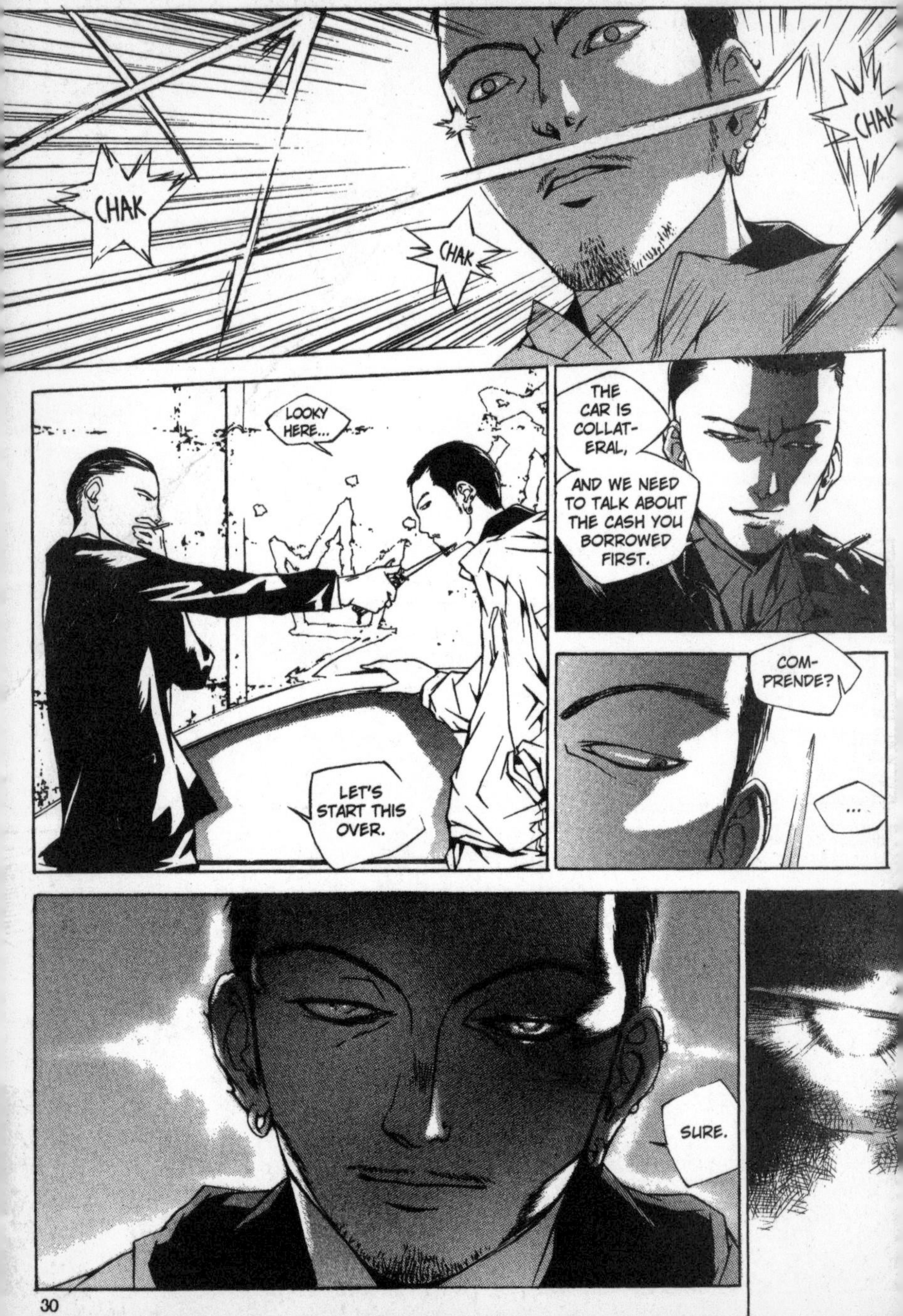
CHAK
CHAK
CHAK
LOOKY HERE...
LET'S START THIS OVER.
THE CAR IS COLLATERAL,
AND WE NEED TO TALK ABOUT THE CASH YOU BORROWED FIRST.
COMPRENDE?
...
SURE.

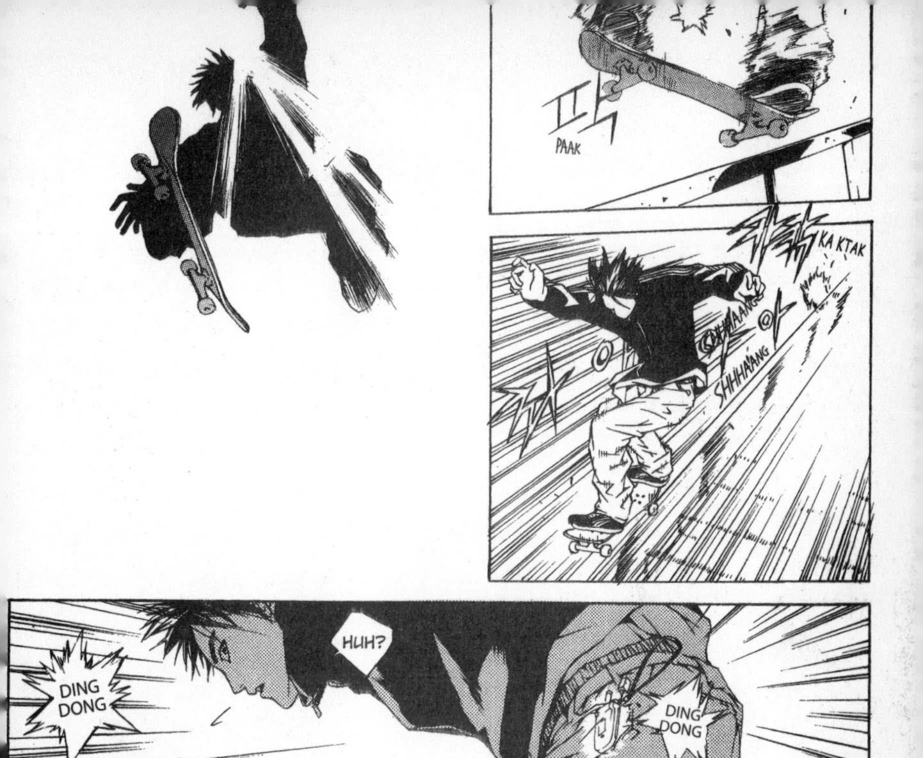
PAAK
KA KTAK
SHHHAANG
DING DONG
HUH?
DING DONG

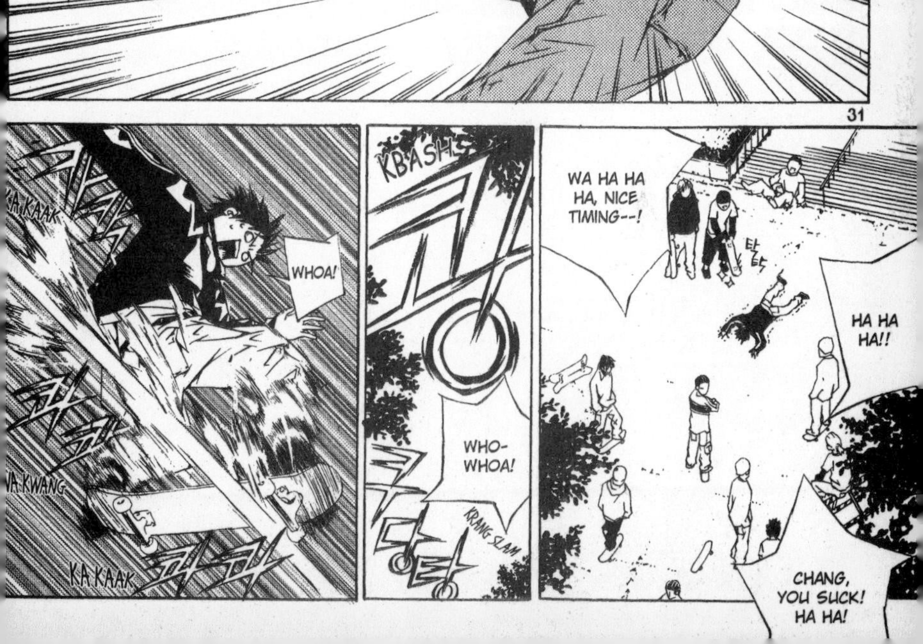
KA KAAK
WHOA!
WA KWANG
KA KAAK
KBASH
WHO-WHOA!
KRANG SLAM
WA HA HA HA, NICE TIMING--!
HA HA HA!!
CHANG, YOU SUCK! HA HA!

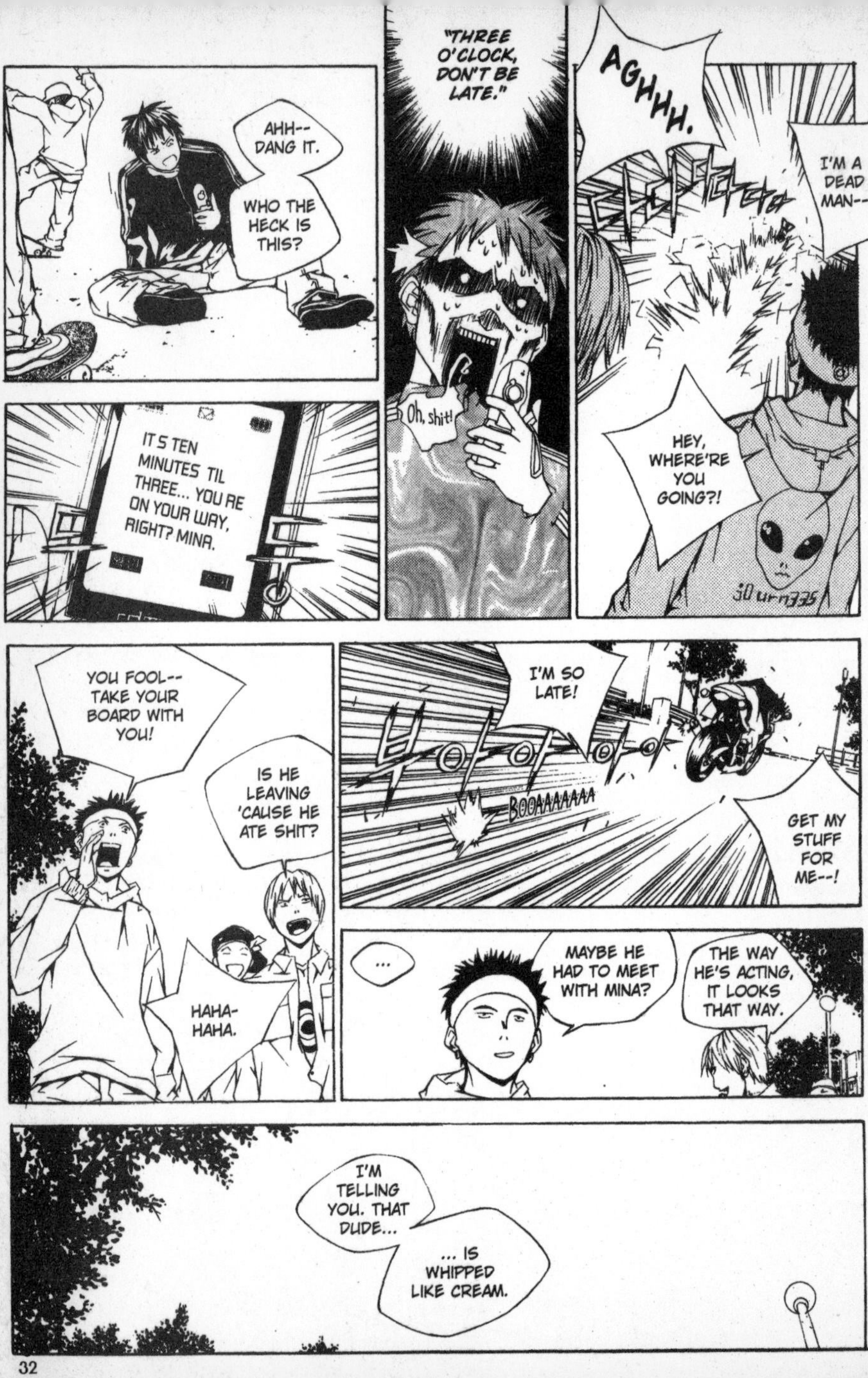
AHH-- DANG IT.
WHO THE HECK IS THIS?
IT'S TEN MINUTES TIL THREE... YOU'RE ON YOUR WAY, RIGHT? MINA.
"THREE O'CLOCK, DON'T BE LATE."
Oh, shit!
AGHHH.
I'M A DEAD MAN--!
HEY, WHERE'RE YOU GOING?!
YOU FOOL-- TAKE YOUR BOARD WITH YOU!
IS HE LEAVING 'CAUSE HE ATE SHIT?
HAHA-HAHA.
I'M SO LATE!
BOOAAAAAAA
GET MY STUFF FOR ME--!
...
MAYBE HE HAD TO MEET WITH MINA?
THE WAY HE'S ACTING, IT LOOKS THAT WAY.
I'M TELLING YOU. THAT DUDE...
... IS WHIPPED LIKE CREAM.

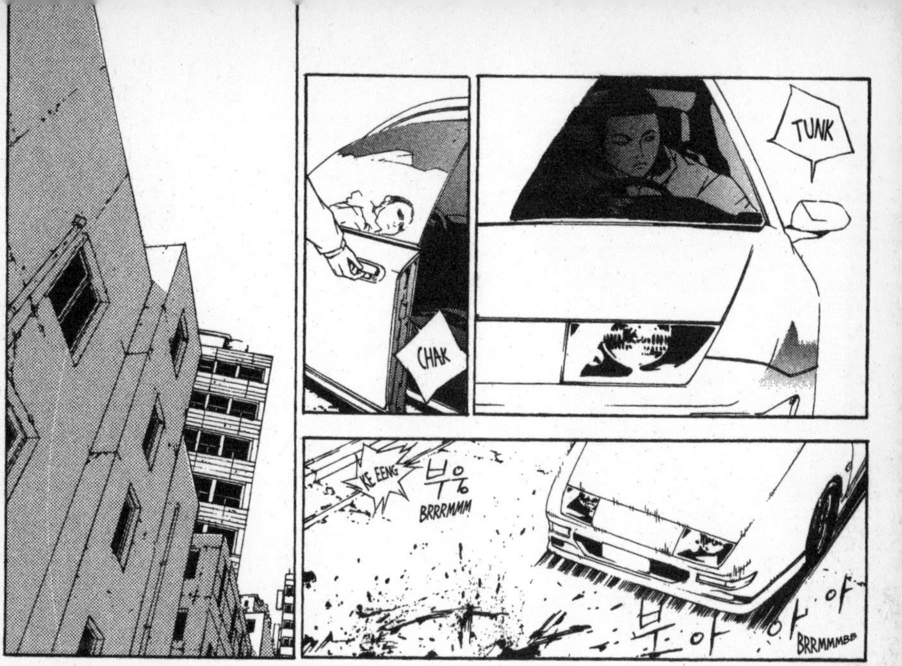
CHAK
TUNK
KE EENG
붕
BRRRMMM
부아아아
BRRMMMBB

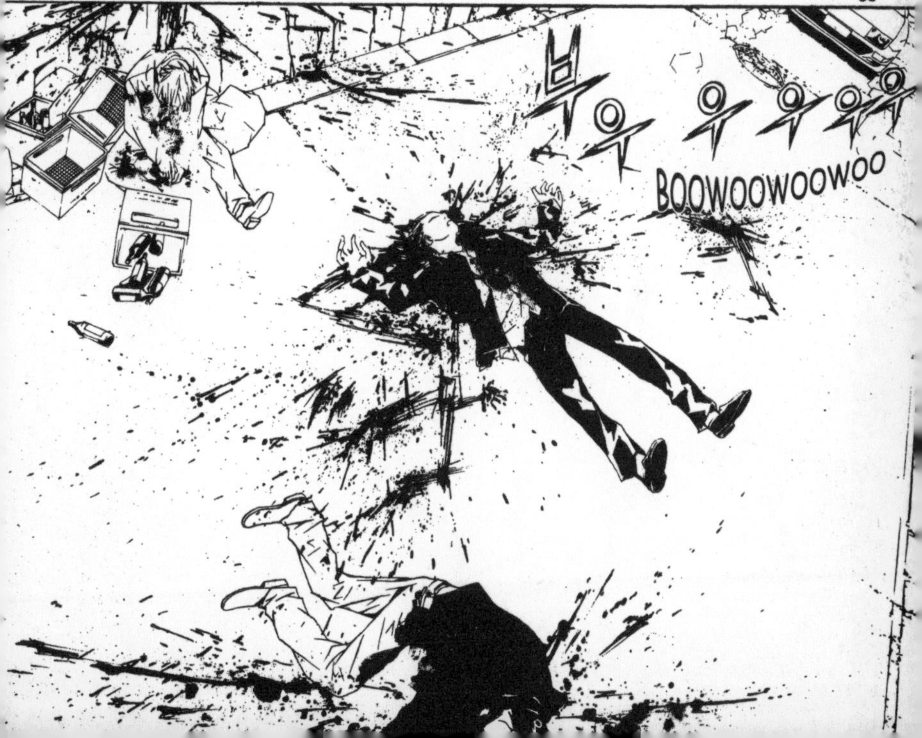
부우우우우
BOOWOOWOOWOO

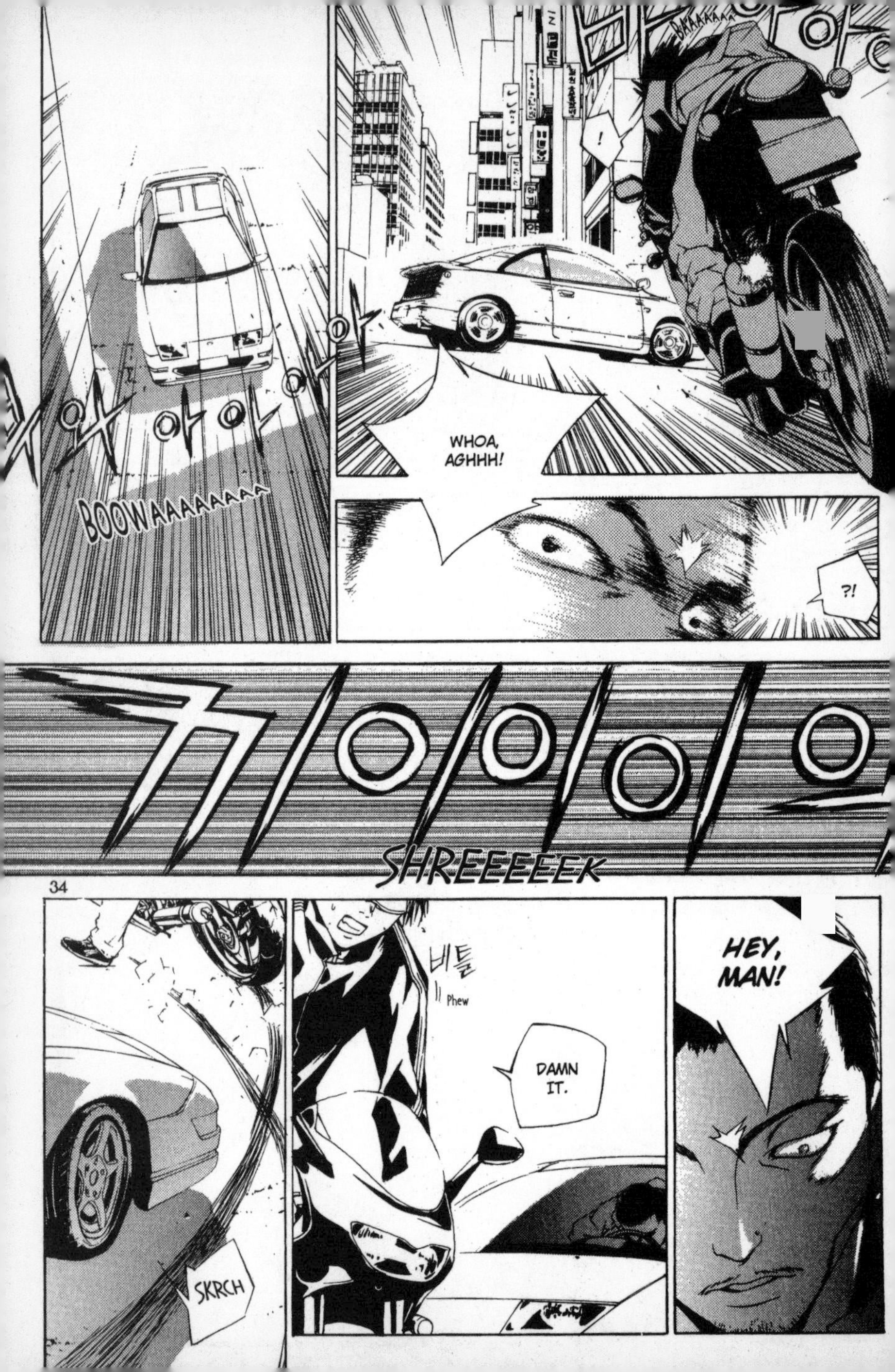
BOOWAAAAAAA
BAAAAAAA
!
WHOA, AGHHH!
?!
SHREEEEEEK
SKRCH
비틀
Phew
DAMN IT.
HEY, MAN!

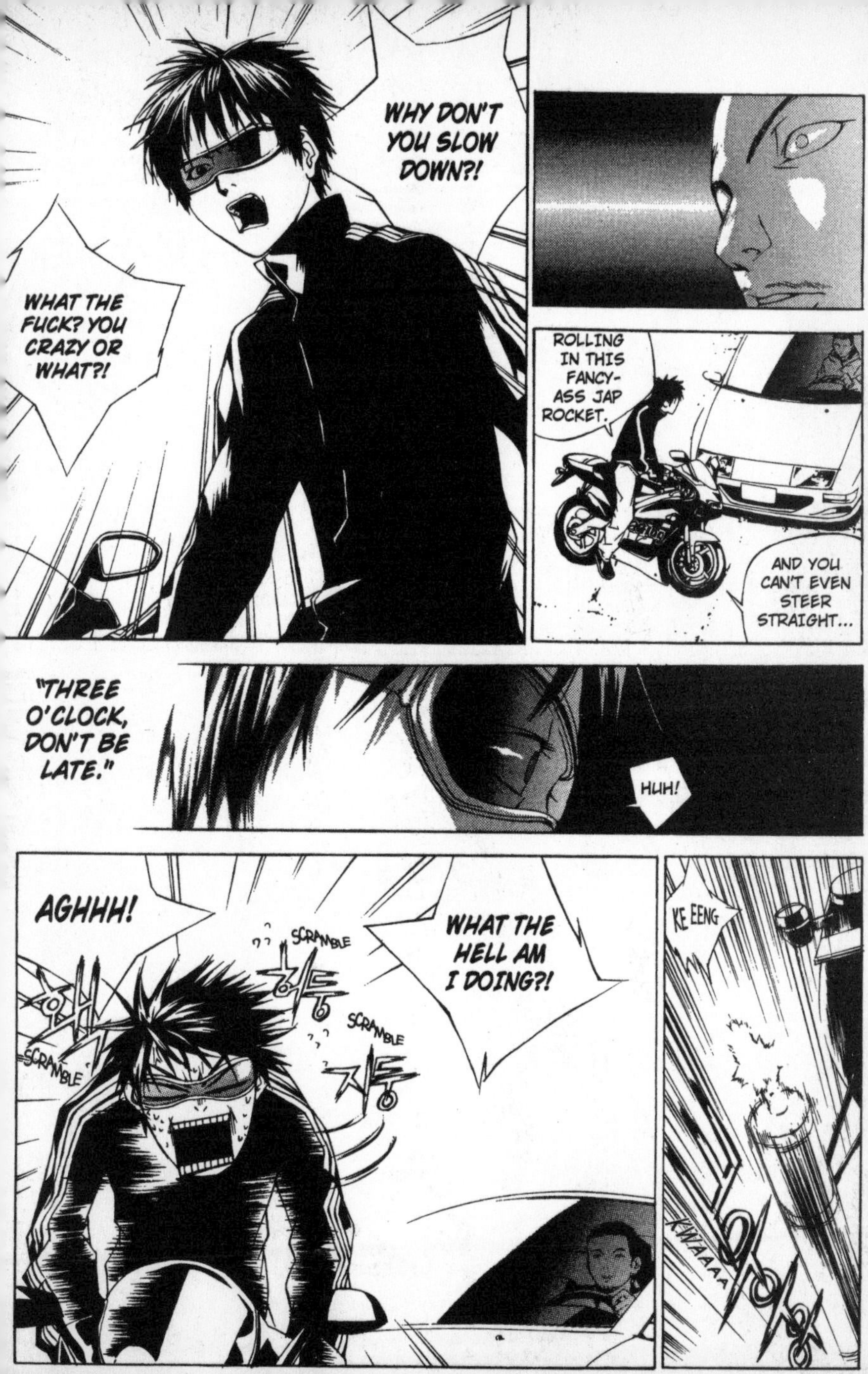

WHY DON'T YOU SLOW DOWN?!
WHAT THE FUCK? YOU CRAZY OR WHAT?!
ROLLING IN THIS FANCY-ASS JAP ROCKET.
AND YOU CAN'T EVEN STEER STRAIGHT...
"THREE O'CLOCK, DON'T BE LATE."
HUH!
AGHHH!
SCRAMBLE
SCRAMBLE
SCRAMBLE
WHAT THE HELL AM I DOING?!
KE EENG
KWAAAA

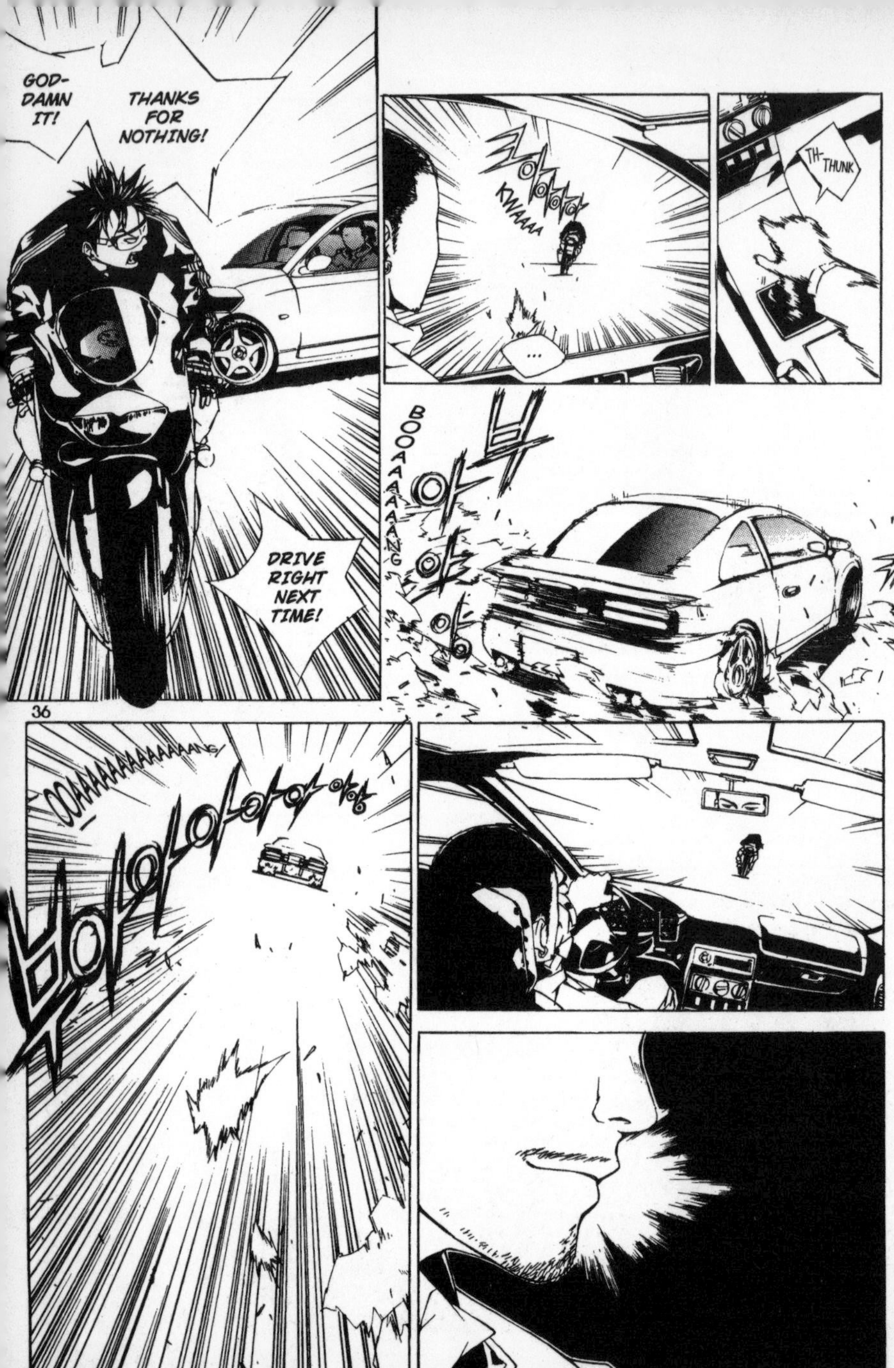
GOD-DAMN IT!
THANKS FOR NOTHING!
DRIVE RIGHT NEXT TIME!
KWAAAA
...
TH-THUNK
BOOAAAAAAAANG
OOAAAAAAAAAAAAANG!

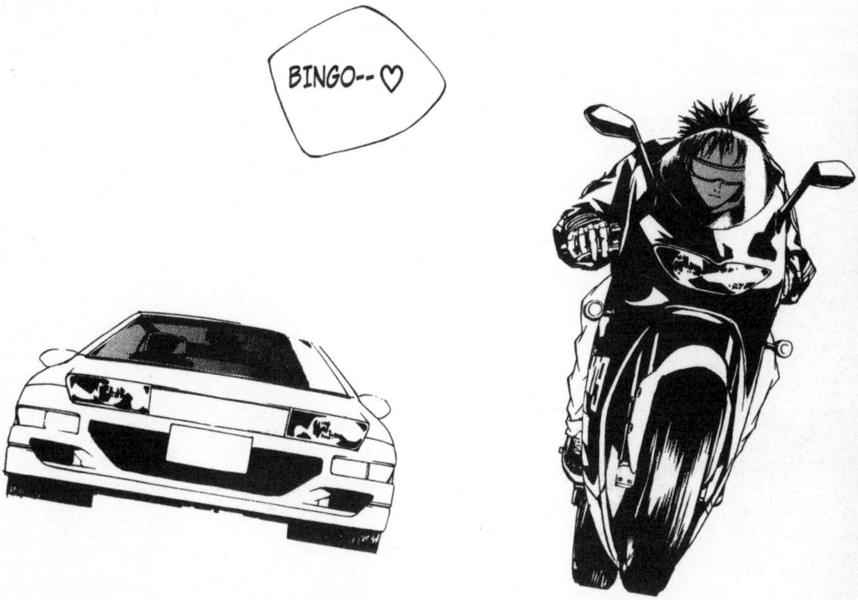
BINGO--♡

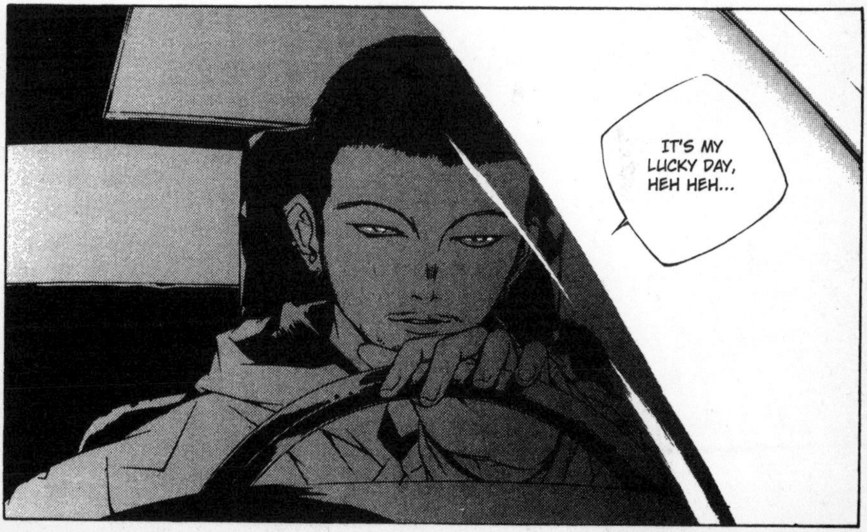
IT'S MY LUCKY DAY, HEH HEH...

Log-1 END

LOG_2: Access

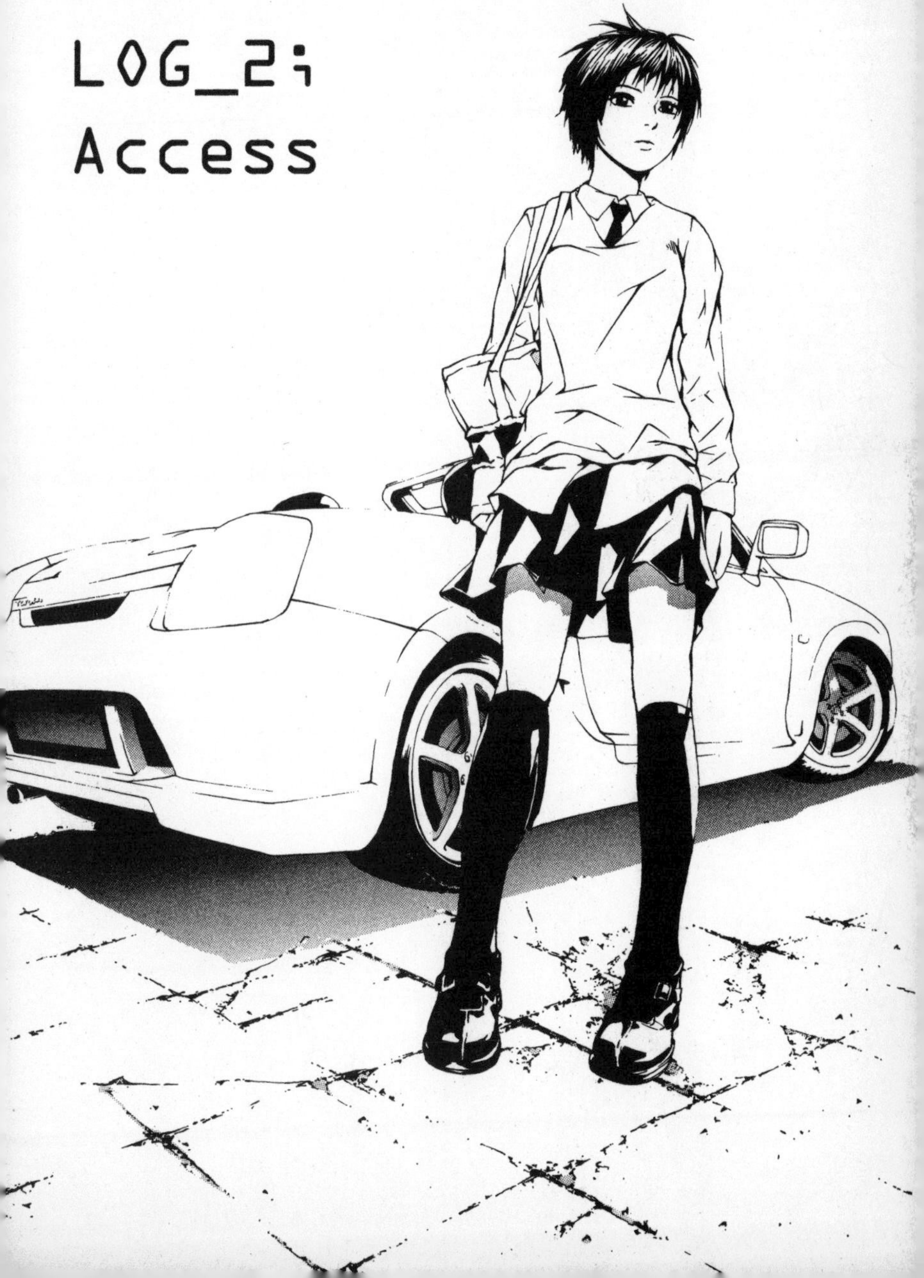

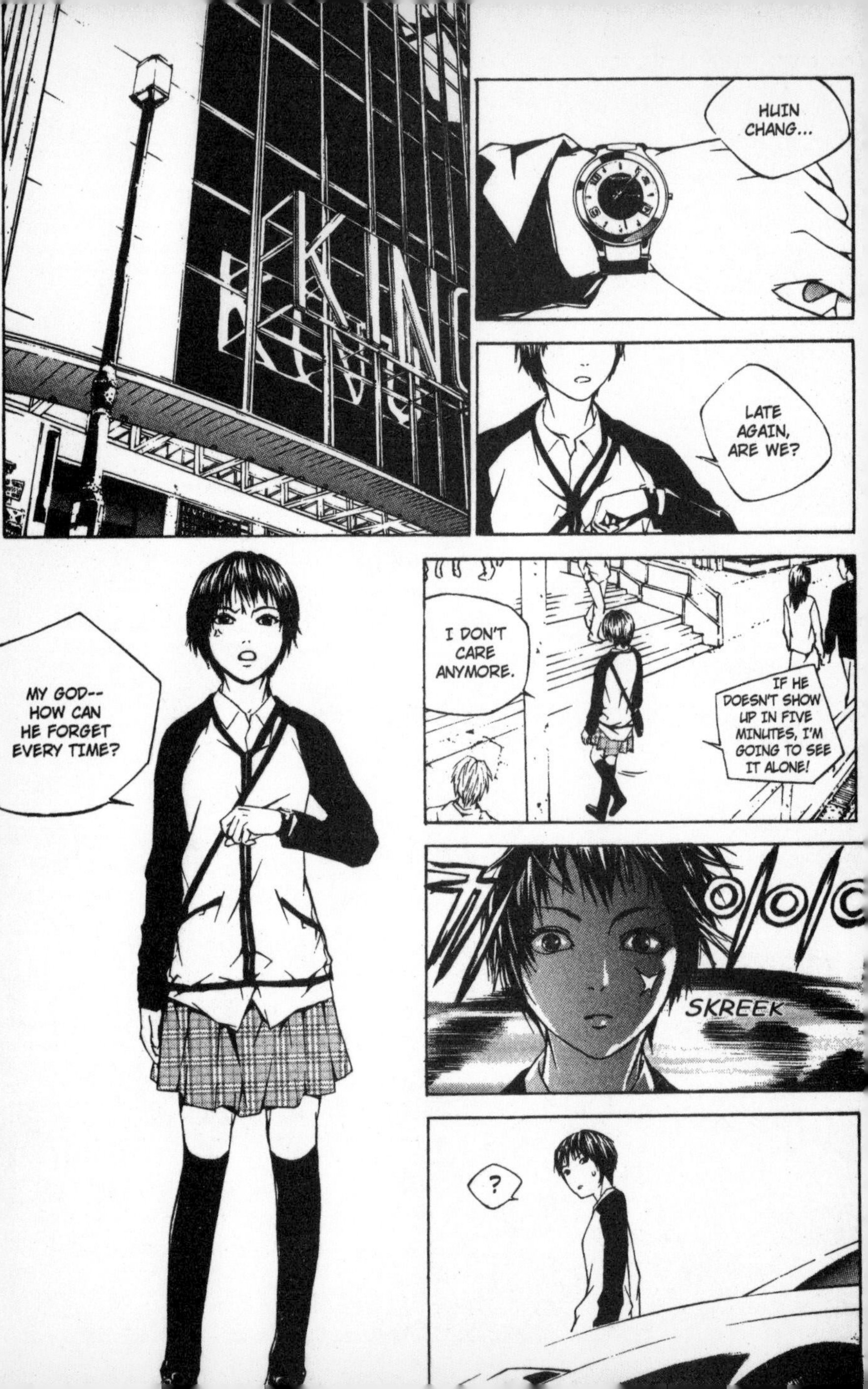
HUIN CHANG...
LATE AGAIN, ARE WE?
MY GOD-- HOW CAN HE FORGET EVERY TIME?
I DON'T CARE ANYMORE.
IF HE DOESN'T SHOW UP IN FIVE MINUTES, I'M GOING TO SEE IT ALONE!
SKREEK
?

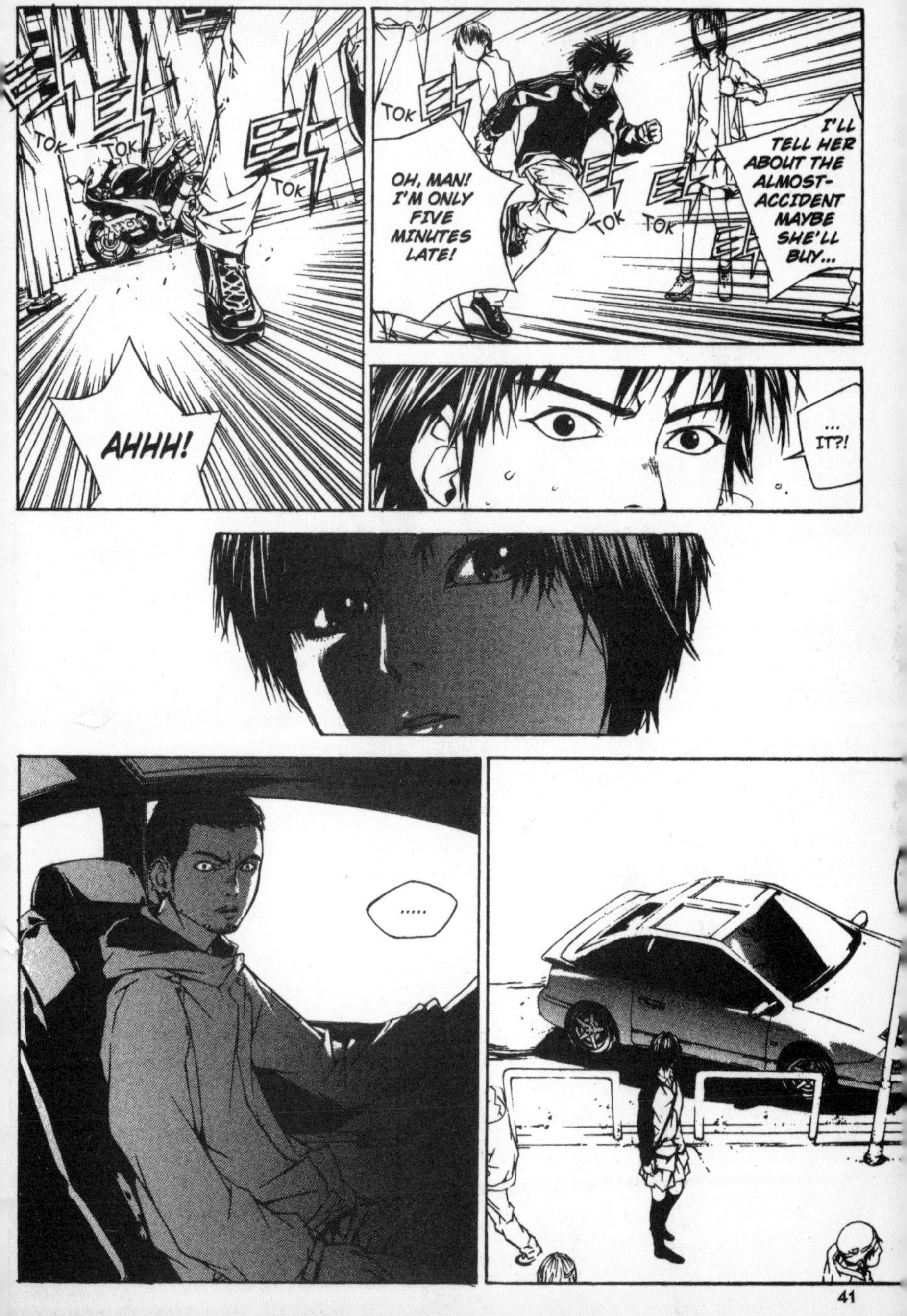
TOK
TOK
TOK
AHHH!
TOK
OH, MAN! I'M ONLY FIVE MINUTES LATE!
TOK
TOK
I'LL TELL HER ABOUT THE ALMOST-ACCIDENT MAYBE SHE'LL BUY...
... IT?!
......

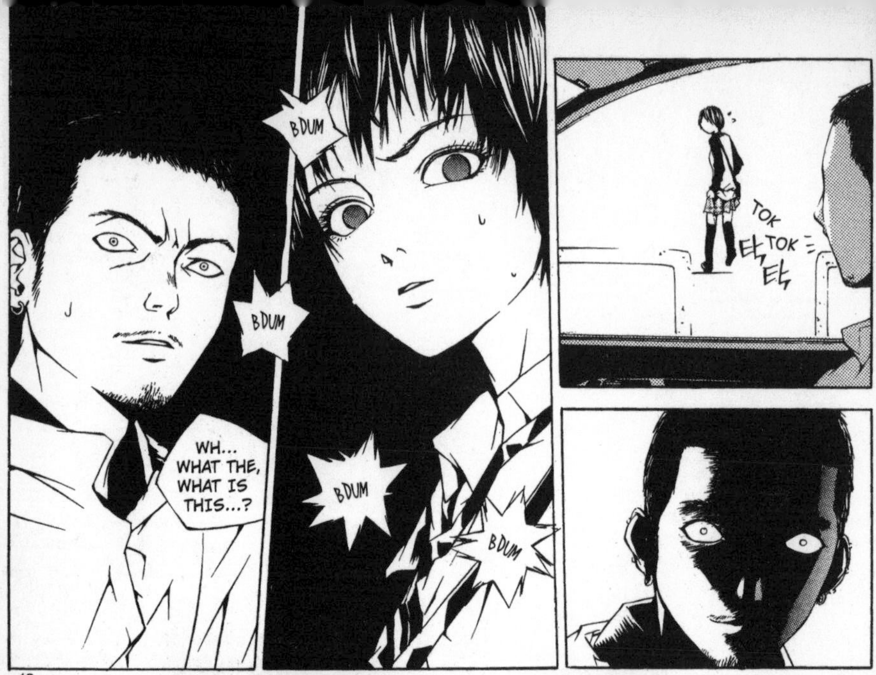
BDUM
WH... WHAT THE, WHAT IS THIS...?
BDUM
BDUM
BDUM
TOK TOK

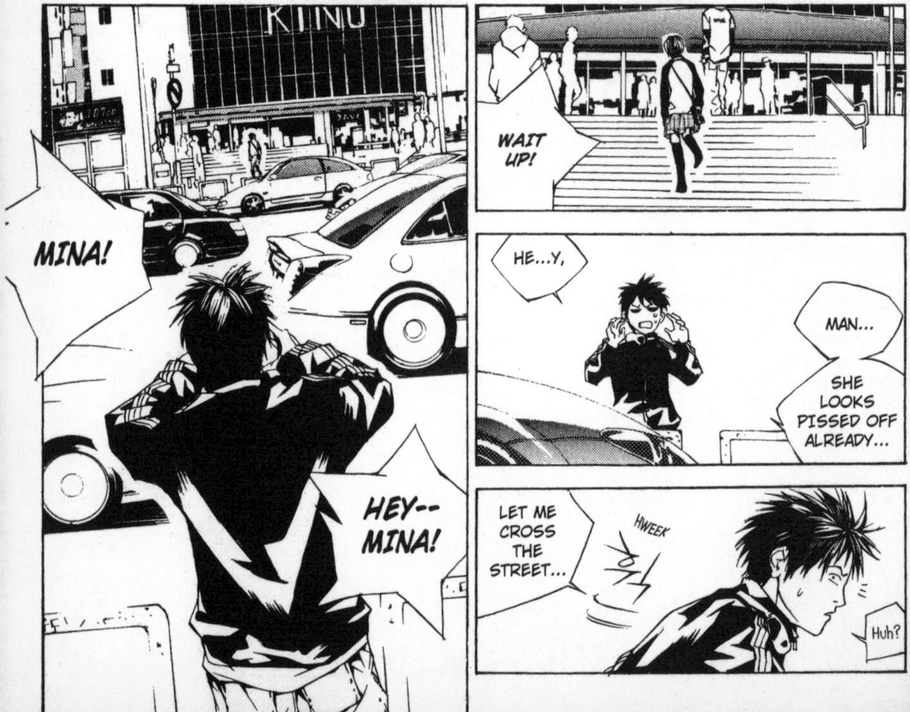
MINA!
HEY-- MINA!
WAIT UP!
HE...Y,
MAN...
SHE LOOKS PISSED OFF ALREADY...
LET ME CROSS THE STREET...
HWEEK
Huh?

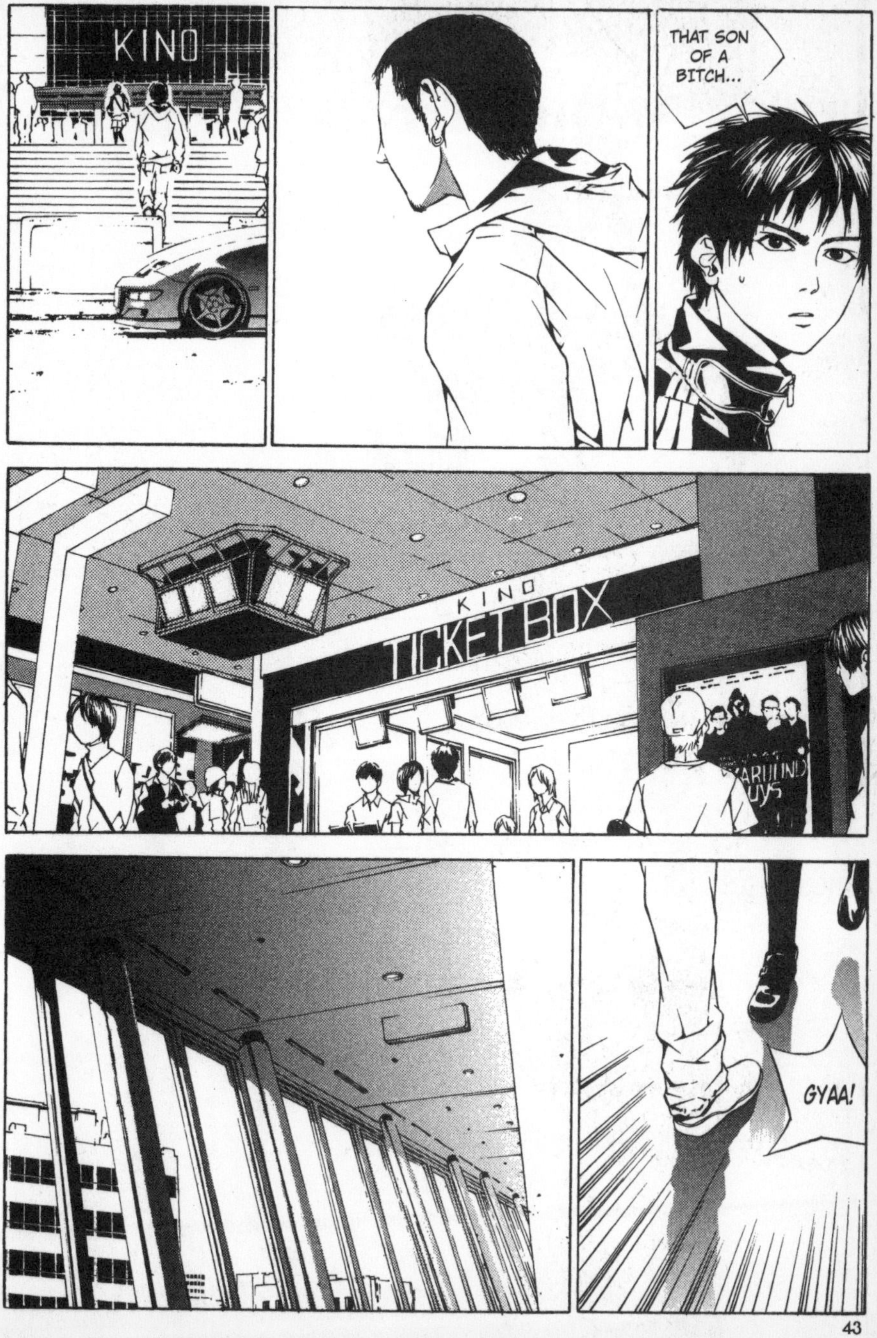
KINO
THAT SON OF A BITCH...
KINO
TICKET BOX
GYAA!

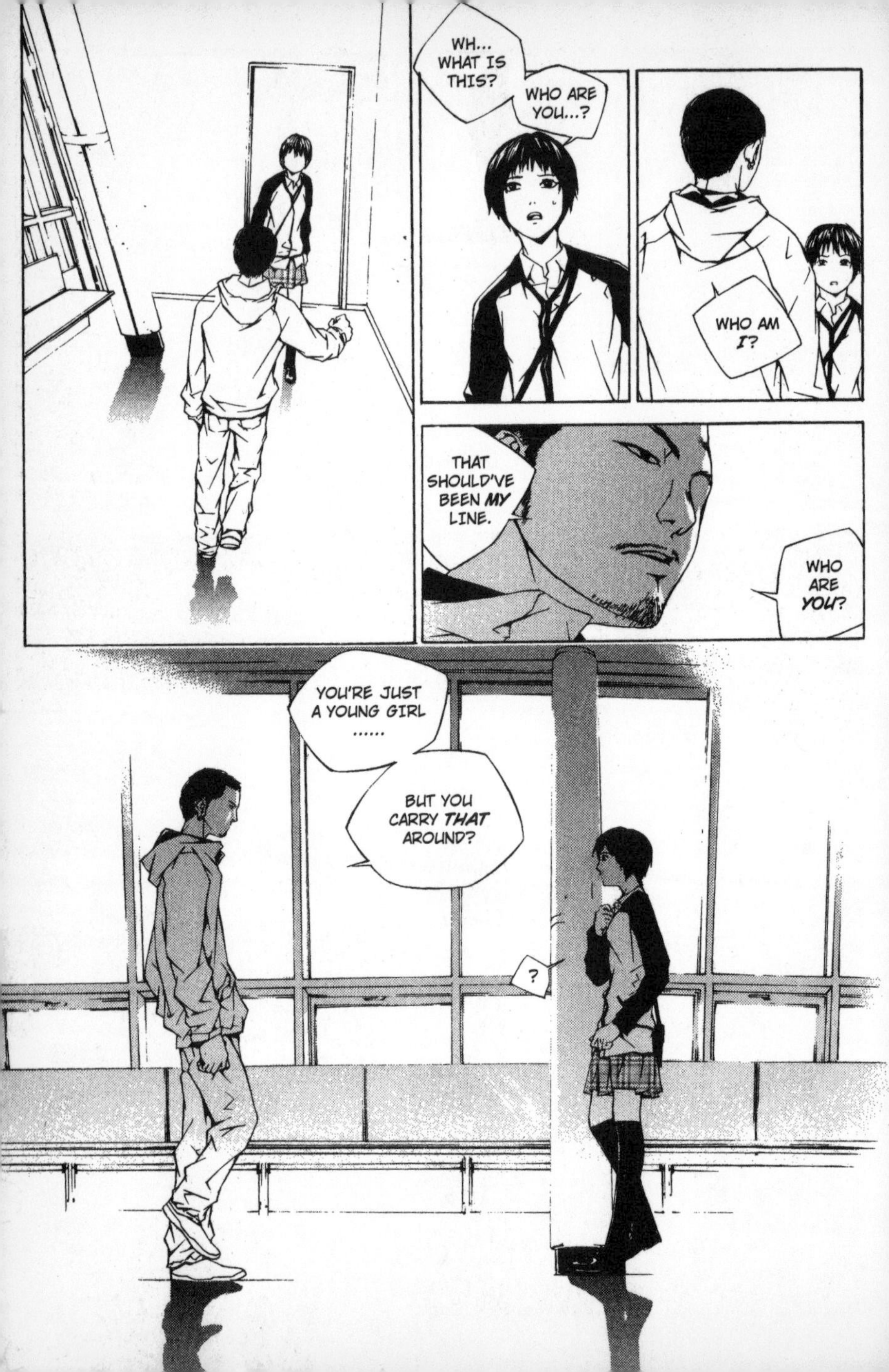
WH... WHAT IS THIS?
WHO ARE YOU...?
WHO AM I?
THAT SHOULD'VE BEEN MY LINE.
WHO ARE YOU?
YOU'RE JUST A YOUNG GIRL ......
BUT YOU CARRY THAT AROUND?
?

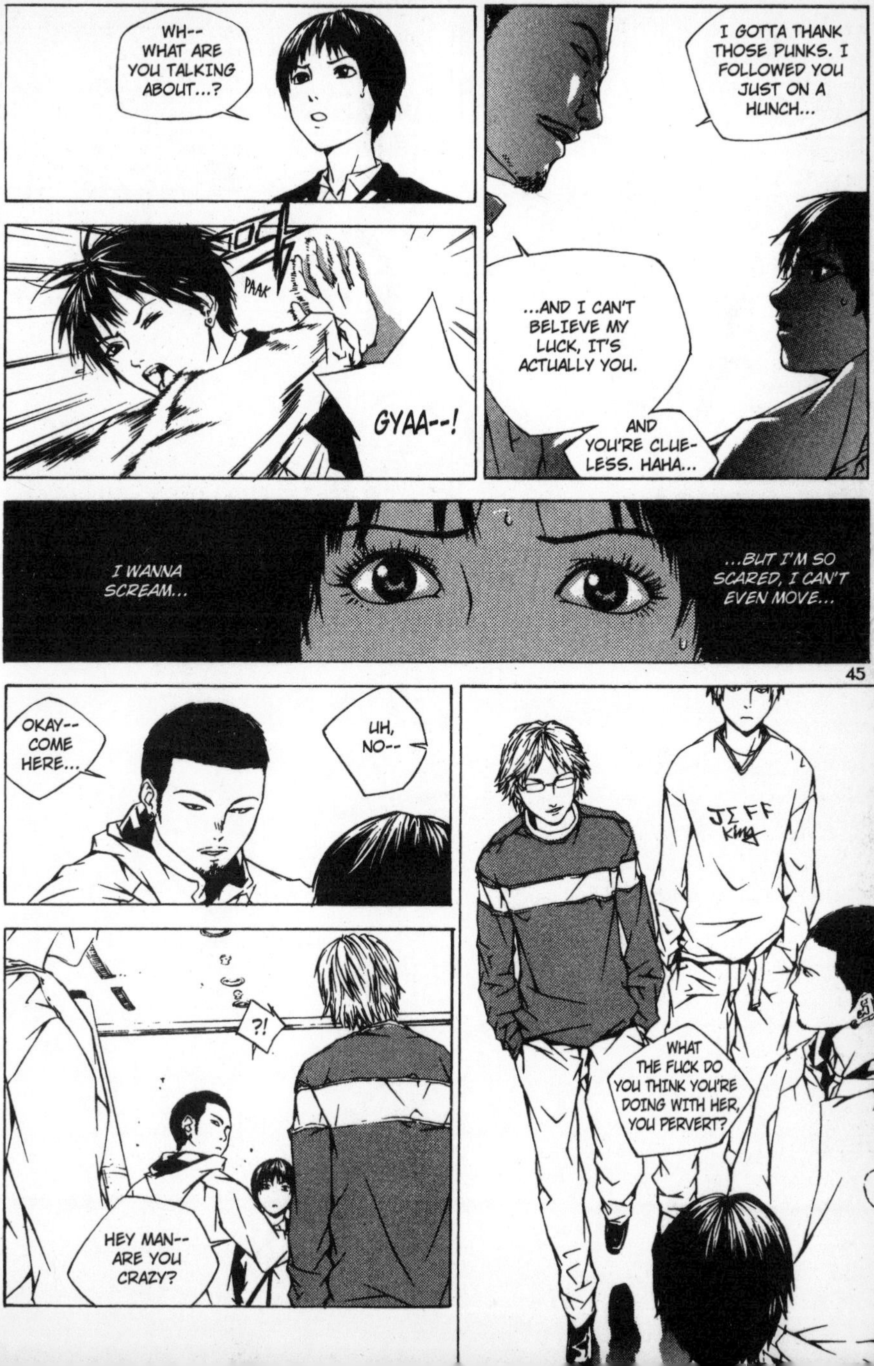
WH-- WHAT ARE YOU TALKING ABOUT...?
I GOTTA THANK THOSE PUNKS. I FOLLOWED YOU JUST ON A HUNCH...
PAAK
GYAA--!
...AND I CAN'T BELIEVE MY LUCK, IT'S ACTUALLY YOU.
AND YOU'RE CLUE-LESS. HAHA...
I WANNA SCREAM...
...BUT I'M SO SCARED, I CAN'T EVEN MOVE...
OKAY-- COME HERE...
UH, NO--
?!
HEY MAN-- ARE YOU CRAZY?
WHAT THE FUCK DO YOU THINK YOU'RE DOING WITH HER, YOU PERVERT?

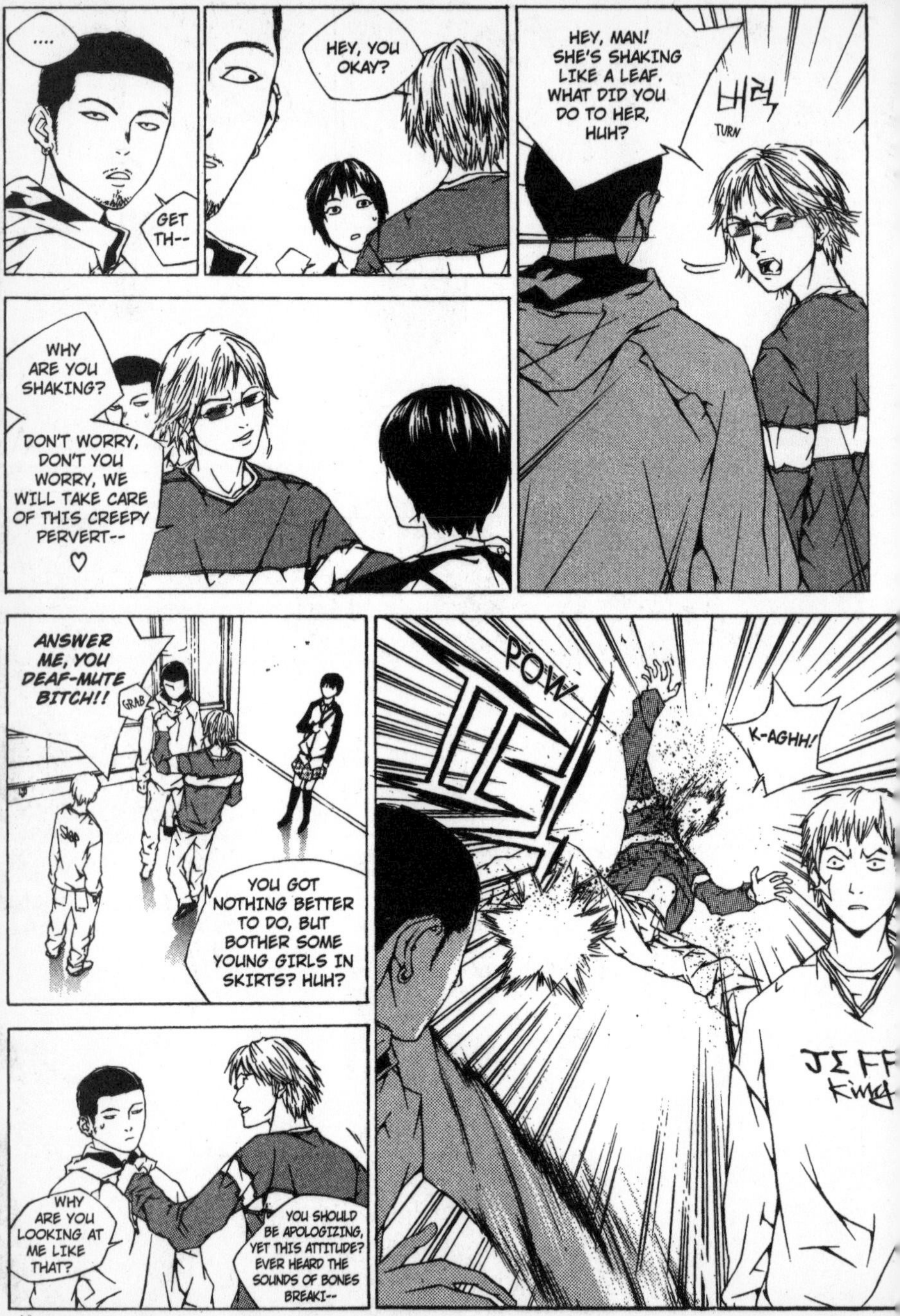
....
GET TH--
HEY, YOU OKAY?
WHY ARE YOU SHAKING?
DON'T WORRY, DON'T YOU WORRY, WE WILL TAKE CARE OF THIS CREEPY PERVERT-- ♡
HEY, MAN! SHE'S SHAKING LIKE A LEAF. WHAT DID YOU DO TO HER, HUH?
버럭
TURN
ANSWER ME, YOU DEAF-MUTE BITCH!!
GRAB
YOU GOT NOTHING BETTER TO DO, BUT BOTHER SOME YOUNG GIRLS IN SKIRTS? HUH?
WHY ARE YOU LOOKING AT ME LIKE THAT?
YOU SHOULD BE APOLOGIZING, YET THIS ATTITUDE? EVER HEARD THE SOUNDS OF BONES BREAKI--
POW
K-AGHH!
JEFF King

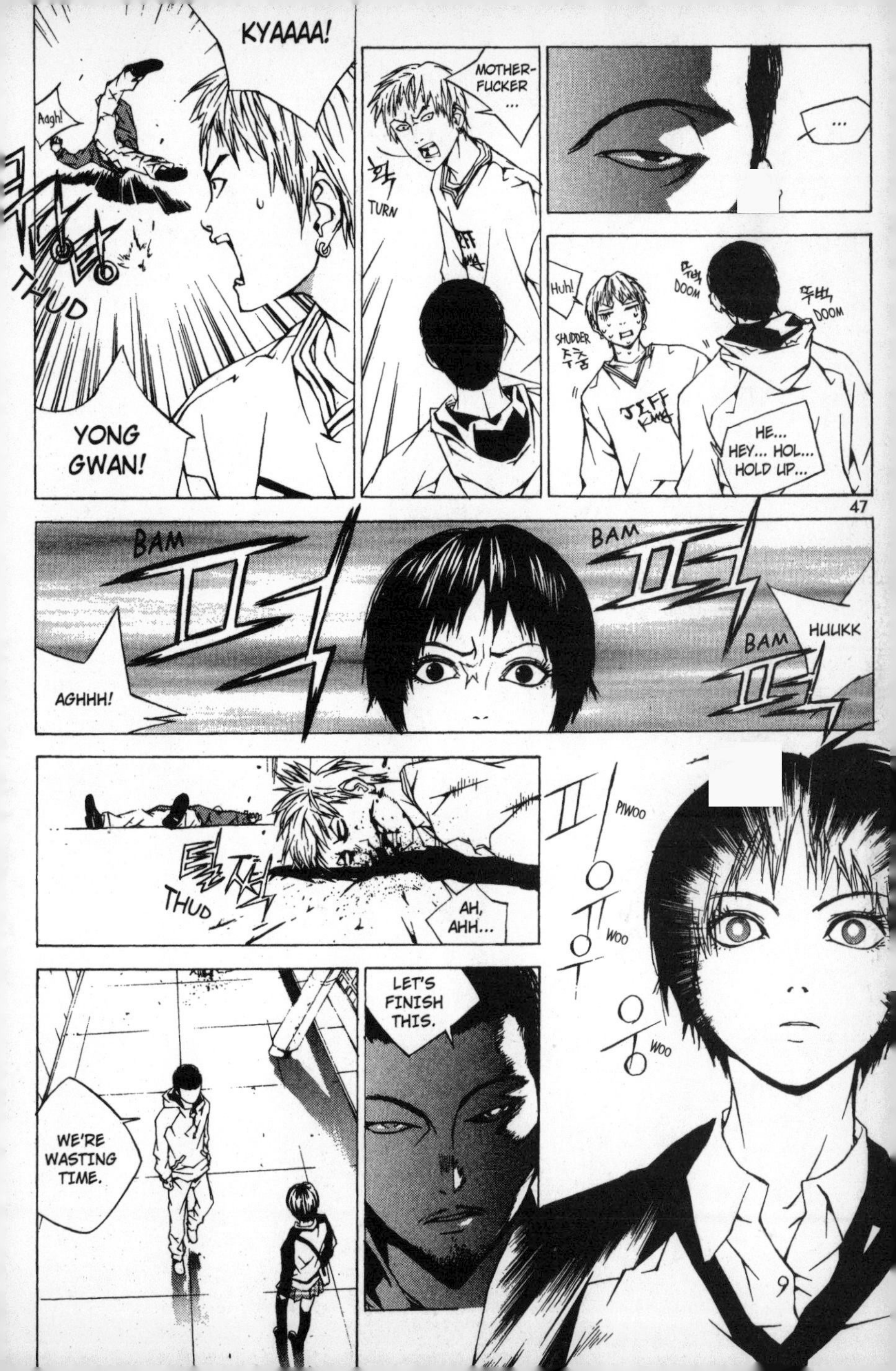
KYAAAA!
Aagh!
THUD
YONG GWAN!
MOTHER-FUCKER ...
TURN
...
Huh!
DOOM
DOOM
SHUDDER
HE... HEY... HOL... HOLD UP...
BAM
AGHHH!
BAM
BAM
HUUKK
THUD
AH, AHH...
WE'RE WASTING TIME.
LET'S FINISH THIS.
PIWOO
WOO
WOO

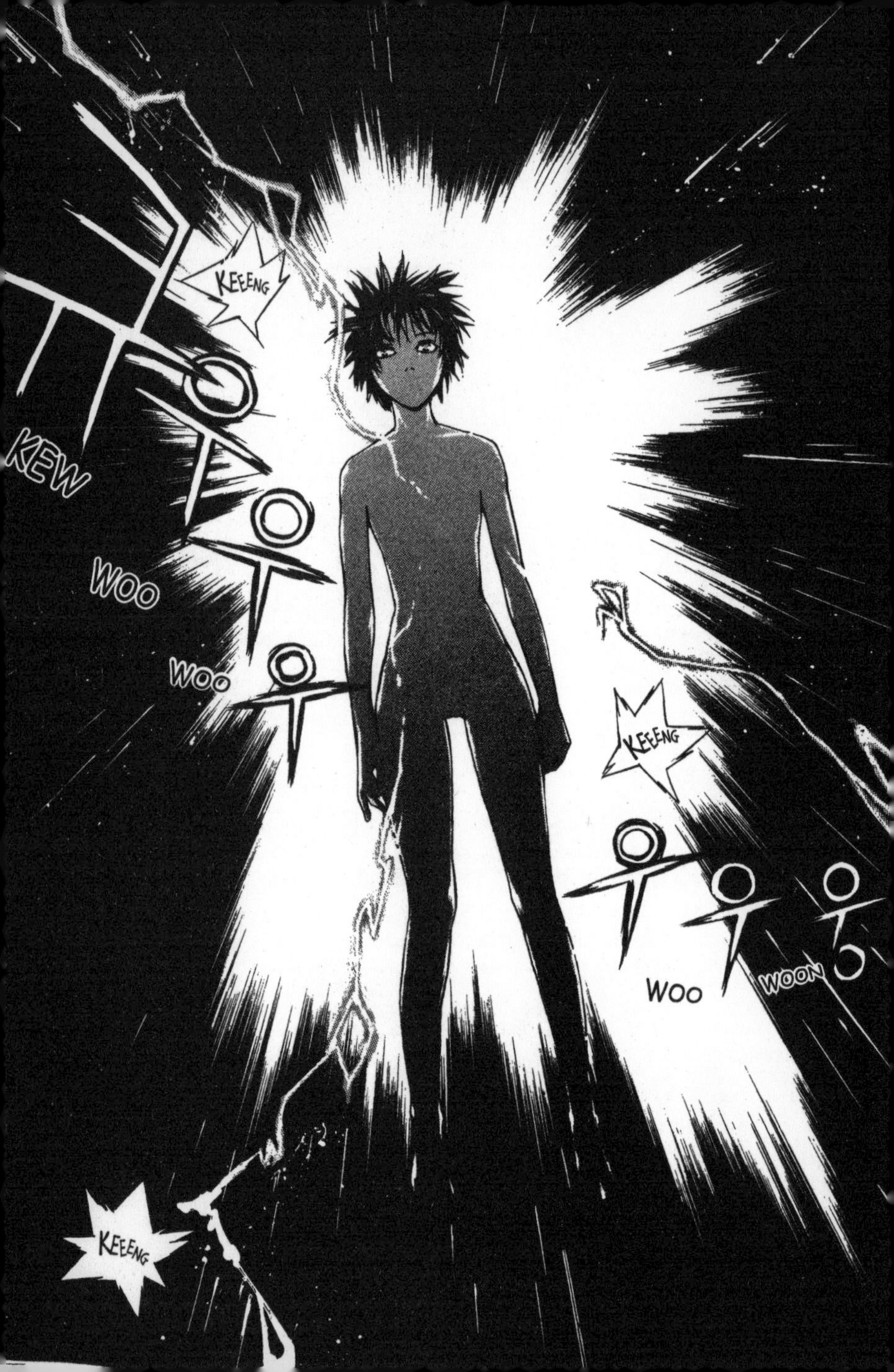
KEEENG
KEW
WOO
WOO
KEEENG
WOO
WOON
KEEENG

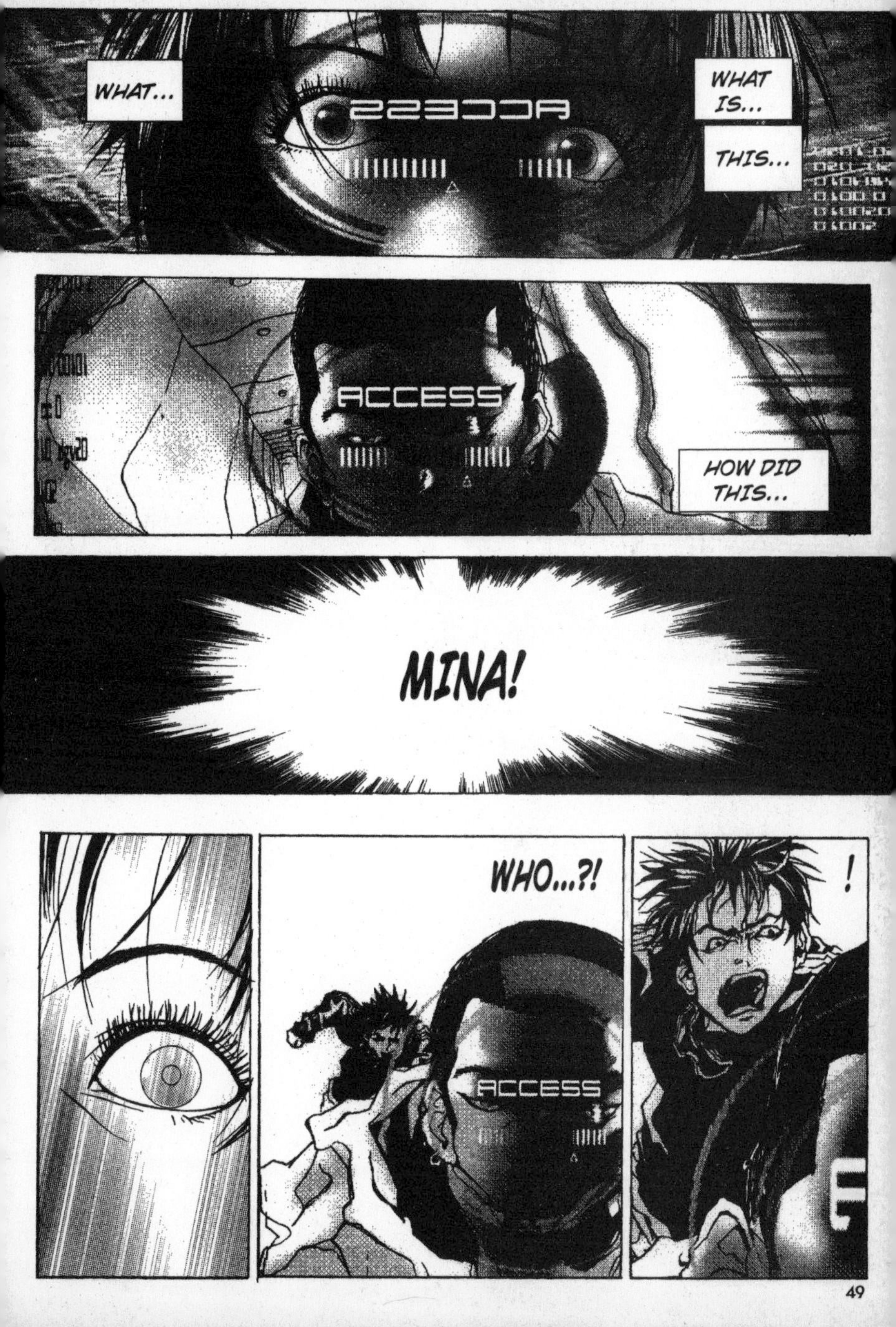
WHAT...
WHAT IS...
THIS...
ACCESS
HOW DID THIS...
MINA!
WHO...?!
ACCESS
!

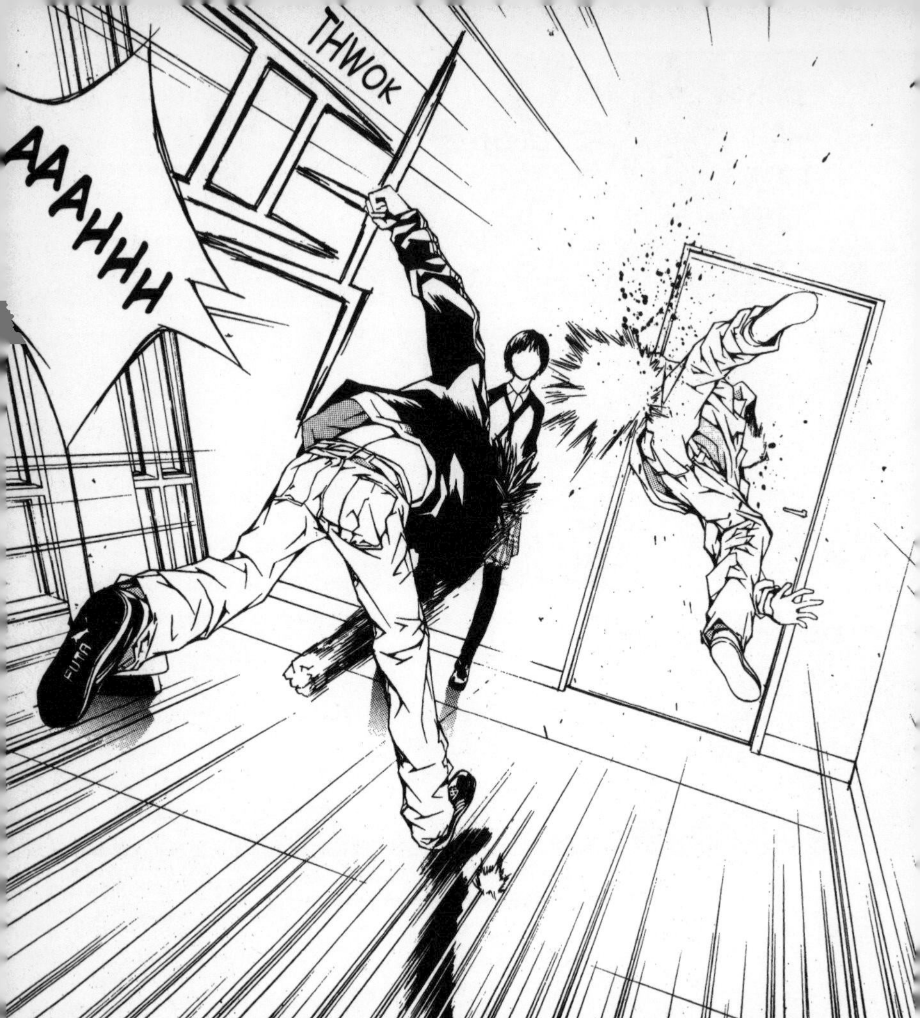
THWOK
AAAHHHH
FUTA

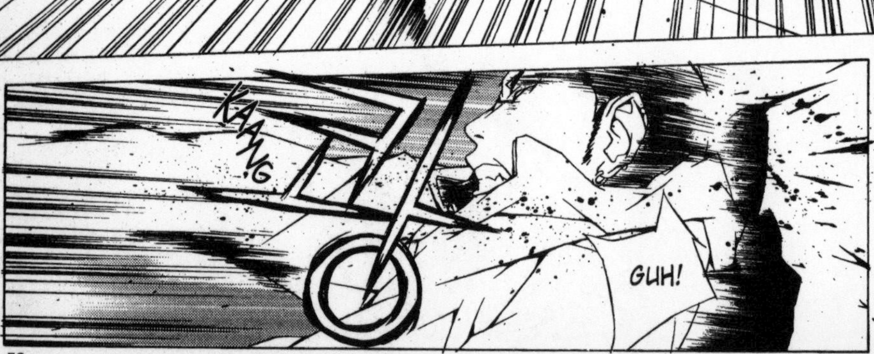
KAAANG
GUH!

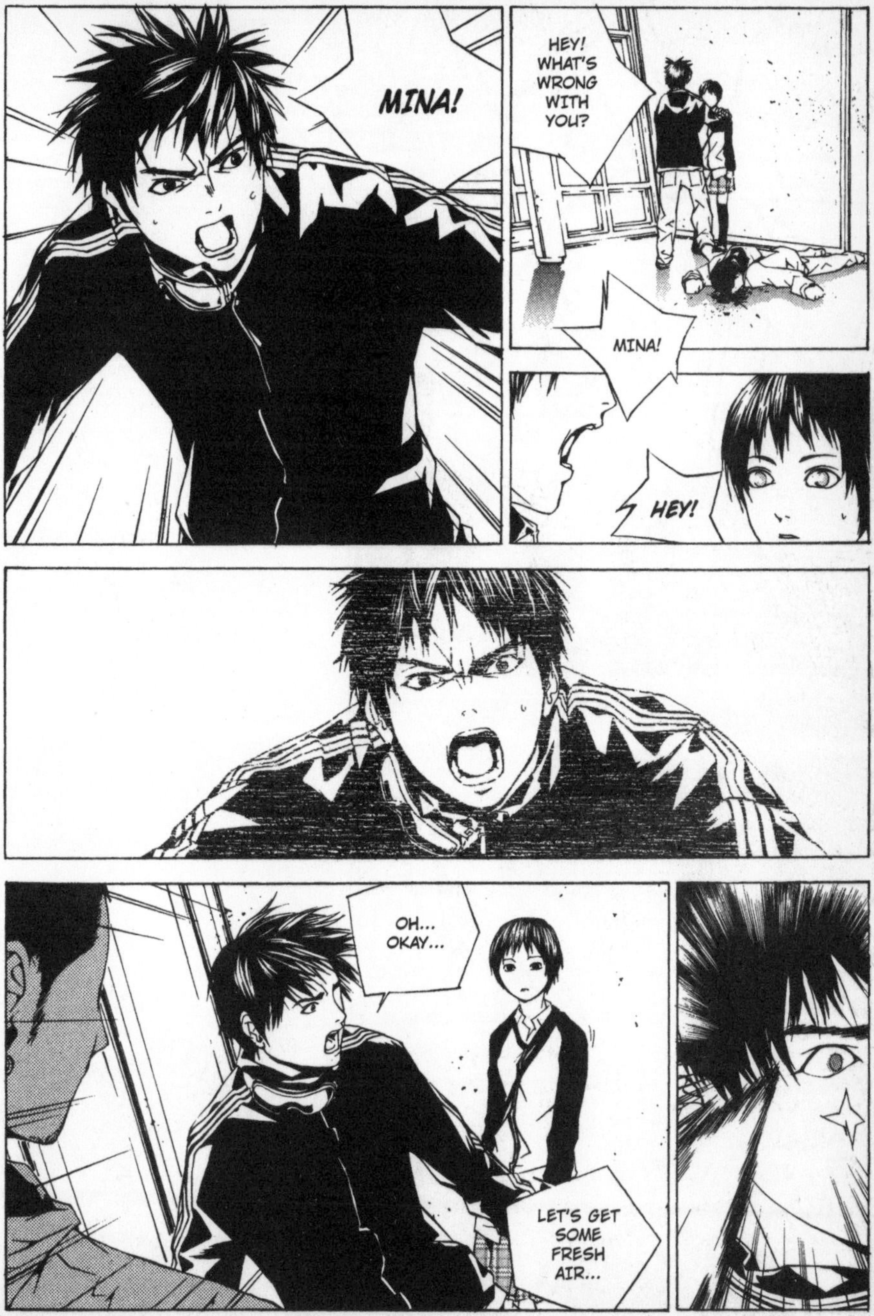
MINA!
HEY! WHAT'S WRONG WITH YOU?
MINA!
HEY!
OH... OKAY...
LET'S GET SOME FRESH AIR...

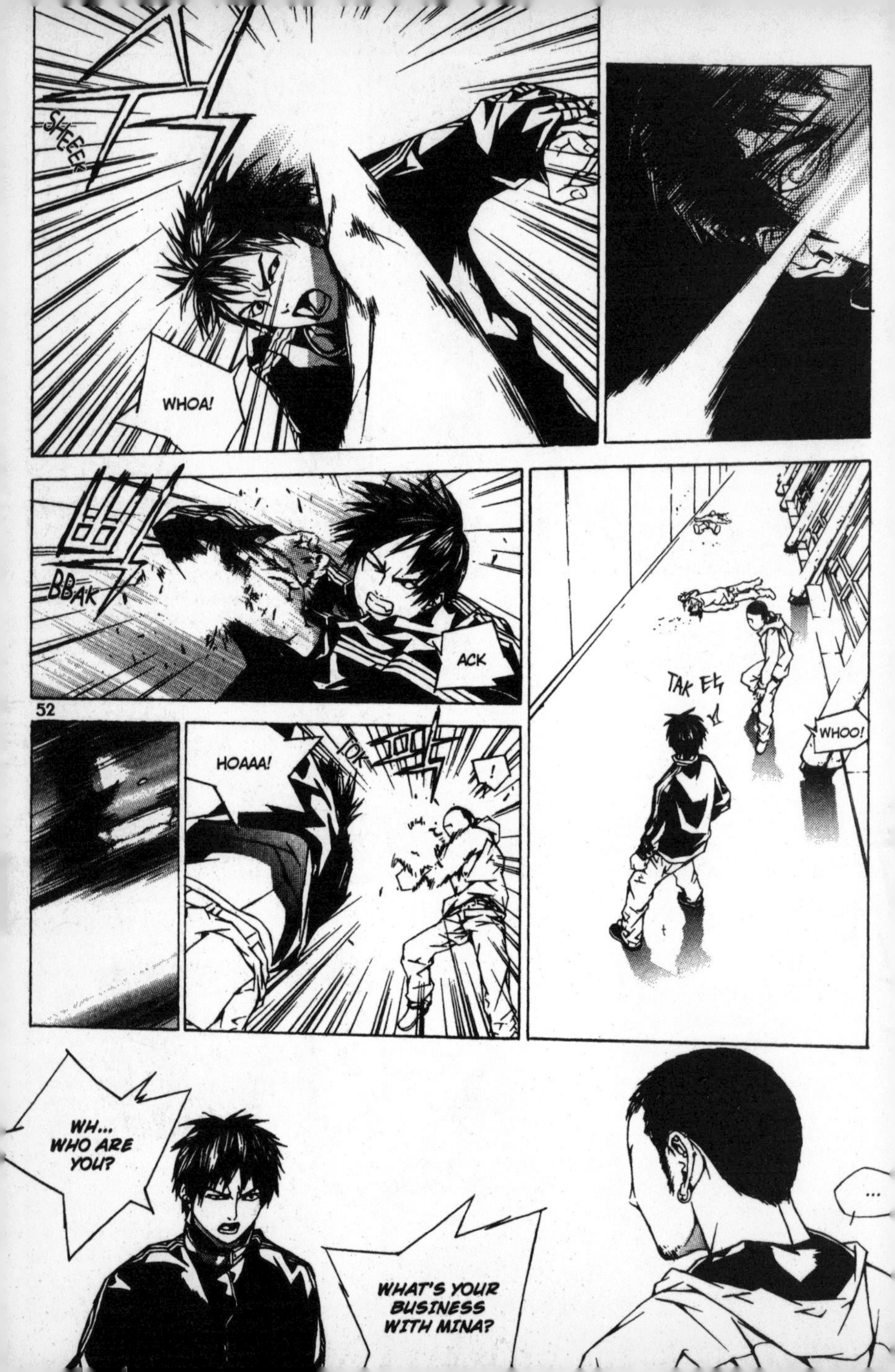
SHEEEK
WHOA!
BBAK
ACK
HOAAA!
TOK
!
TAK EK
WHOO!
WH... WHO ARE YOU?
WHAT'S YOUR BUSINESS WITH MINA?
...

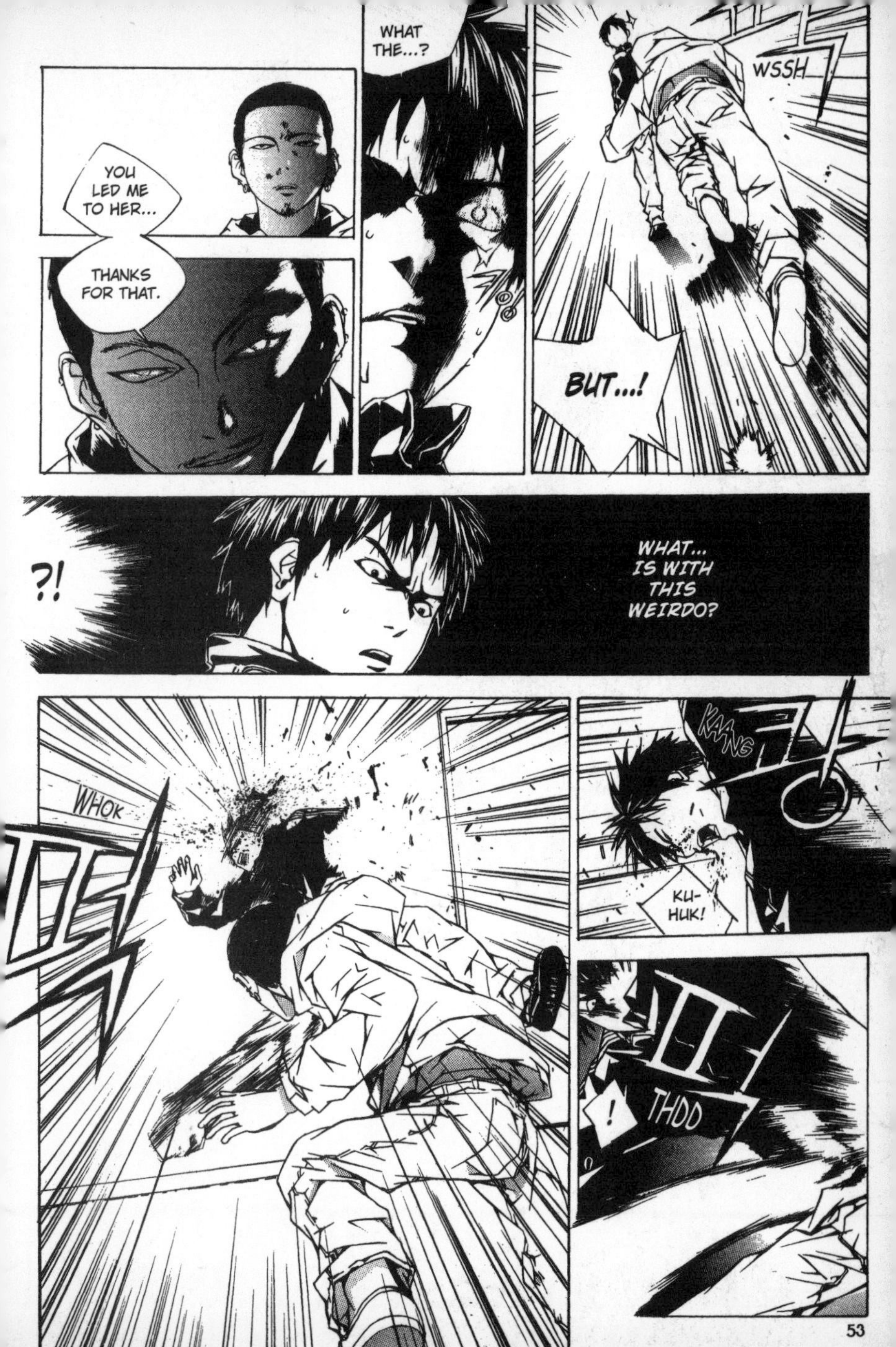

YOU LED ME TO HER...
THANKS FOR THAT.
WHAT THE...?
WSSH
BUT...!
?!
WHAT... IS WITH THIS WEIRDO?
WHOK
KAANG
KU-HUK!
!
THDD

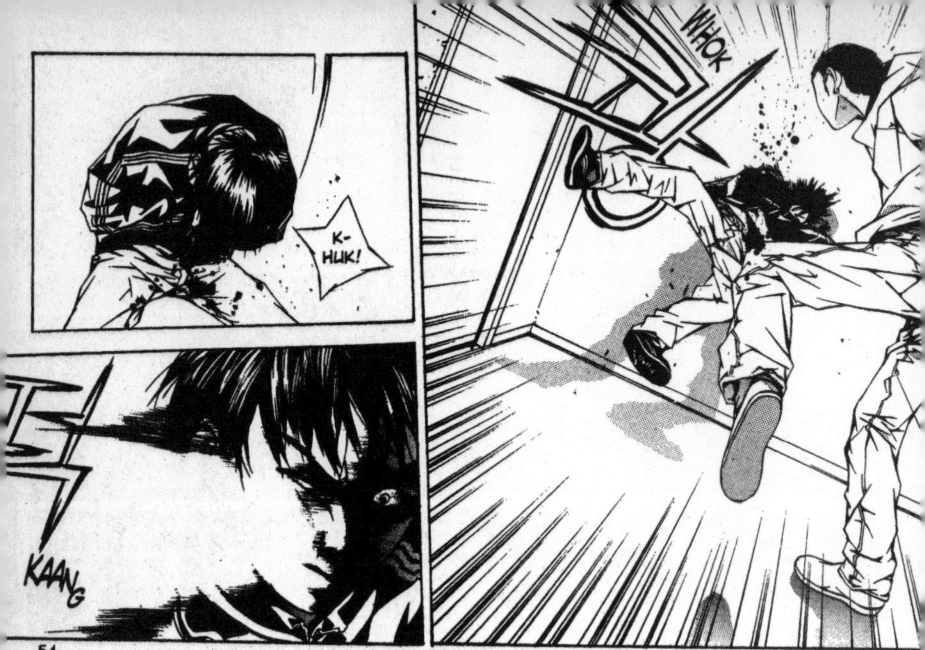
K-HUK!
KAANG
WHOK

54

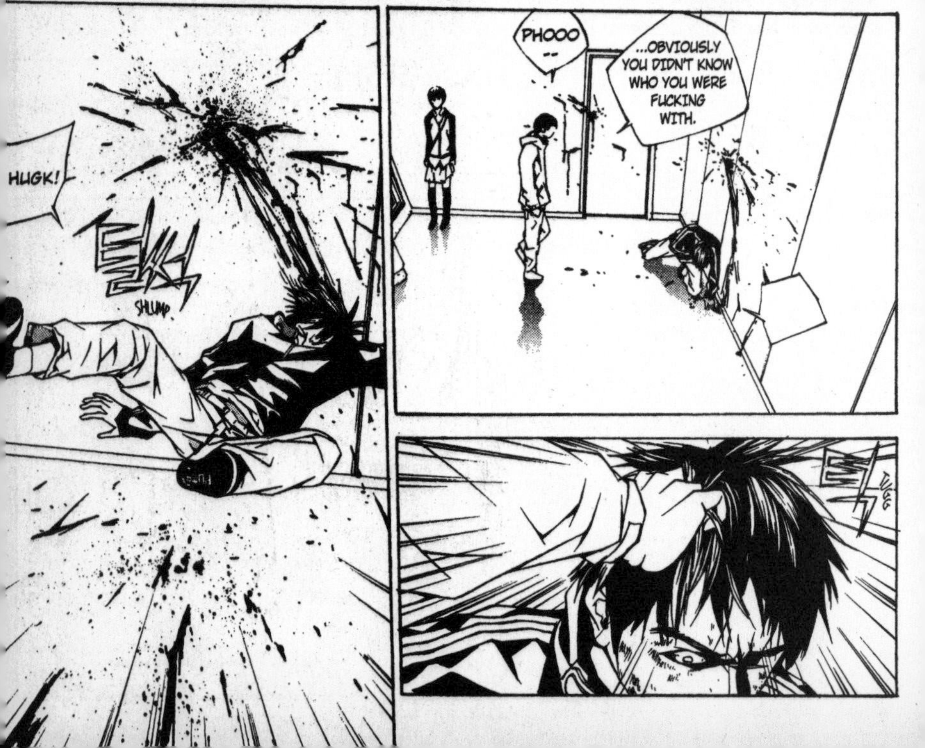
HUGK!
SHUMP
PHOOO--
...OBVIOUSLY YOU DIDN'T KNOW WHO YOU WERE FUCKING WITH.
TUGG

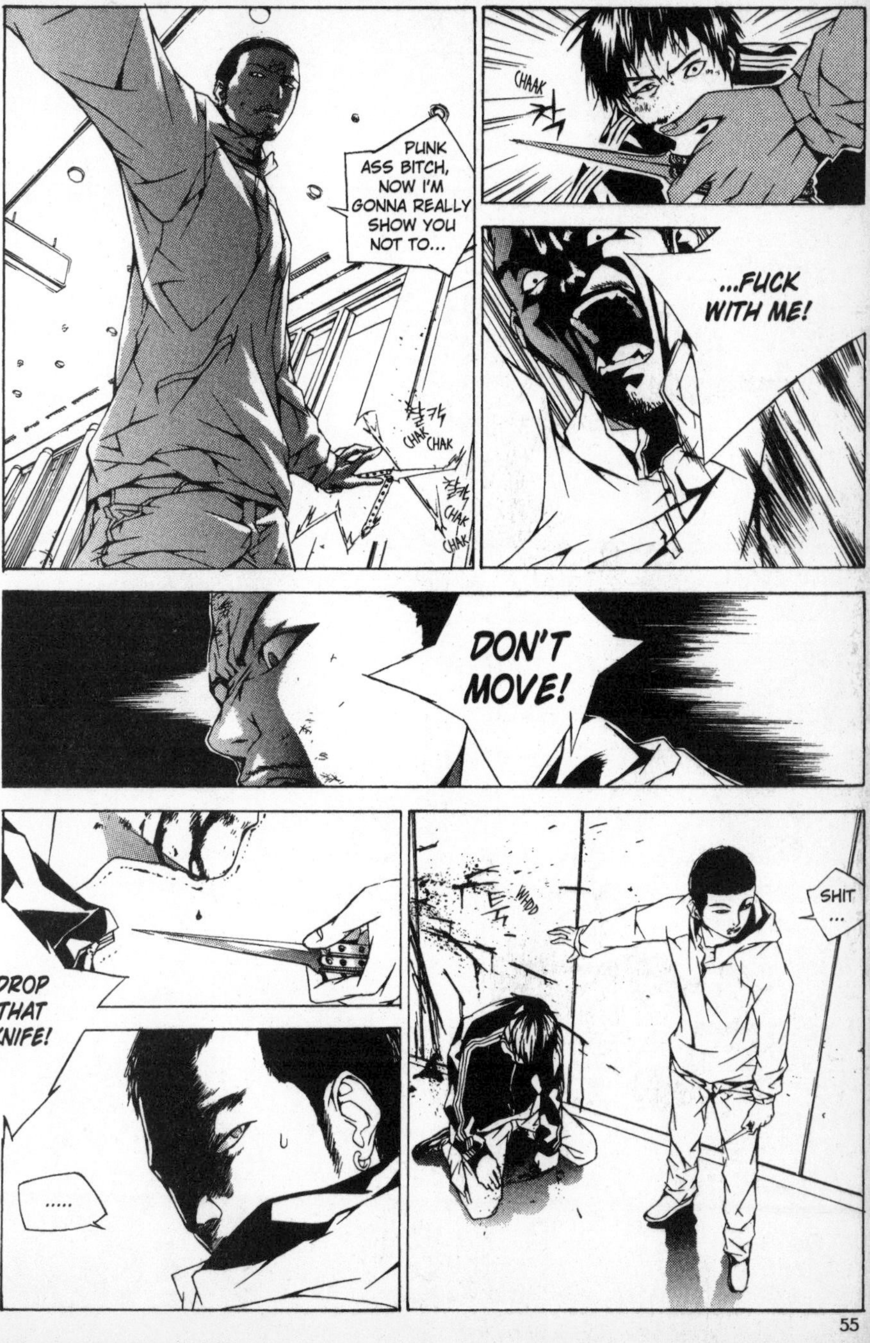
PUNK ASS BITCH, NOW I'M GONNA REALLY SHOW YOU NOT TO...
CHAK CHAK
CHAK CHAK
CHAAK
...FUCK WITH ME!
DON'T MOVE!
DROP THAT KNIFE!
.....
WHDD
SHIT ...

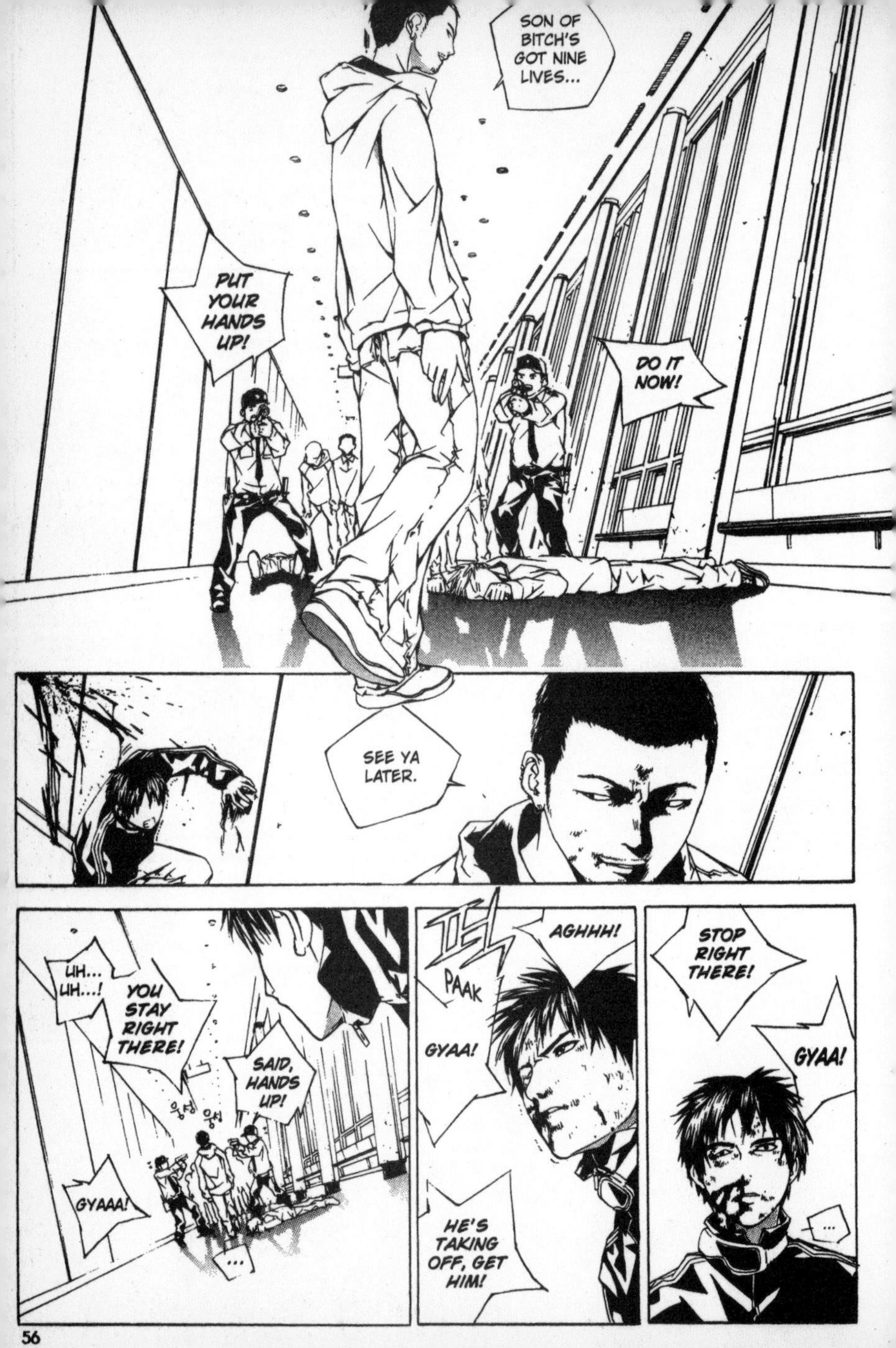
SON OF BITCH'S GOT NINE LIVES...
PUT YOUR HANDS UP!
DO IT NOW!
SEE YA LATER.
UH... UH...!
YOU STAY RIGHT THERE!
SAID, HANDS UP!
웅성 웅성
GYAAA!
...
AGHHH!
PAAK
GYAA!
HE'S TAKING OFF, GET HIM!
STOP RIGHT THERE!
GYAA!
...

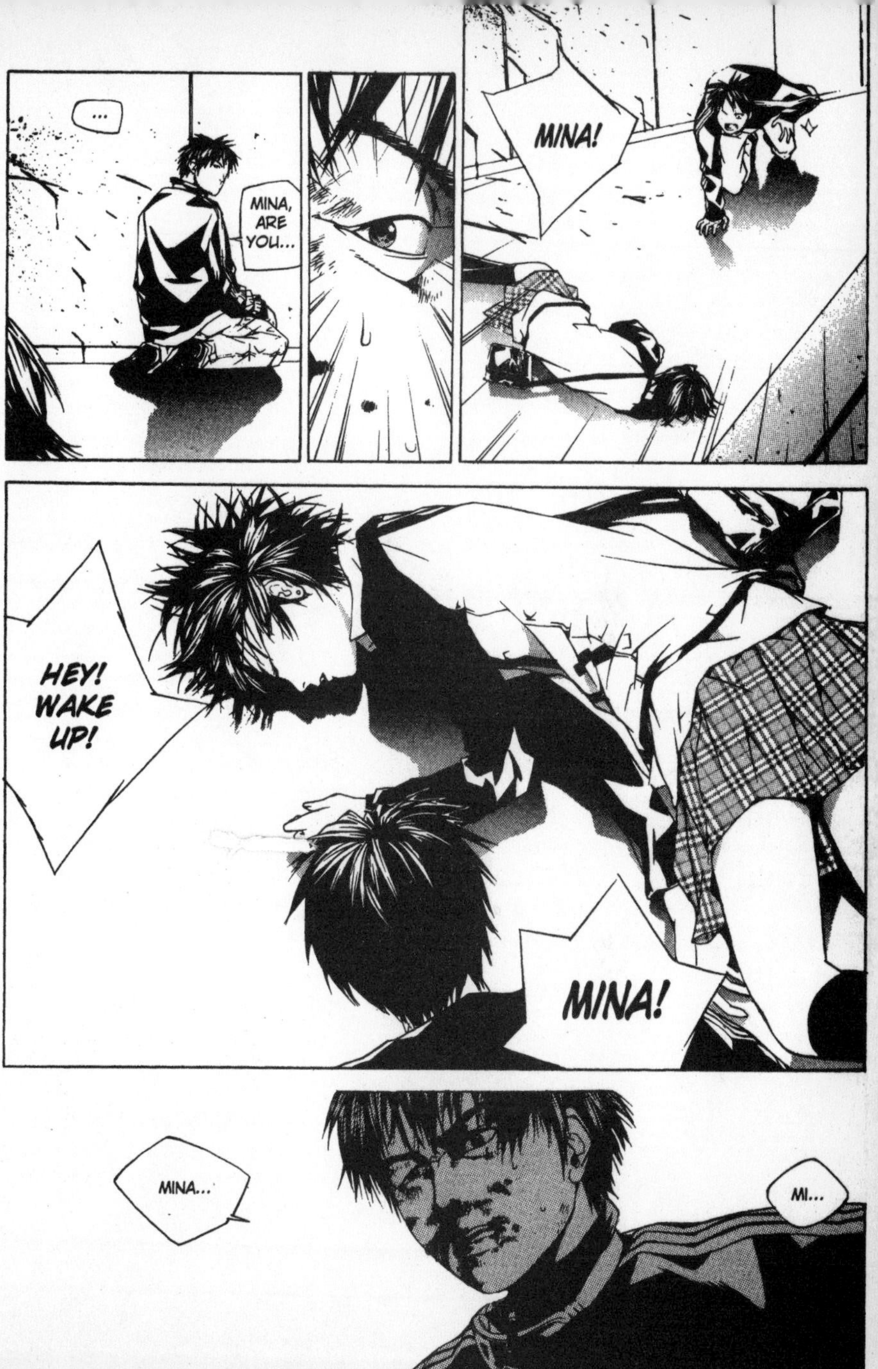
...
MINA, ARE YOU...
MINA!
HEY! WAKE UP!
MINA!
MINA...
MI...

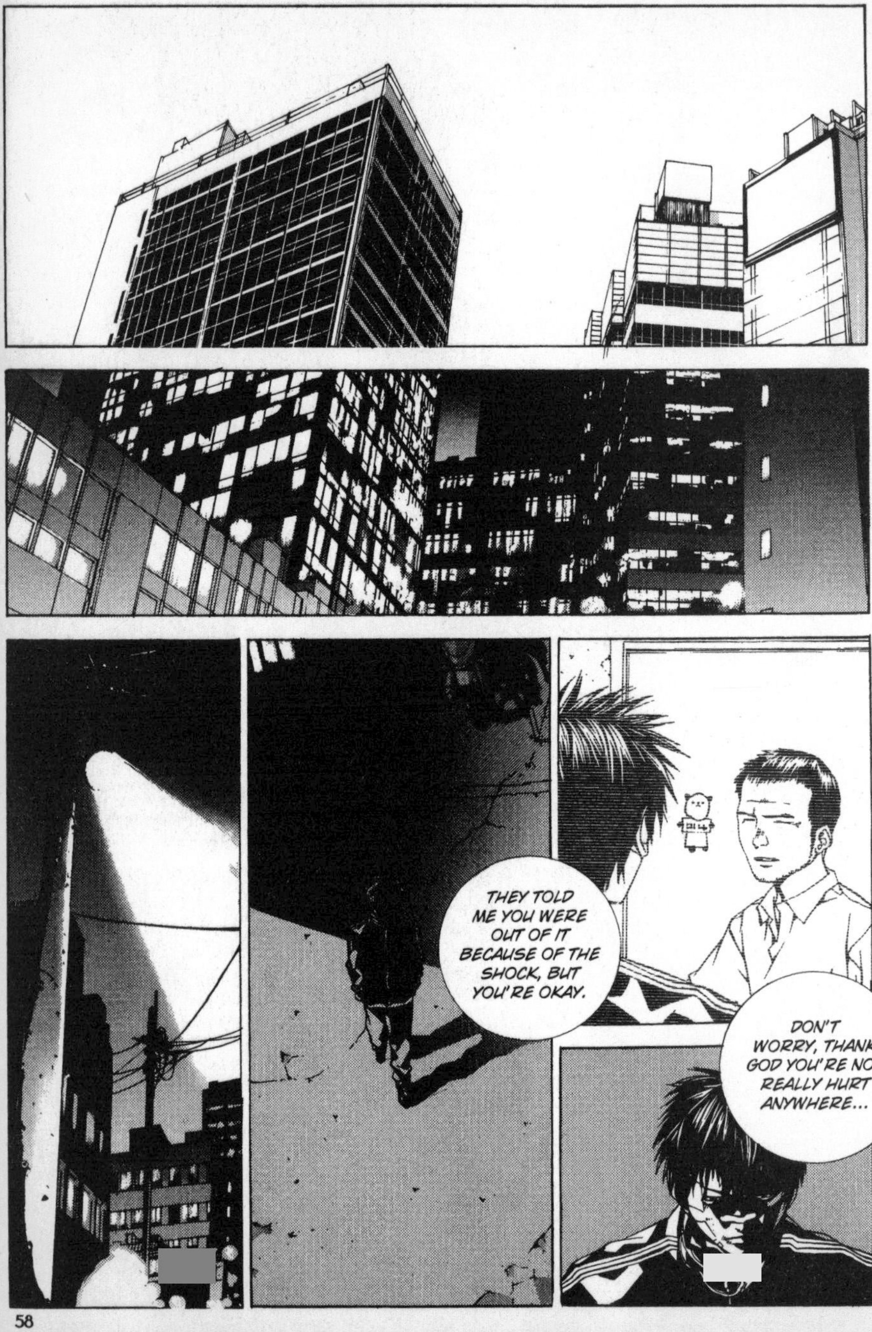
THEY TOLD ME YOU WERE OUT OF IT BECAUSE OF THE SHOCK, BUT YOU'RE OKAY.
DON'T WORRY, THANK GOD YOU'RE NOT REALLY HURT ANYWHERE...

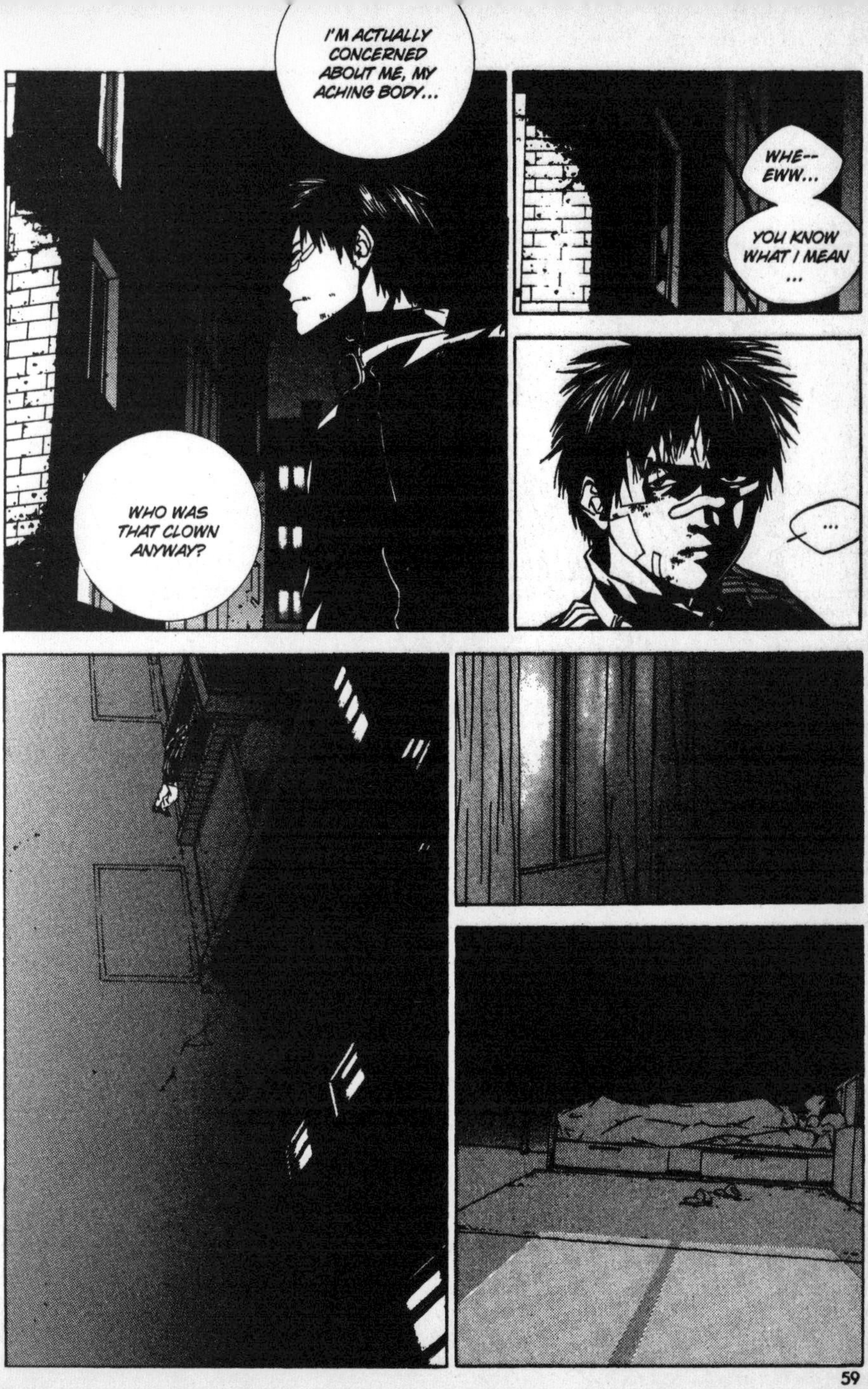
I'M ACTUALLY CONCERNED ABOUT ME, MY ACHING BODY...
WHO WAS THAT CLOWN ANYWAY?
WHE-- EWW...
YOU KNOW WHAT I MEAN ...
...

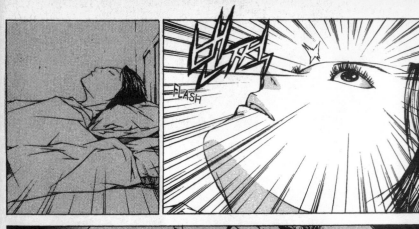

FLASH

.....

...?

WH.

WHO IS...?

TURN

WEE EE EE

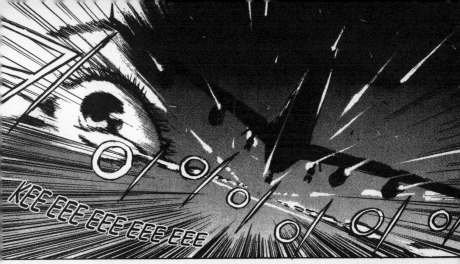

KEE EEE EEE EEE EEE

INCHON
INTERNATIONAL AIRPORT

Ahem
흠끔

......

PASSPORT

PM
생/SUN

PAR
PYG

BACH...

...NAM
JUNG...?

PMKORPARK<<NA

YOU JUST
LOOK A BIT
DIFFERENT...

WOULD YOU
MIND TAKING
OFF THE SUN-
GLASSES?

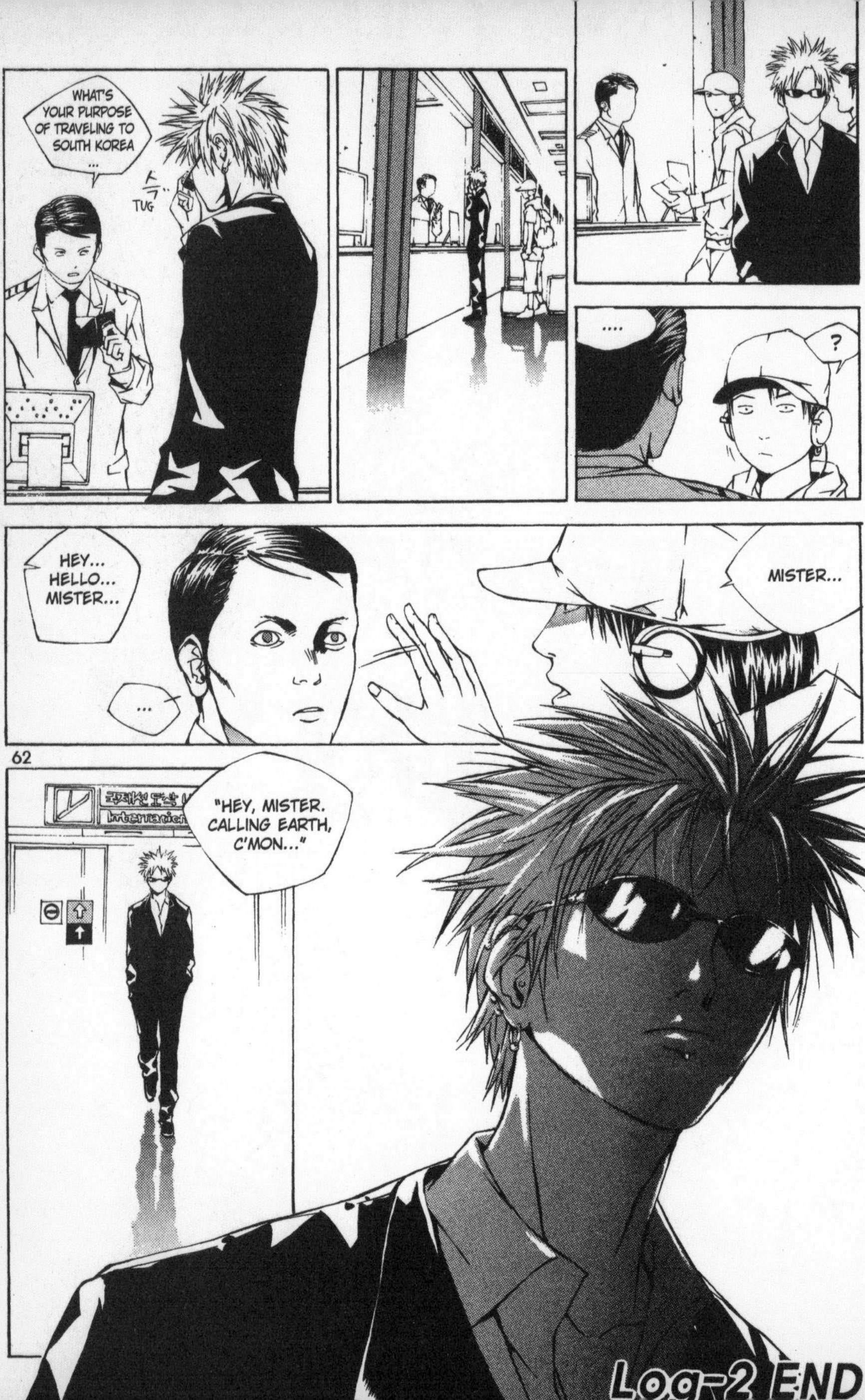
WHAT'S YOUR PURPOSE OF TRAVELING TO SOUTH KOREA ...
TUG
....
?
HEY... HELLO... MISTER...
...
MISTER...
"HEY, MISTER. CALLING EARTH, C'MON..."
Log-2 END

LOG_3;Kali

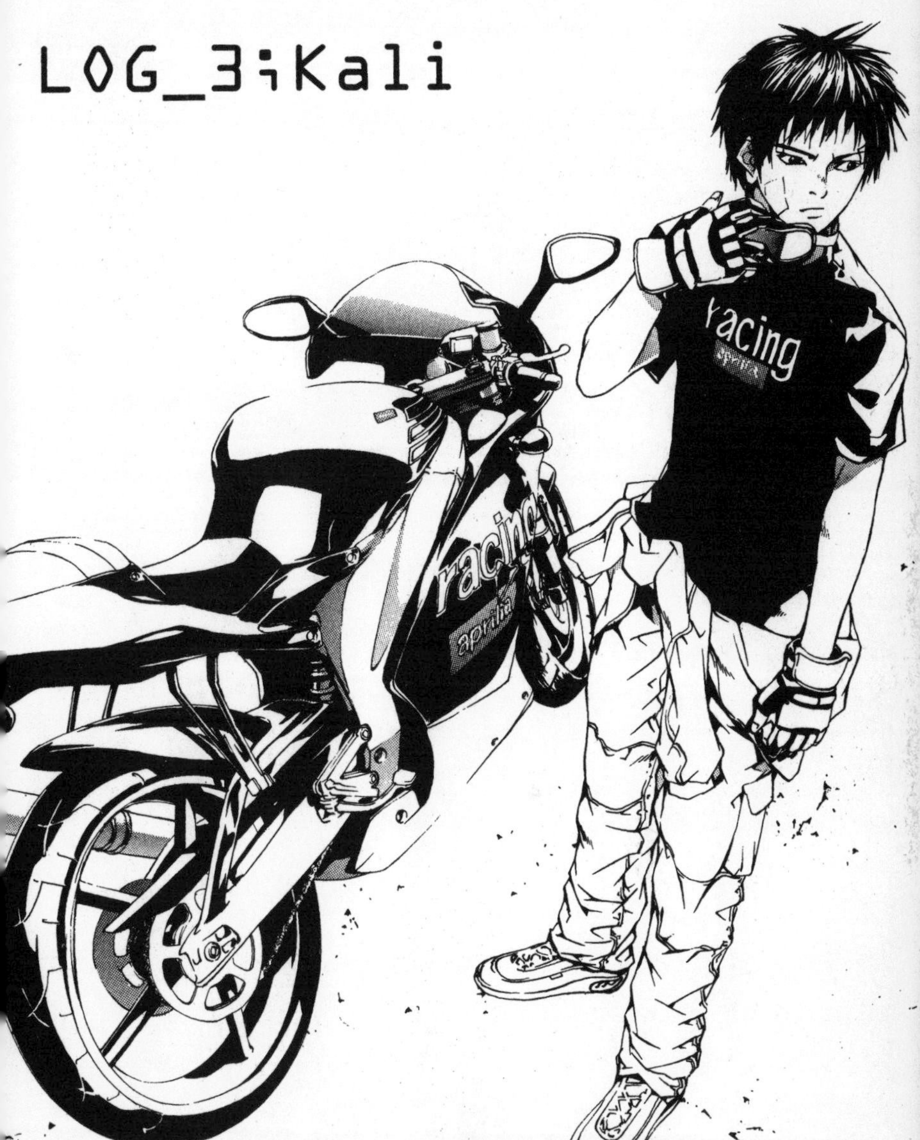
racing
racing
aprilia

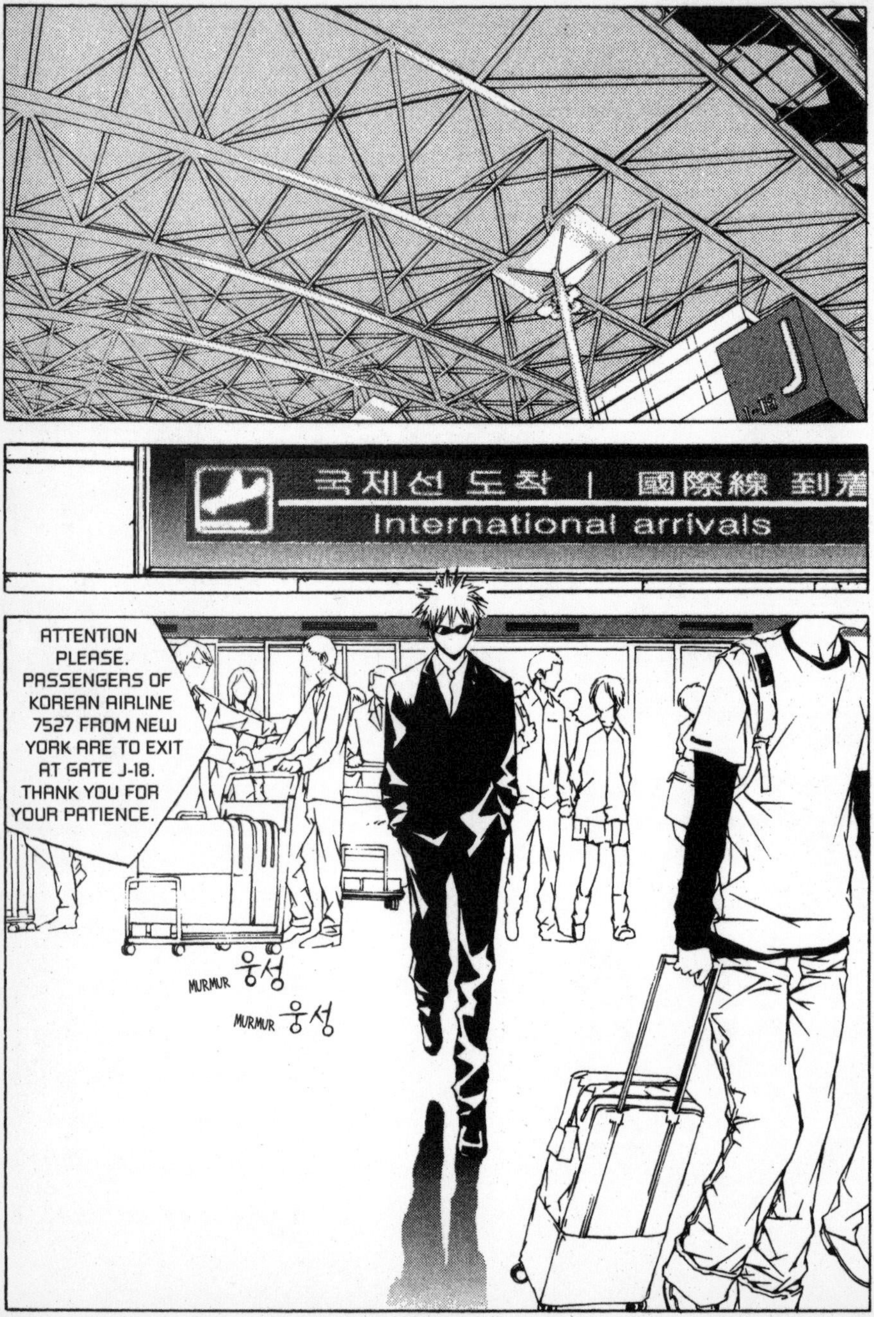
국제선 도착 | 國際線 到着
International arrivals
ATTENTION PLEASE. PASSENGERS OF KOREAN AIRLINE 7527 FROM NEW YORK ARE TO EXIT AT GATE J-18. THANK YOU FOR YOUR PATIENCE.
MURMUR 웅성
MURMUR 웅성

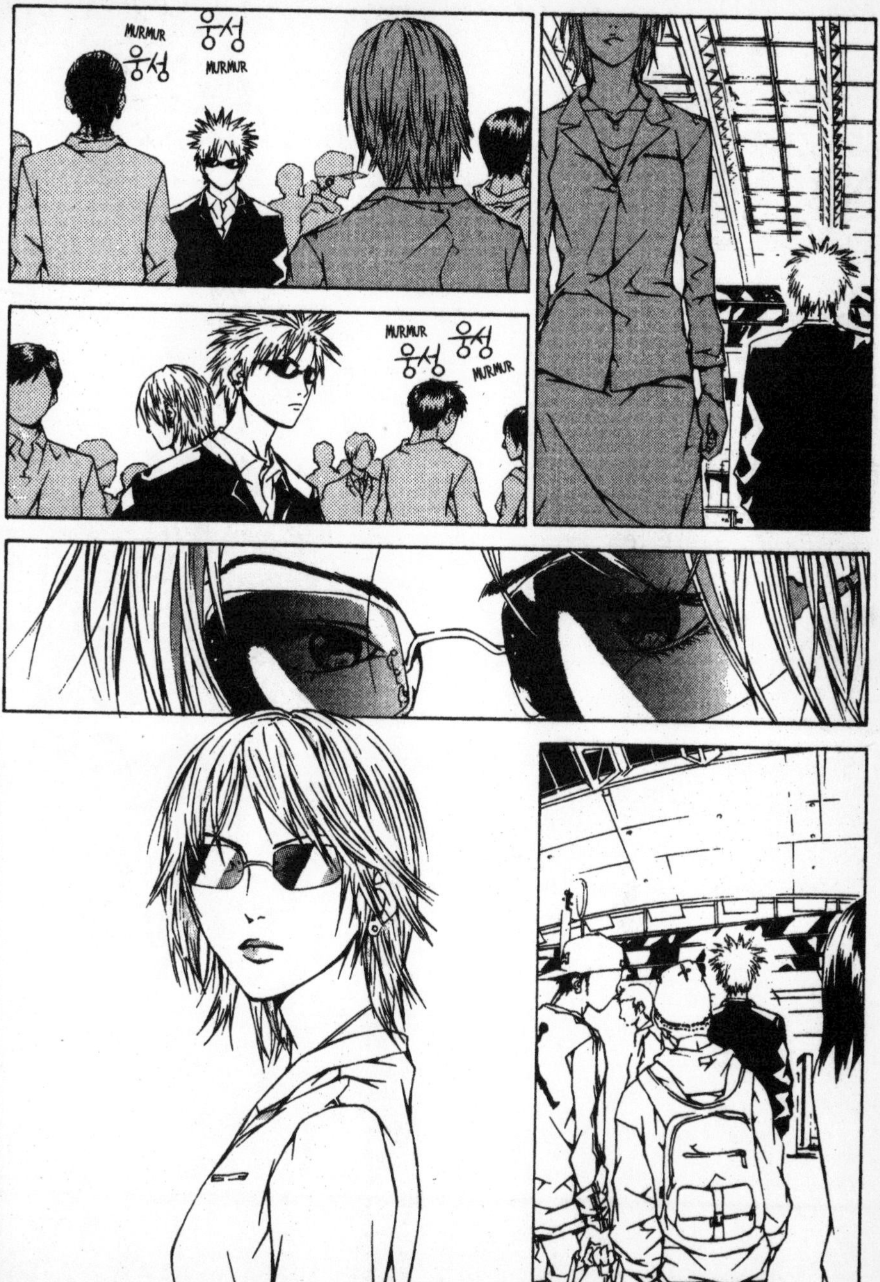
MURMUR
웅성
웅성
MURMUR
MURMUR
웅성
웅성
MURMUR

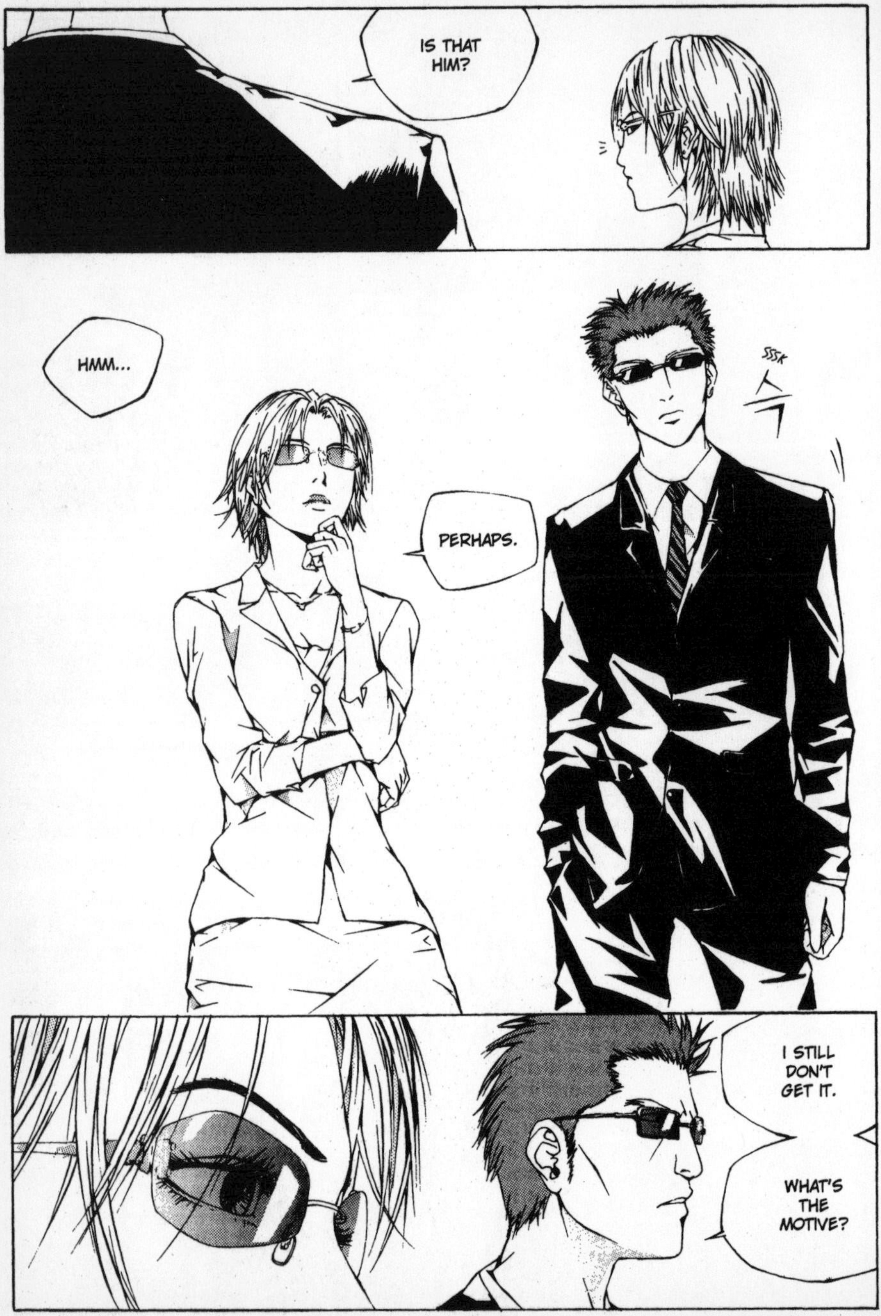
IS THAT HIM?
HMM...
SSSK
PERHAPS.
I STILL DON'T GET IT.
WHAT'S THE MOTIVE?

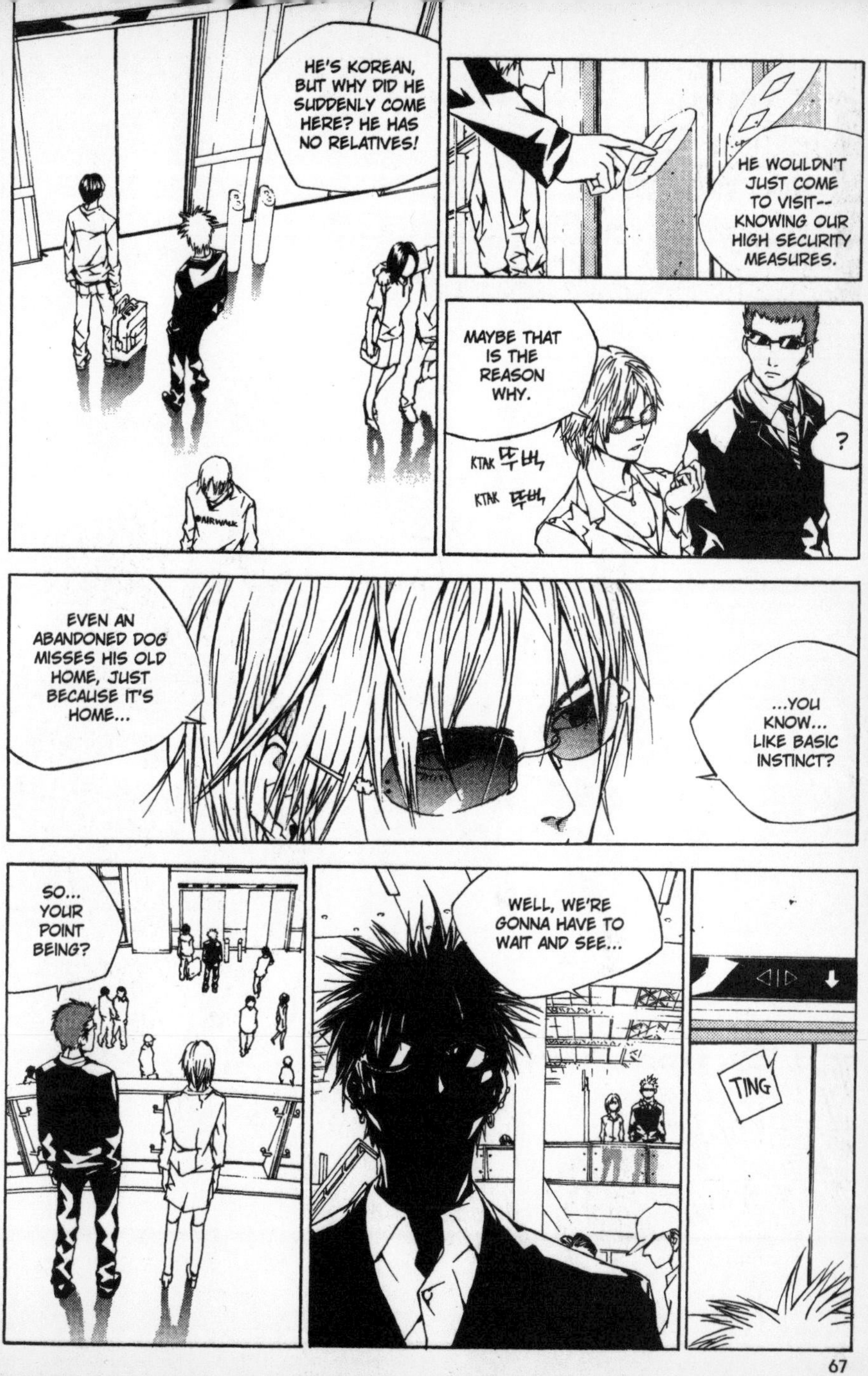
HE'S KOREAN, BUT WHY DID HE SUDDENLY COME HERE? HE HAS NO RELATIVES!
HE WOULDN'T JUST COME TO VISIT-- KNOWING OUR HIGH SECURITY MEASURES.
MAYBE THAT IS THE REASON WHY.
KTAK 뚜벅
KTAK 뚜벅
?
EVEN AN ABANDONED DOG MISSES HIS OLD HOME, JUST BECAUSE IT'S HOME...
...YOU KNOW... LIKE BASIC INSTINCT?
SO... YOUR POINT BEING?
WELL, WE'RE GONNA HAVE TO WAIT AND SEE...
TING

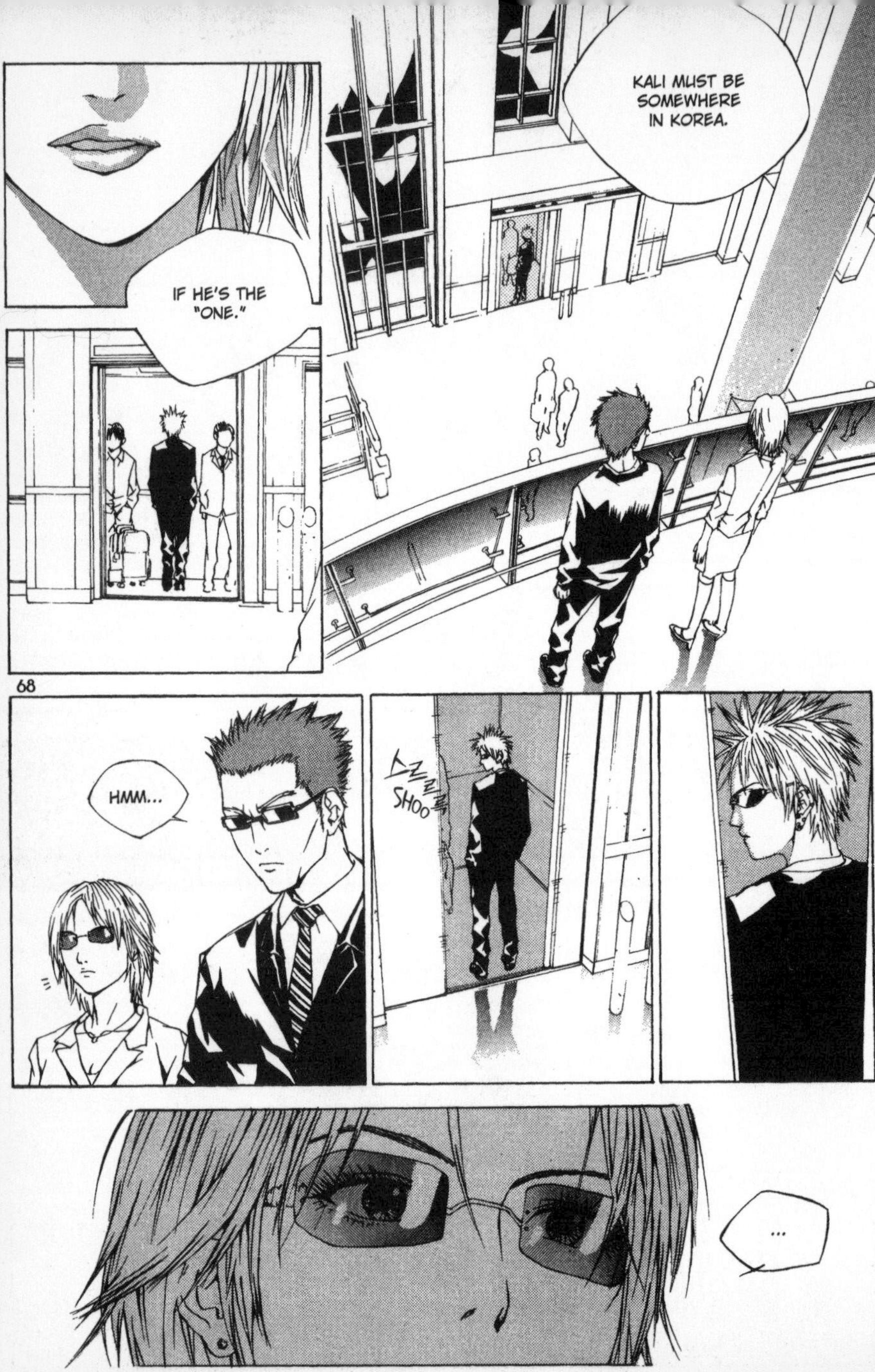
IF HE'S THE "ONE."
KALI MUST BE SOMEWHERE IN KOREA.
HMM...
SHOO
...

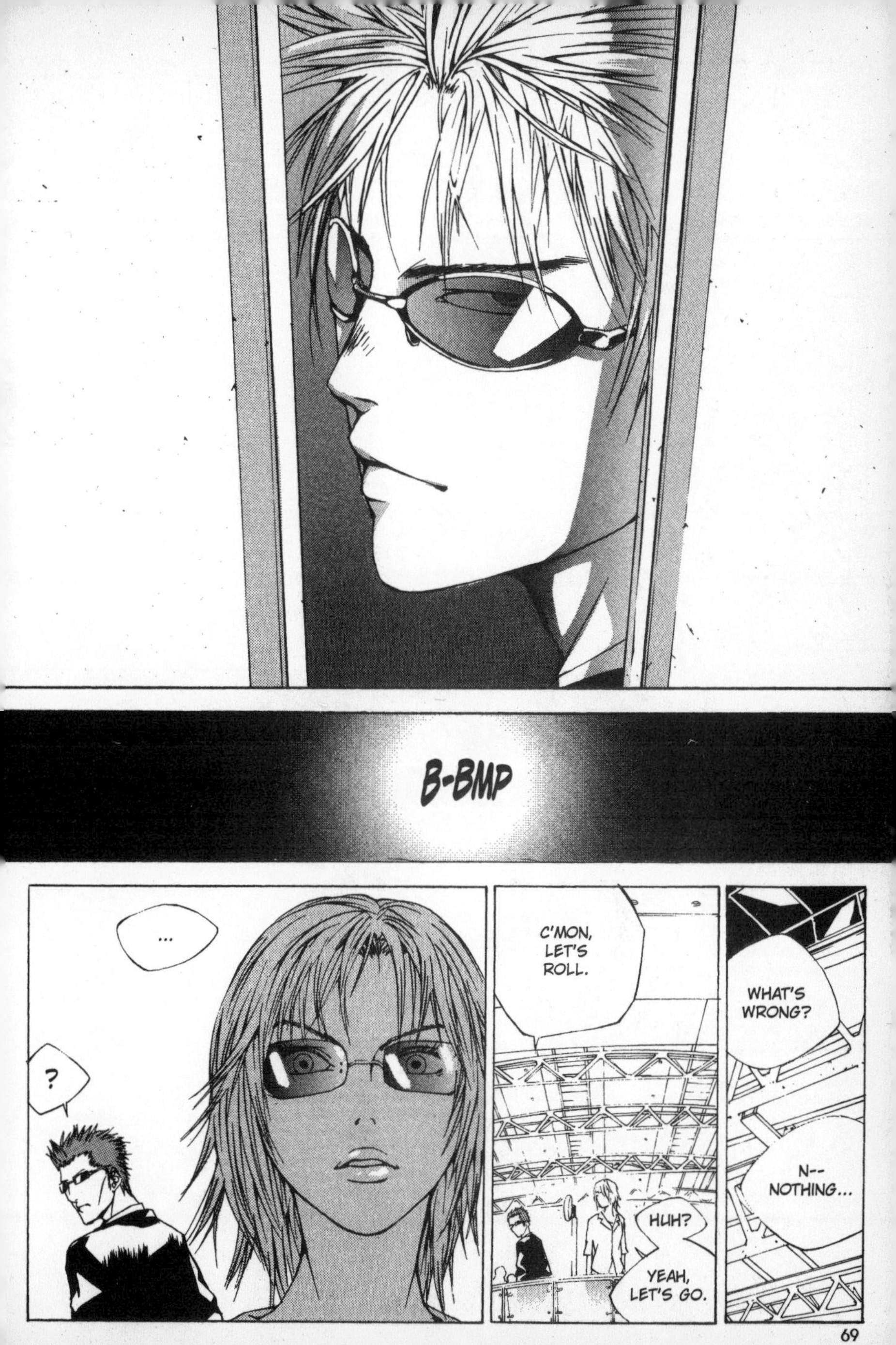
B-BMP
...
?
C'MON, LET'S ROLL.
HUH?
YEAH, LET'S GO.
WHAT'S WRONG?
N-- NOTHING...

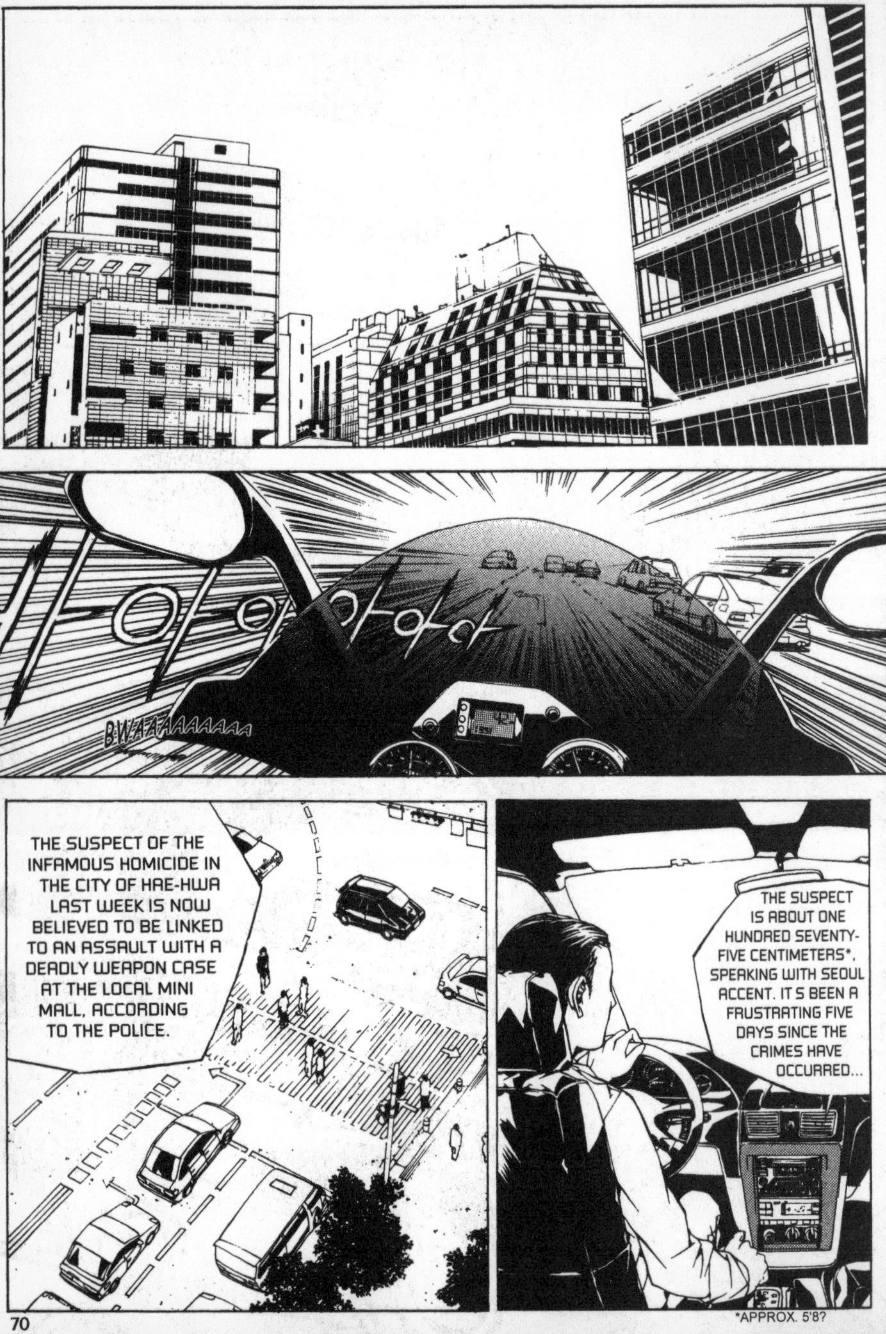
BWAAAAAAAAAA
THE SUSPECT OF THE INFAMOUS HOMICIDE IN THE CITY OF HAE-HWA LAST WEEK IS NOW BELIEVED TO BE LINKED TO AN ASSAULT WITH A DEADLY WEAPON CASE AT THE LOCAL MINI MALL, ACCORDING TO THE POLICE.
THE SUSPECT IS ABOUT ONE HUNDRED SEVENTY-FIVE CENTIMETERS*, SPEAKING WITH SEOUL ACCENT. IT S BEEN A FRUSTRATING FIVE DAYS SINCE THE CRIMES HAVE OCCURRED...

*APPROX. 5'8?

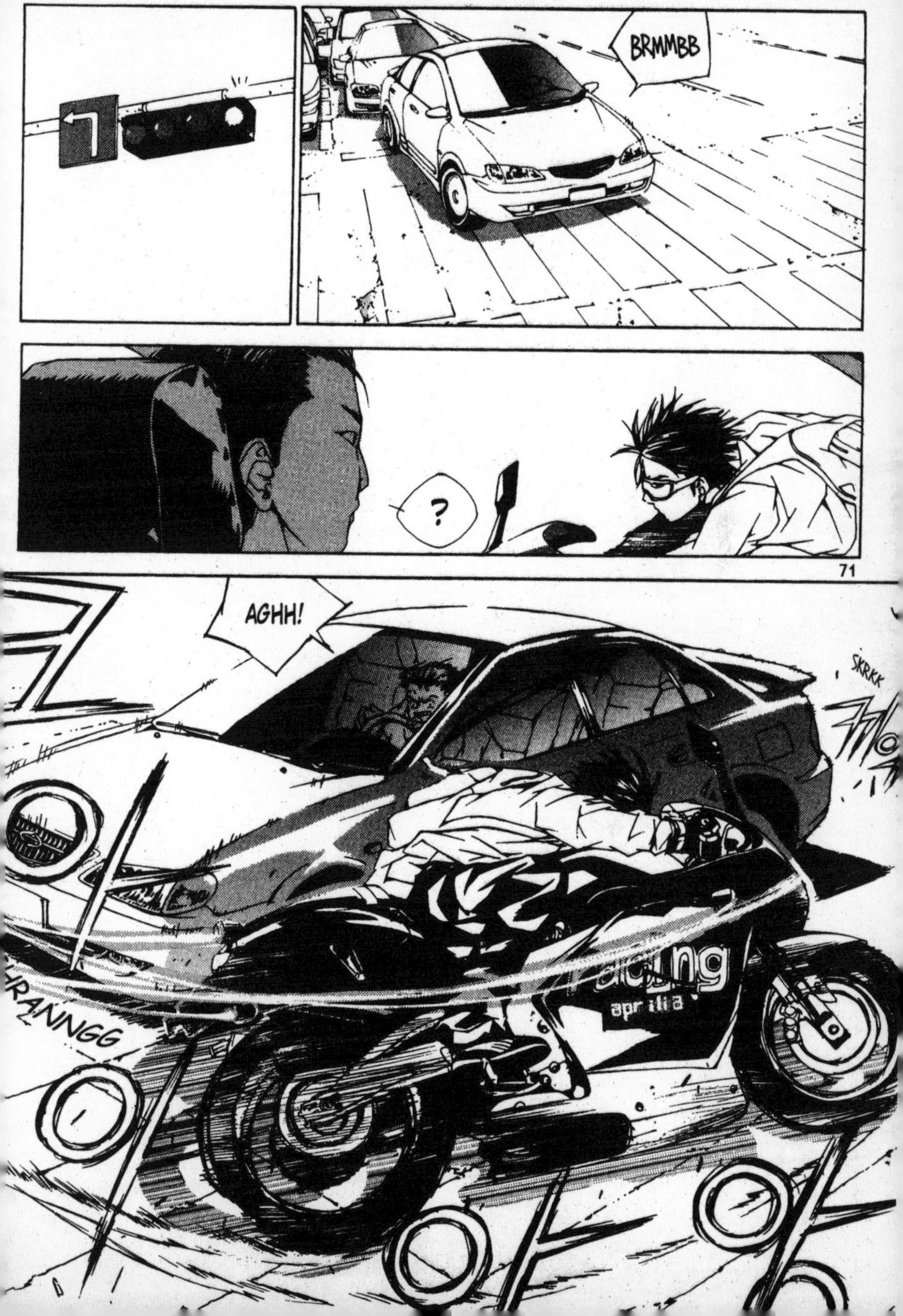
BRMMBB
?
AGHH!
SKRKK
RANNGG

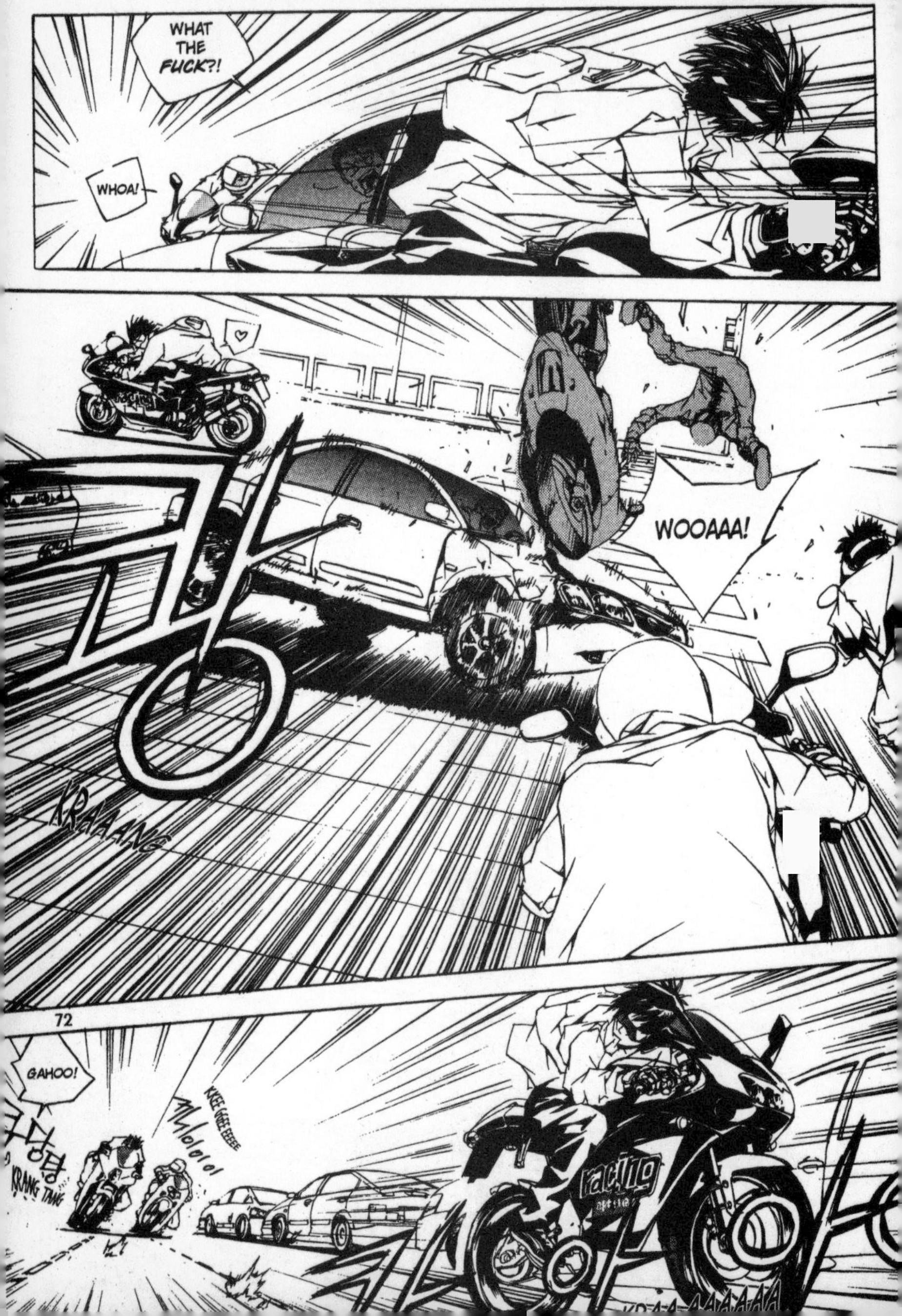
WHAT THE FUCK?!
WHOA!
WOOAAA!
KRAAAANG
GAHOO!
KRANG TANG
KKEE GGEE EEEEE

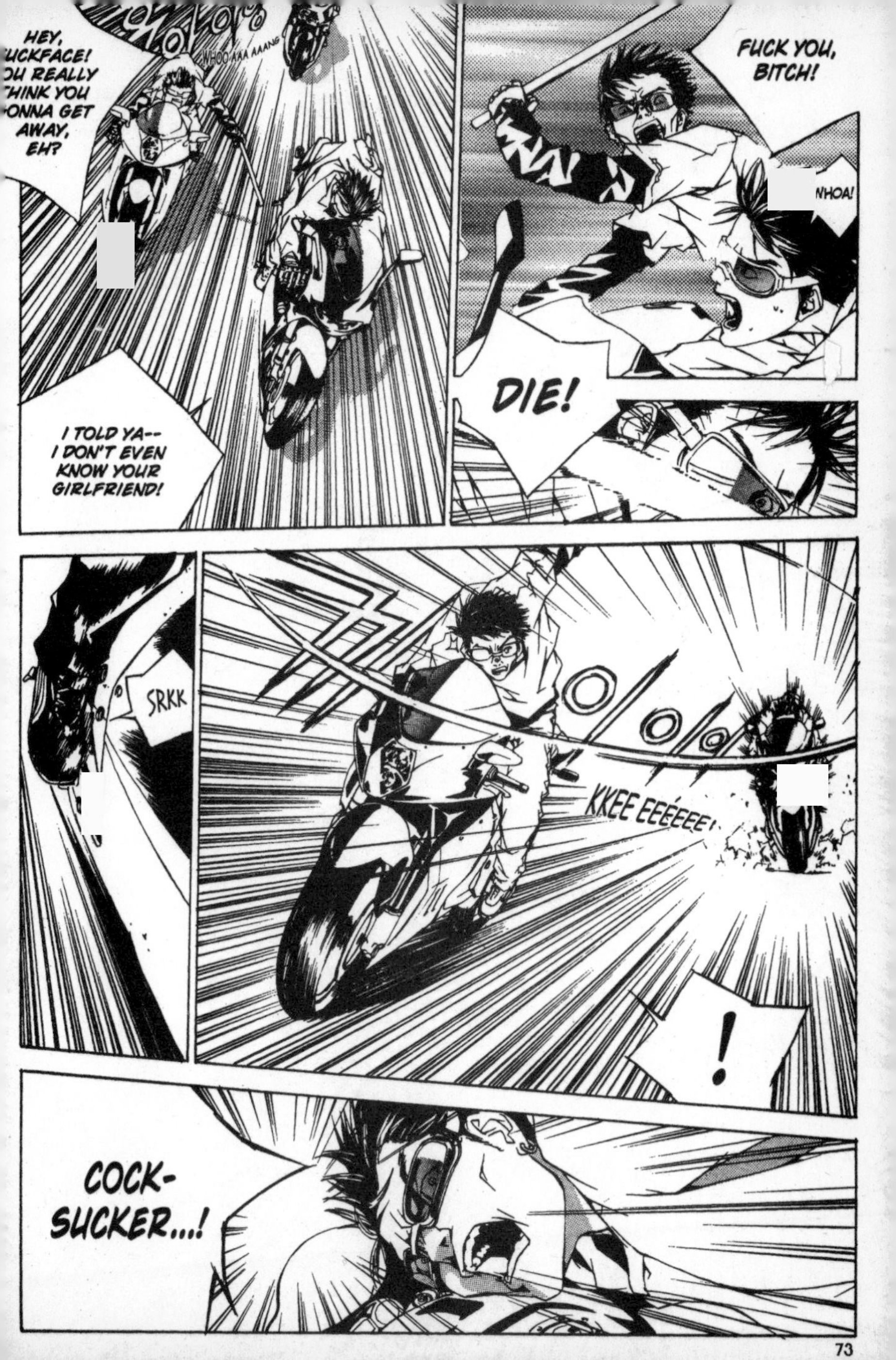
HEY,
UCKFACE!
OU REALLY
THINK YOU
ONNA GET
AWAY,
EH?
WHOO AAA AAANG
I TOLD YA--
I DON'T EVEN
KNOW YOUR
GIRLFRIEND!
FUCK YOU,
BITCH!
WHOA!
DIE!
SRKK
KKEE EEÉEEE!
!
COCK-
SUCKER...!

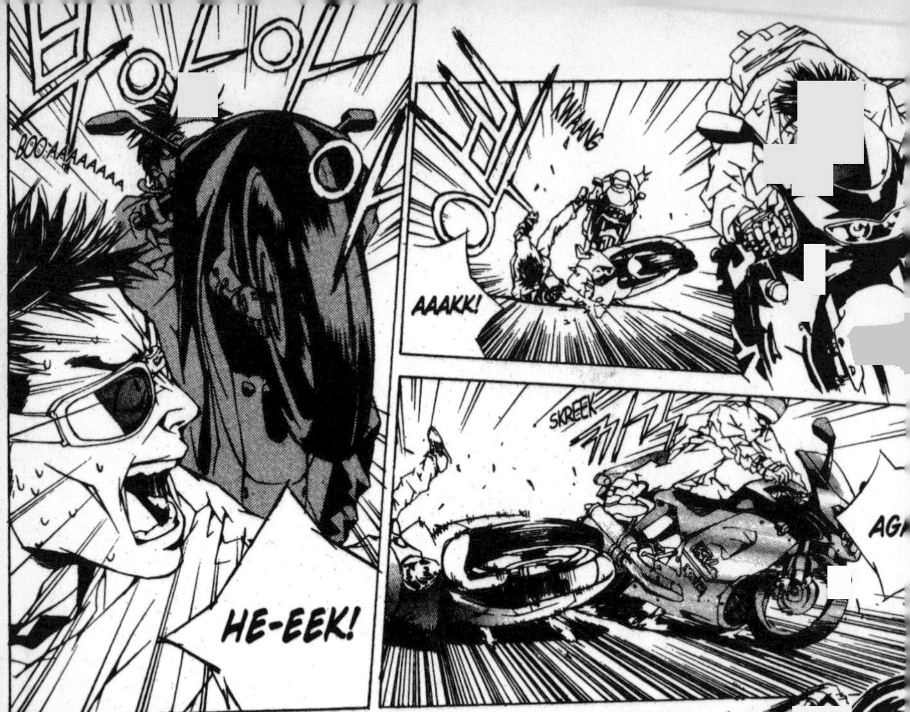
BOO-AAAAAAAA
HE-EEK!
KWANG
AAAKK!
SKREEK

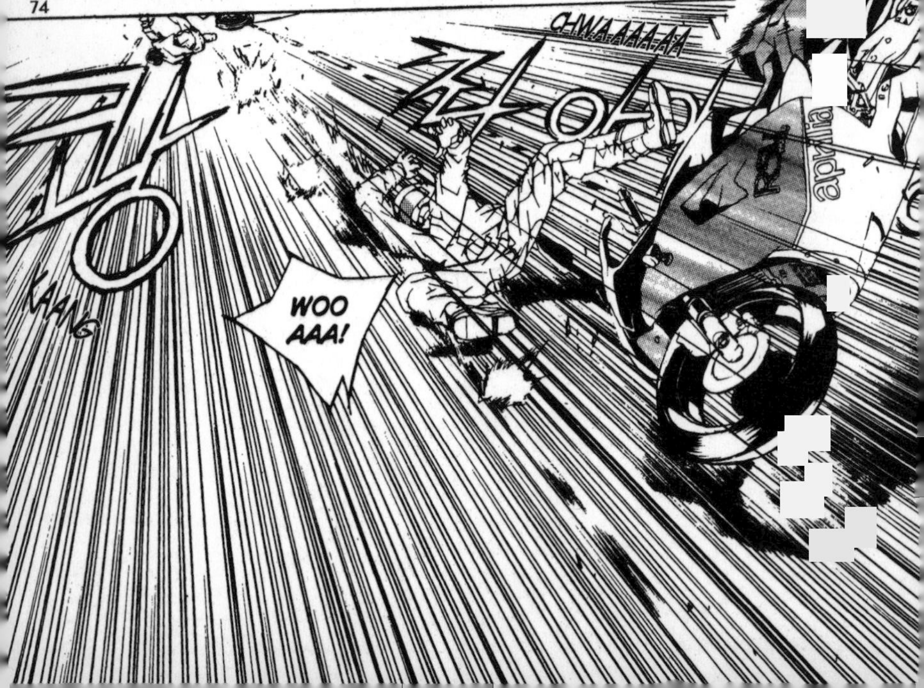
CHWAAAAAAA
KAANG
WOO AAA!
aprilia

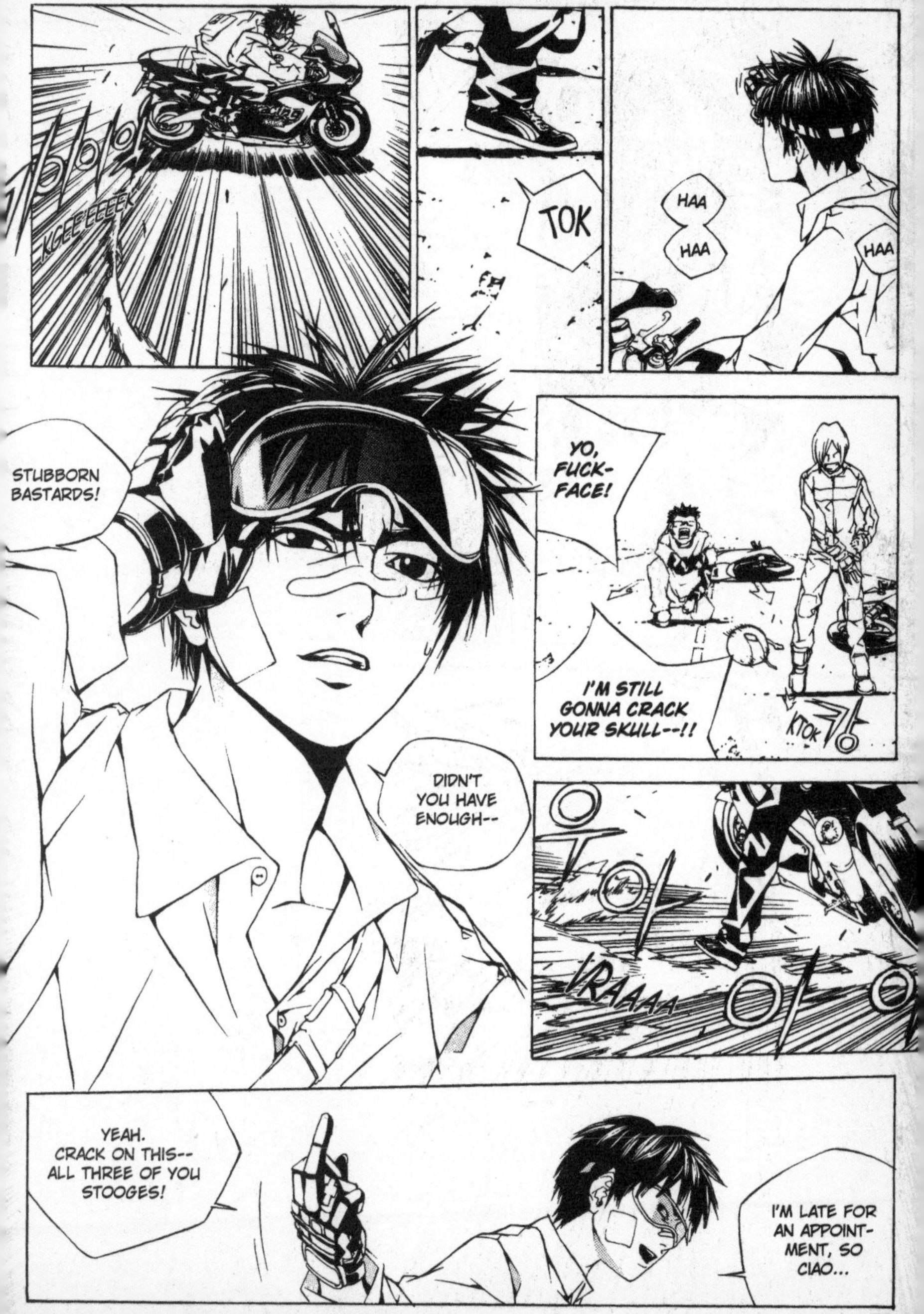
KGEEEEEEK
TOK
HAA
HAA
HAA
STUBBORN BASTARDS!
YO, FUCK-FACE!
I'M STILL GONNA CRACK YOUR SKULL--!!
KTOK
DIDN'T YOU HAVE ENOUGH--
VRAAAA
YEAH. CRACK ON THIS-- ALL THREE OF YOU STOOGES!
I'M LATE FOR AN APPOINT-MENT, SO CIAO...

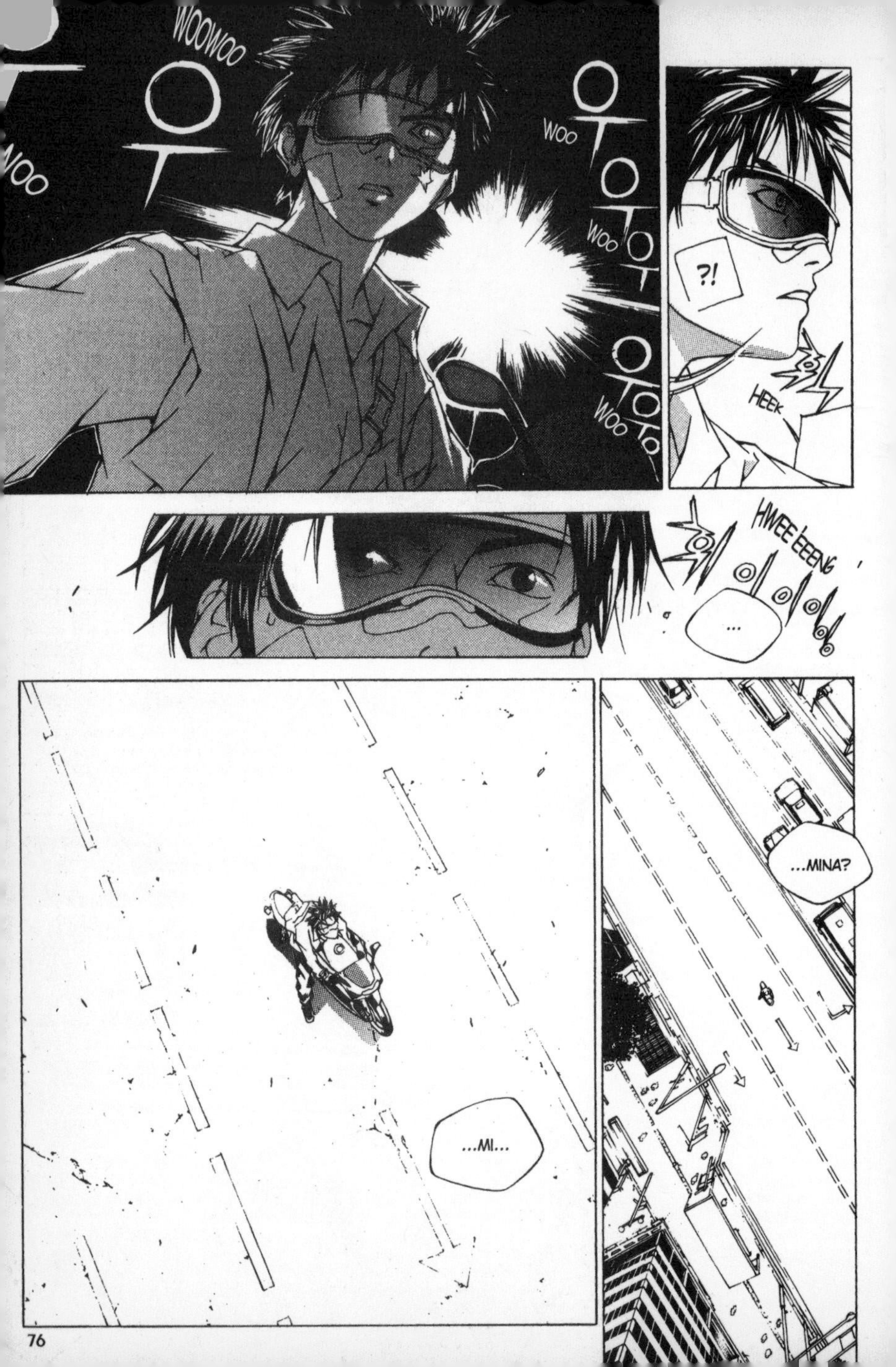
WOOWOO
WOO
WOO
WOO
WOO
?!
HEEK
HWEE EEENG
...
...MI...
...MINA?

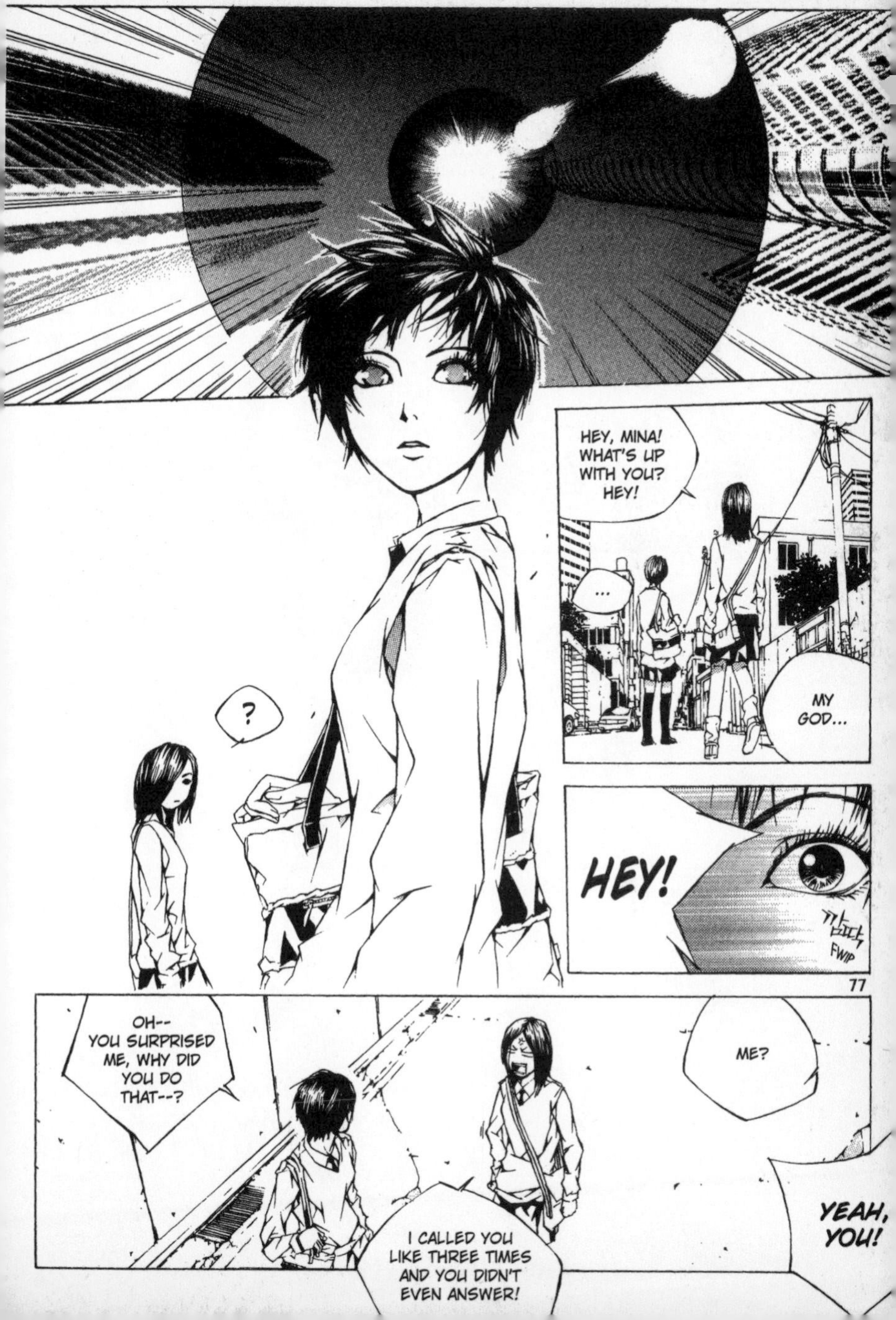
?
HEY, MINA! WHAT'S UP WITH YOU? HEY!
...
MY GOD...
HEY!
깜빡
FWIP
OH-- YOU SURPRISED ME, WHY DID YOU DO THAT--?
ME?
I CALLED YOU LIKE THREE TIMES AND YOU DIDN'T EVEN ANSWER!
YEAH, YOU!

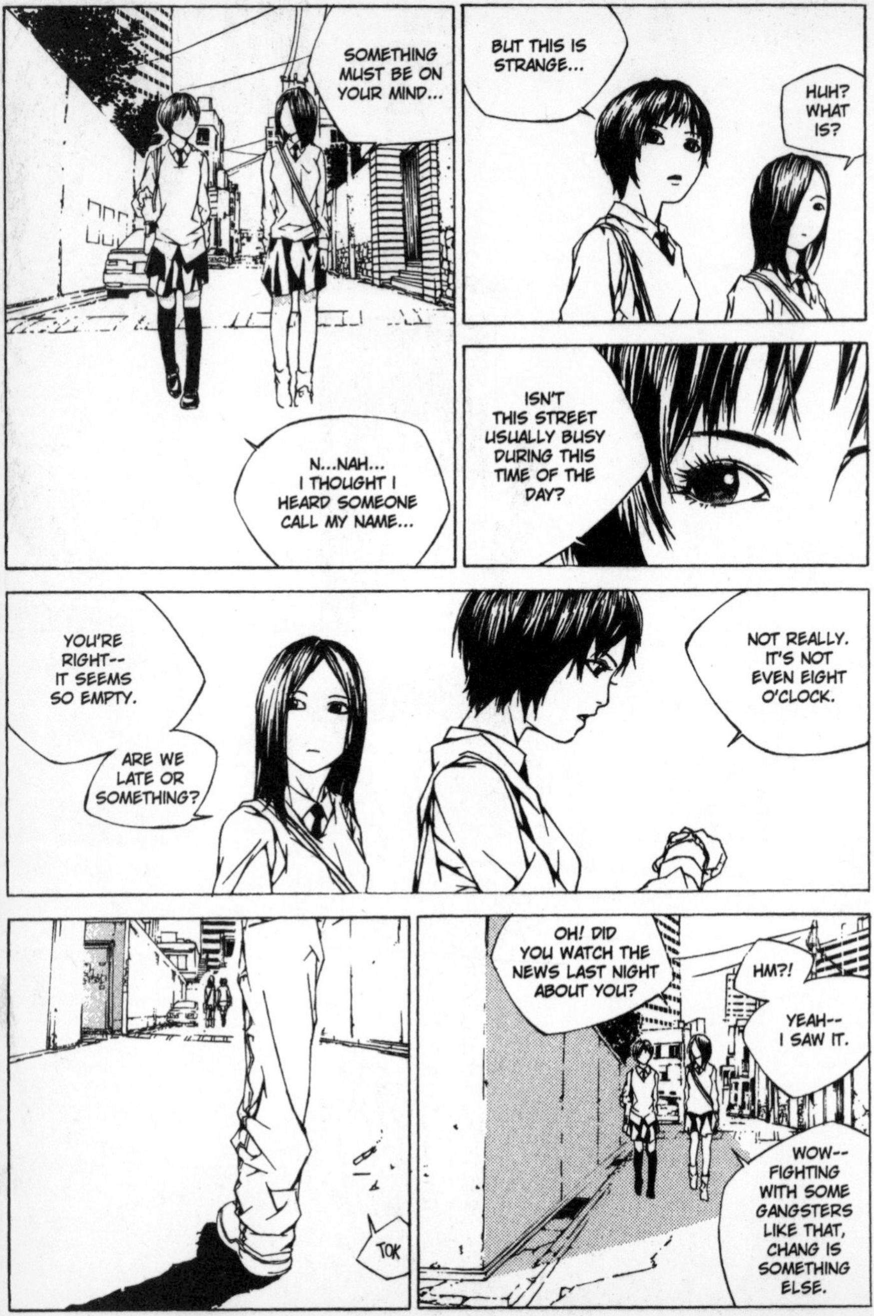
SOMETHING MUST BE ON YOUR MIND...
N...NAH... I THOUGHT I HEARD SOMEONE CALL MY NAME...
BUT THIS IS STRANGE...
HUH? WHAT IS?
ISN'T THIS STREET USUALLY BUSY DURING THIS TIME OF THE DAY?
YOU'RE RIGHT-- IT SEEMS SO EMPTY.
ARE WE LATE OR SOMETHING?
NOT REALLY. IT'S NOT EVEN EIGHT O'CLOCK.
TOK
OH! DID YOU WATCH THE NEWS LAST NIGHT ABOUT YOU?
HM?!
YEAH-- I SAW IT.
WOW-- FIGHTING WITH SOME GANGSTERS LIKE THAT, CHANG IS SOMETHING ELSE.

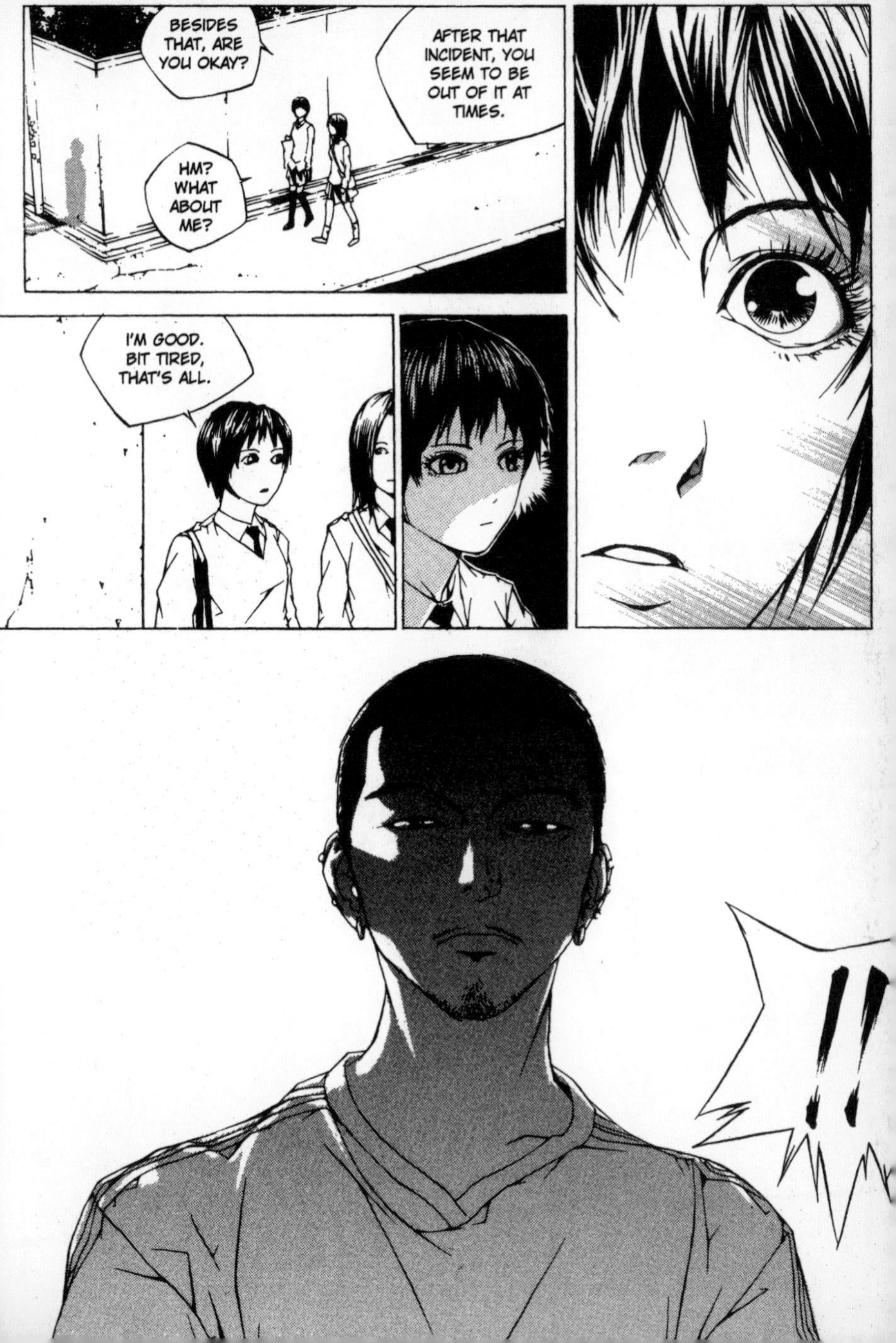
BESIDES THAT, ARE YOU OKAY?
HM? WHAT ABOUT ME?
AFTER THAT INCIDENT, YOU SEEM TO BE OUT OF IT AT TIMES.
I'M GOOD. BIT TIRED, THAT'S ALL.
!!

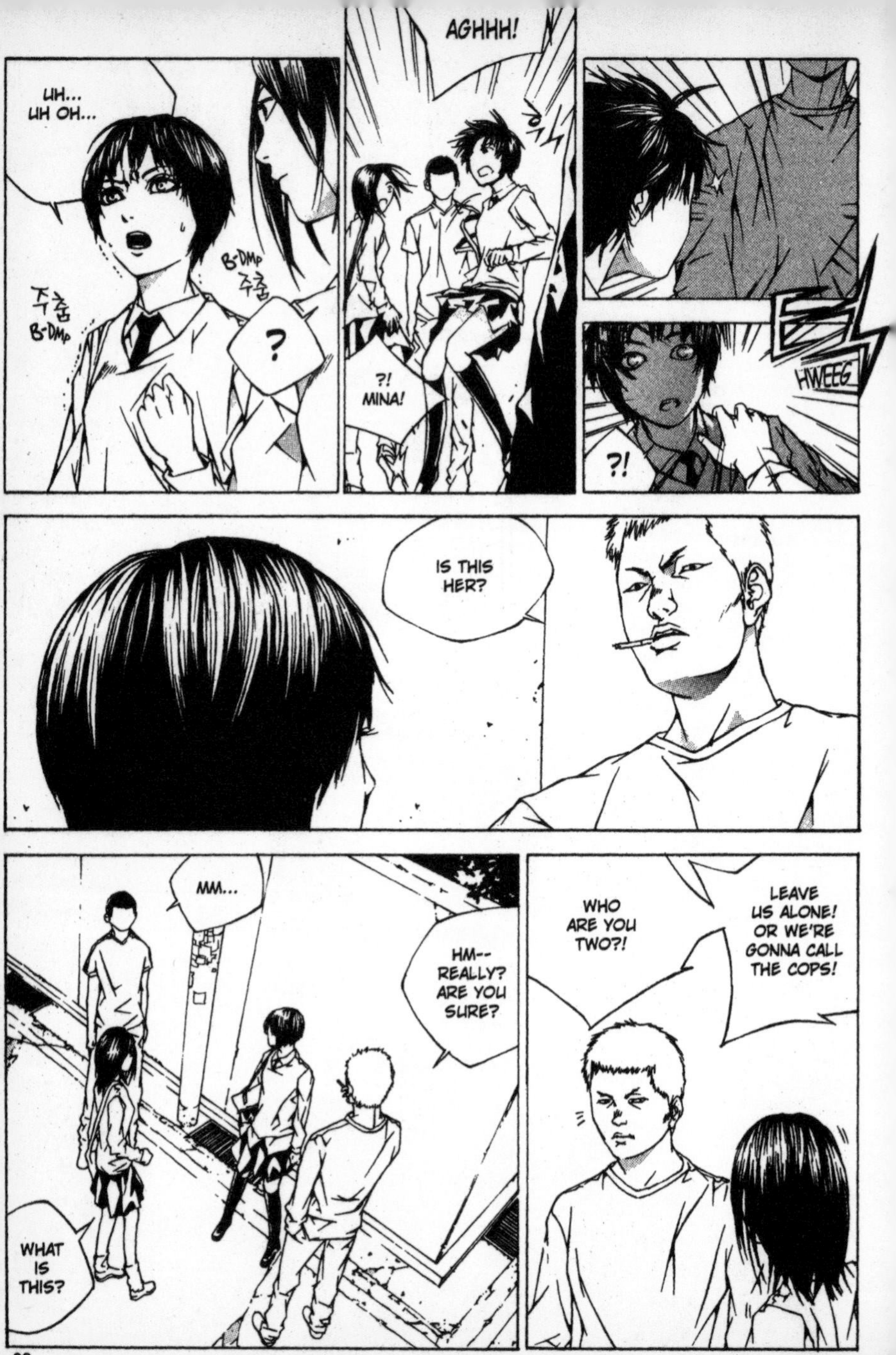
UH...
UH OH...
B-DMP
주춤
주춤
B-DMP
?
AGHHH!
?!
MINA!
?!
HWEEG
IS THIS
HER?
MM...
WHAT
IS
THIS?
HM--
REALLY?
ARE YOU
SURE?
WHO
ARE YOU
TWO?!
LEAVE
US ALONE!
OR WE'RE
GONNA CALL
THE COPS!

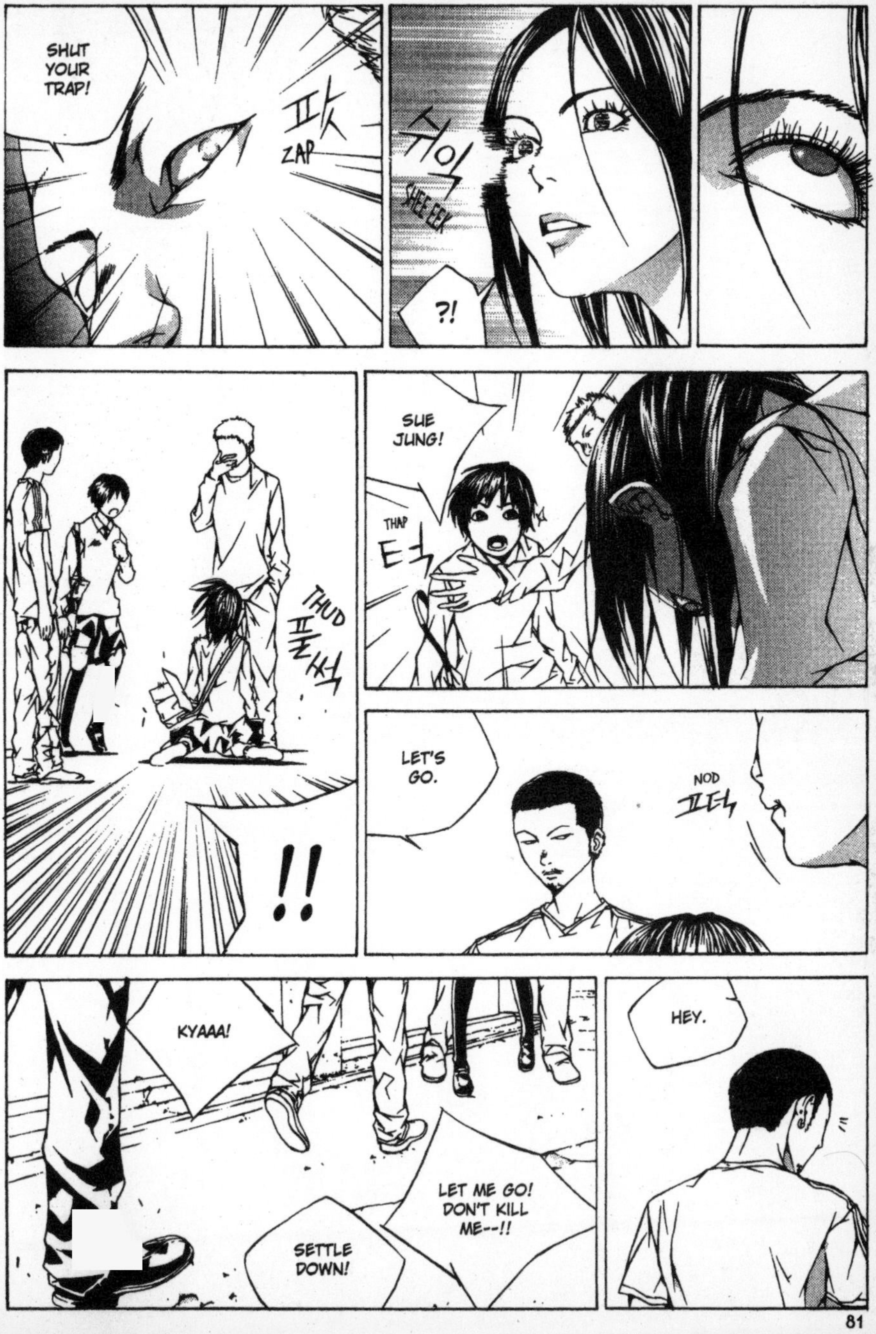
SHUT YOUR TRAP!
ZAP
SHEE-EEK
?!
THUD
!!
SUE JUNG!
THAP
LET'S GO.
NOD
KYAAA!
LET ME GO! DON'T KILL ME--!!
SETTLE DOWN!
HEY.

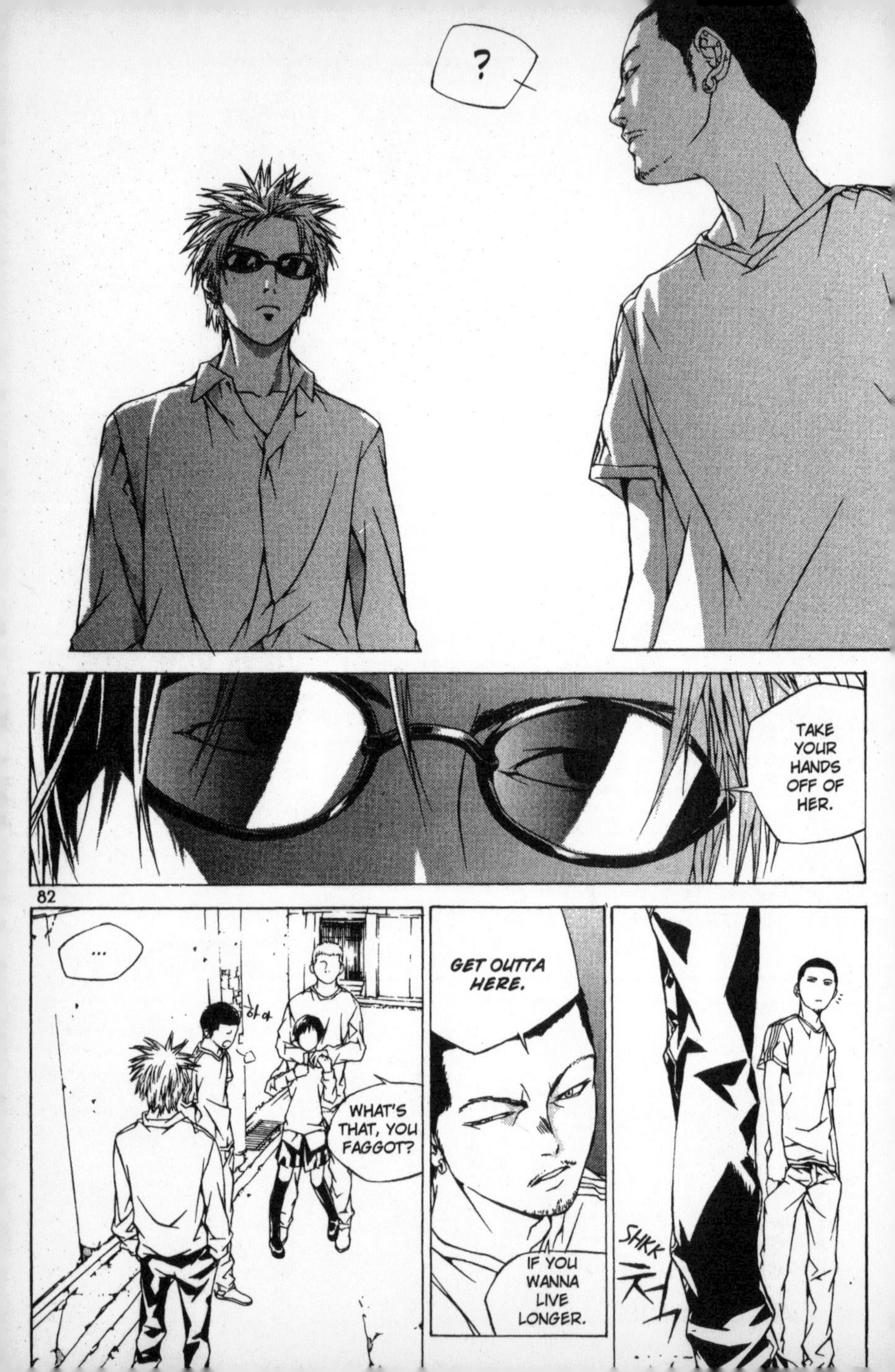
?
TAKE YOUR HANDS OFF OF HER.
...
하아
WHAT'S THAT, YOU FAGGOT?
GET OUTTA HERE.
IF YOU WANNA LIVE LONGER.
SHKK

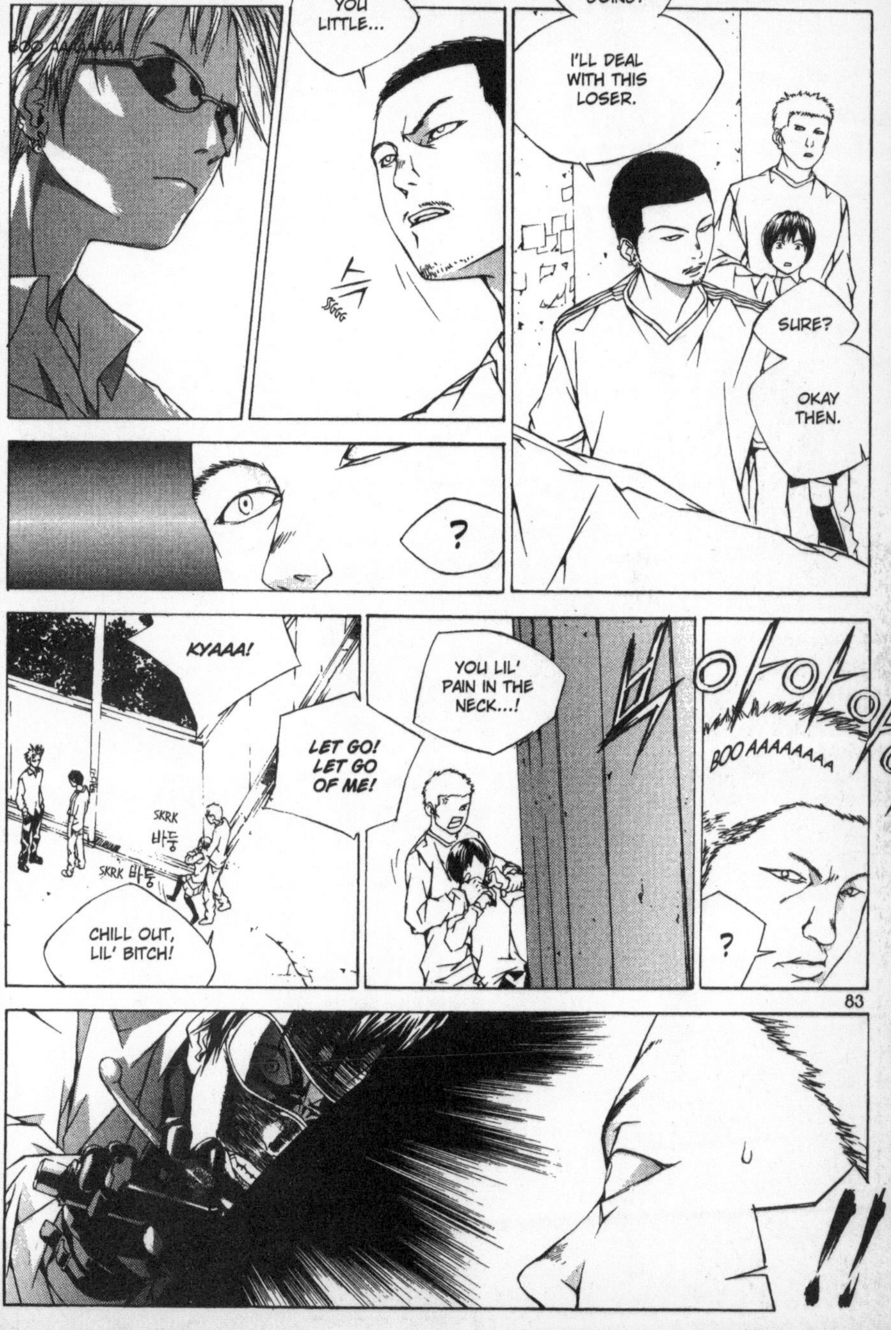

YOU LITTLE...
SSGGG
......GET GOING.
I'LL DEAL WITH THIS LOSER.
SURE?
OKAY THEN.
?
KYAAA!
LET GO! LET GO OF ME!
SKRK 바둥
SKRK 바둥
CHILL OUT, LIL' BITCH!
YOU LIL' PAIN IN THE NECK...!
BOO AAAAAAAA
?
!!

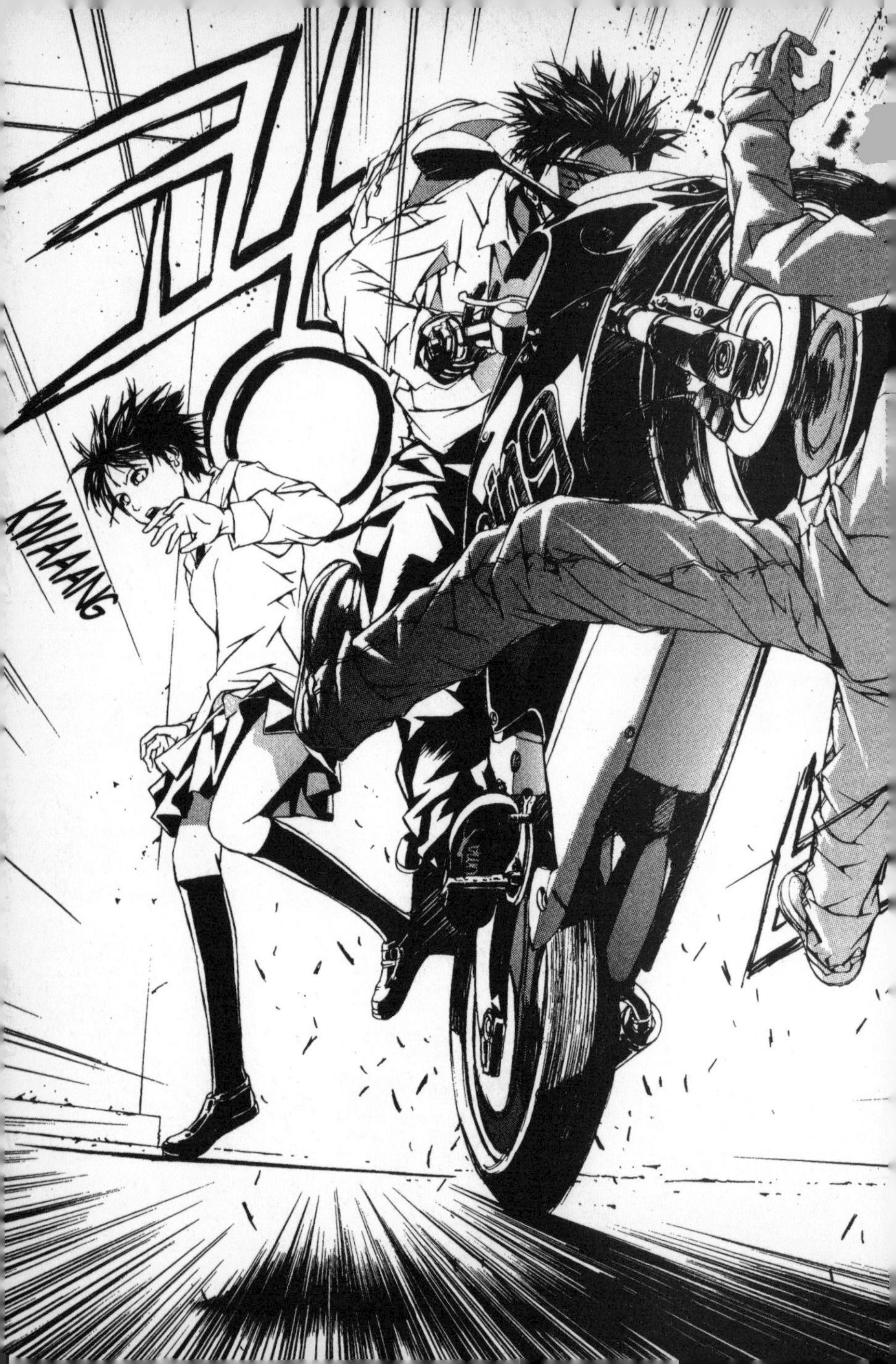
KWAAANG

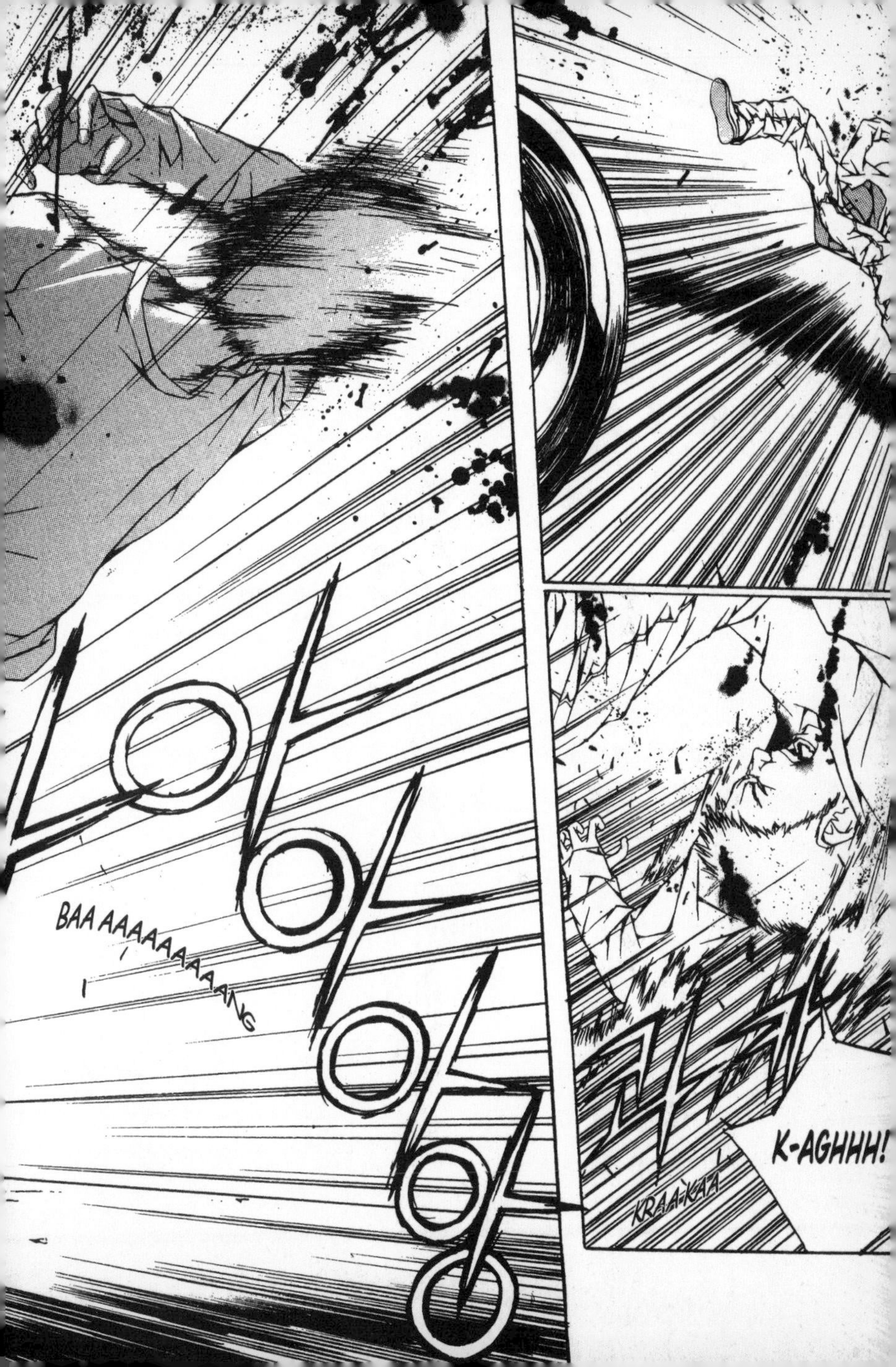
BAAAAAAAAAAAAANG
K-AGHHH!
KRAA-KAA

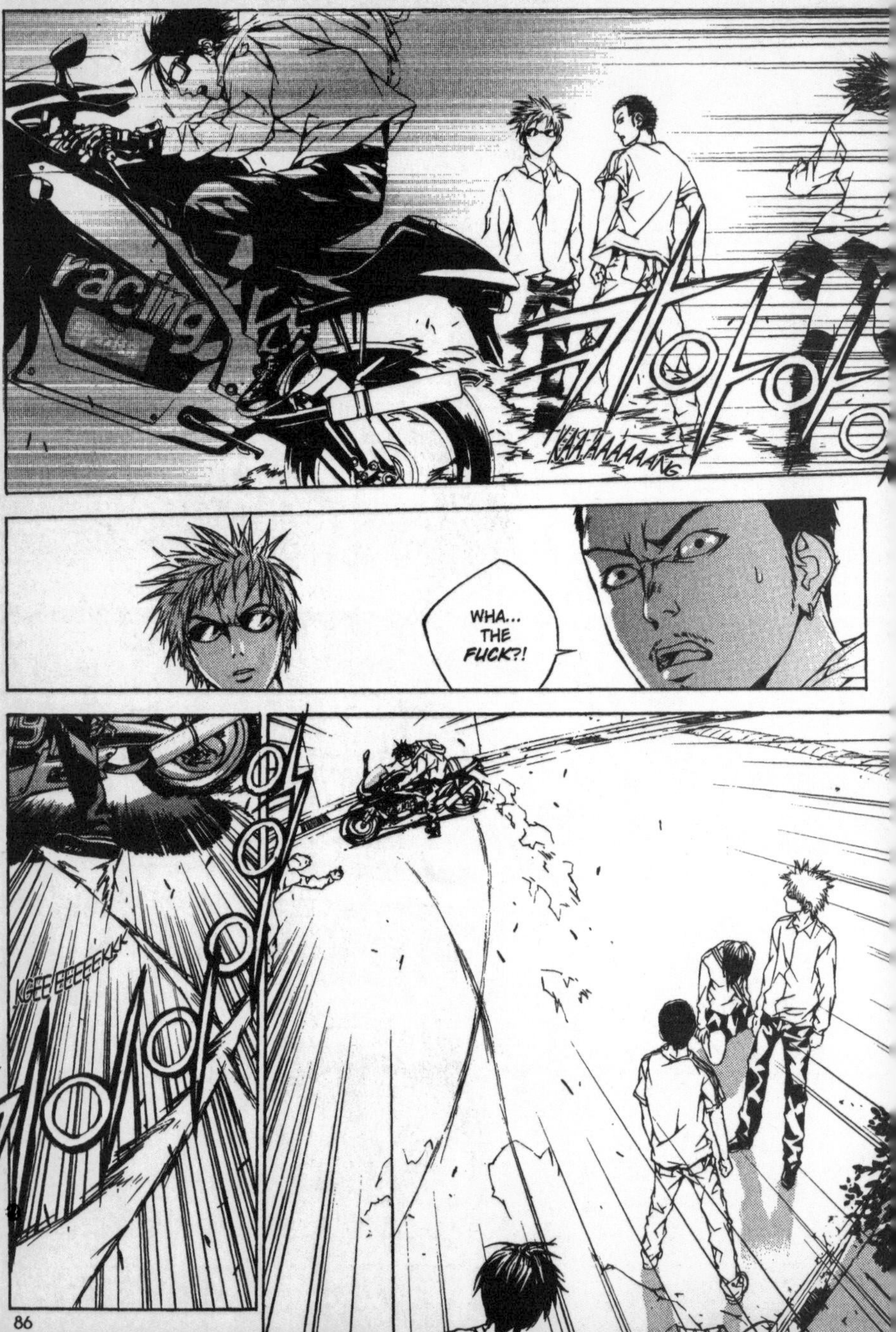
KAAAAAAAAAANG
WHA... THE FUCK?!
KGEEEEEEEEKKK

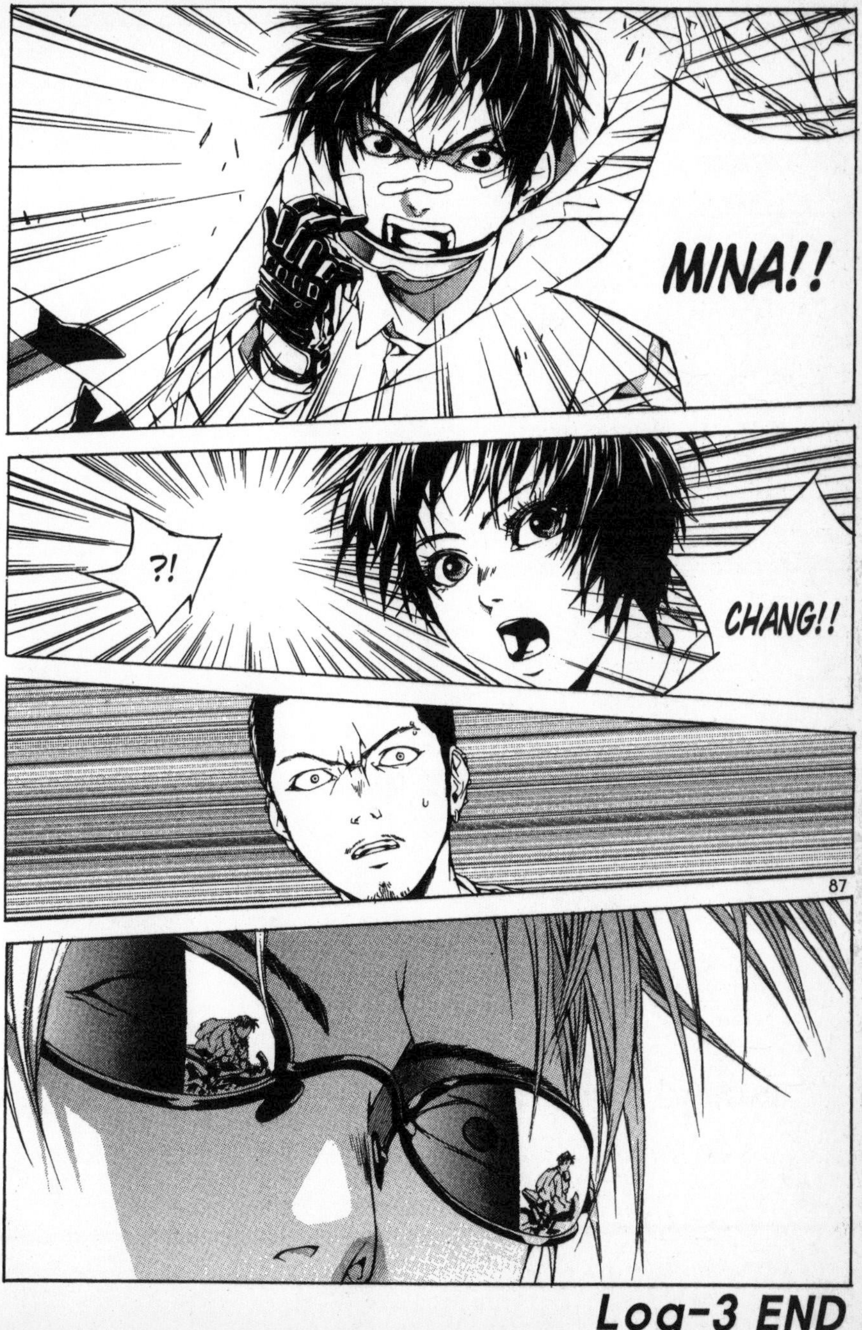
MINA!!
?!
CHANG!!

Log-3 END

LOG_4;J

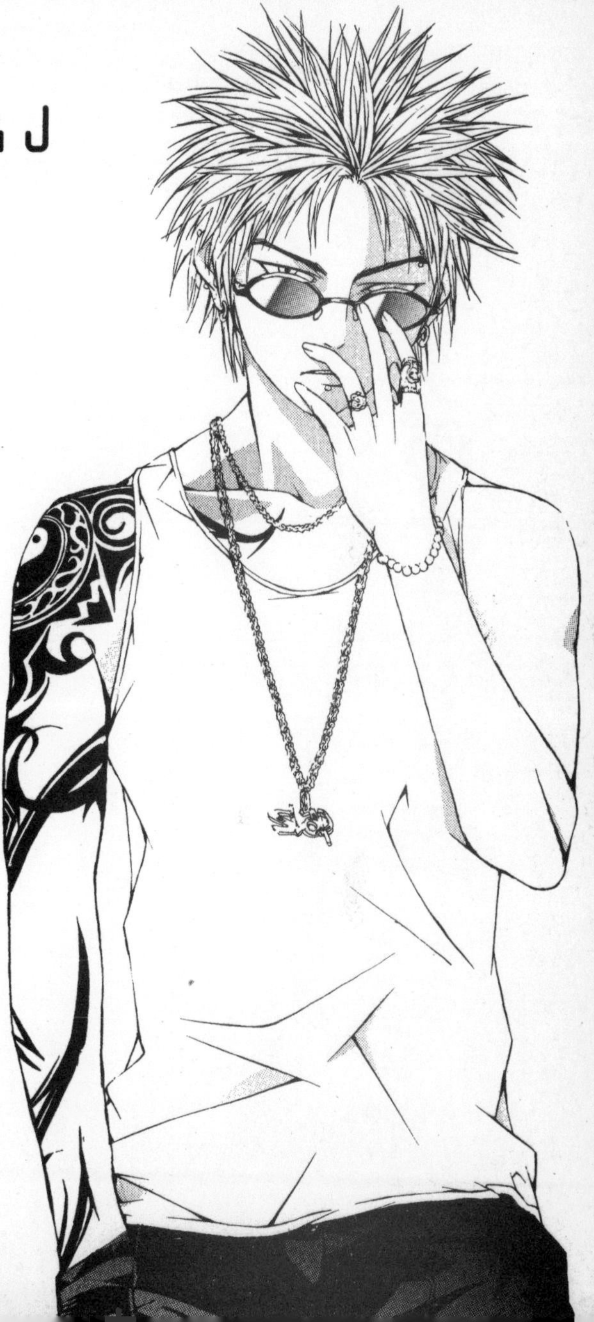

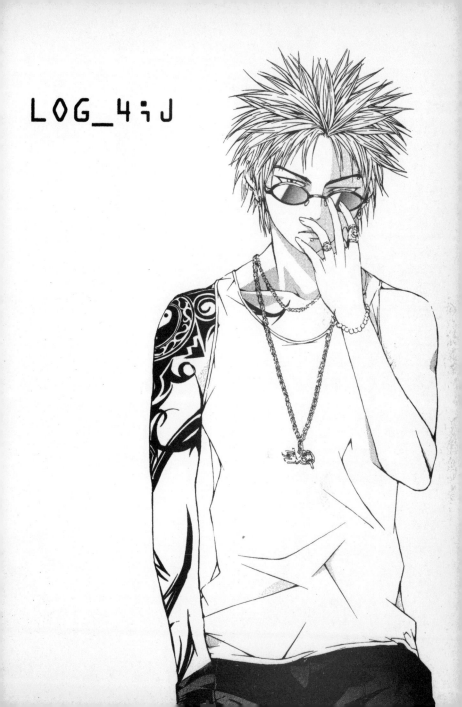

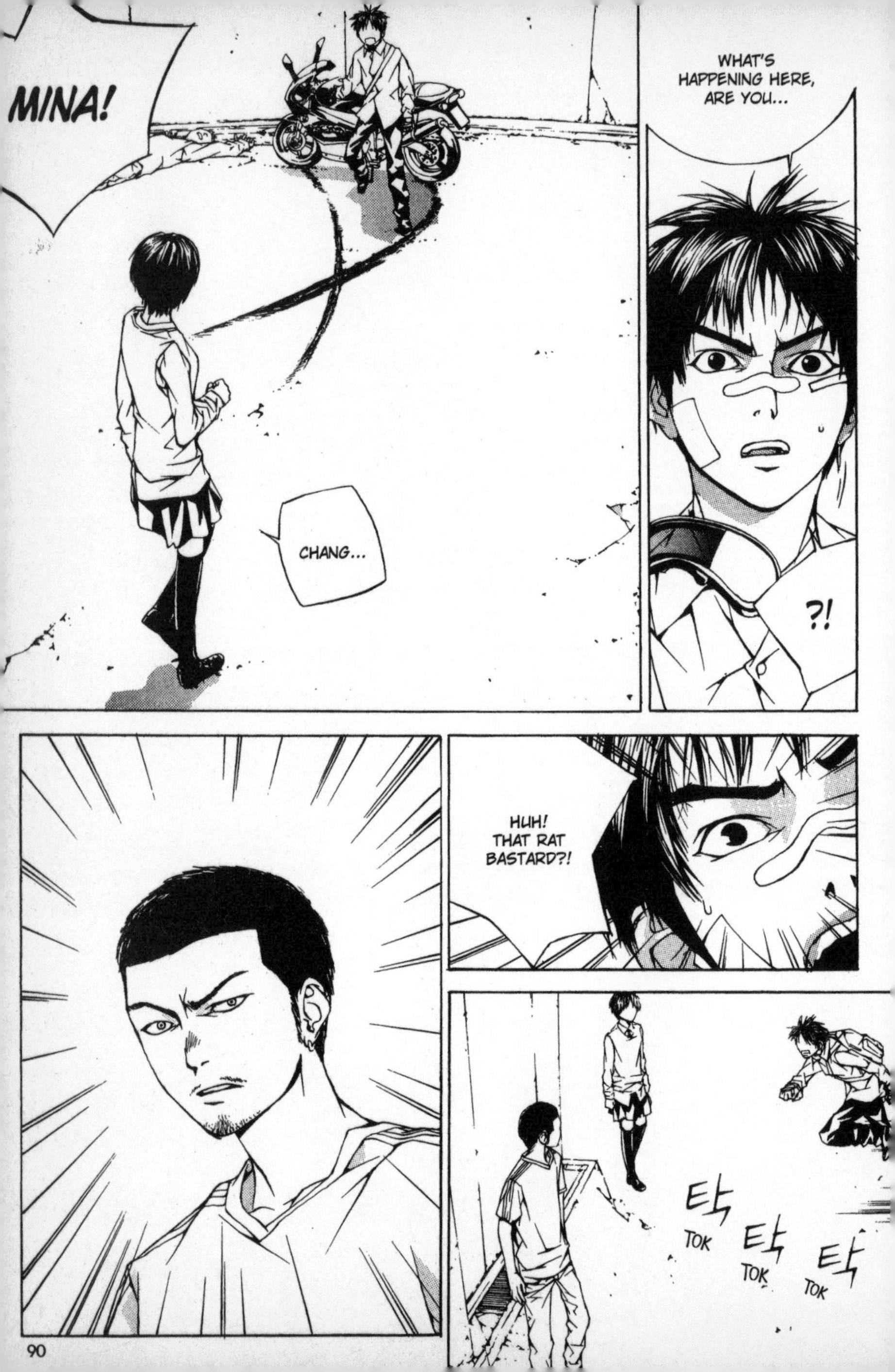
MINA!
CHANG...
WHAT'S HAPPENING HERE, ARE YOU...
?!
HUH! THAT RAT BASTARD?!
타
TOK
타
TOK
타
TOK

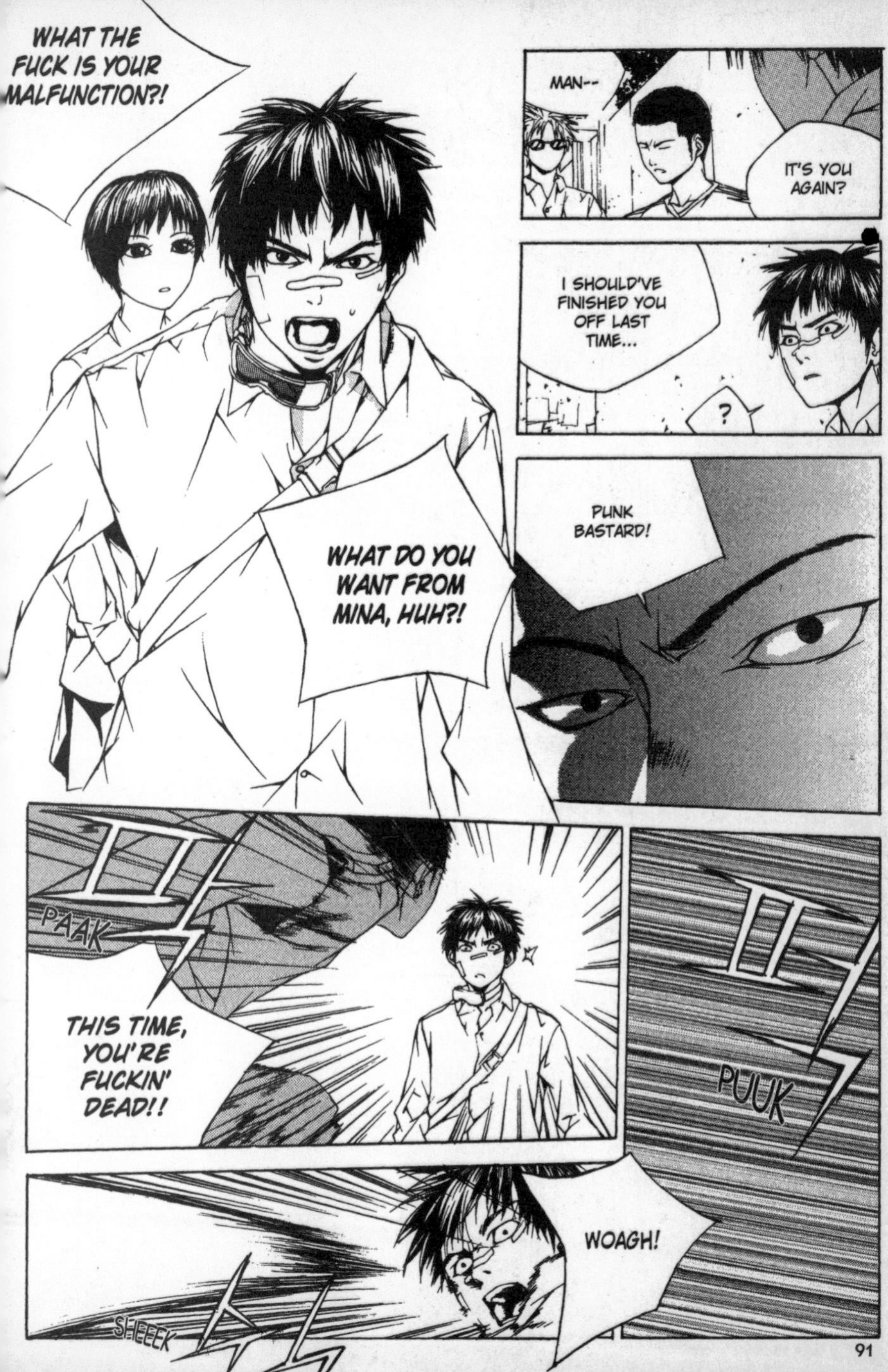

WHAT THE FUCK IS YOUR MALFUNCTION?!
WHAT DO YOU WANT FROM MINA, HUH?!
MAN--
IT'S YOU AGAIN?
I SHOULD'VE FINISHED YOU OFF LAST TIME...
?
PUNK BASTARD!
PAAK
THIS TIME, YOU'RE FUCKIN' DEAD!!
PUUK
WOAGH!
SHEEEK

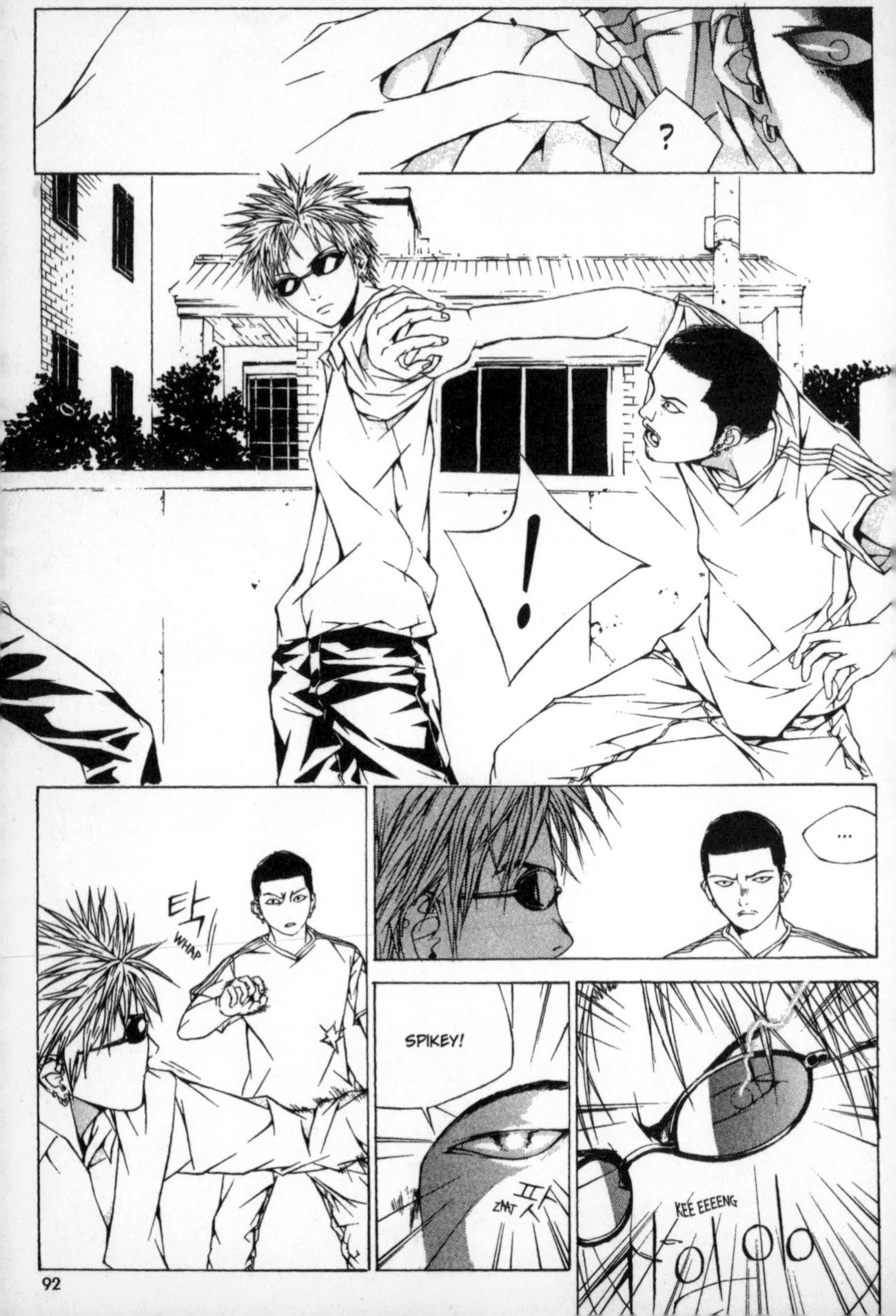
?
!
탁
WHAP
...
SPIKEY!
ZZAT
KEE EEEENG

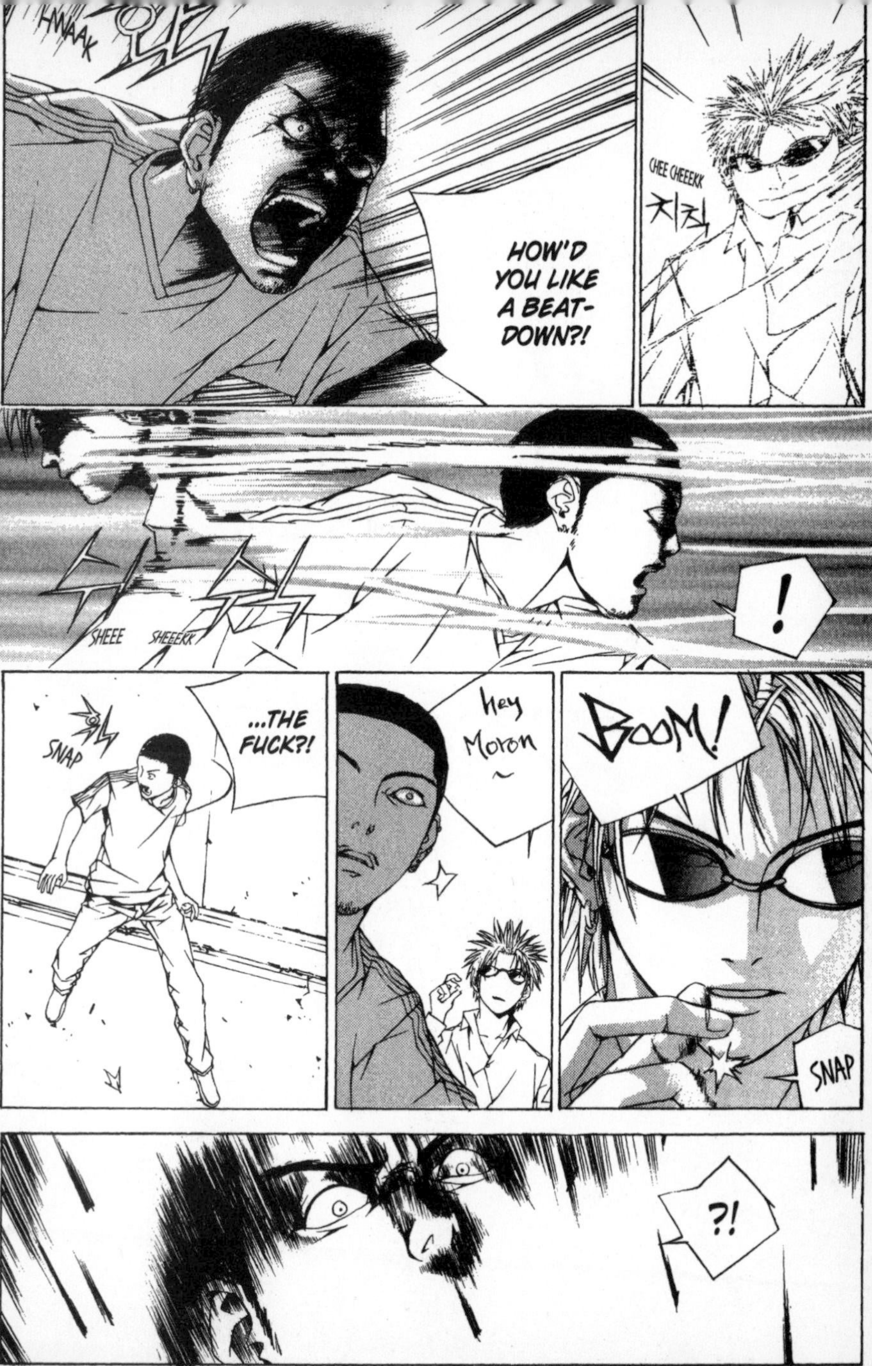
HWAAK
HOW'D YOU LIKE A BEAT-DOWN?!
CHEE CHEEEKK
치칙
SHEEE
SHEEEKK
!
SNAP
...THE FUCK?!
hey Moron ~
BOOM!
SNAP
?!

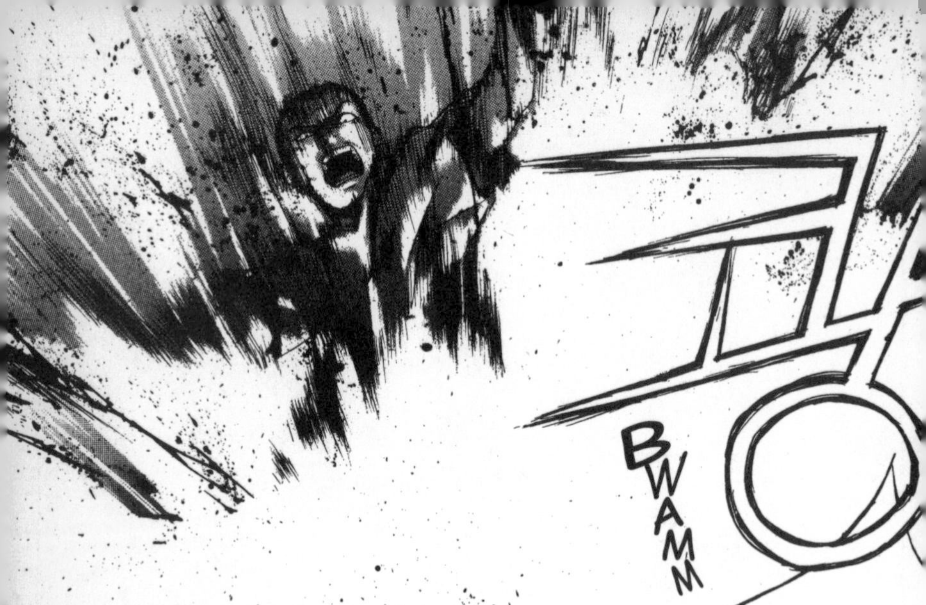
BWAMM
WOO AHH AGHH

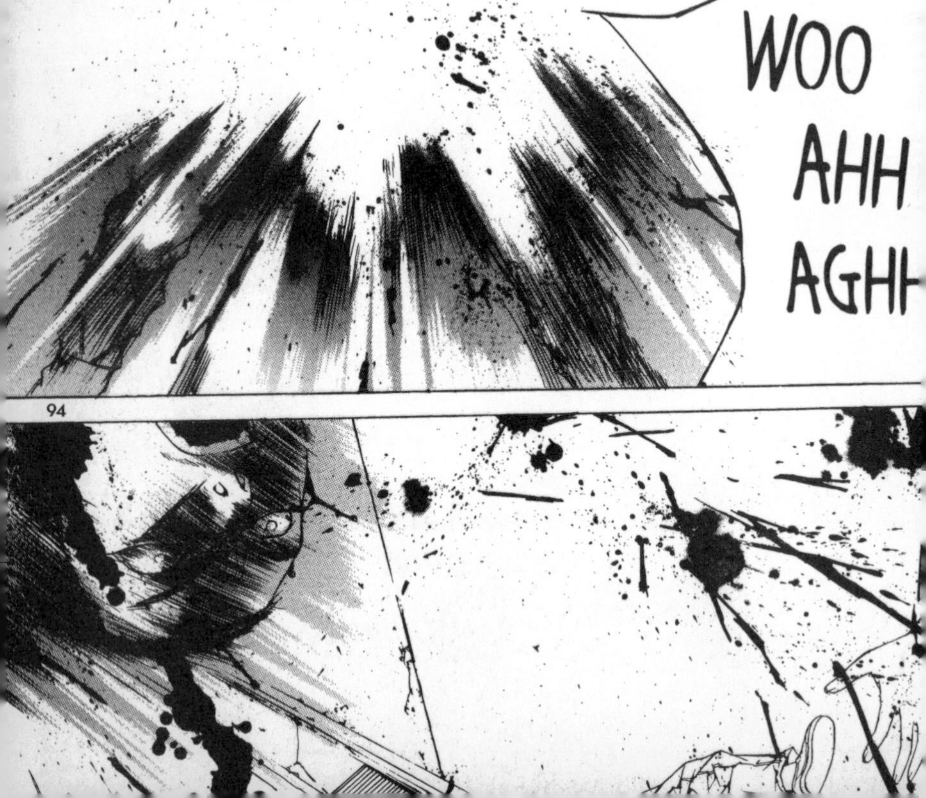

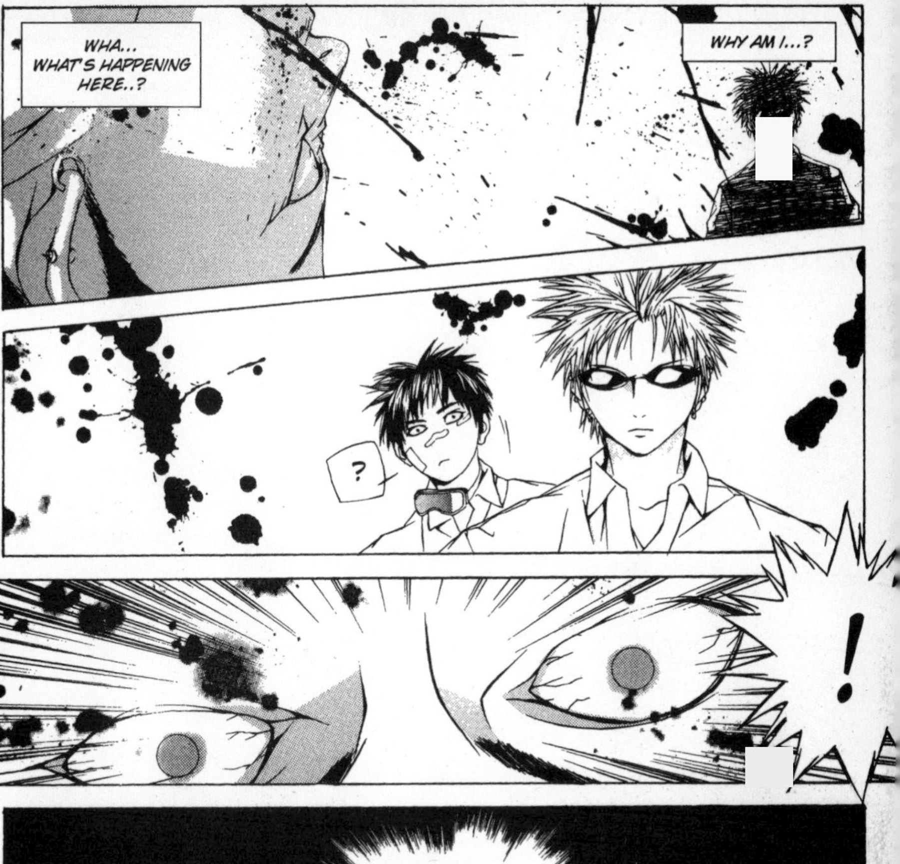
WHA...
WHAT'S HAPPENING
HERE..?
WHY AM I...?
?
!
...G...
GODDAMN
IT...!

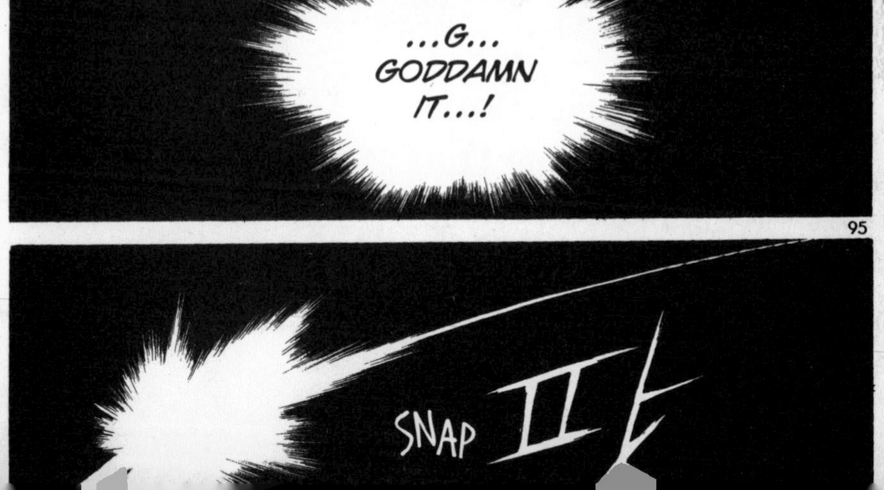
SNAP

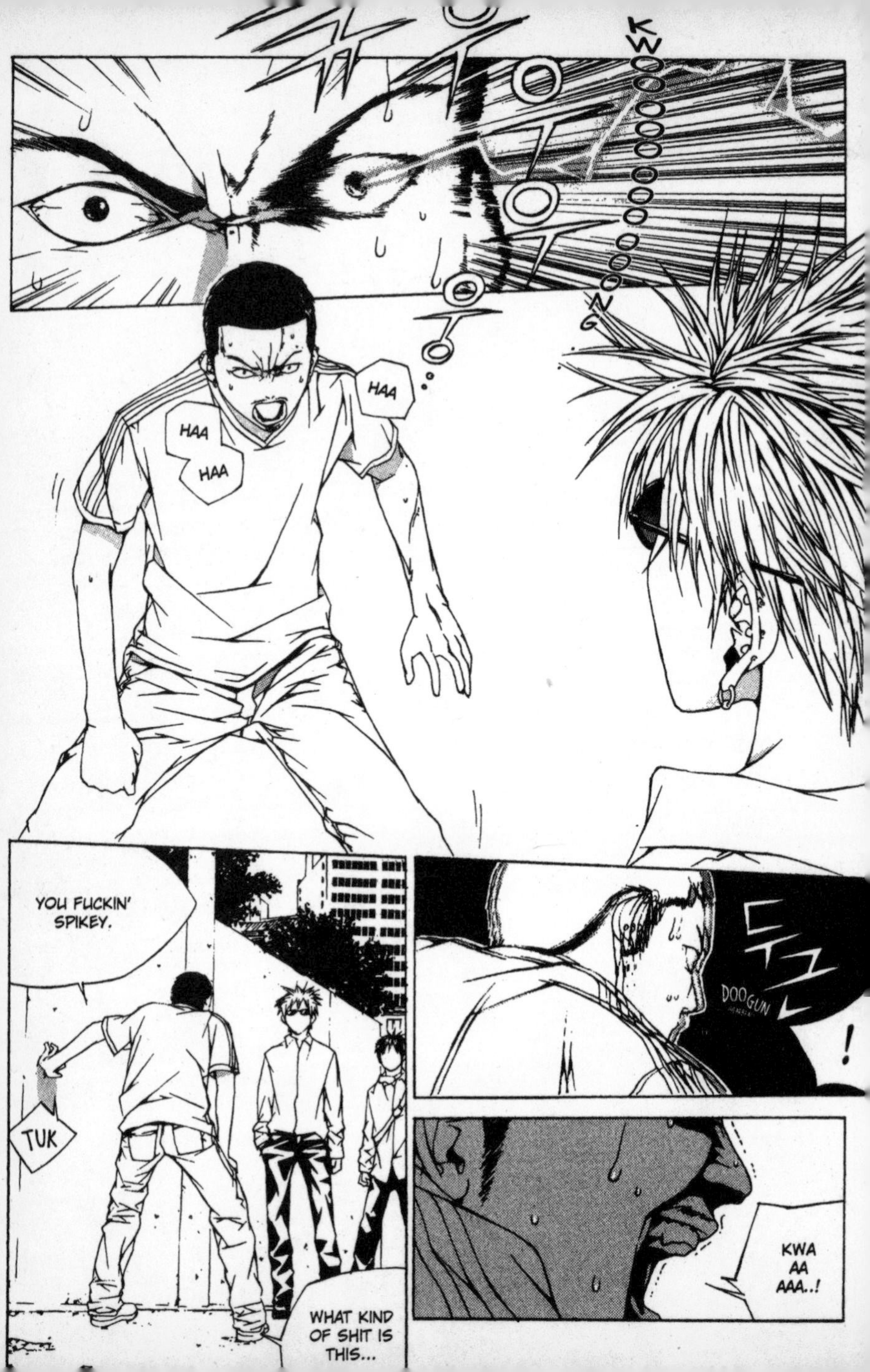
KWOOOOOOOOOOONG
HAA
HAA
HAA
YOU FUCKIN' SPIKEY.
TUK
WHAT KIND OF SHIT IS THIS...
DOOGUN
!
KWA AA AAA..!

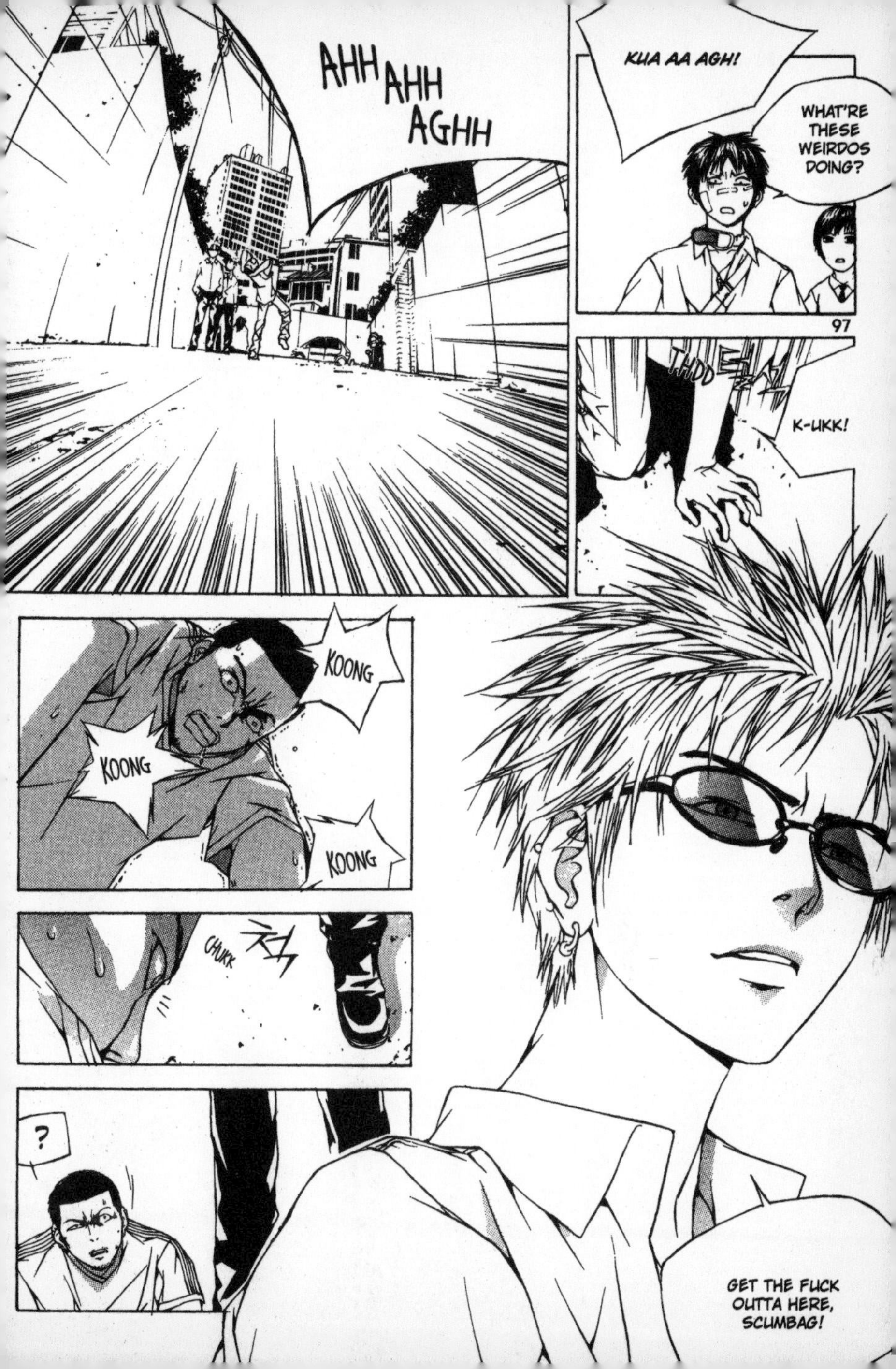

AHH AHH AGHH
KUA AA AGH!
WHAT'RE THESE WEIRDOS DOING?
THDD
K-UKK!
KOONG
KOONG
KOONG
CHUKK
?
GET THE FUCK OUTTA HERE, SCUMBAG!

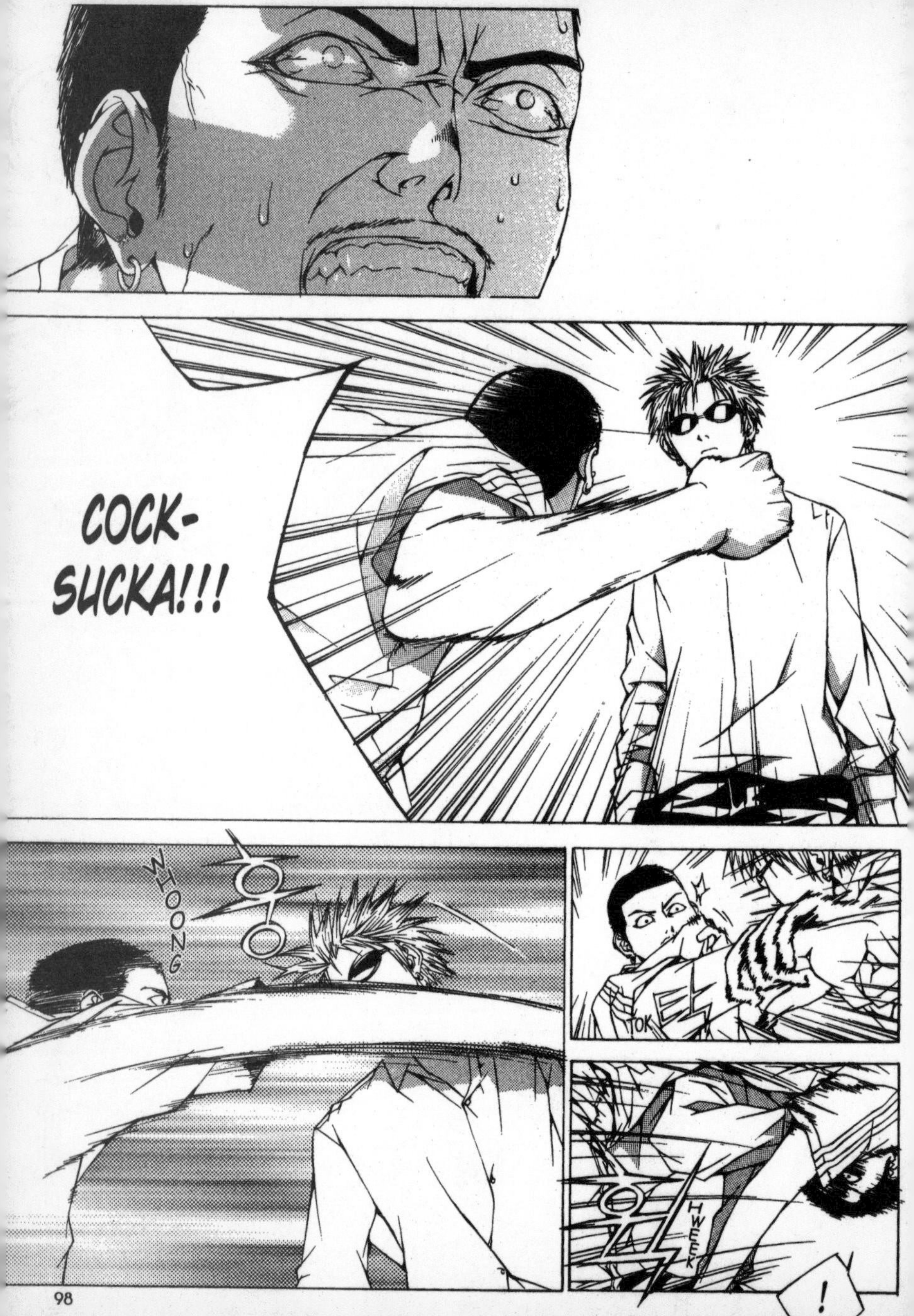
COCK-
SUCKA!!!
WHOONG
TOK
HWEEK
!

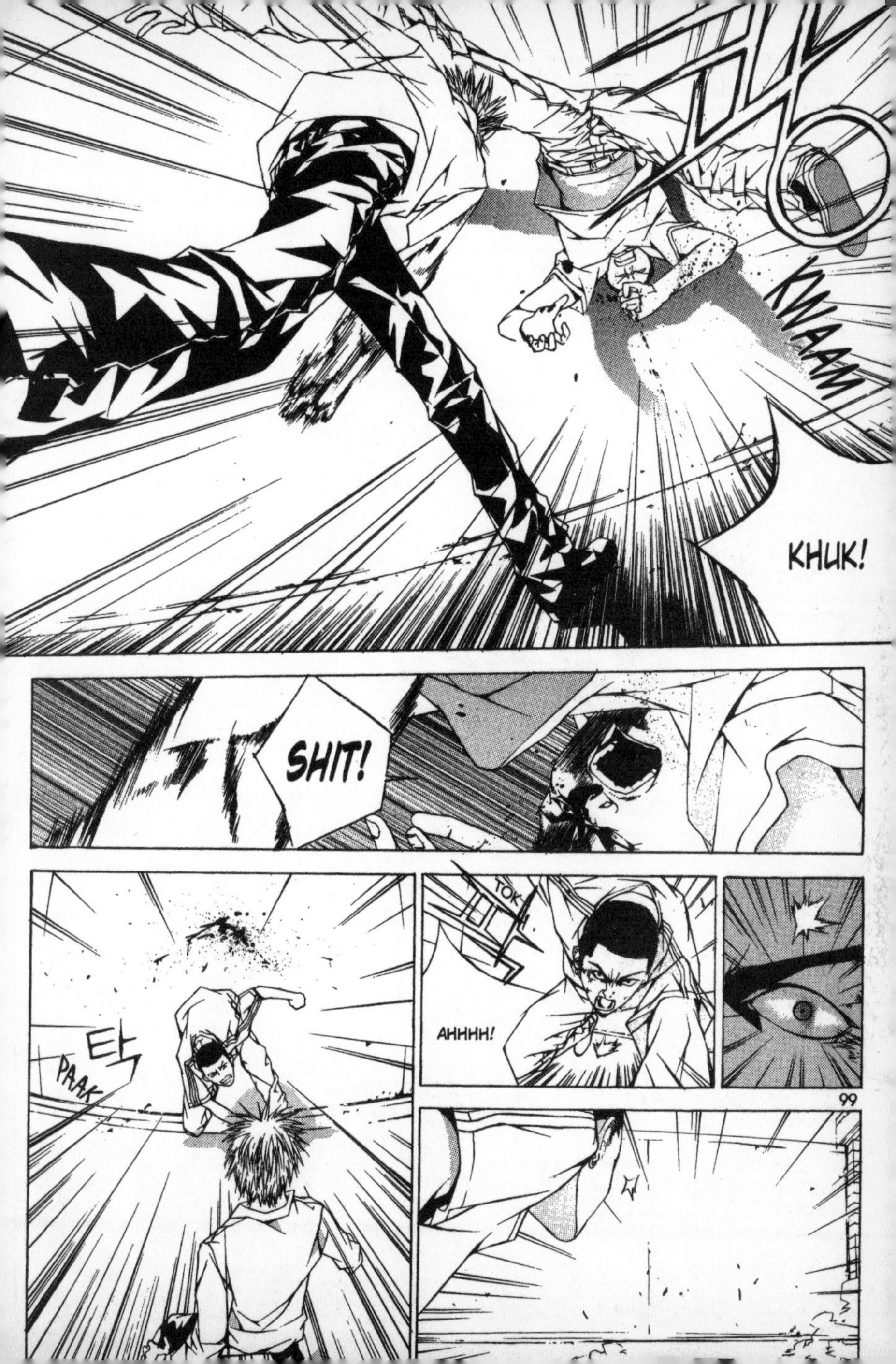
KWAAM
KHUK!
SHIT!
PAAK
TOK
AHHHH!

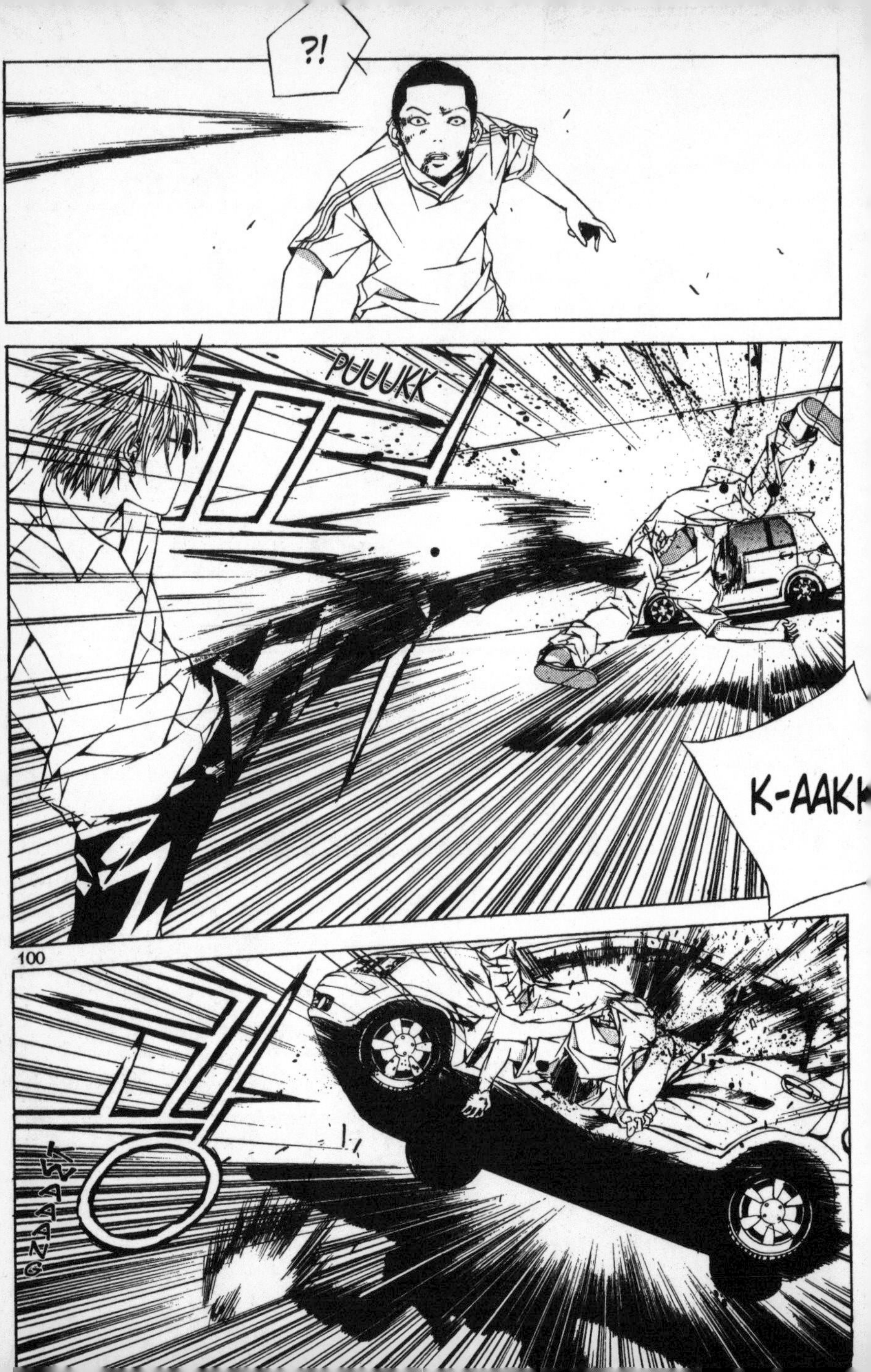
?!
PUUUKK
K-AAKK
KWAAAANG

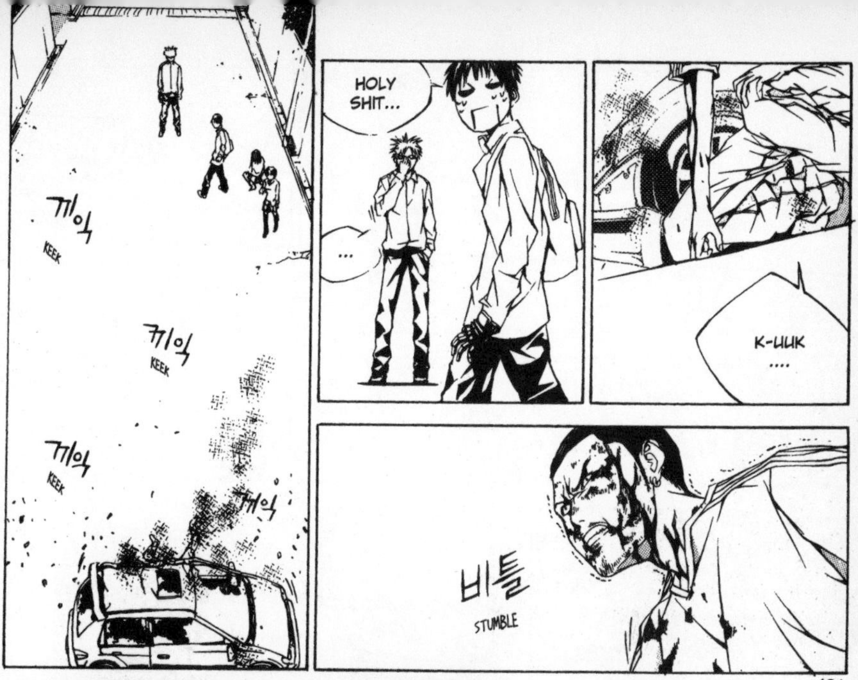
끼익
KEEK
끼익
KEEK
끼익
KEEK
끼익
HOLY SHIT...
...
K-UUK ....
비틀
STUMBLE

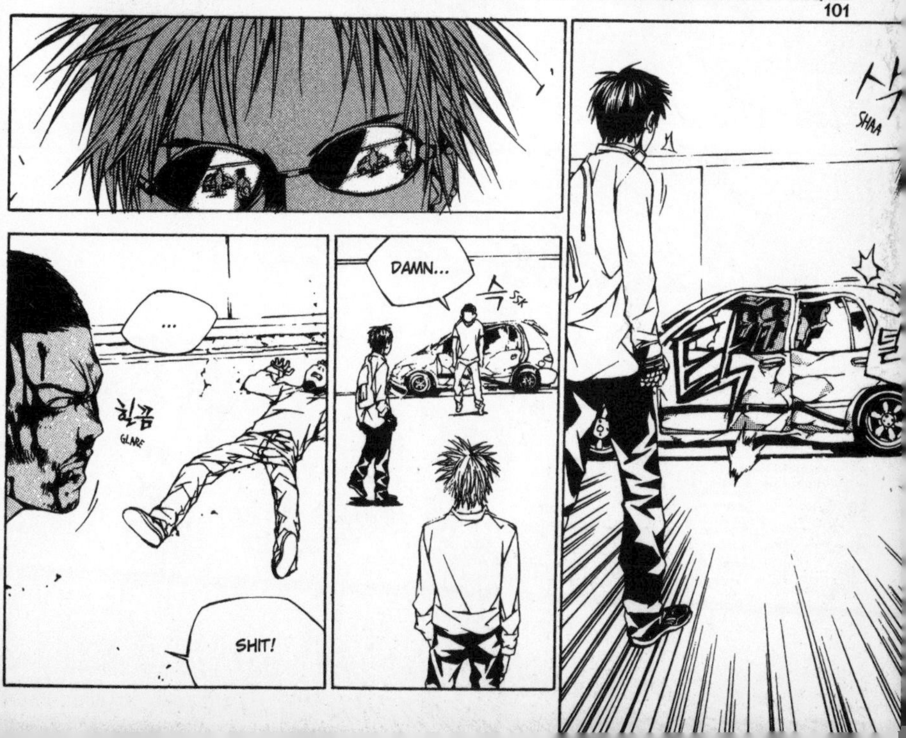
...
힐끔
GLARE
SHIT!
DAMN...
슥 SSK
SHAA

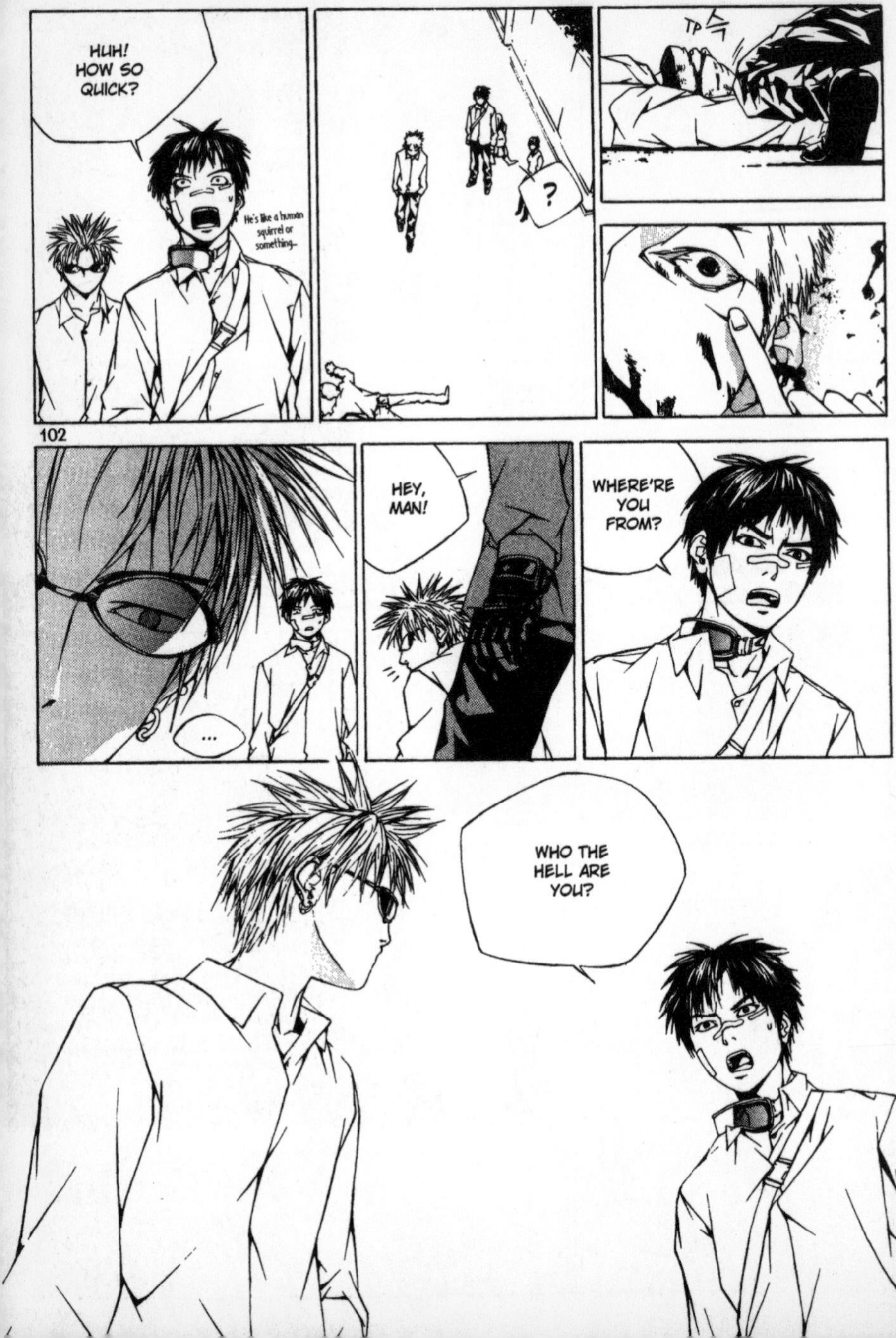
HUH! HOW SO QUICK?
He's like a human squirrel or something...
?
TP
...
HEY, MAN!
WHERE'RE YOU FROM?
WHO THE HELL ARE YOU?

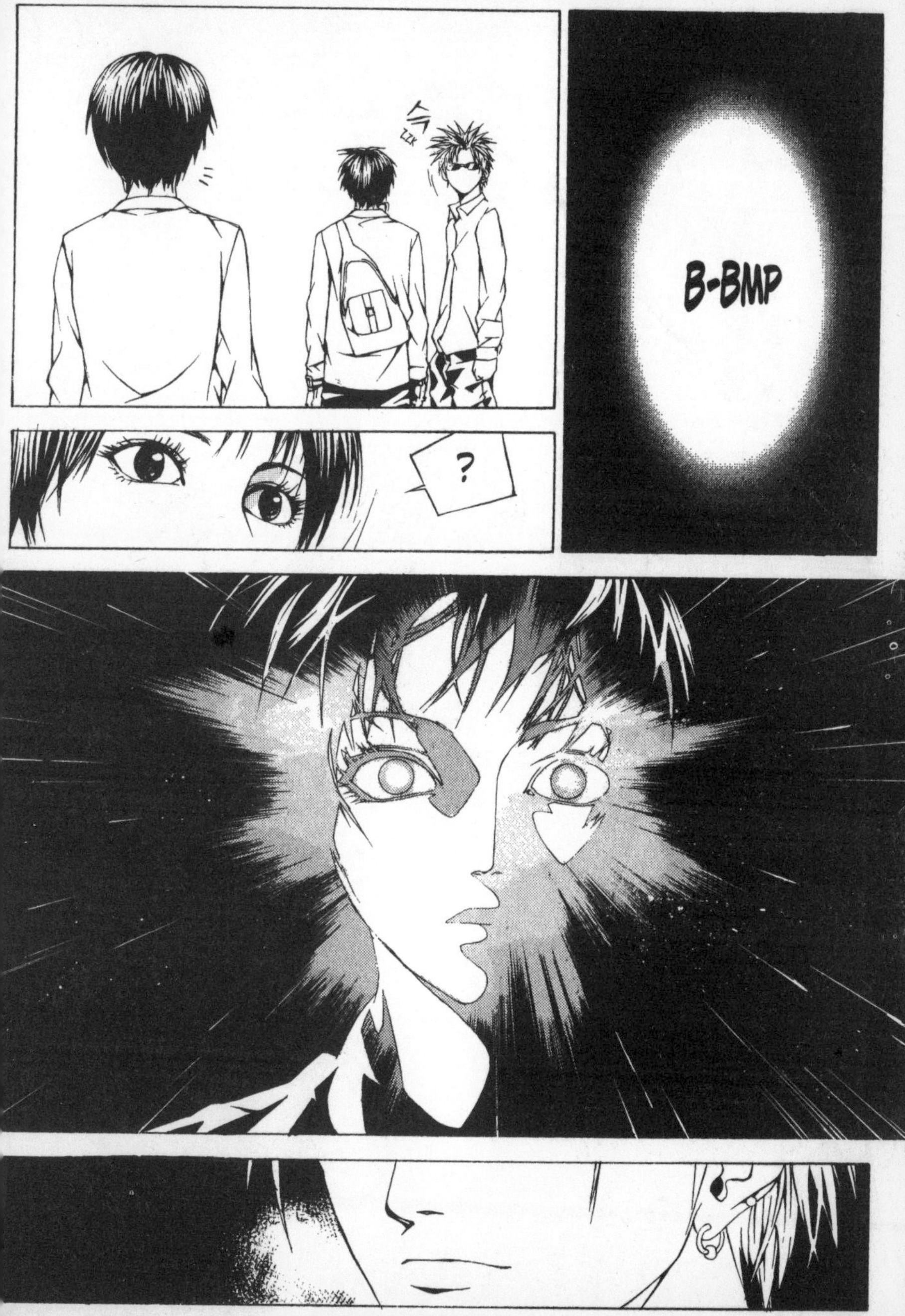
ZZK
?
B-BMP

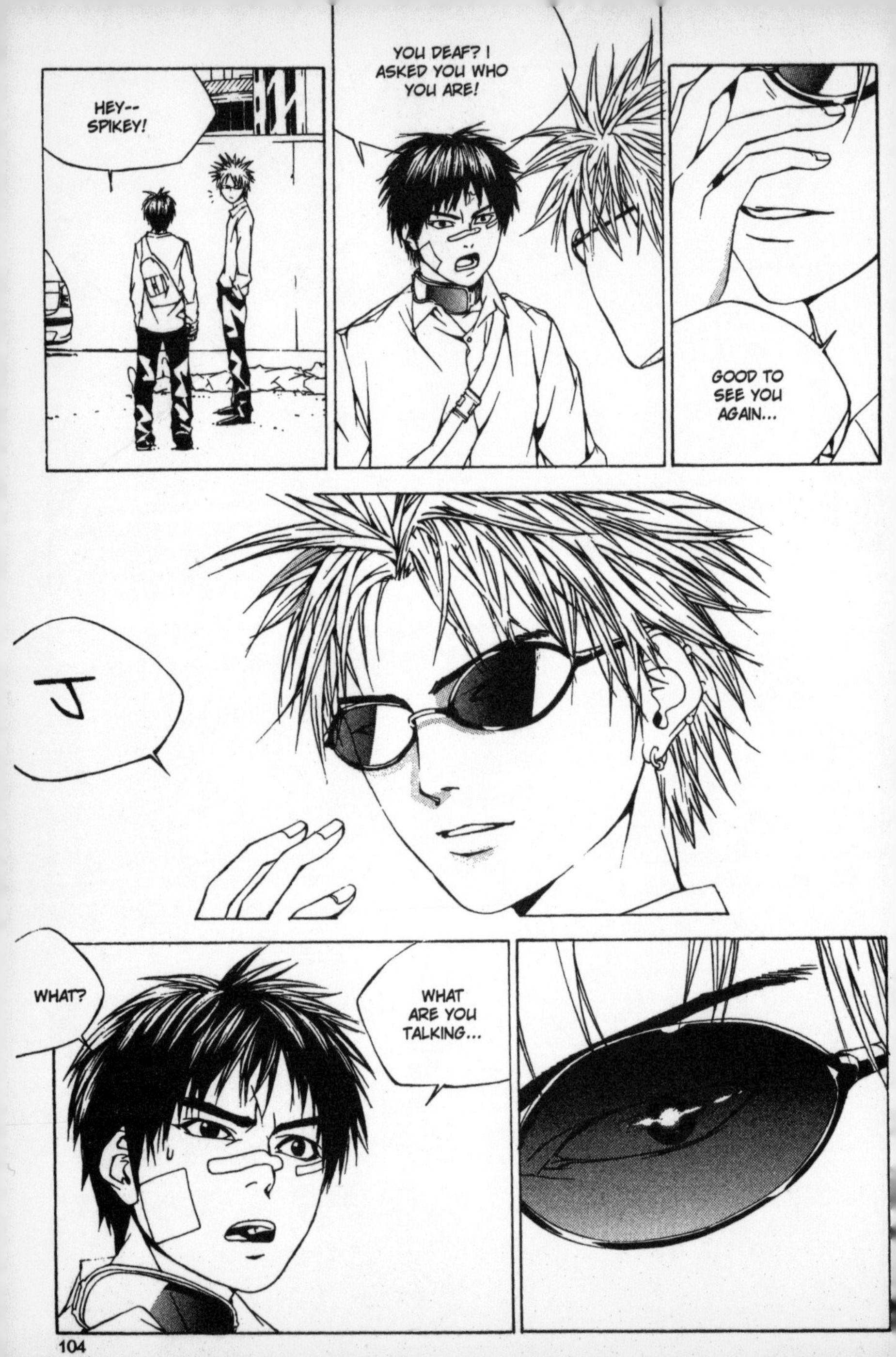
HEY--
SPIKEY!
YOU DEAF? I ASKED YOU WHO YOU ARE!
GOOD TO SEE YOU AGAIN...
J
WHAT?
WHAT ARE YOU TALKING...

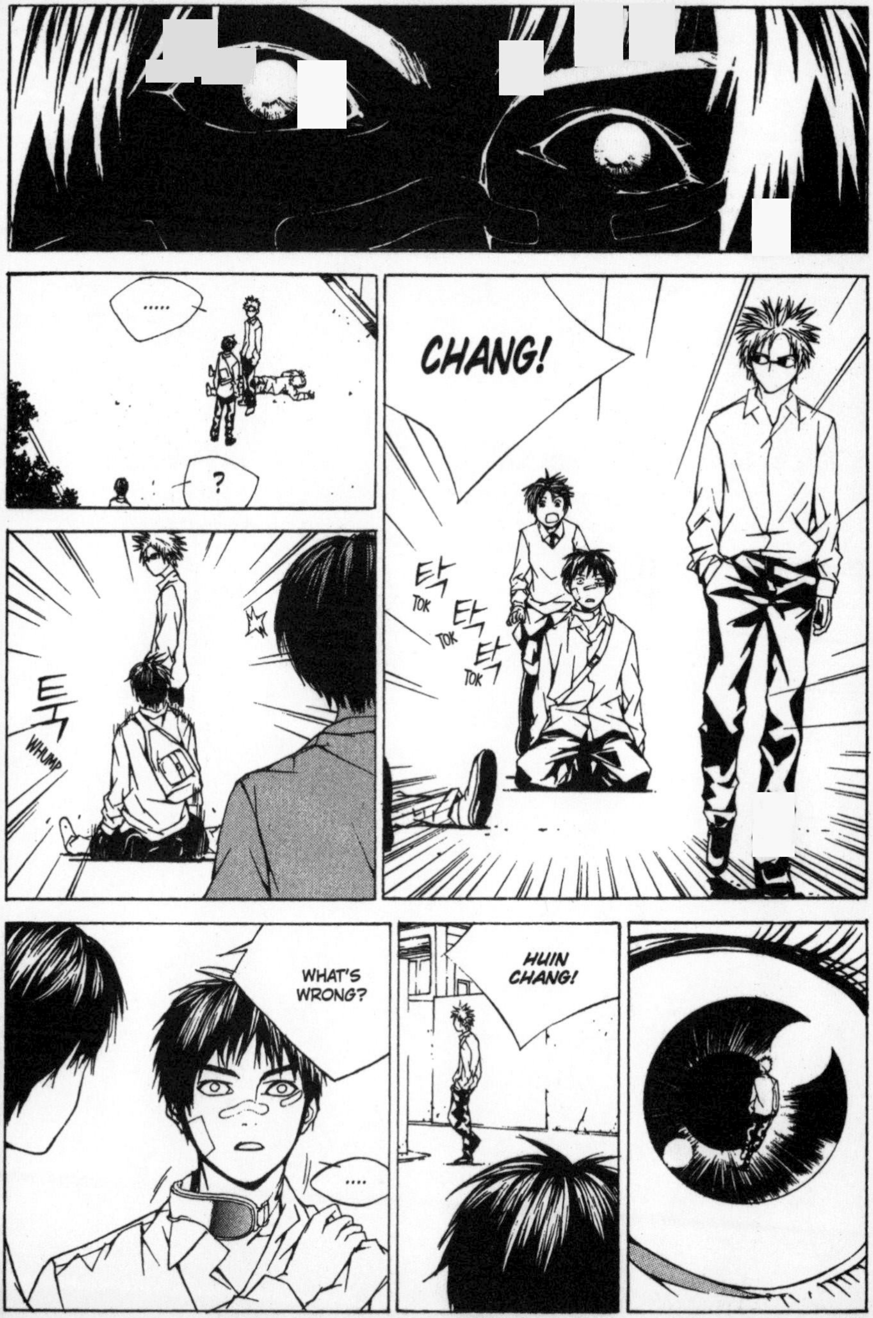

.....
?
툭
WHUMP
CHANG!
탁
TOK
탁
TOK
탁
TOK
WHAT'S WRONG?
....
HUIN CHANG!

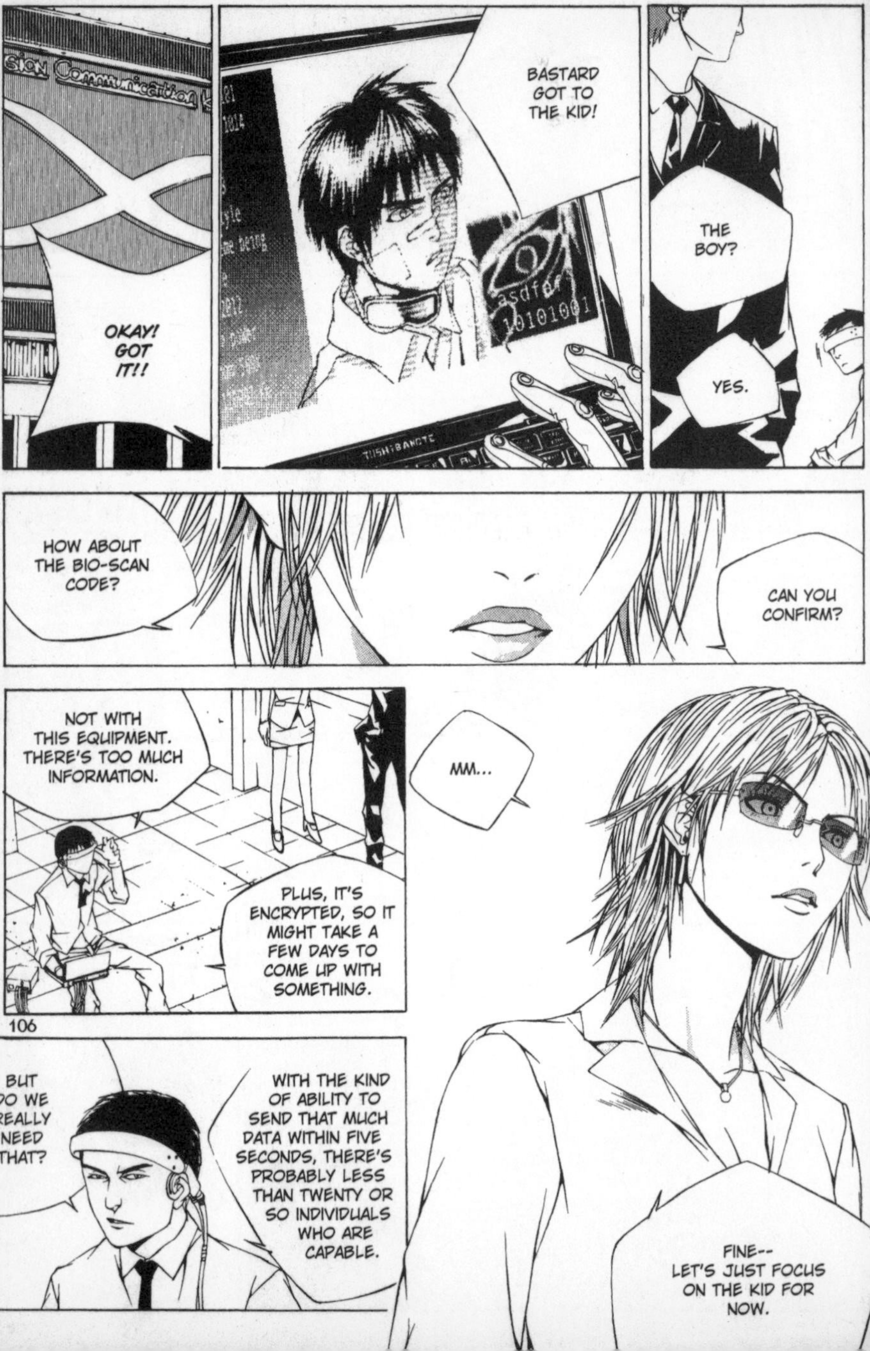
OKAY! GOT IT!!
BASTARD GOT TO THE KID!
THE BOY?
YES.
HOW ABOUT THE BIO-SCAN CODE?
CAN YOU CONFIRM?
NOT WITH THIS EQUIPMENT. THERE'S TOO MUCH INFORMATION.
PLUS, IT'S ENCRYPTED, SO IT MIGHT TAKE A FEW DAYS TO COME UP WITH SOMETHING.
BUT DO WE REALLY NEED THAT?
WITH THE KIND OF ABILITY TO SEND THAT MUCH DATA WITHIN FIVE SECONDS, THERE'S PROBABLY LESS THAN TWENTY OR SO INDIVIDUALS WHO ARE CAPABLE.
MM...
FINE-- LET'S JUST FOCUS ON THE KID FOR NOW.

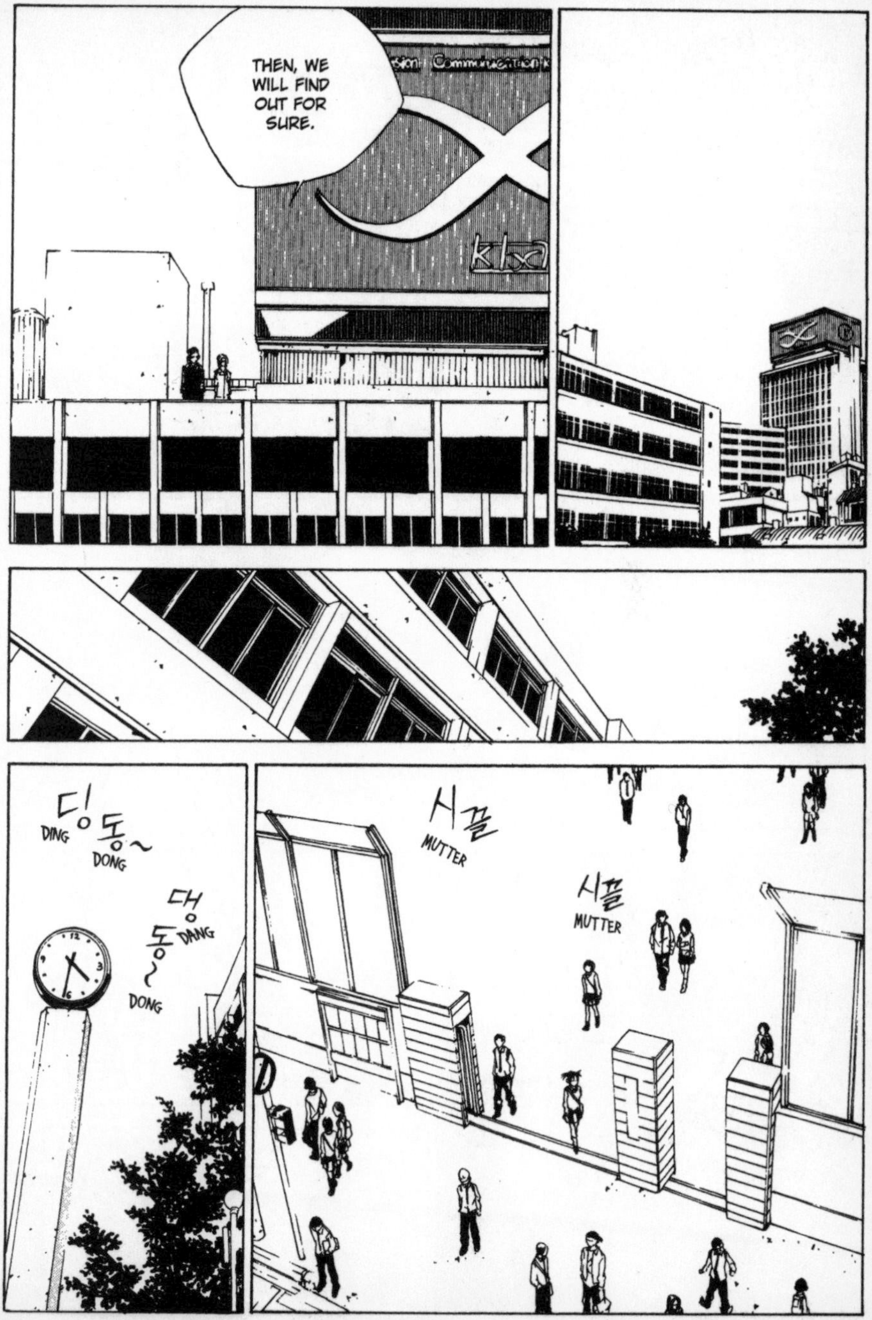
THEN, WE WILL FIND OUT FOR SURE.
딩 DING
동~ DONG
댕 DANG
동~ DONG
시끌 MUTTER
시끌 MUTTER

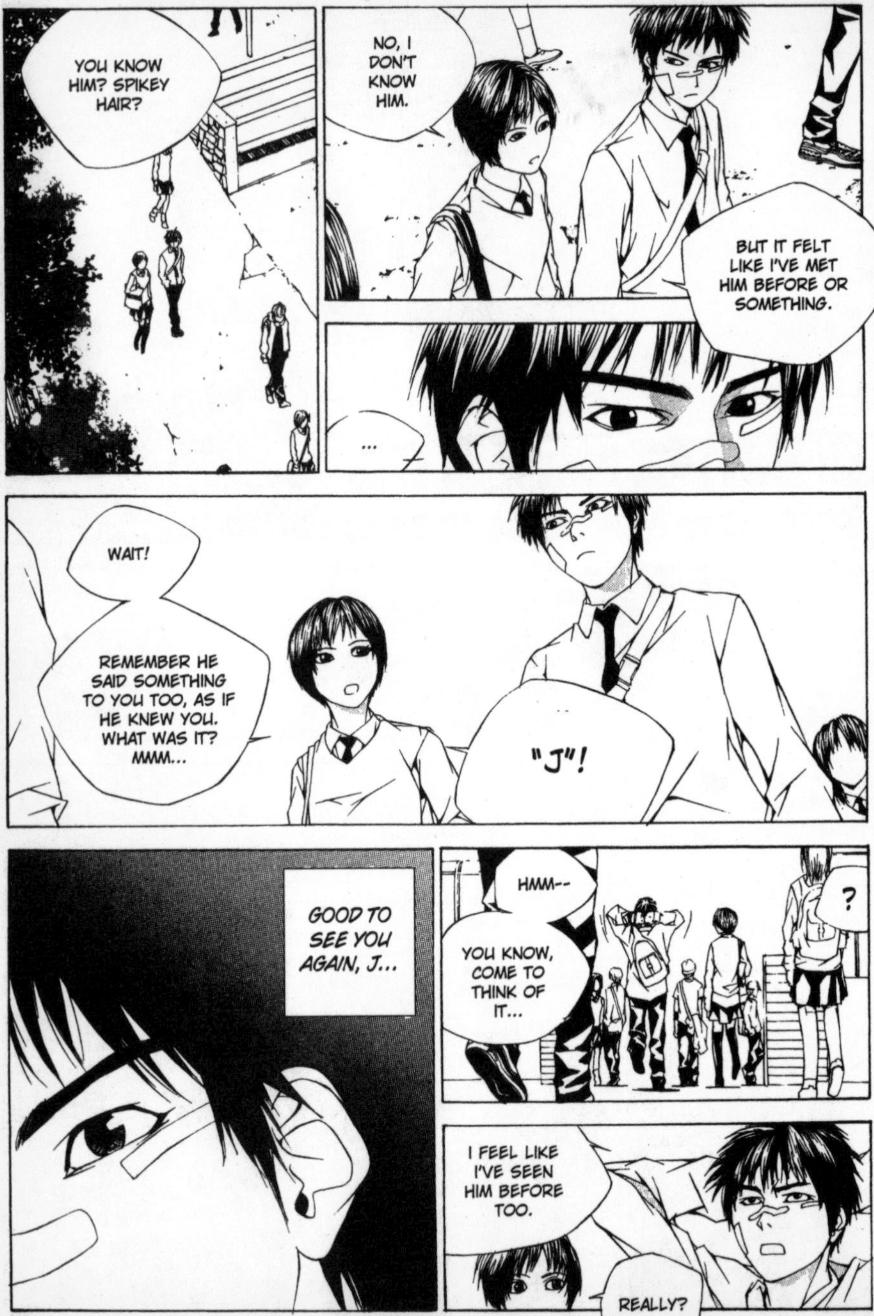
YOU KNOW HIM? SPIKEY HAIR?
NO, I DON'T KNOW HIM.
BUT IT FELT LIKE I'VE MET HIM BEFORE OR SOMETHING.
...
WAIT!
REMEMBER HE SAID SOMETHING TO YOU TOO, AS IF HE KNEW YOU. WHAT WAS IT? MMM...
"J"!
GOOD TO SEE YOU AGAIN, J...
HMM--
YOU KNOW, COME TO THINK OF IT...
?
I FEEL LIKE I'VE SEEN HIM BEFORE TOO.
REALLY?

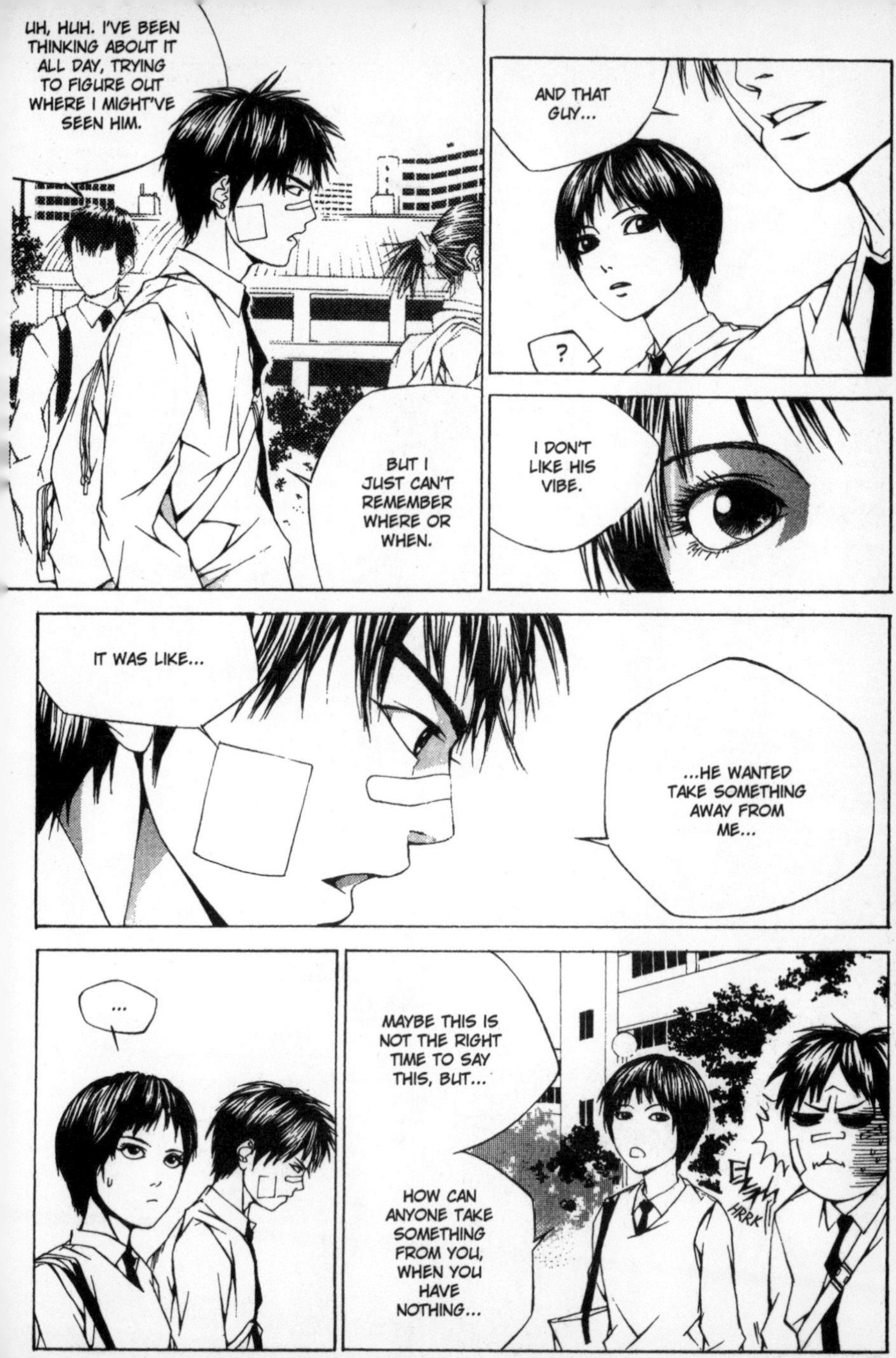
UH, HUH. I'VE BEEN THINKING ABOUT IT ALL DAY, TRYING TO FIGURE OUT WHERE I MIGHT'VE SEEN HIM.
BUT I JUST CAN'T REMEMBER WHERE OR WHEN.
AND THAT GUY...
?
I DON'T LIKE HIS VIBE.
IT WAS LIKE...
...HE WANTED TAKE SOMETHING AWAY FROM ME...
...
MAYBE THIS IS NOT THE RIGHT TIME TO SAY THIS, BUT...
HOW CAN ANYONE TAKE SOMETHING FROM YOU, WHEN YOU HAVE NOTHING...
HRRK

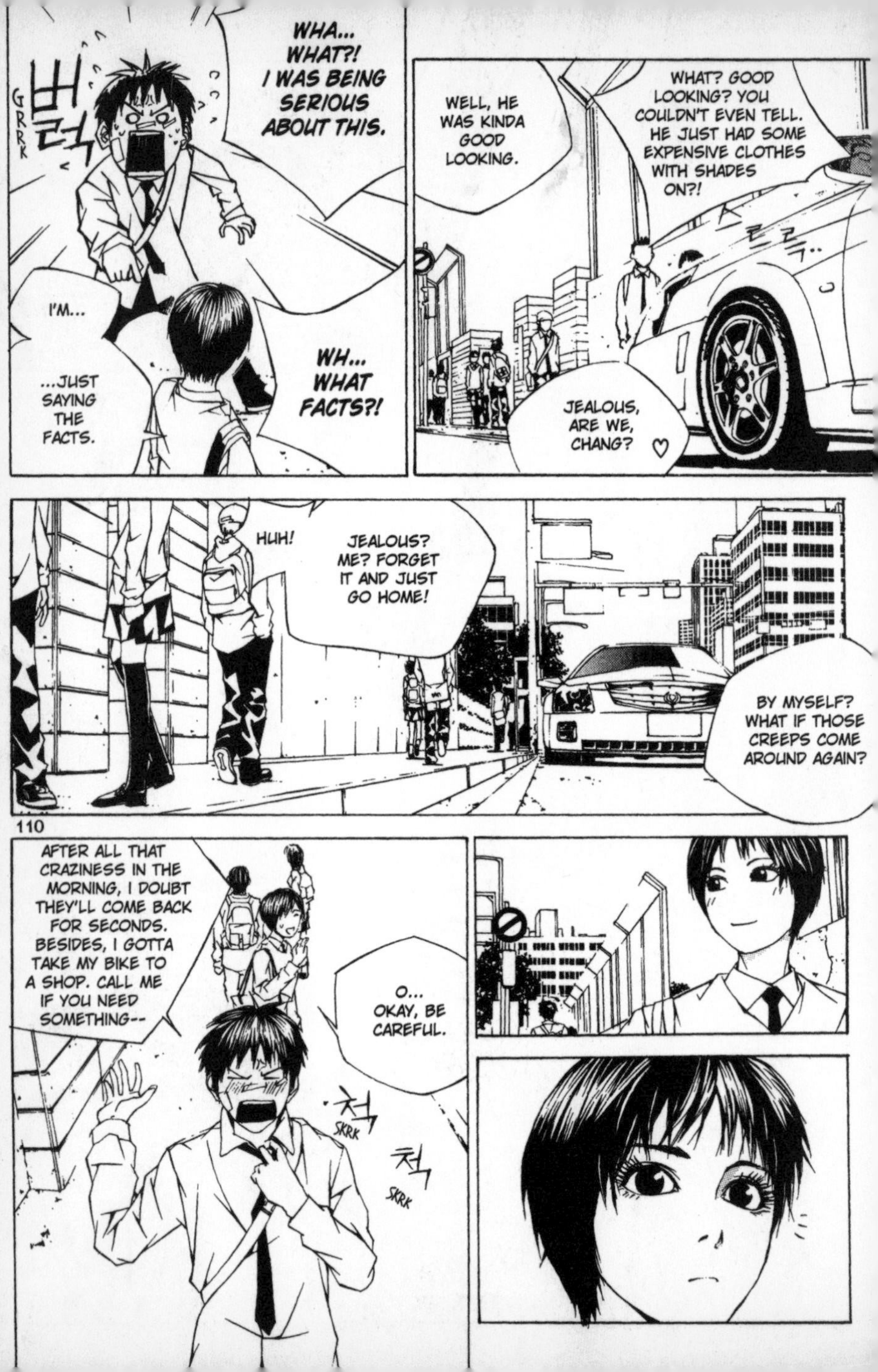
GRRK
WHA... WHAT?! I WAS BEING SERIOUS ABOUT THIS.
I'M...
...JUST SAYING THE FACTS.
WH... WHAT FACTS?!
WELL, HE WAS KINDA GOOD LOOKING.
WHAT? GOOD LOOKING? YOU COULDN'T EVEN TELL. HE JUST HAD SOME EXPENSIVE CLOTHES WITH SHADES ON?!
JEALOUS, ARE WE, CHANG? ♡
HUH!
JEALOUS? ME? FORGET IT AND JUST GO HOME!
BY MYSELF? WHAT IF THOSE CREEPS COME AROUND AGAIN?
AFTER ALL THAT CRAZINESS IN THE MORNING, I DOUBT THEY'LL COME BACK FOR SECONDS. BESIDES, I GOTTA TAKE MY BIKE TO A SHOP. CALL ME IF YOU NEED SOMETHING--
O... OKAY, BE CAREFUL.
SKRK
SKRK

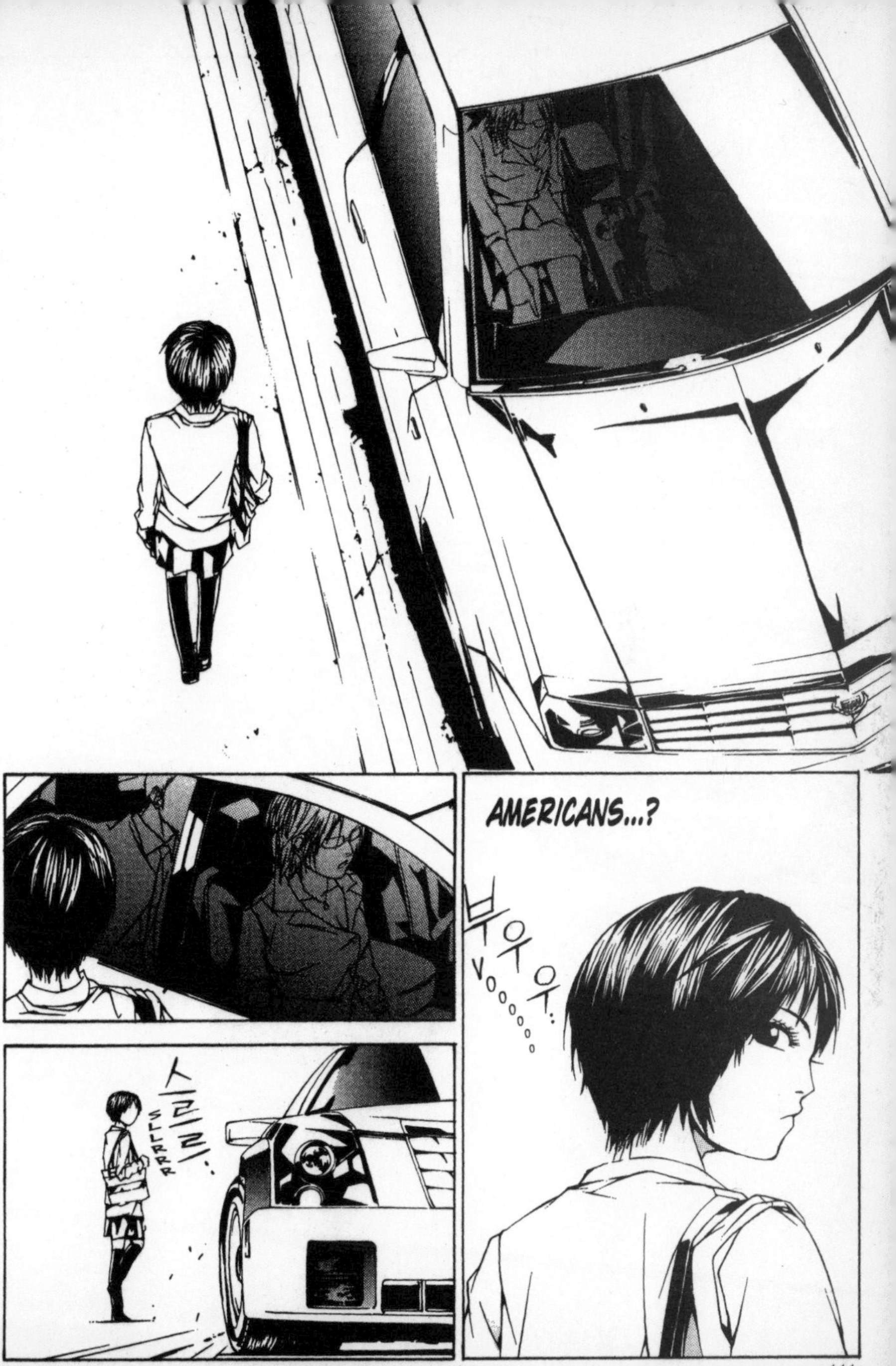
스르르..
SLLRRR
AMERICANS...?
부우우..
VOOOOOO

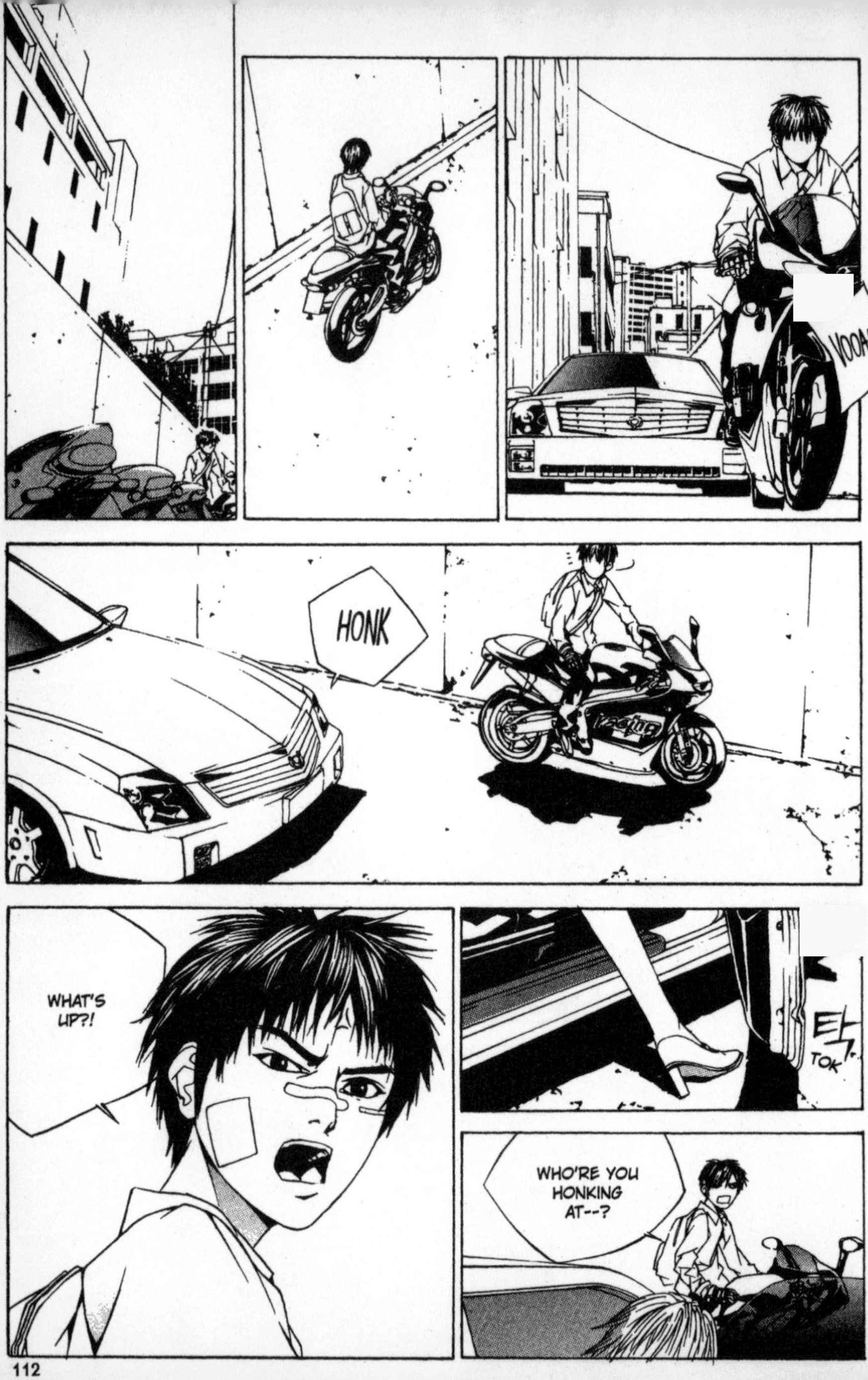
VOOANG
HONK
WHAT'S UP?!
탁
TOK
WHO'RE YOU HONKING AT--?

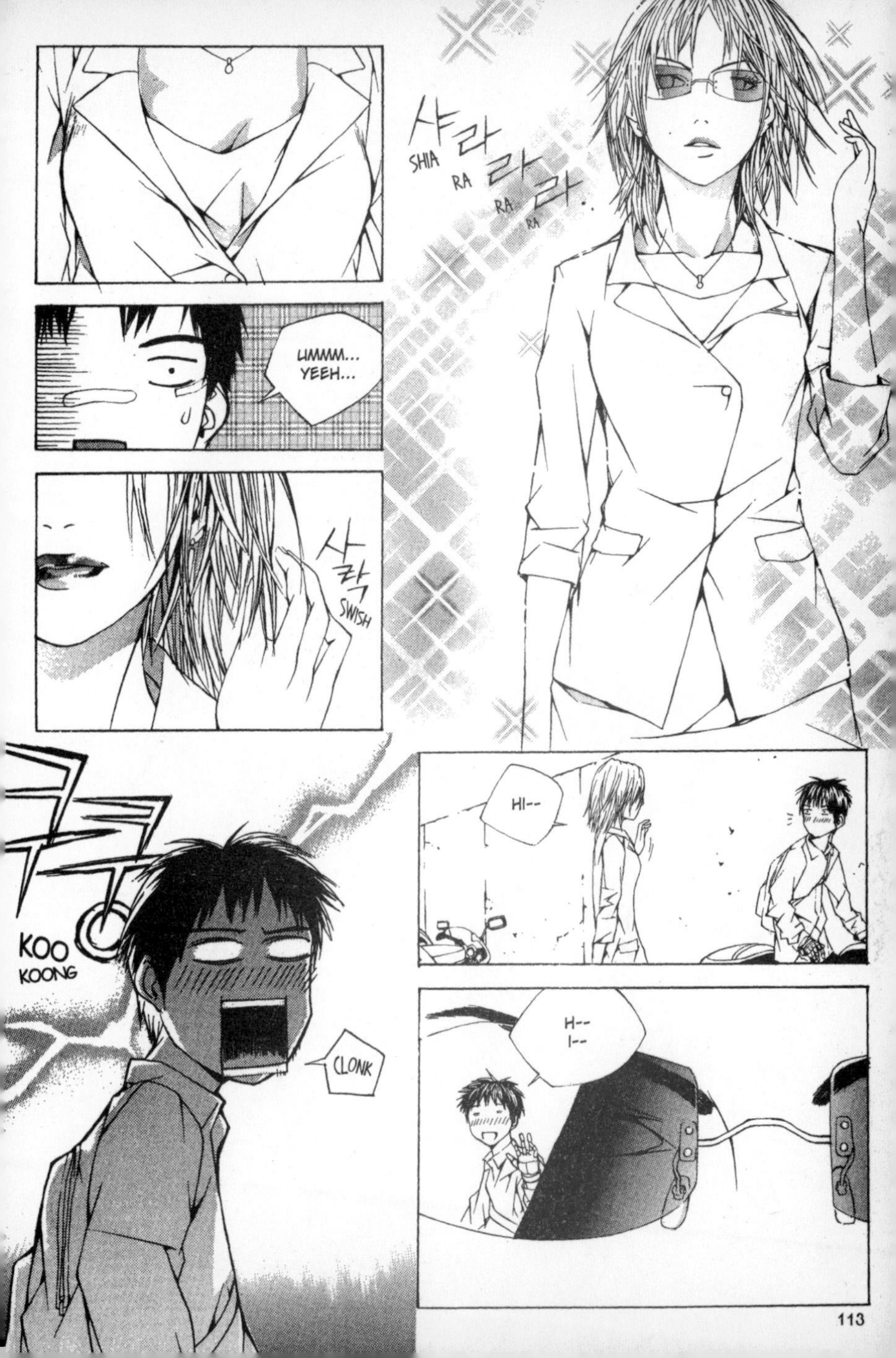
UMMM... YEEH...
사락
SWISH
샤라라라
SHIA RA RA RA
KOO KOONG
CLONK
HI--
H-- I--

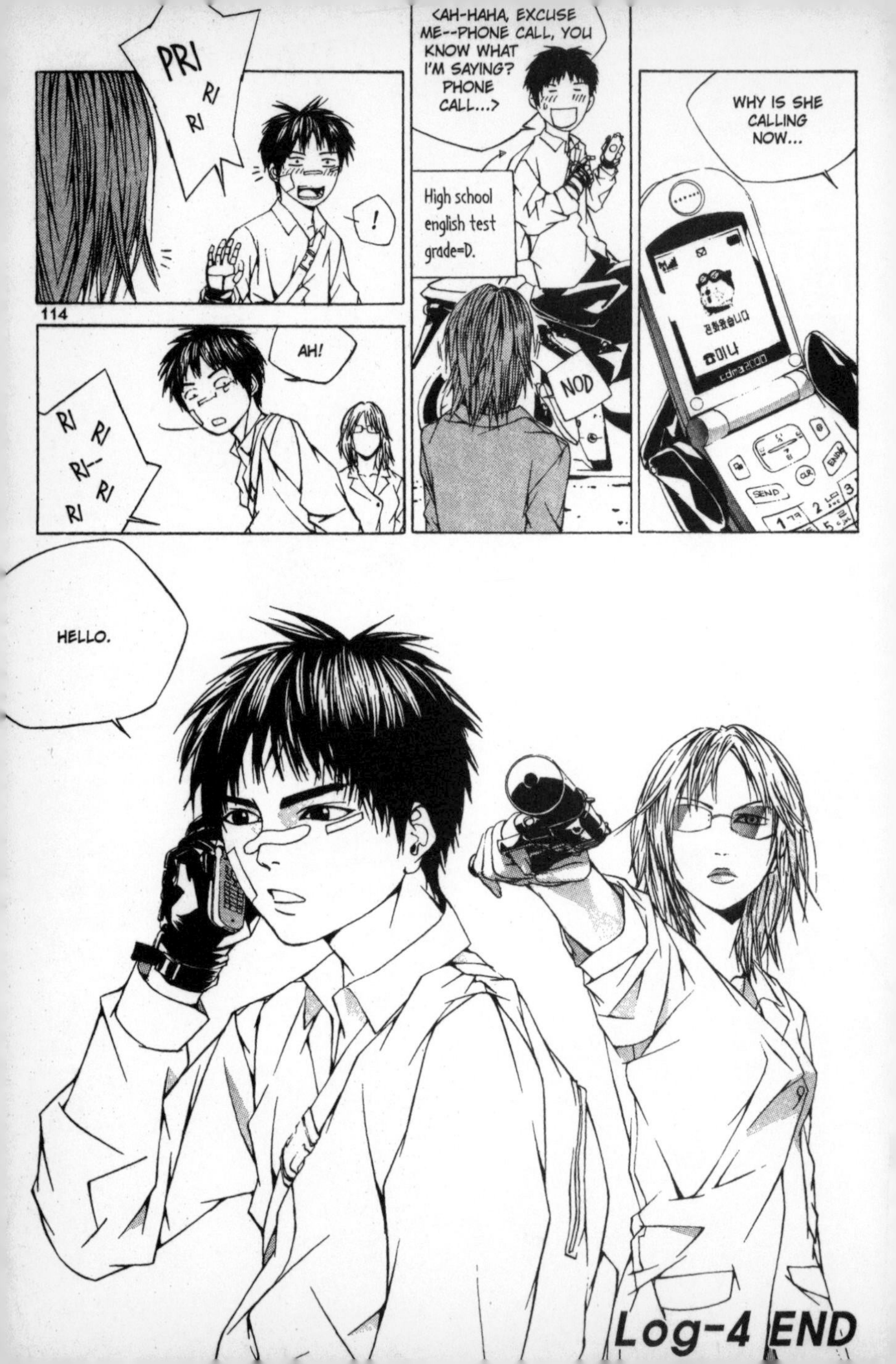
PRI
RI
RI
!
AH!
RI
RI
RI--
RI
RI
<AH-HAHA, EXCUSE ME--PHONE CALL, YOU KNOW WHAT I'M SAYING? PHONE CALL...>
High school english test grade=D.
NOD
WHY IS SHE CALLING NOW...
HELLO.
Log-4 END

LOG_5;Access Denied

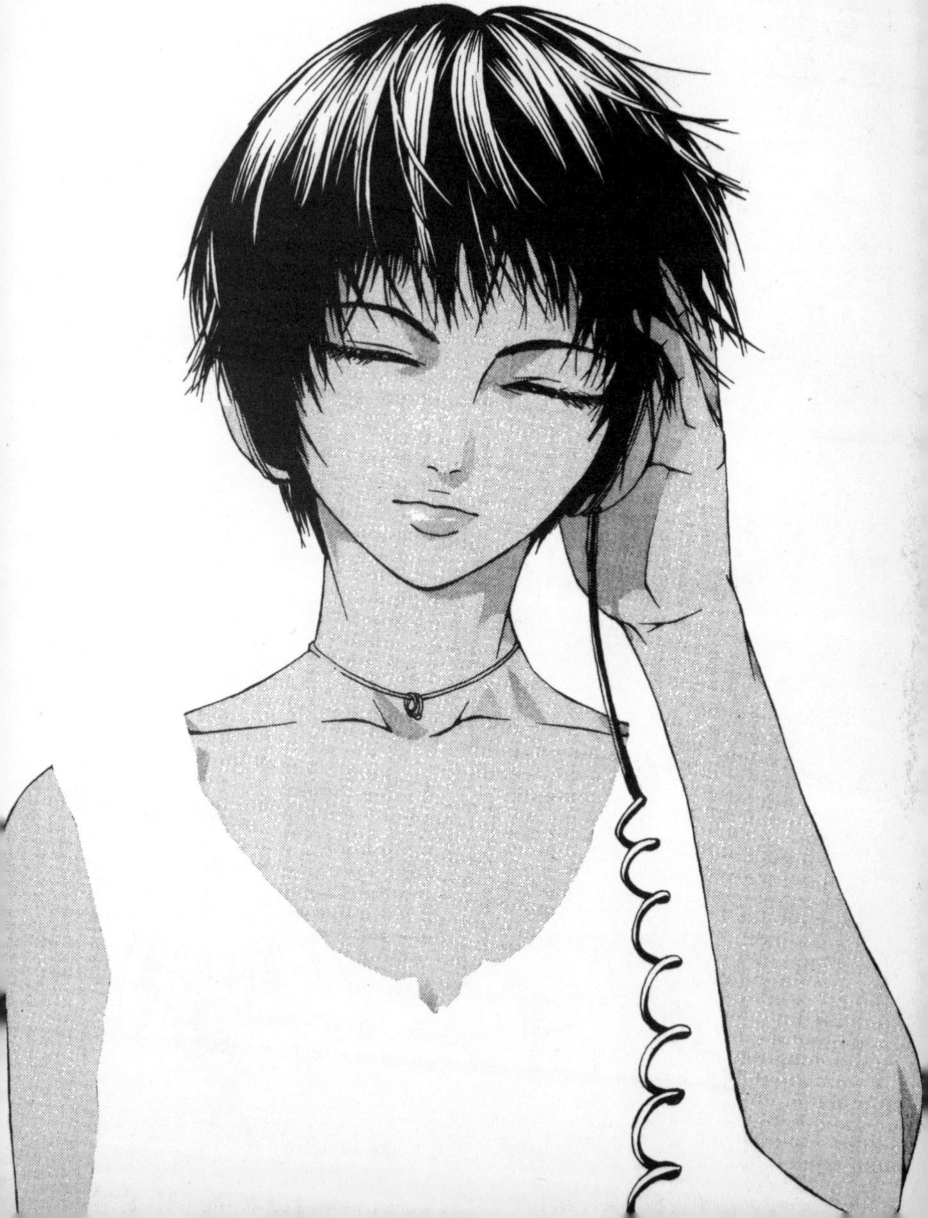

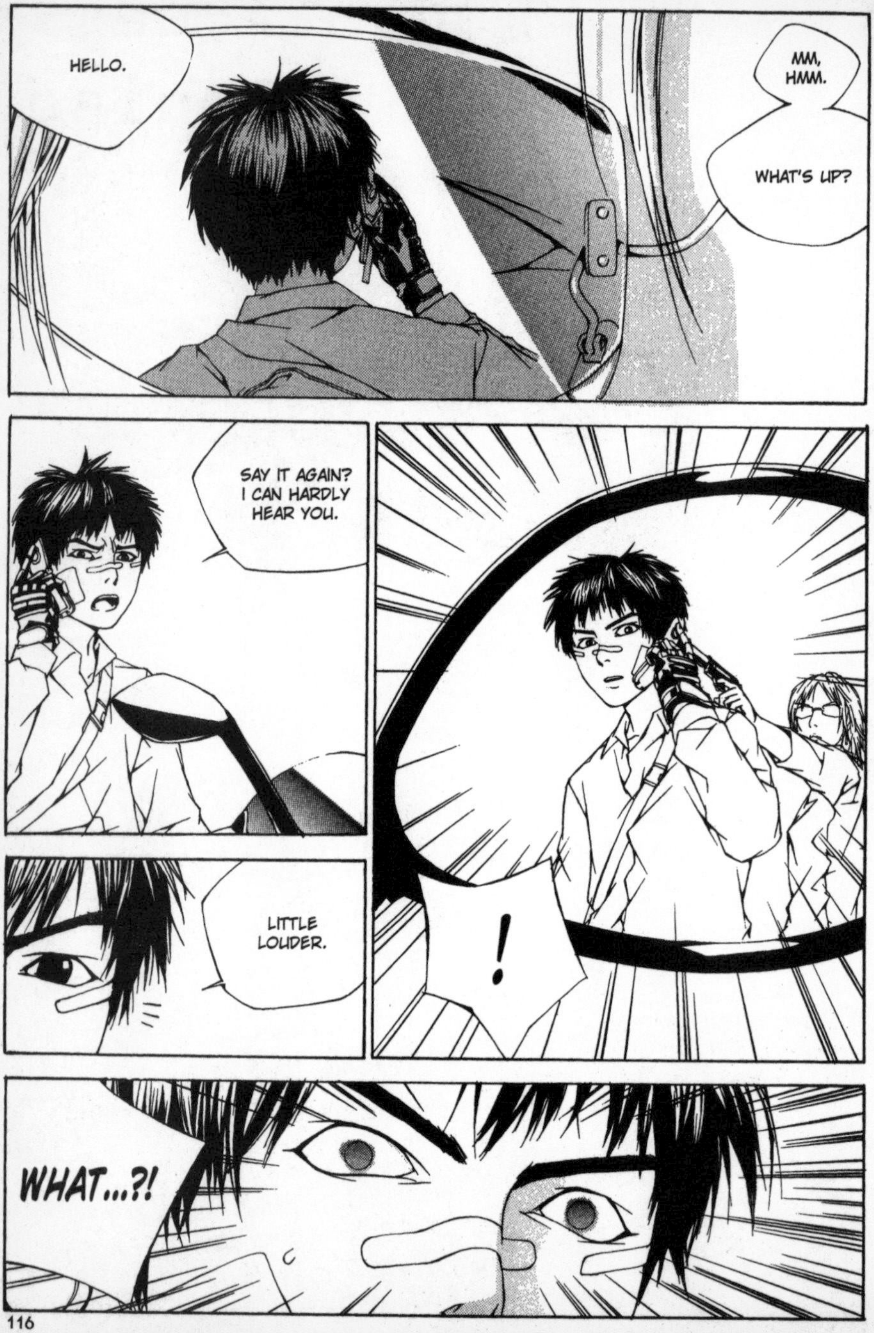
HELLO.
MM, HMM.
WHAT'S UP?
SAY IT AGAIN? I CAN HARDLY HEAR YOU.
LITTLE LOUDER.
!
WHAT...?!

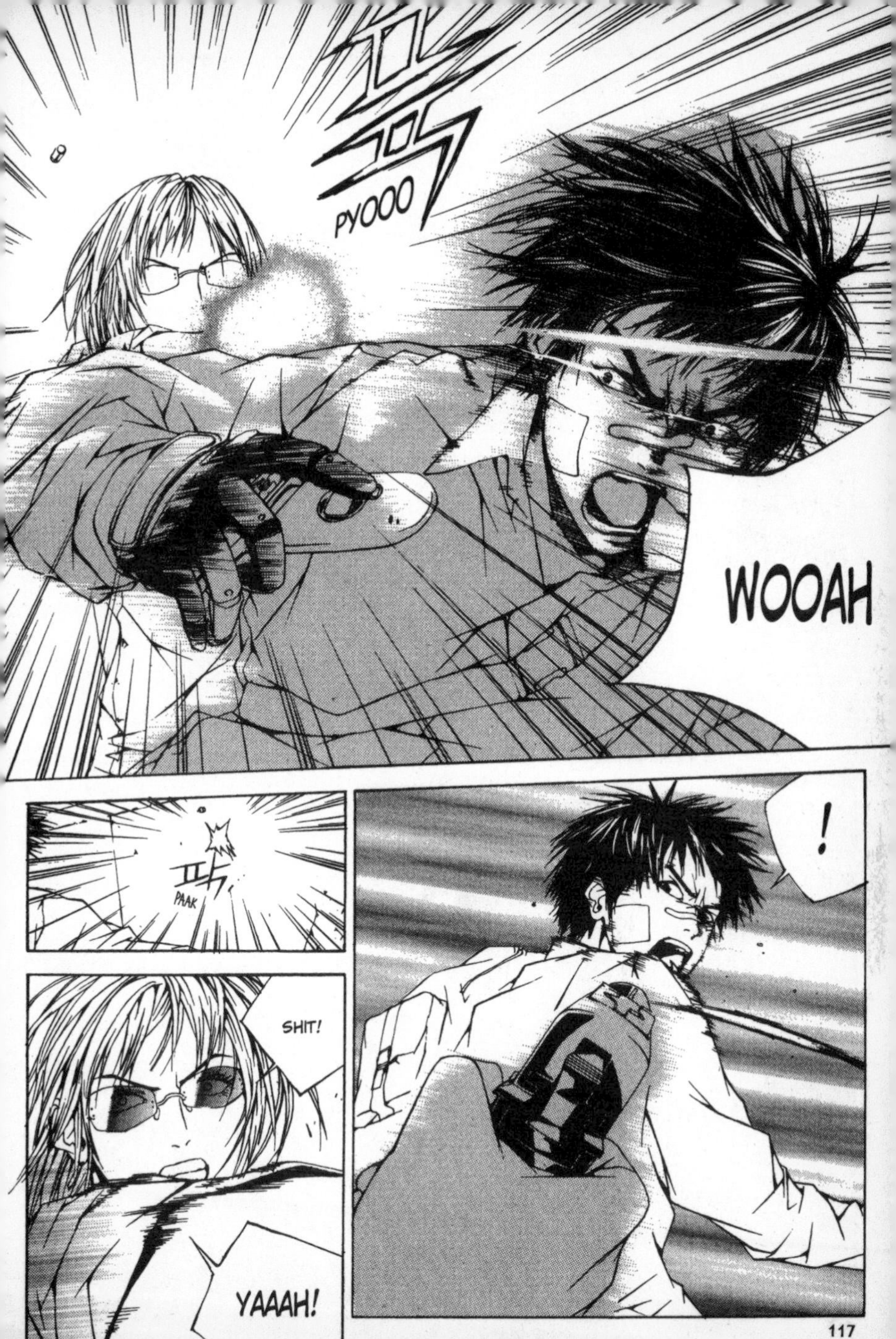
PYOOO
WOOAH
PAAK
SHIT!
YAAAH!
!

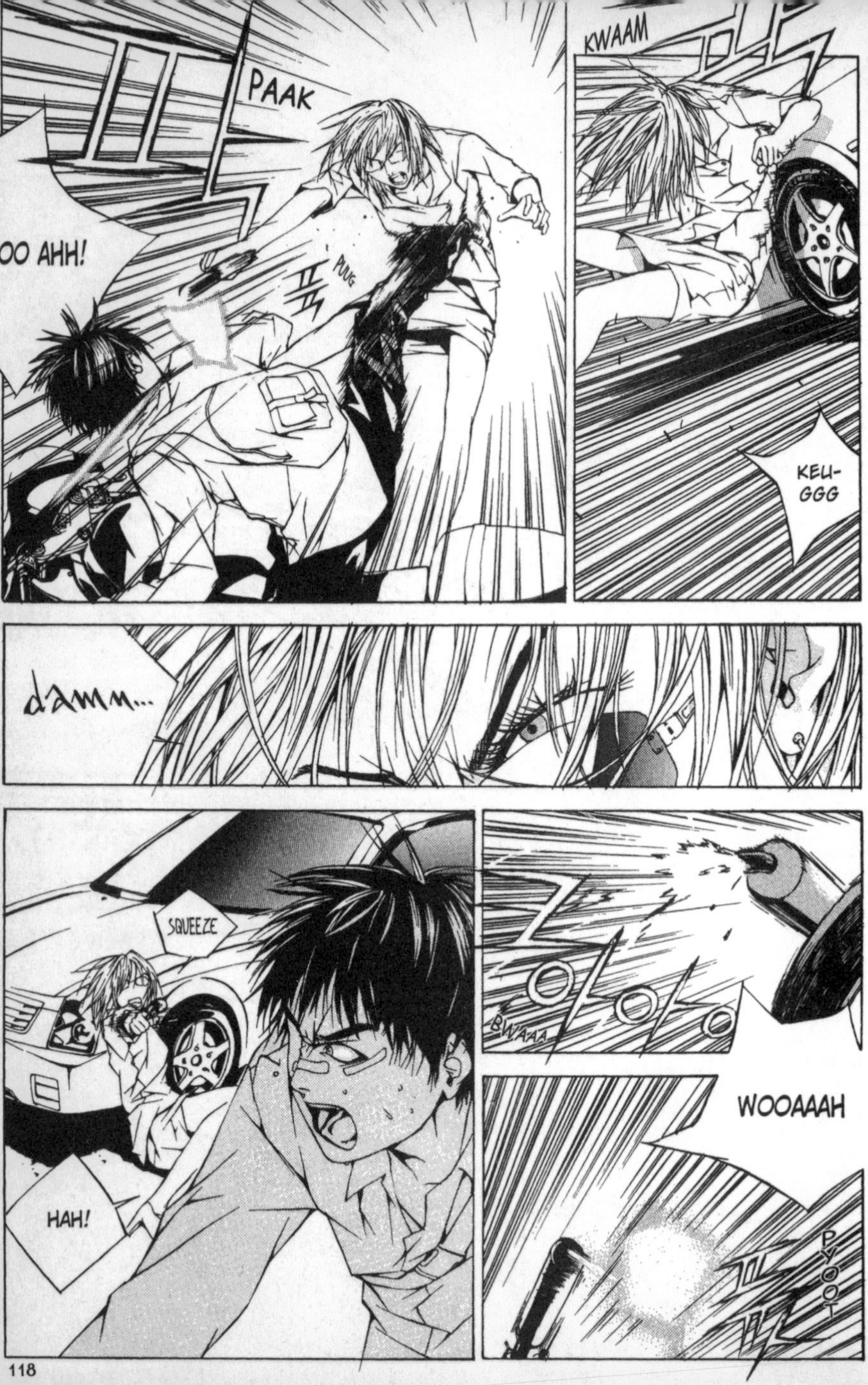
PAAK
WOO AHH!
PUUG
KWAAM
KEU-GGG
damn...
SQUEEZE
HAH!
BWAAA
WOOAAAH
PYOOT

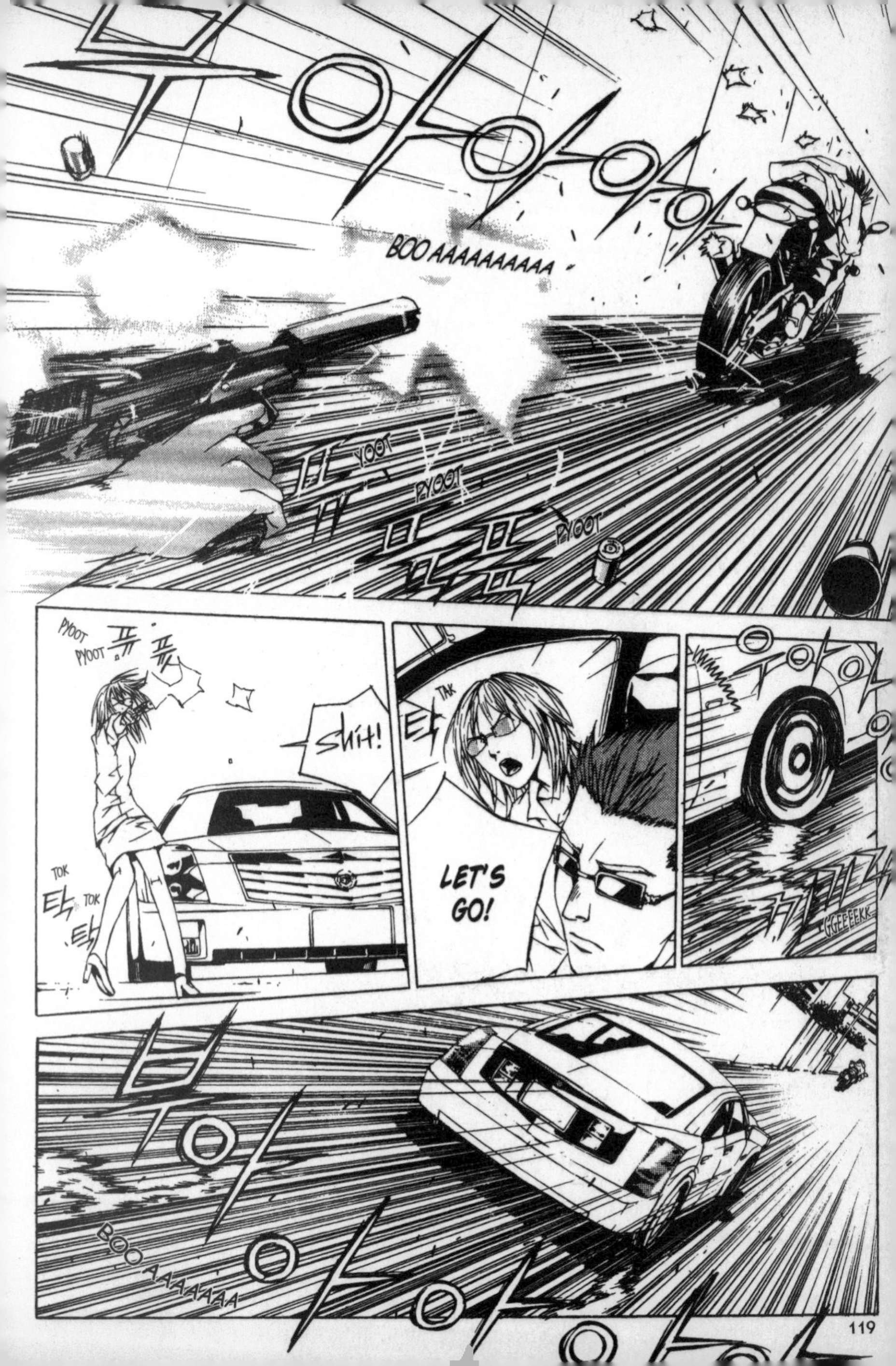

BOO AAAAAAAAAA
YOOT
PYOOT
PYOOT
PYOOT
PYOOT
퓨 퓻
SHIT!
TOK
탁
TOK
탁
TAK
탁
LET'S GO!
GGEEEEKK
BOO AAAAAAA

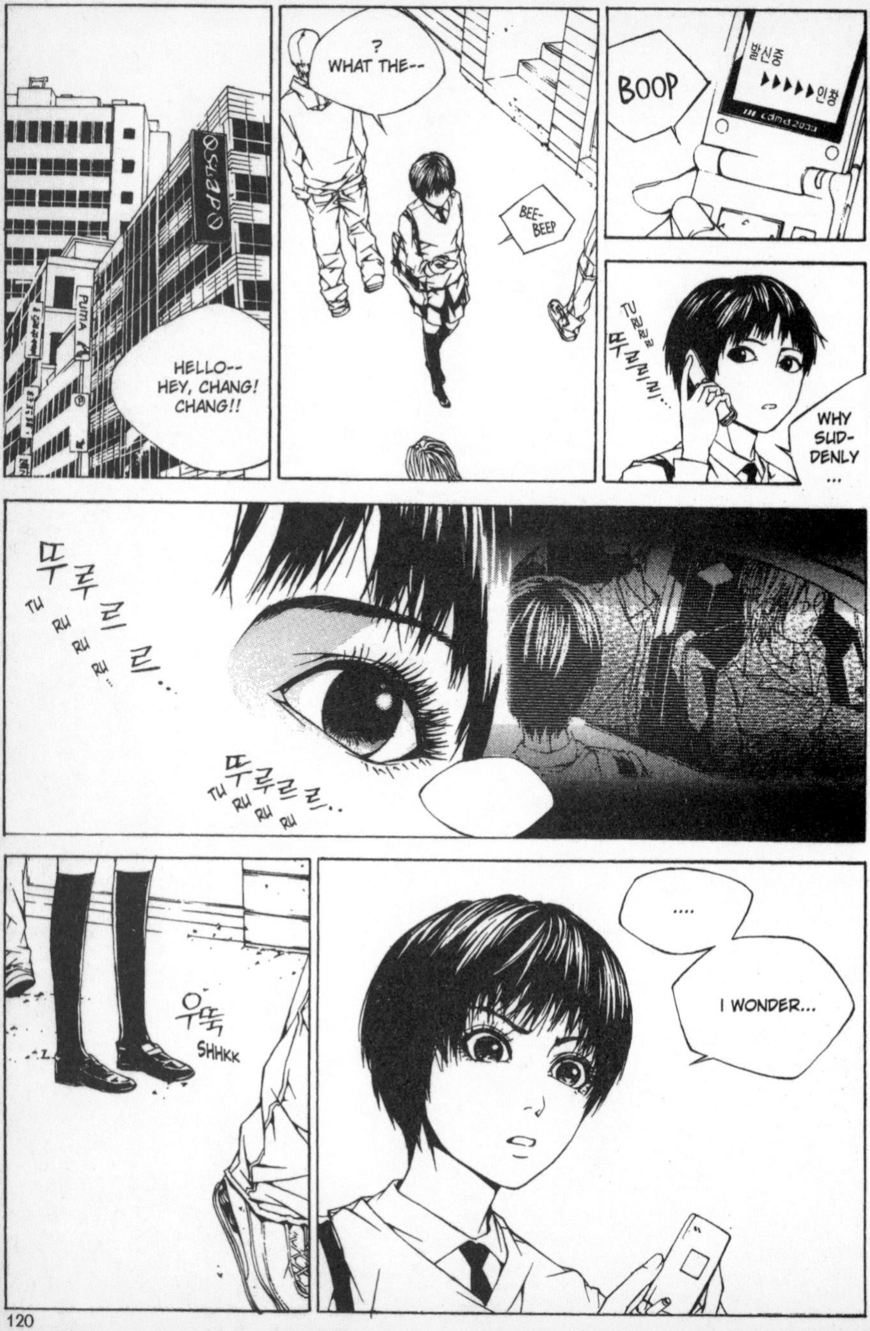
HELLO-- HEY, CHANG! CHANG!!
? WHAT THE--
BEE-BEEP
BOOP
발신중
▶▶▶▶▶인창
TU RU RU RU
뚜르르르...
WHY SUD-DENLY ...
뚜루르르...
TU RU RU RU...
뚜루르르..
TU RU RU RU
우뚝
SHHKK
....
I WONDER...

IT'S HIM AGAIN...

I CAN'T REALLY SEE, BUT HE'S THERE...

WHAT AM I GONNA DO...?

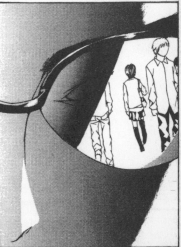

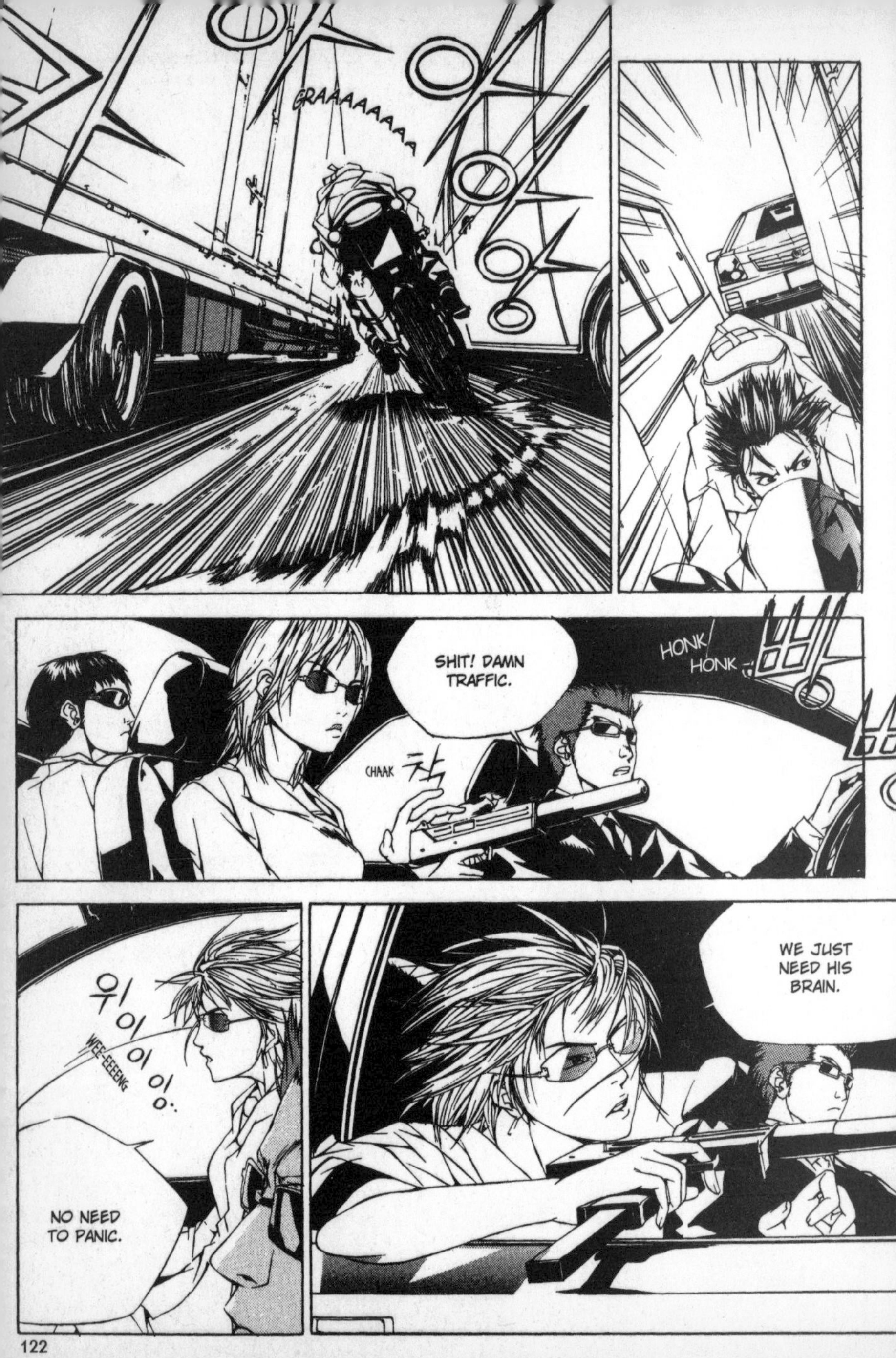
GRAAAAAAAAA
SHIT! DAMN TRAFFIC.
CHAAK
착
HONK/ HONK
우이이잉..
WEE-EEEENG
NO NEED TO PANIC.
WE JUST NEED HIS BRAIN.

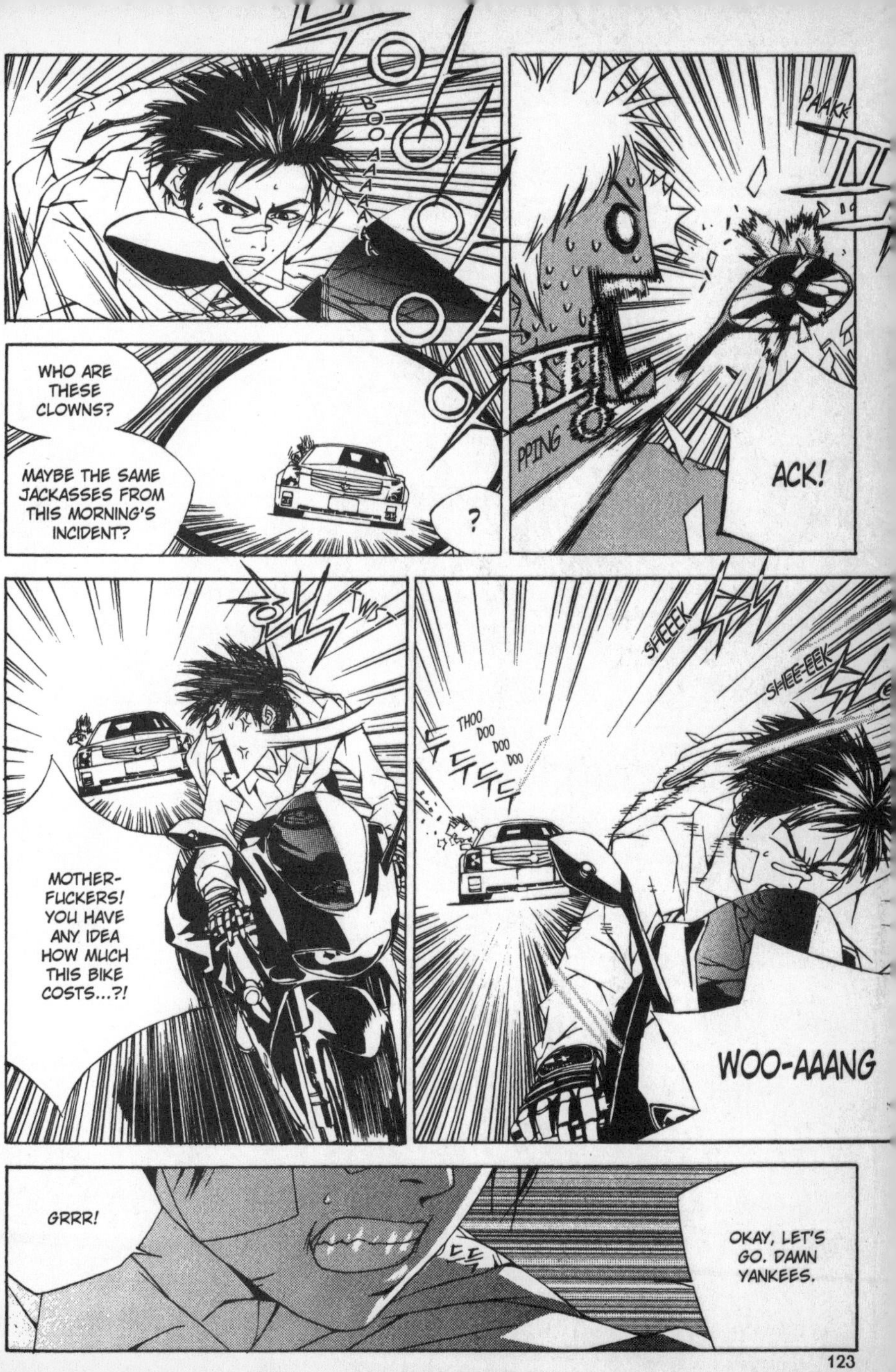
BOOAAAAAA
WHO ARE THESE CLOWNS?
MAYBE THE SAME JACKASSES FROM THIS MORNING'S INCIDENT?
?
PAAKK!
PPING
ACK!
TWIST
MOTHER-FUCKERS! YOU HAVE ANY IDEA HOW MUCH THIS BIKE COSTS...?!
SHEEEK
SHEE-EEK
THOO DOO DOO DOO
WOO-AAANG
GRRR!
OKAY, LET'S GO. DAMN YANKEES.

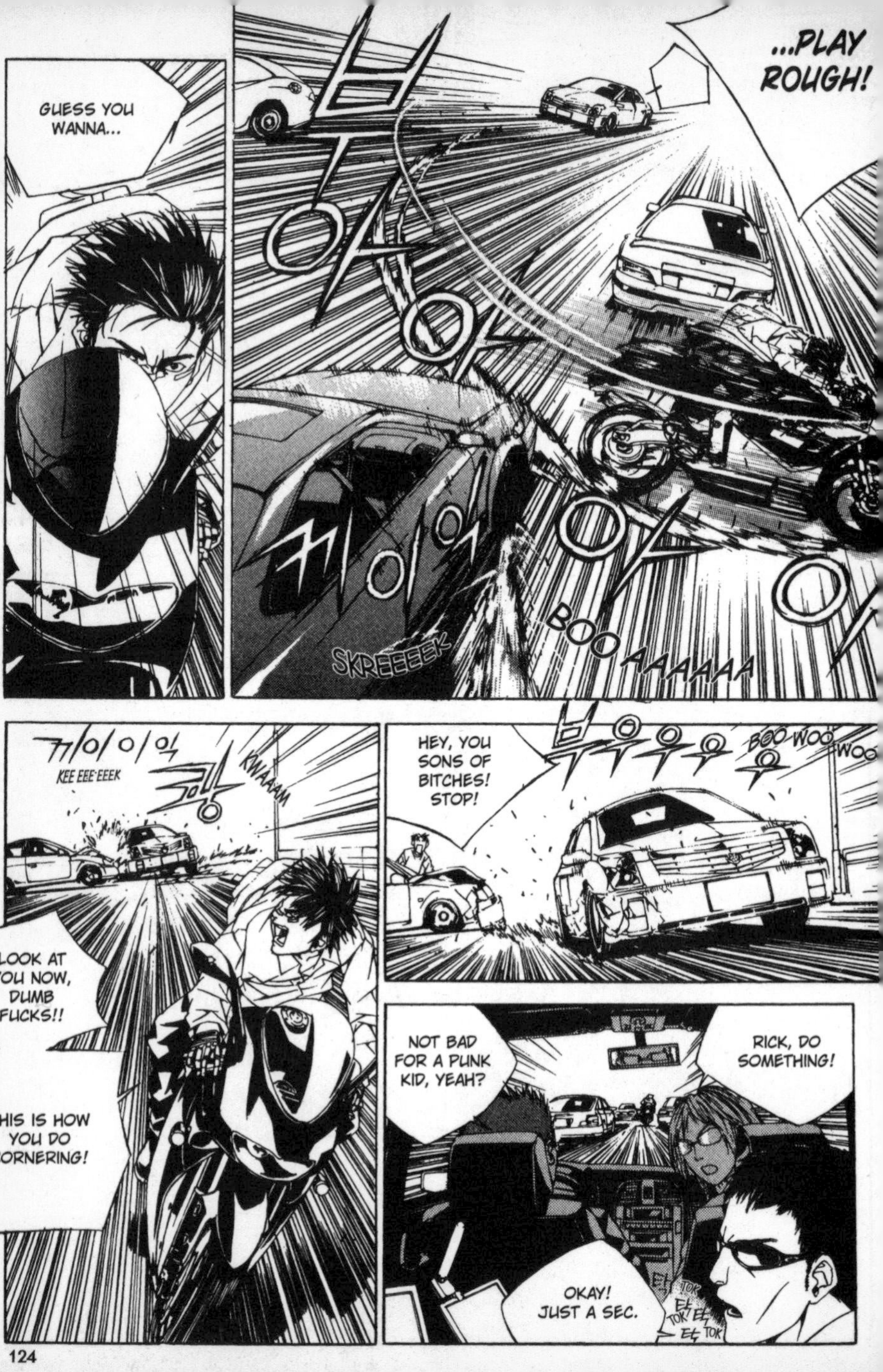

GUESS YOU WANNA...
...PLAY ROUGH!
SKREEEEEK
BOOAAAAAA
끼이이익
KEE EEE EEEK
쾅
KWAAAM
LOOK AT YOU NOW, DUMB FUCKS!!
THIS IS HOW YOU DO CORNERING!
HEY, YOU SONS OF BITCHES! STOP!
부우우우우
BOO WOO WOO
NOT BAD FOR A PUNK KID, YEAH?
RICK, DO SOMETHING!
OKAY! JUST A SEC.
탁 TOK
탁 TOK
탁 TOK
탁 TOK

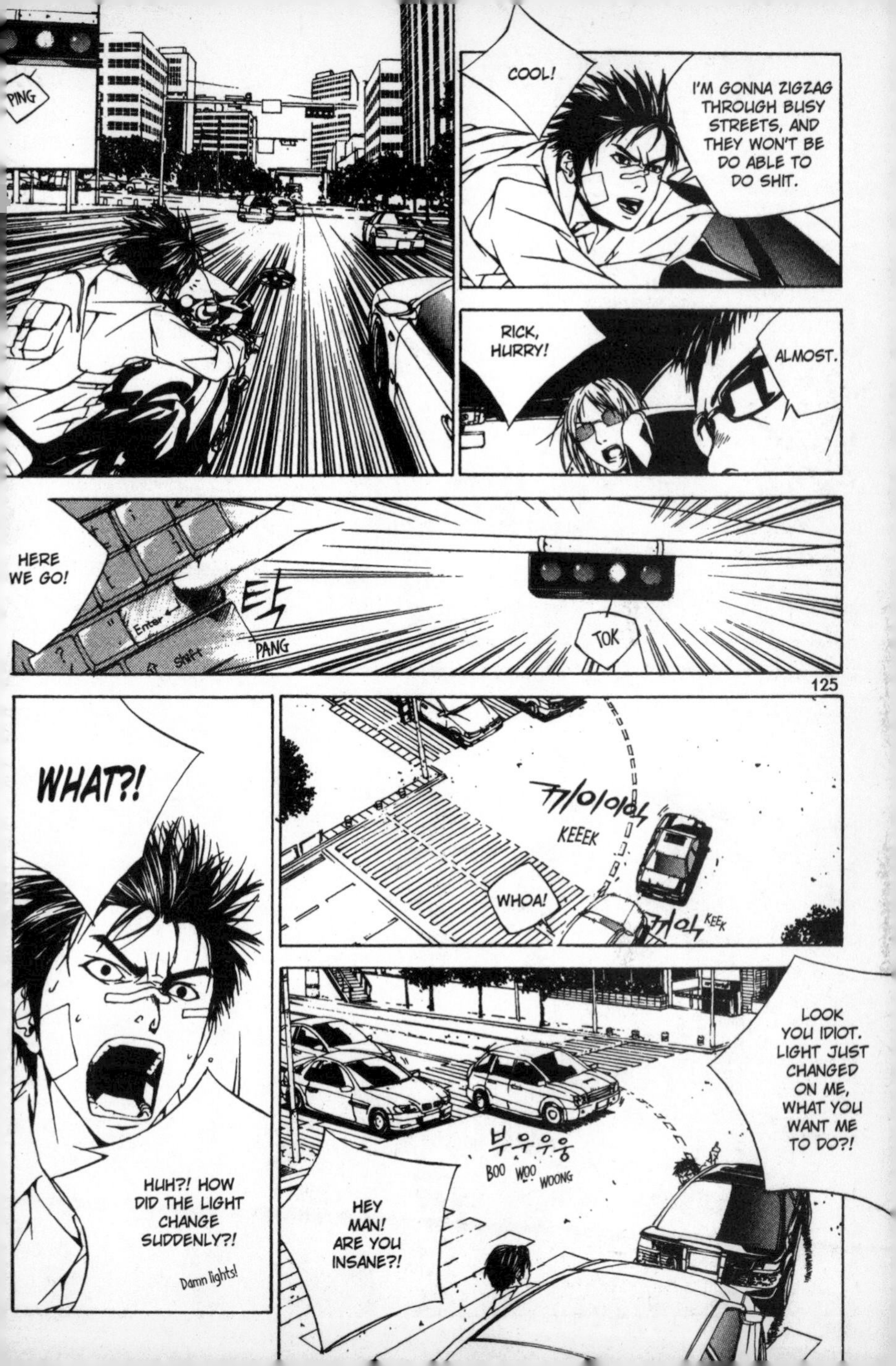
PING
COOL!
I'M GONNA ZIGZAG THROUGH BUSY STREETS, AND THEY WON'T BE DO ABLE TO DO SHIT.
RICK, HURRY!
ALMOST.
HERE WE GO!
Enter
Shift
탁
PANG
TOK
WHAT?!
HUH?! HOW DID THE LIGHT CHANGE SUDDENLY?!
Damn lights!
끼이이익
KEEEK
WHOA!
끼익
KEEK
HEY MAN! ARE YOU INSANE?!
부우우웅
BOO WOO WOONG
LOOK YOU IDIOT. LIGHT JUST CHANGED ON ME, WHAT YOU WANT ME TO DO?!

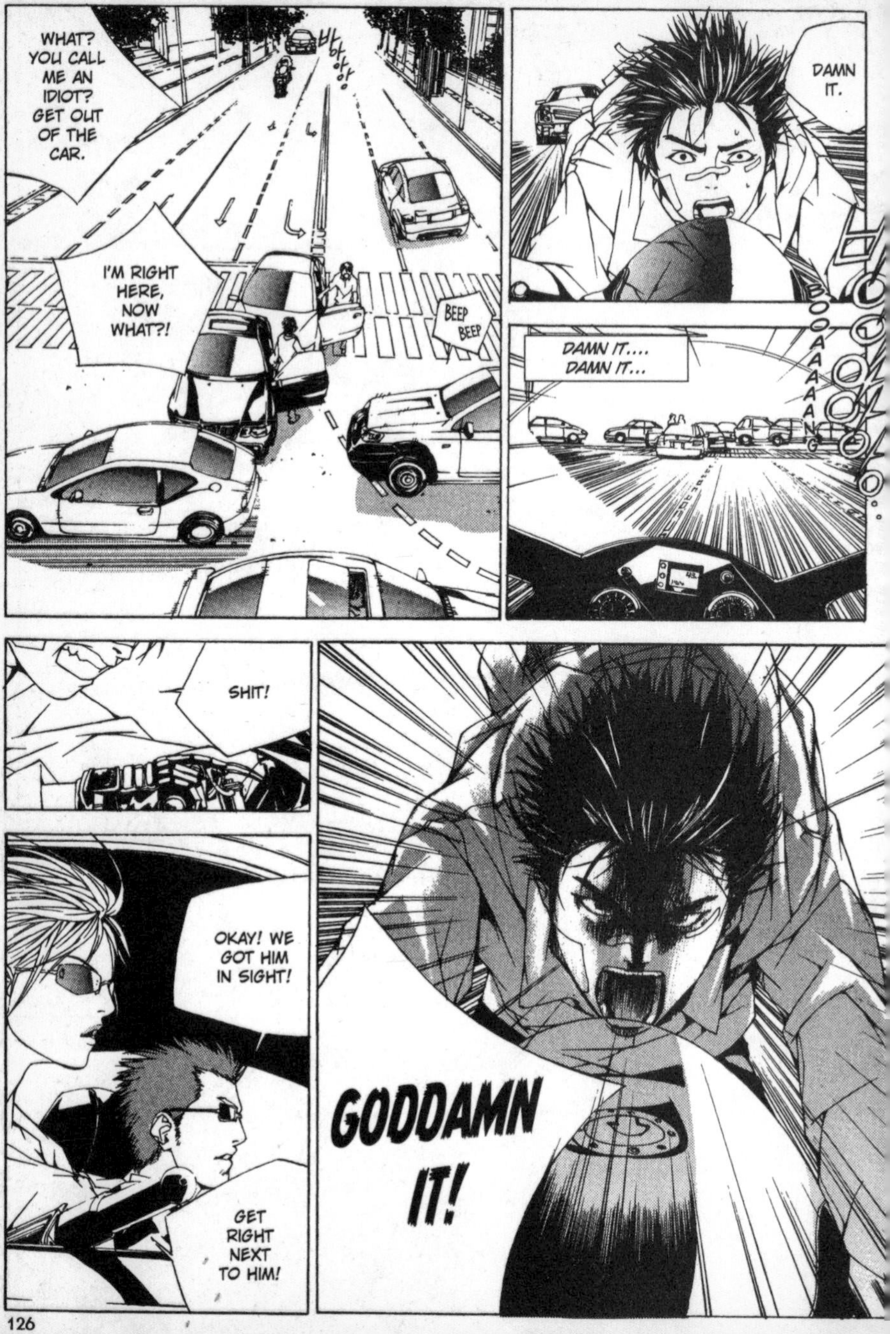
WHAT? YOU CALL ME AN IDIOT? GET OUT OF THE CAR.
I'M RIGHT HERE, NOW WHAT?!
BEEP BEEP
DAMN IT.
DAMN IT.... DAMN IT...
BOOAAAAAANG
SHIT!
OKAY! WE GOT HIM IN SIGHT!
GET RIGHT NEXT TO HIM!
GODDAMN IT!

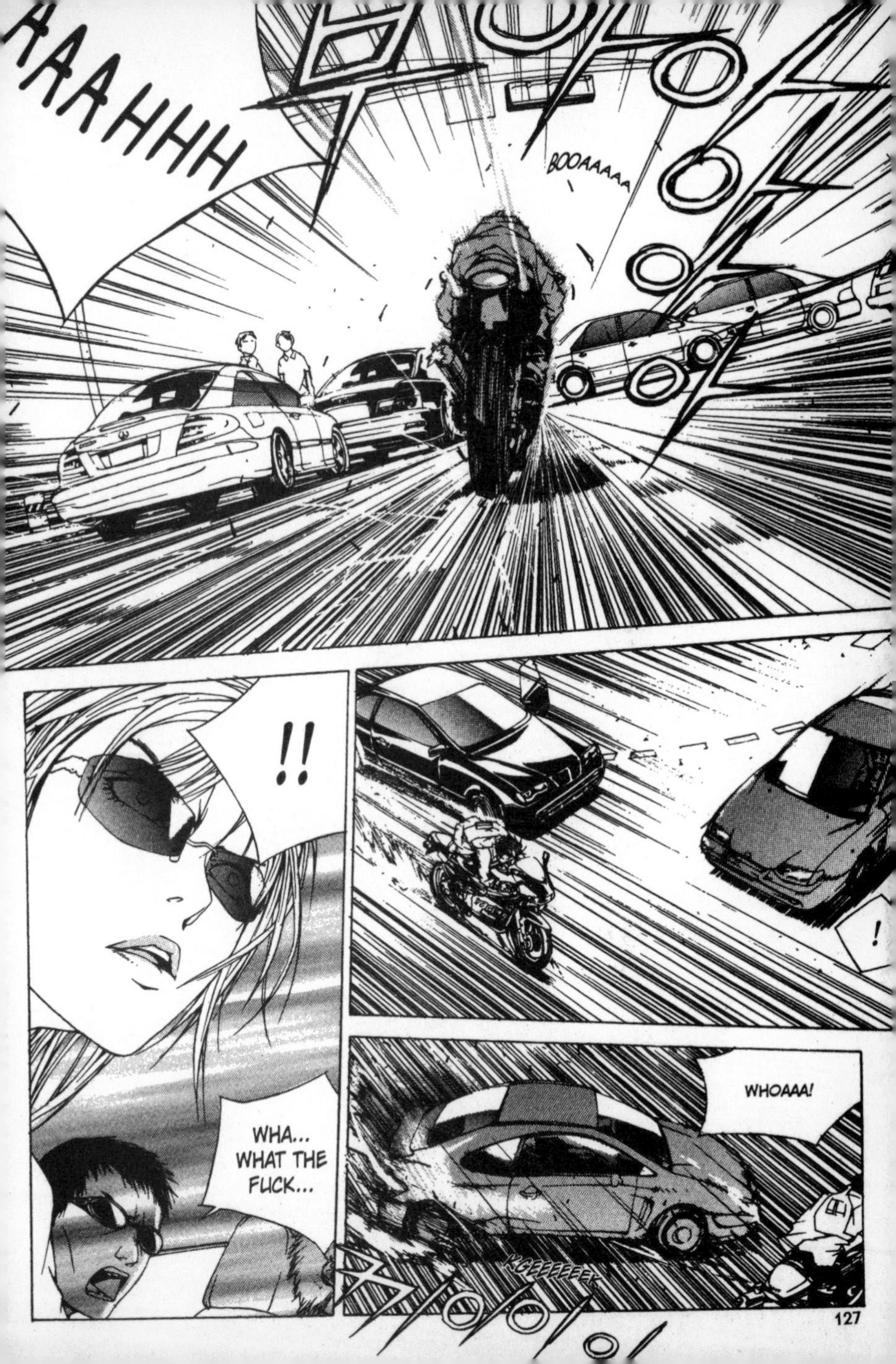
RAAHHHH
BOOAAAAA
!!
WHA... WHAT THE FUCK...
!
WHOAAA!
KGEEEEEEEK

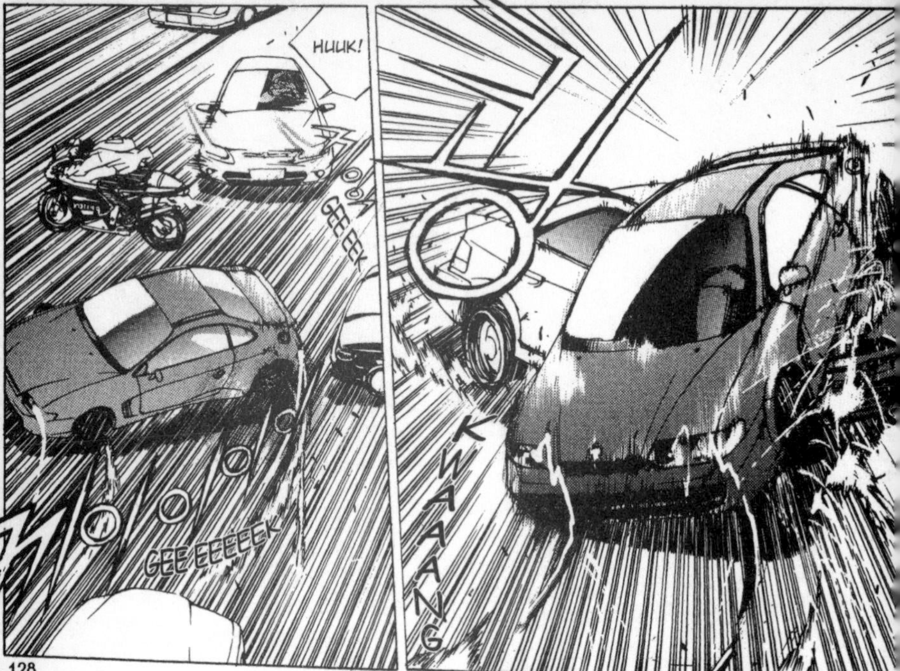
HUUK!
GEEEEK
GEE EEEEEK
KWAAAANG

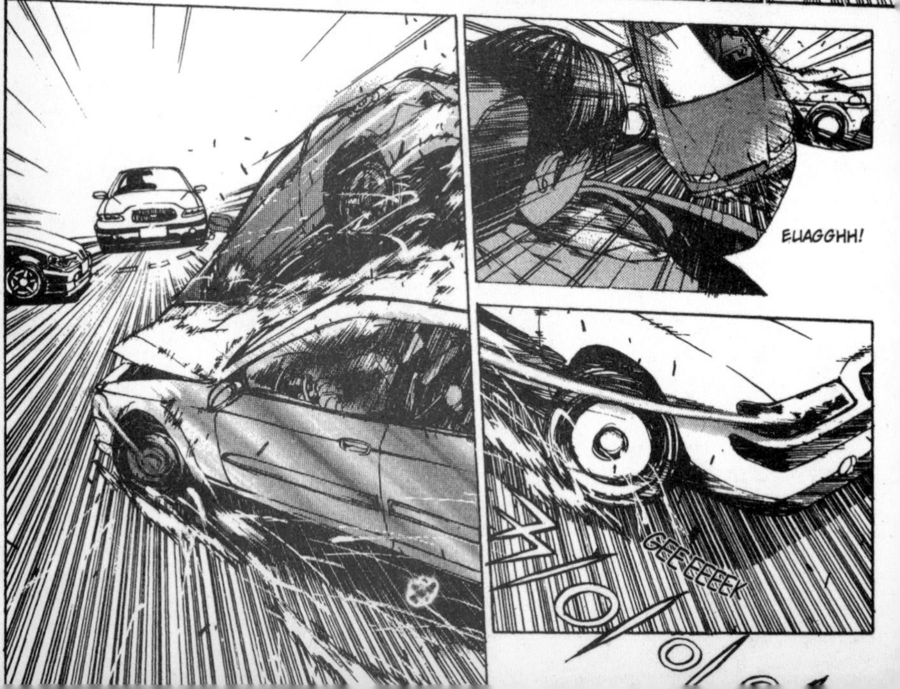
EUAGGHH!
GEE EEEEK

WAAAAM

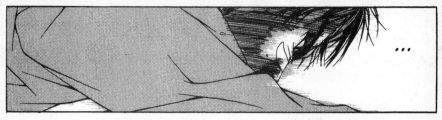

...

GOT AWA--

WOO-OOONG

?!

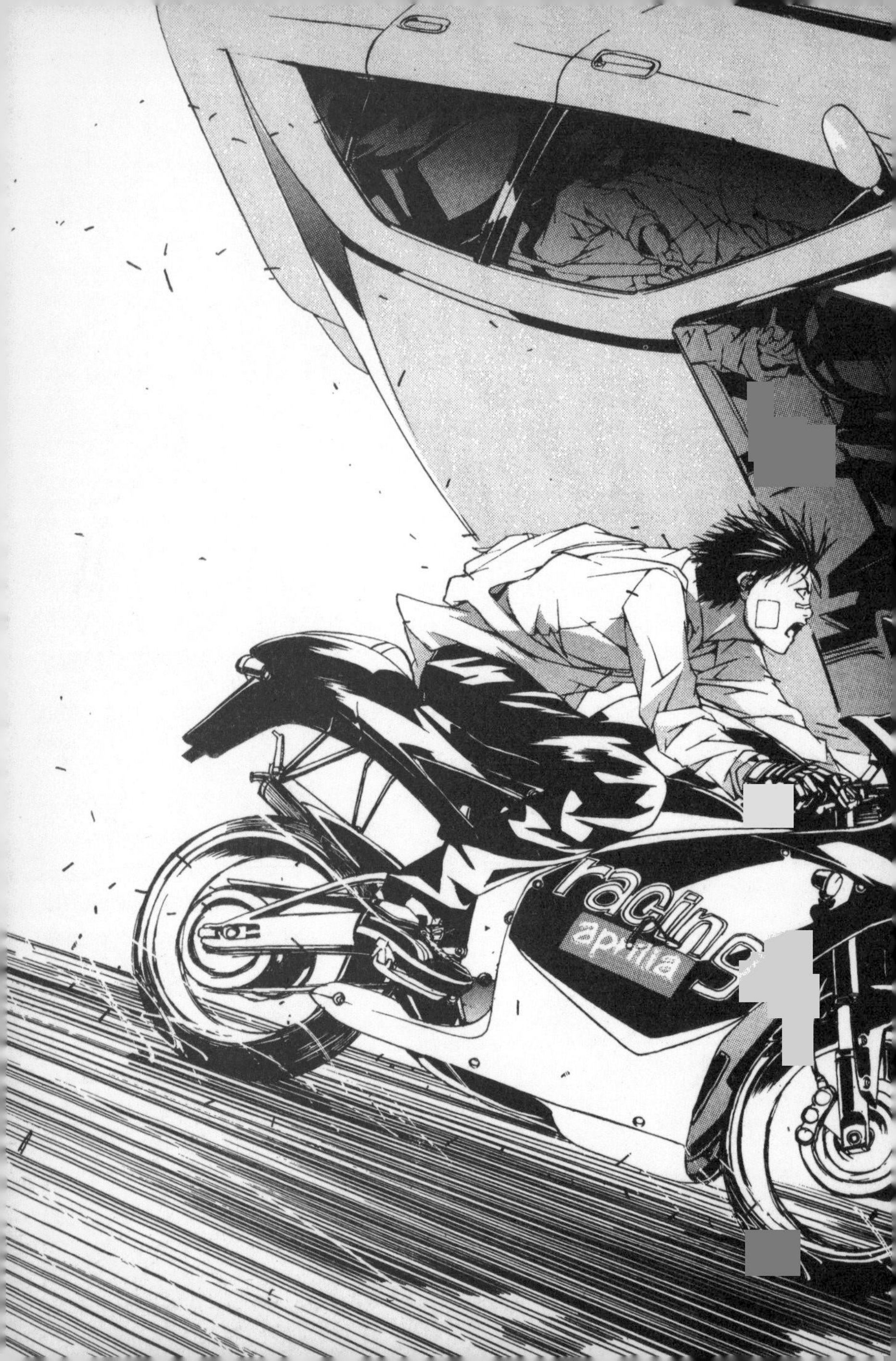
racing
aprilia

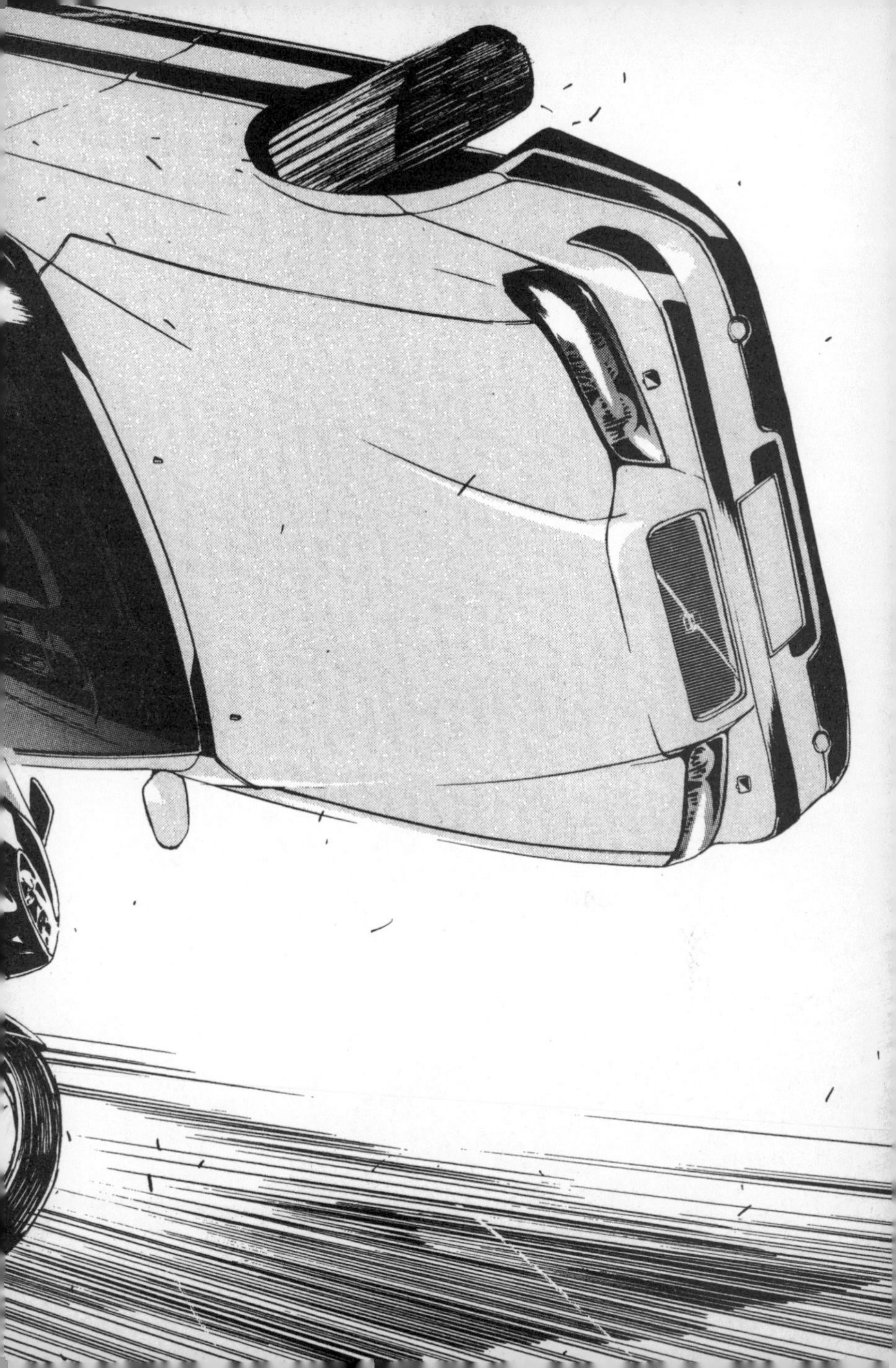

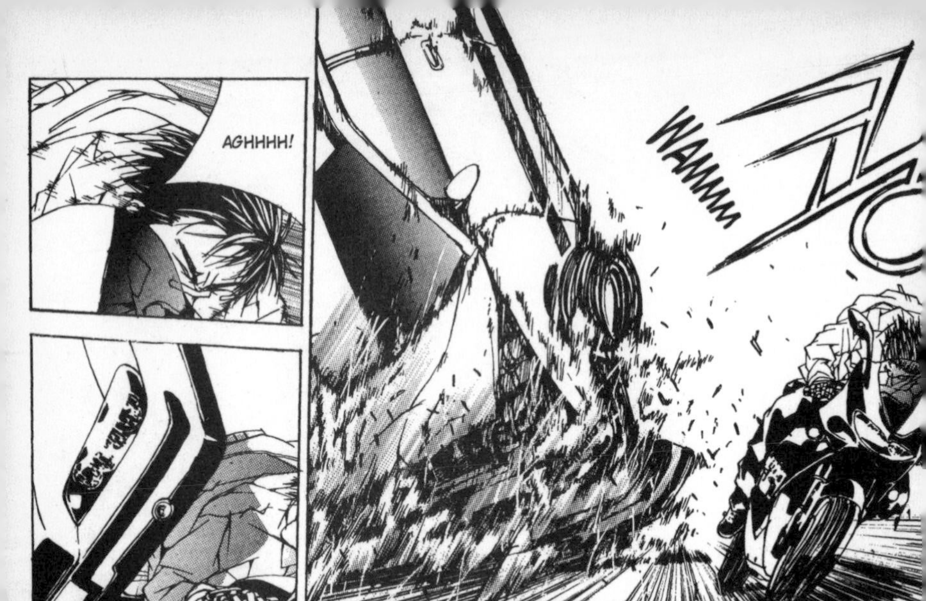
AGHHHH!
WAAAAAA
KAAAANG
KRAAAANG

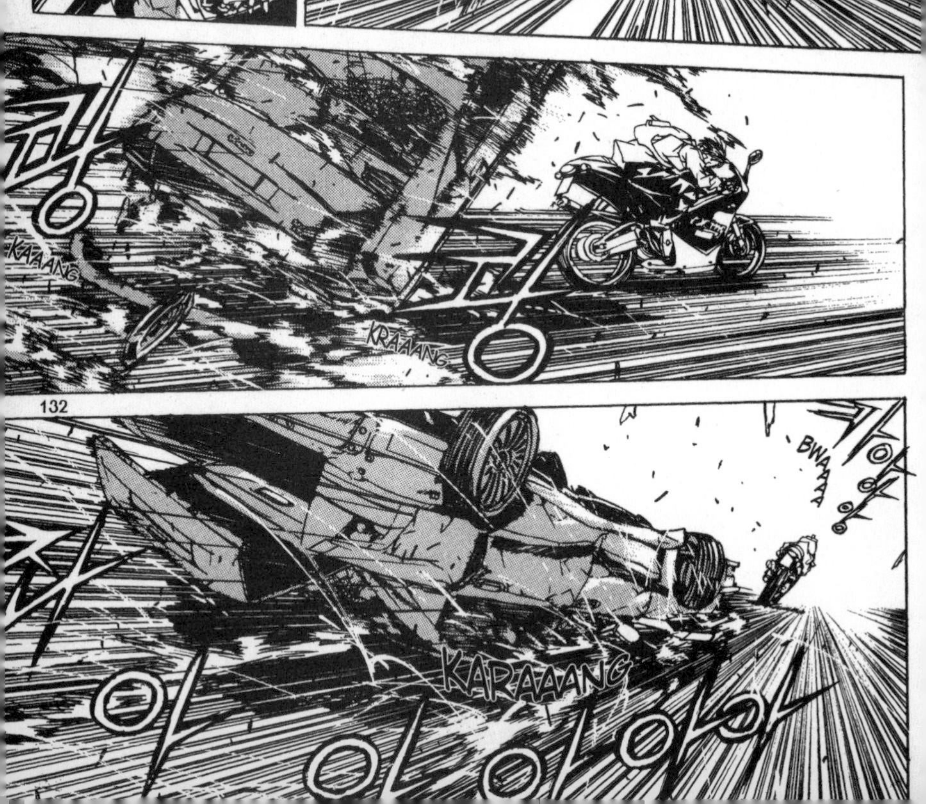
BWAAAAA
KARAAAANG

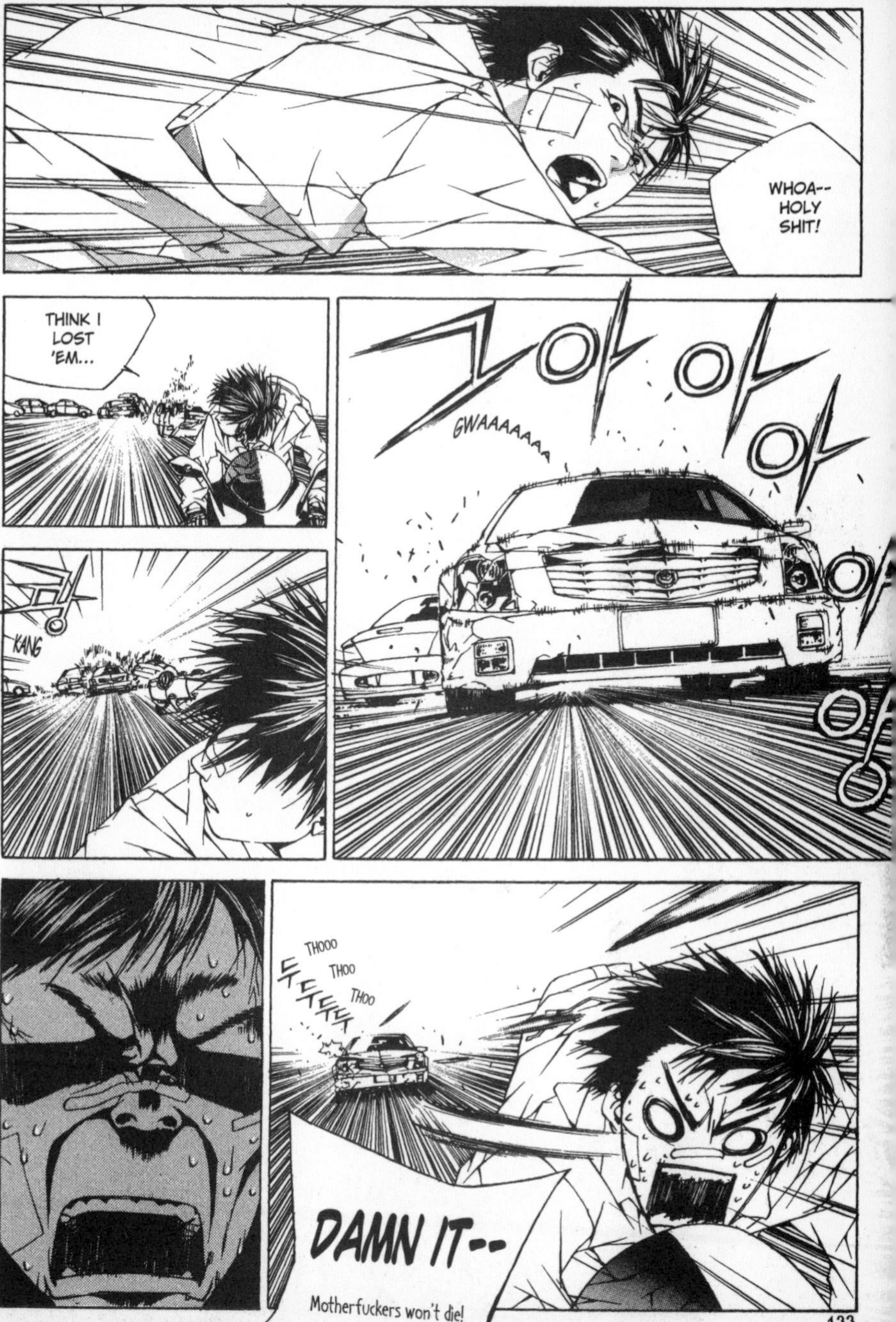
WHOA-- HOLY SHIT!
THINK I LOST 'EM...
KANG
GWAAAAAAA
THOOO
THOO
THOO
DAMN IT--
Motherfuckers won't die!

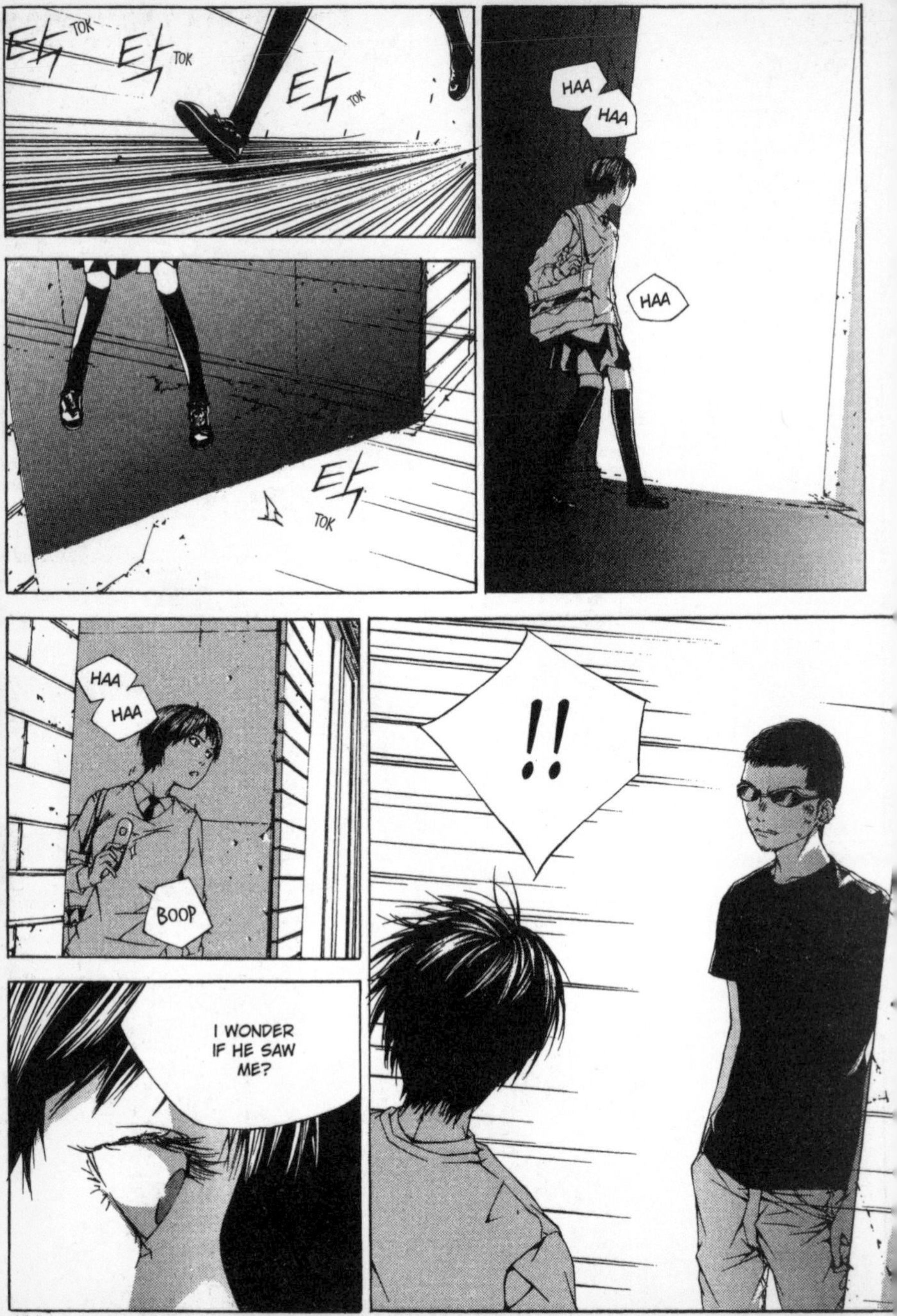

탁 TOK
탁 TOK
탁 TOK
탁 TOK
HAA
HAA
HAA
HAA
HAA
BOOP
I WONDER IF HE SAW ME?
!!

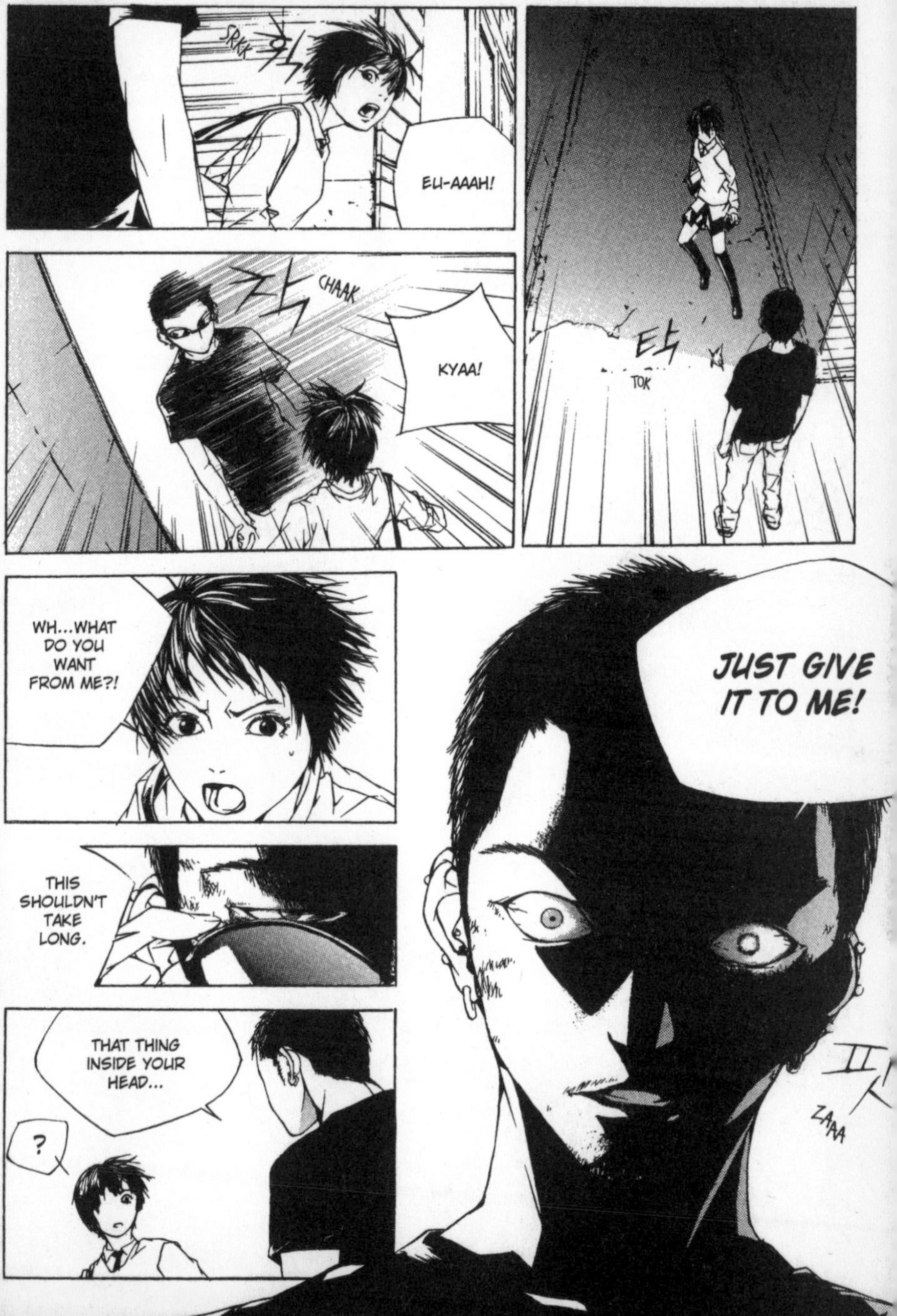
SRKK
EU-AAAH!
CHAAK
KYAA!
TOK
WH...WHAT DO YOU WANT FROM ME?!
THIS SHOULDN'T TAKE LONG.
THAT THING INSIDE YOUR HEAD...
?
JUST GIVE IT TO ME!
ZAAA

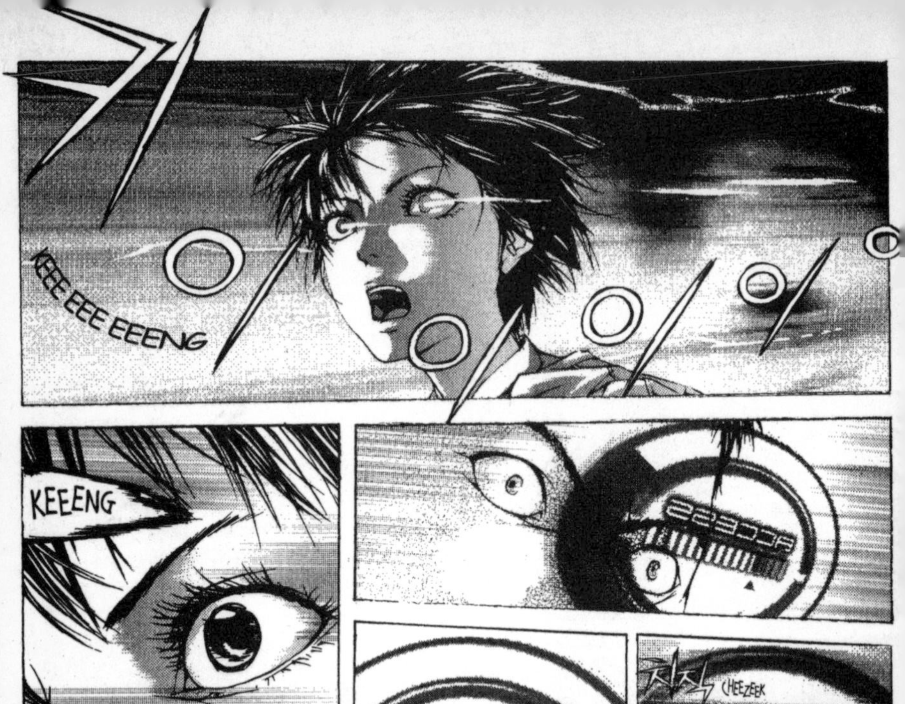
KEEE EEE EEEENG
KEEENG
KEEENG
TH...AT... SOUND AGAIN!
ACCESS
CHEEZEEK
ACCESS
CHEEZEEK
access denied_

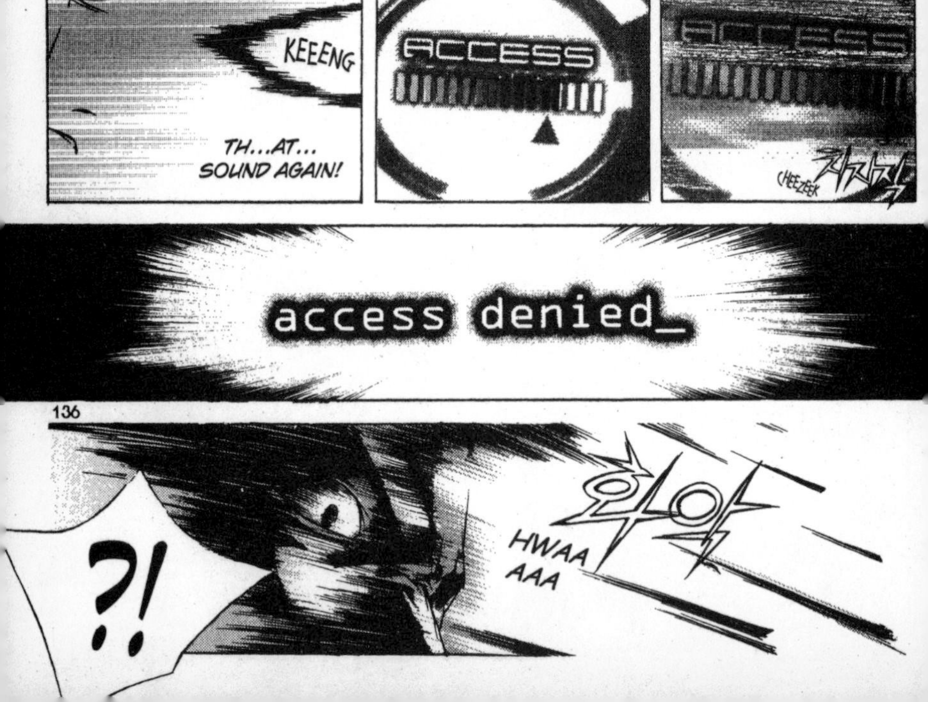
?!
HWAA AAA

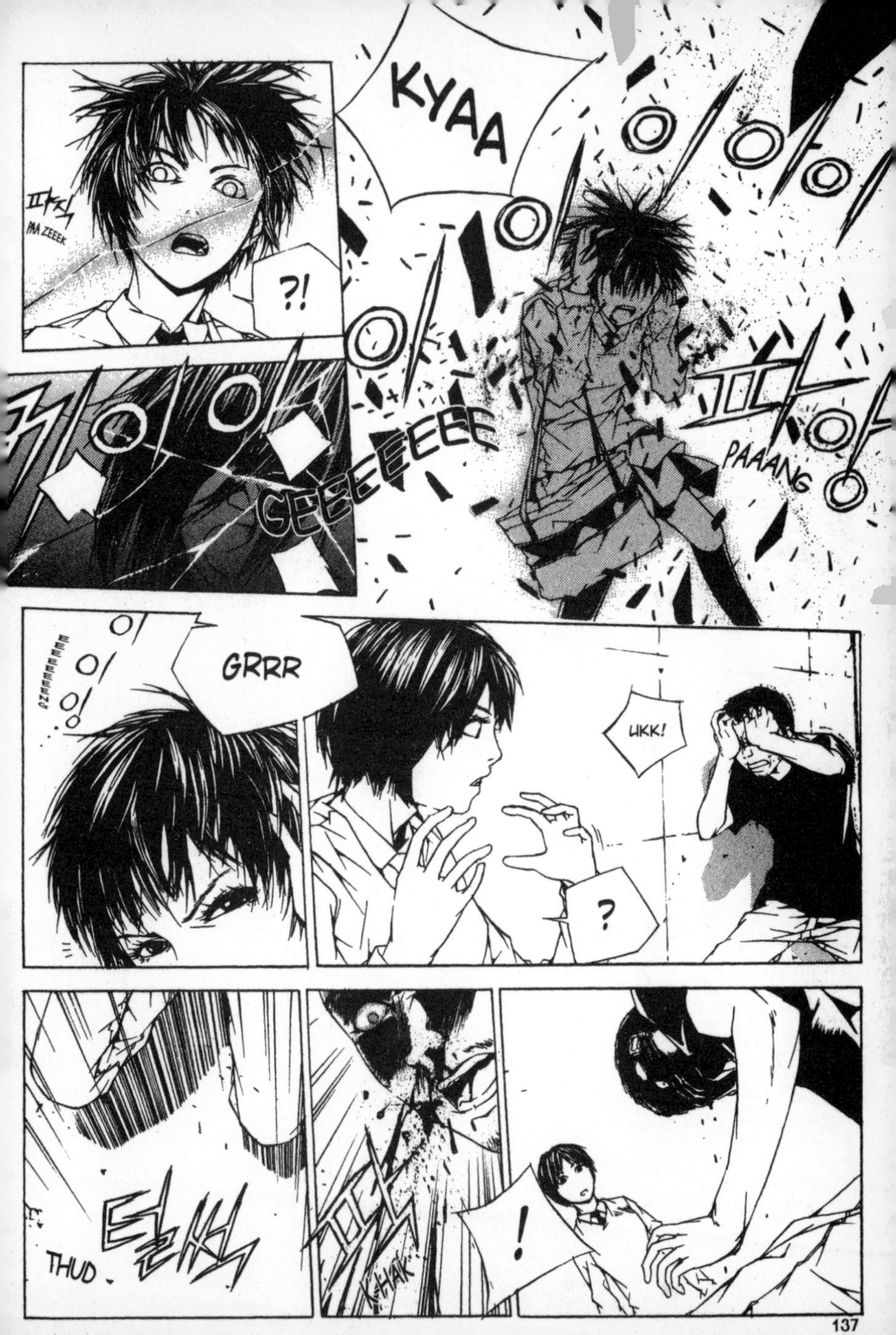
PAA ZEEEK
?!
KYAA
PAAANG
GEEEEEEEE
EEEEEEEEENG
GRRR
UKK!
?
THUD
K-HAK
!

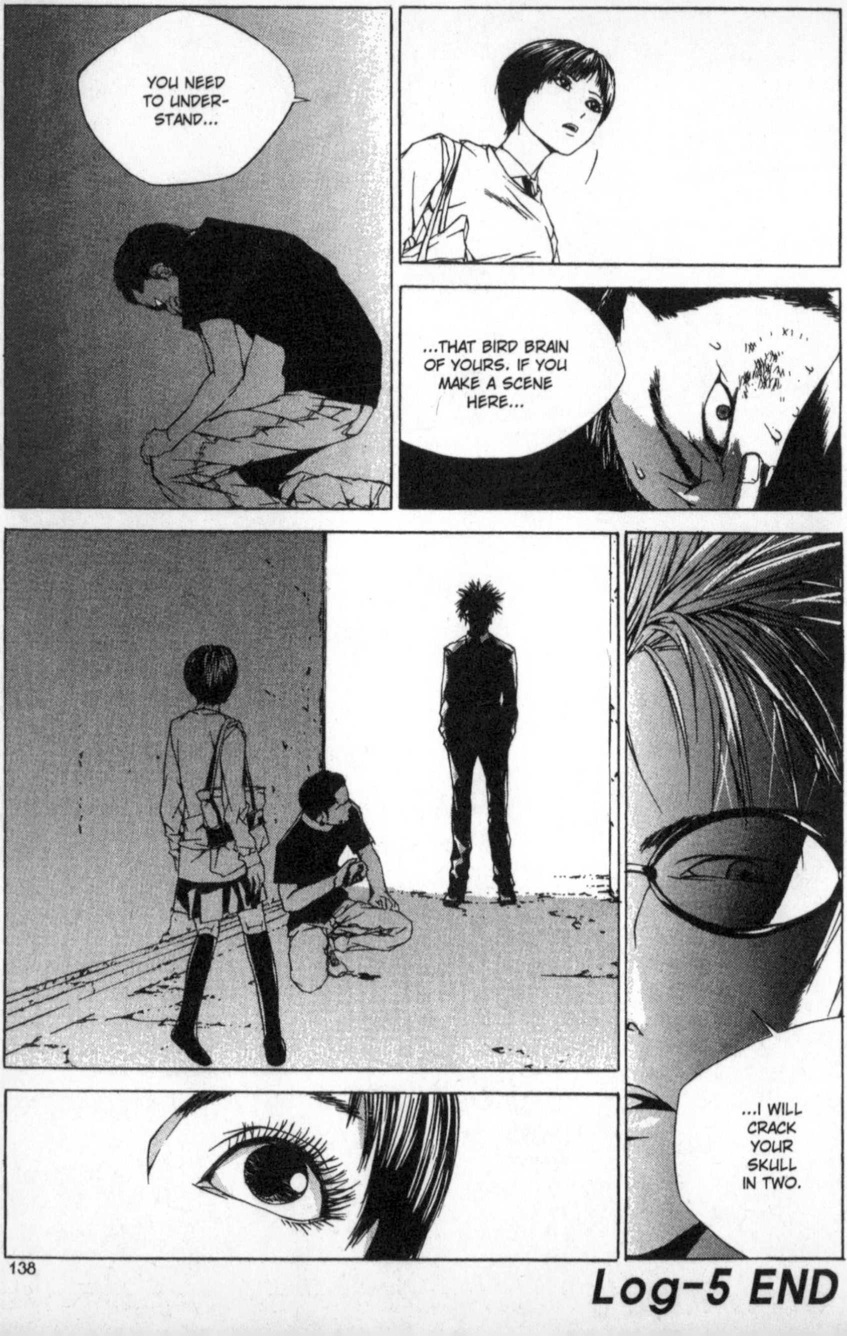
YOU NEED TO UNDER-STAND...
...THAT BIRD BRAIN OF YOURS. IF YOU MAKE A SCENE HERE...
...I WILL CRACK YOUR SKULL IN TWO.

Log-5 END

LOG_6;Delete

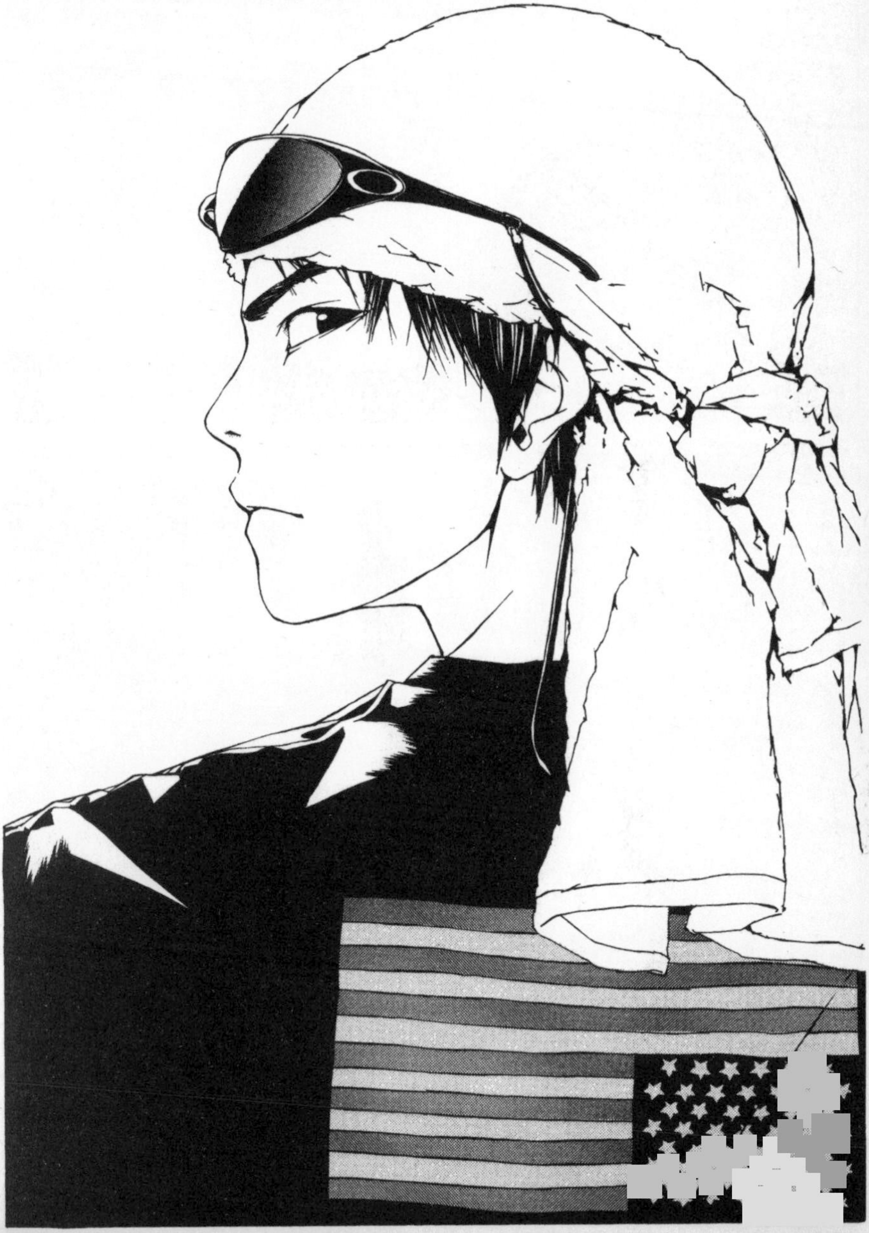

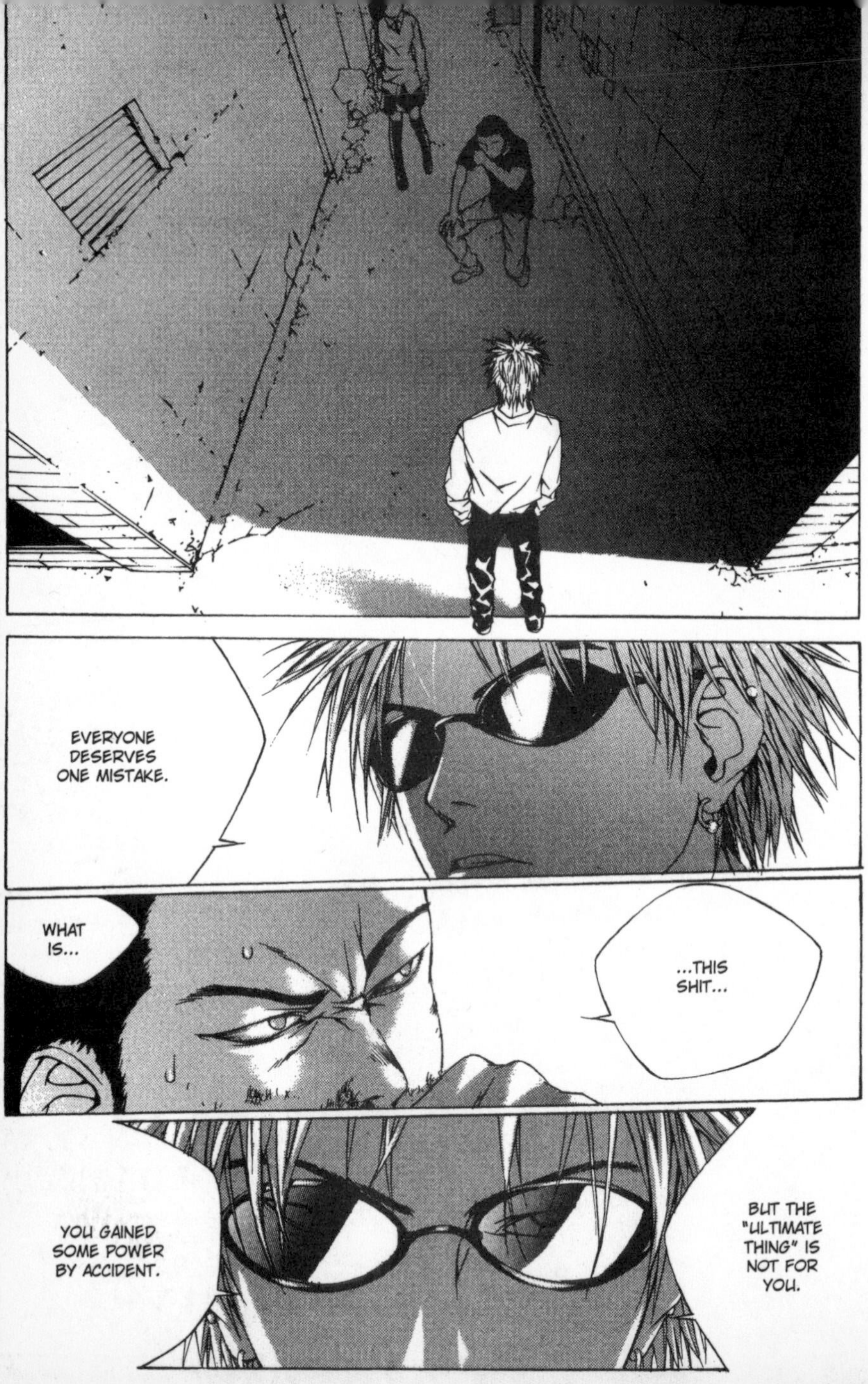
EVERYONE DESERVES ONE MISTAKE.
WHAT IS...
...THIS SHIT...
YOU GAINED SOME POWER BY ACCIDENT.
BUT THE "ULTIMATE THING" IS NOT FOR YOU.

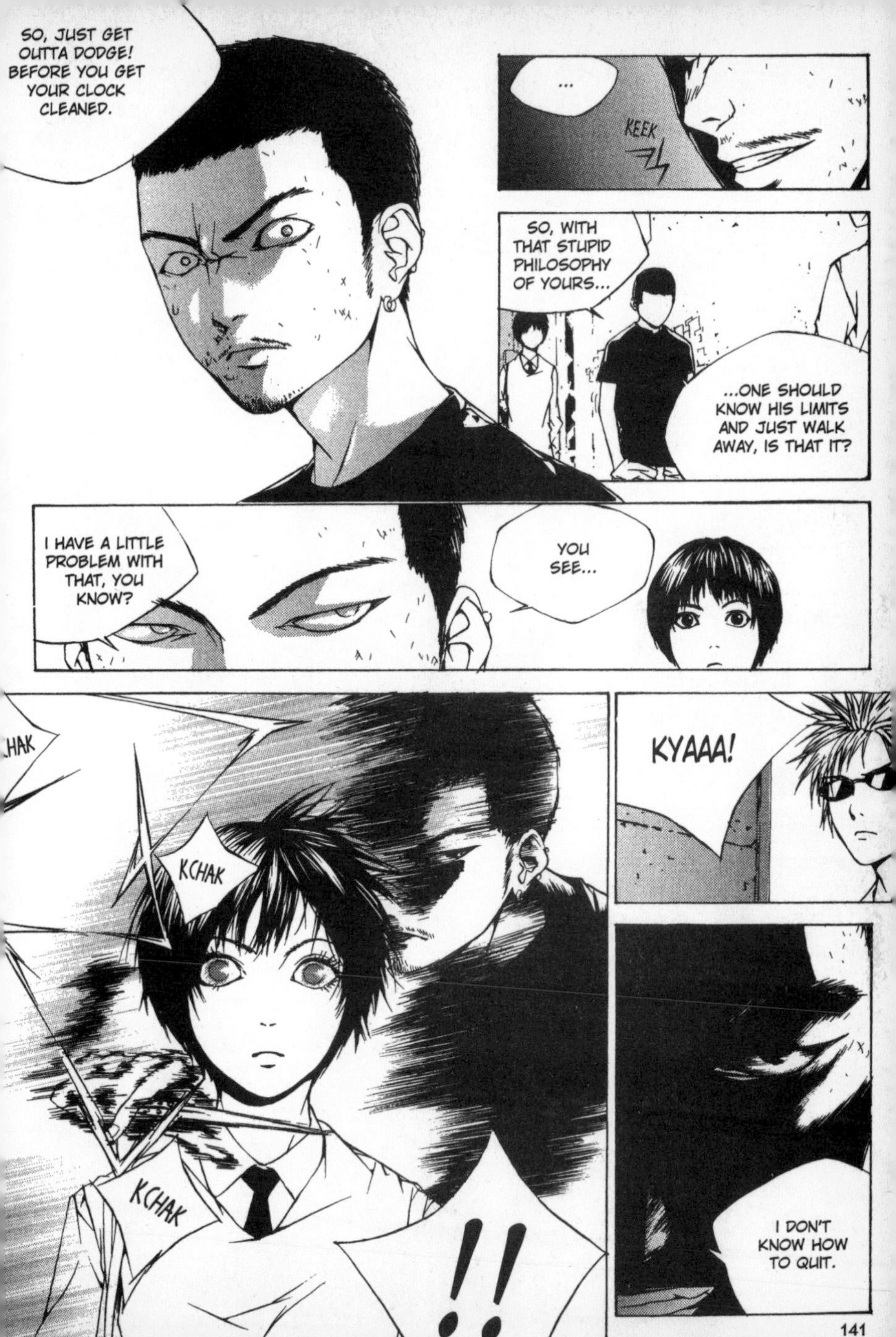
SO, JUST GET OUTTA DODGE! BEFORE YOU GET YOUR CLOCK CLEANED.
...
KEEK
SO, WITH THAT STUPID PHILOSOPHY OF YOURS...
...ONE SHOULD KNOW HIS LIMITS AND JUST WALK AWAY, IS THAT IT?
I HAVE A LITTLE PROBLEM WITH THAT, YOU KNOW?
YOU SEE...
KCHAK
KCHAK
!!
KYAAA!
I DON'T KNOW HOW TO QUIT.

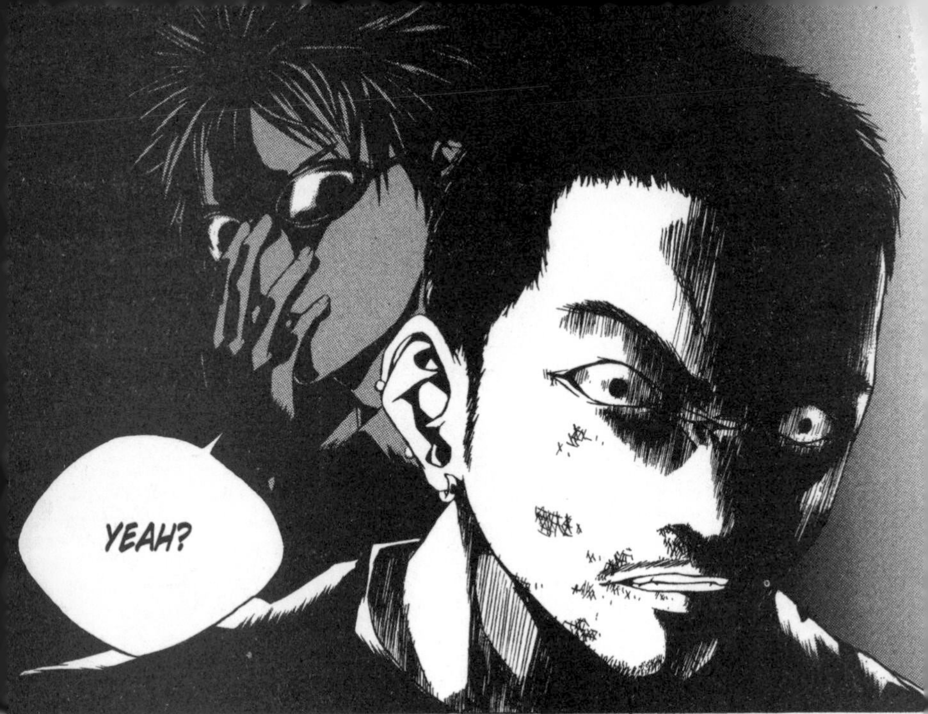
YEAH?

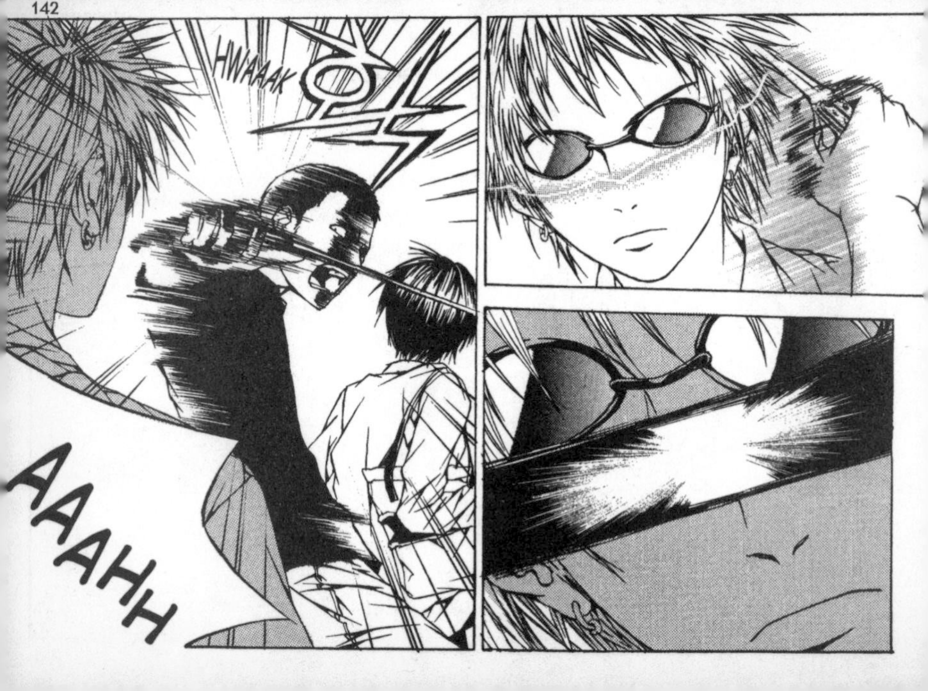
HWAAAK
AAAHH

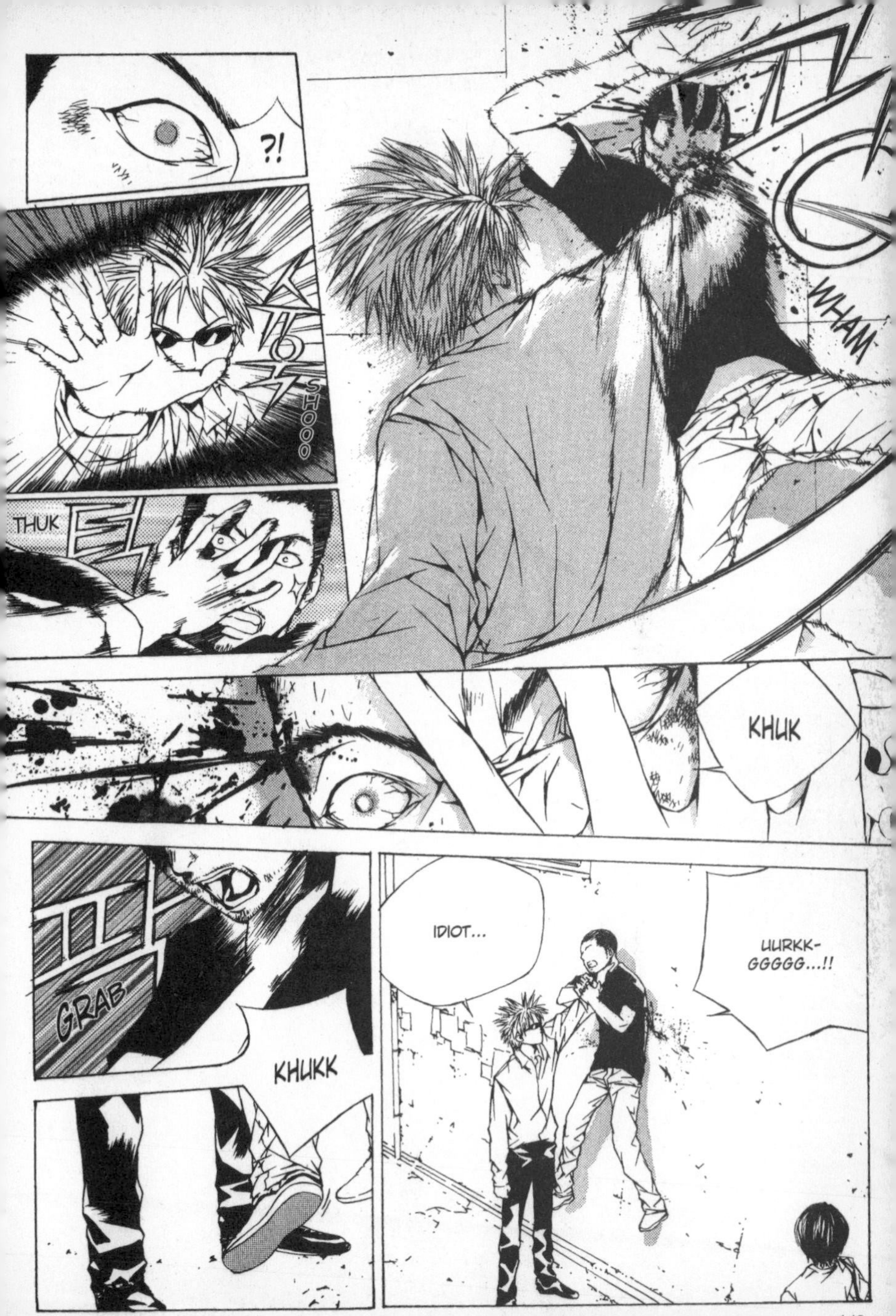
?!
SHOOOO
THUK
WHAM
KHUK
GRAB
KHUKK
IDIOT...
UURKK-GGGGG...!!

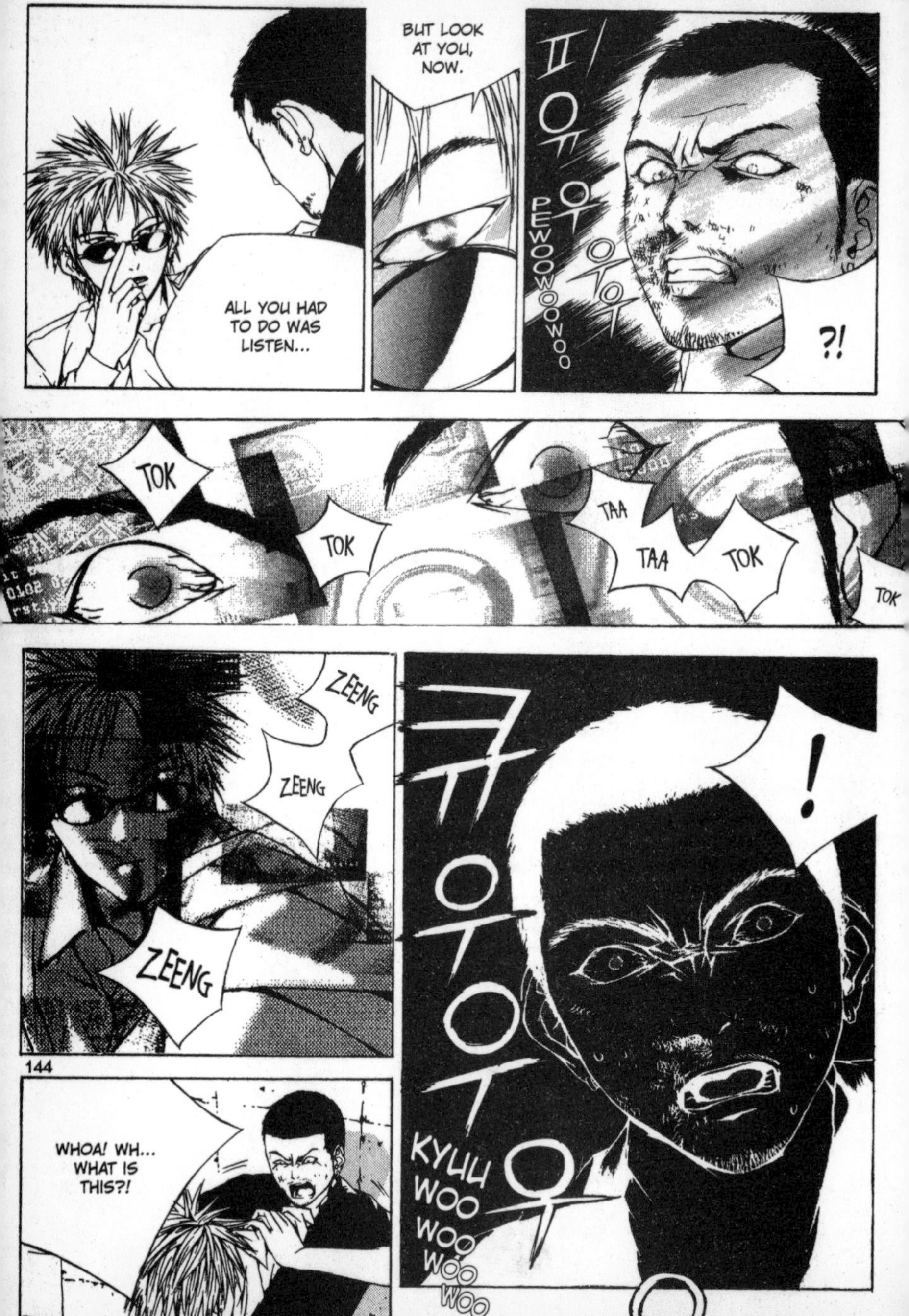
ALL YOU HAD TO DO WAS LISTEN...
BUT LOOK AT YOU, NOW.
PEWOOWOOWOO
?!
TOK
TOK
TAA
TAA
TOK
TOK
ZEENG
ZEENG
ZEENG
WHOA! WH... WHAT IS THIS?!
!
KYUU WOO WOO WOO WOO

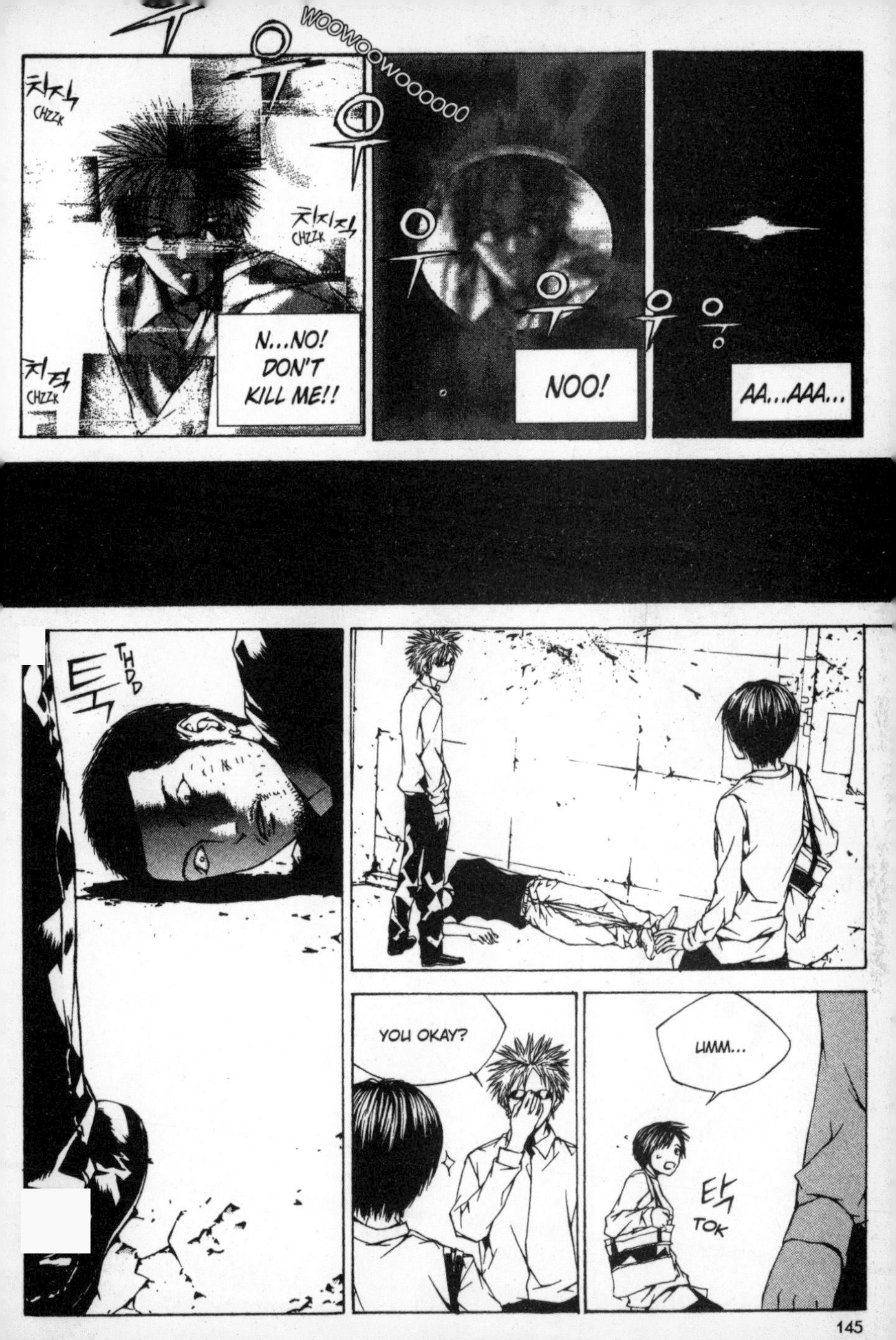
WOOWOOWOOOOOOO
CHZZK
치지직
CHZZK
CHZZK
N...NO! DON'T KILL ME!!
NOO!
AA...AAA...
툭
THDD
YOU OKAY?
UMM...
탁
TOK

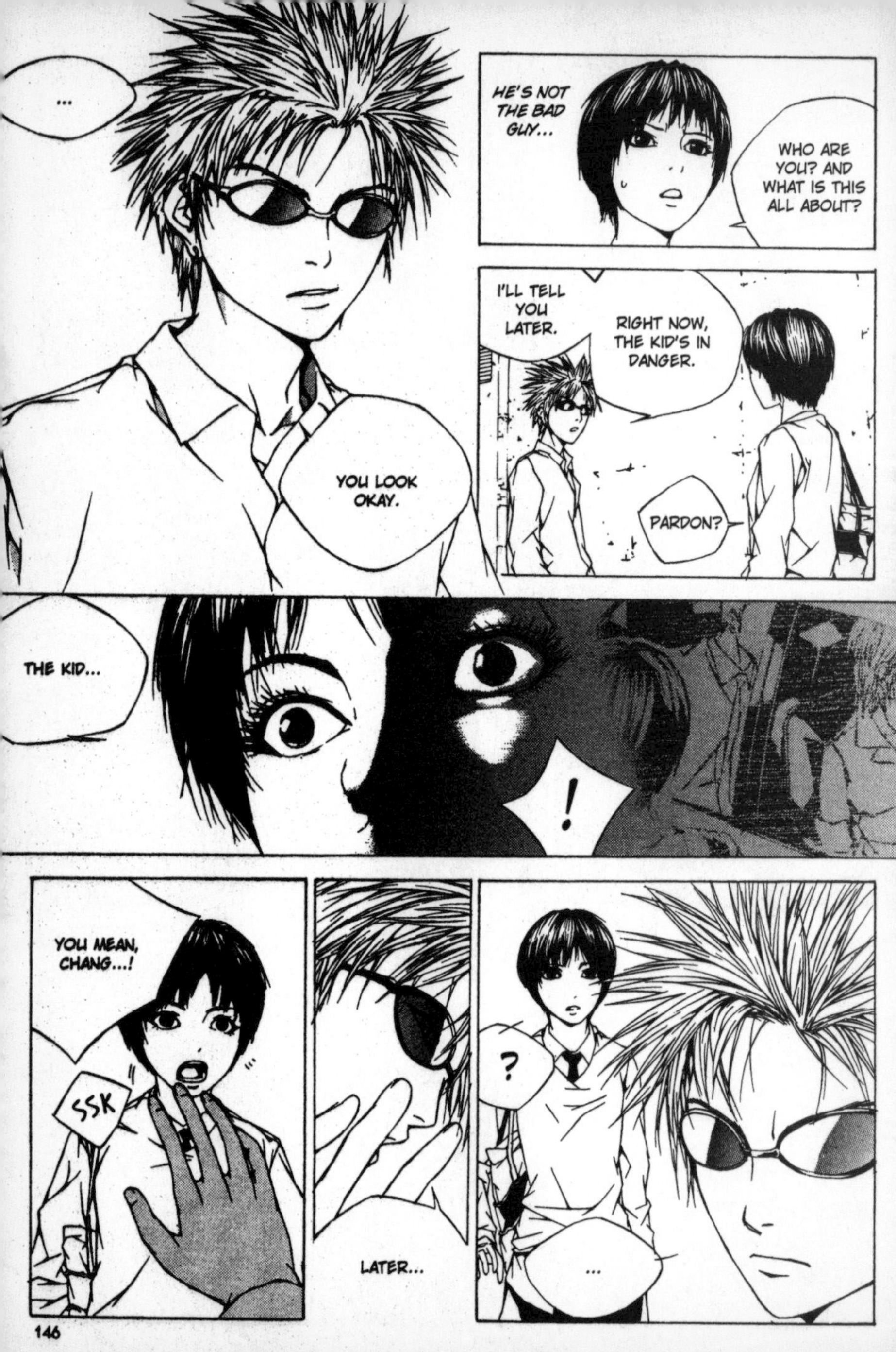
...
YOU LOOK OKAY.
HE'S NOT THE BAD GUY...
WHO ARE YOU? AND WHAT IS THIS ALL ABOUT?
I'LL TELL YOU LATER.
RIGHT NOW, THE KID'S IN DANGER.
PARDON?
THE KID...
!
YOU MEAN, CHANG...!
SSK
LATER...
?
...

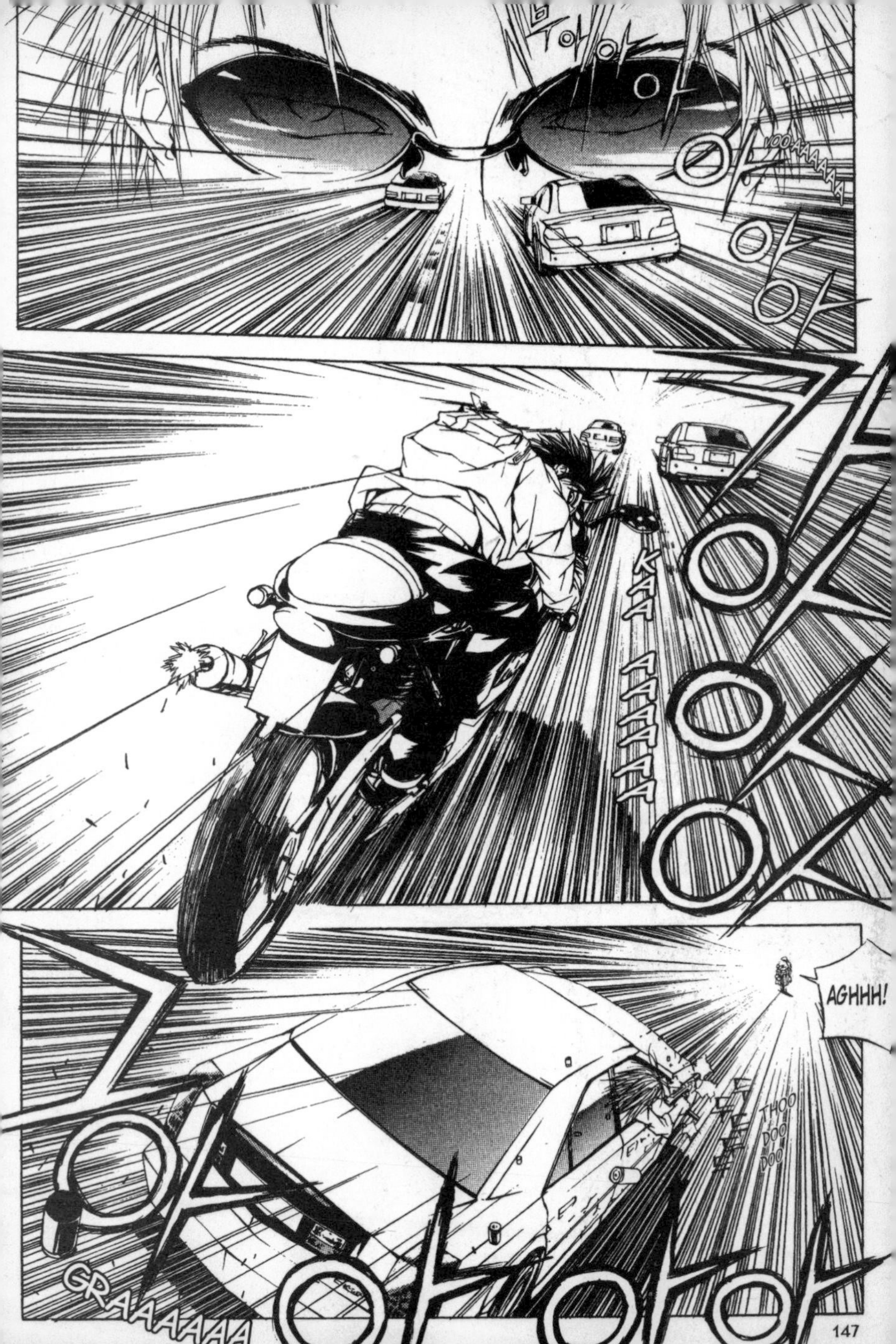
VOOAAAAAAA
KAAAAAAAA
AGHHH!
THOO DOO DOO
GRAAAAAAA

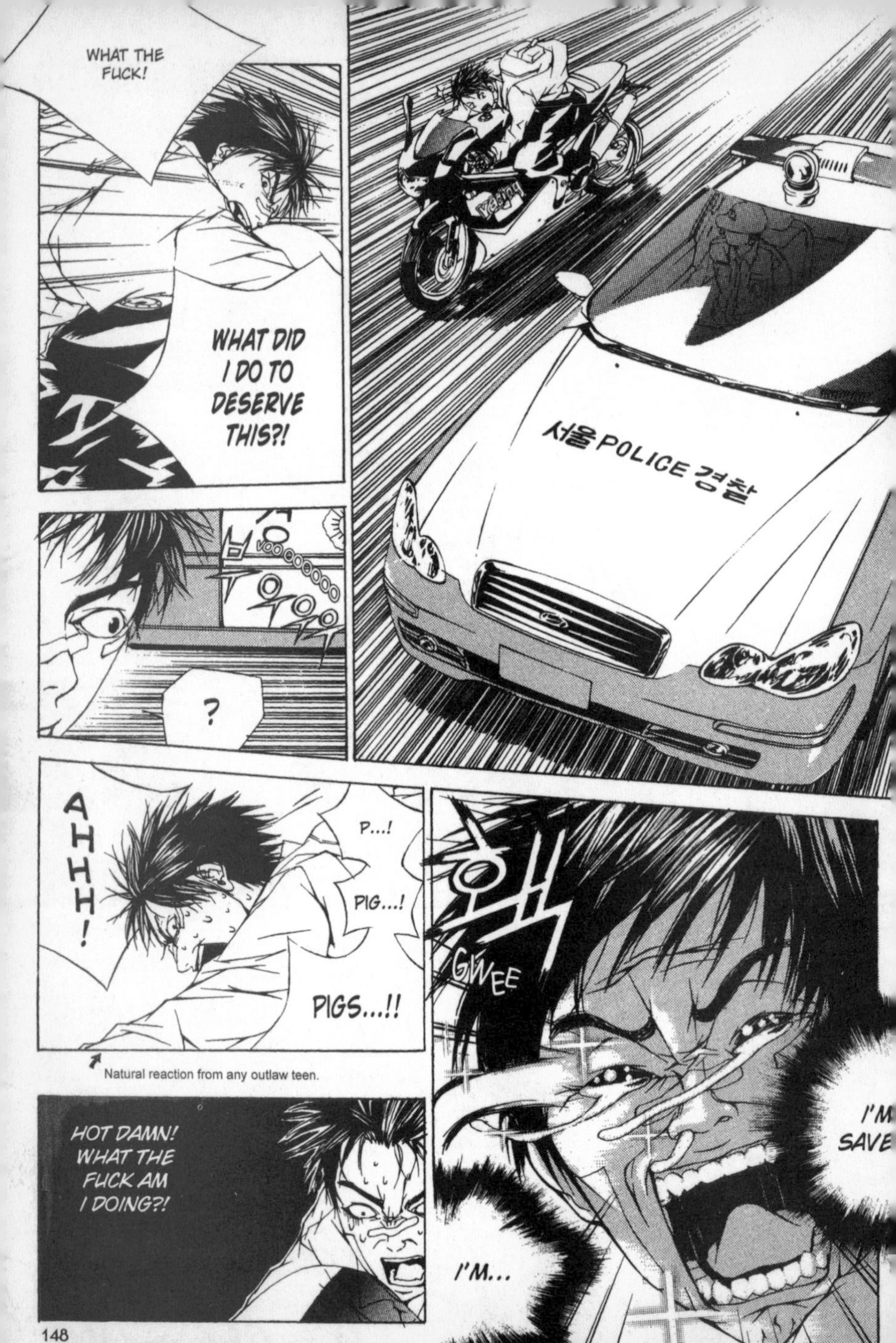
WHAT THE FUCK!
WHAT DID I DO TO DESERVE THIS?!
VOOOOOOOO
?
서울 POLICE 경찰
AHHH!
P...!
PIG...!
PIGS...!!
Natural reaction from any outlaw teen.
HOT DAMN! WHAT THE FUCK AM I DOING?!
GWEE
I'M SAVE
I'M...

Sign lingo translation: Those motherfuckers are trying to kill me. Help!!

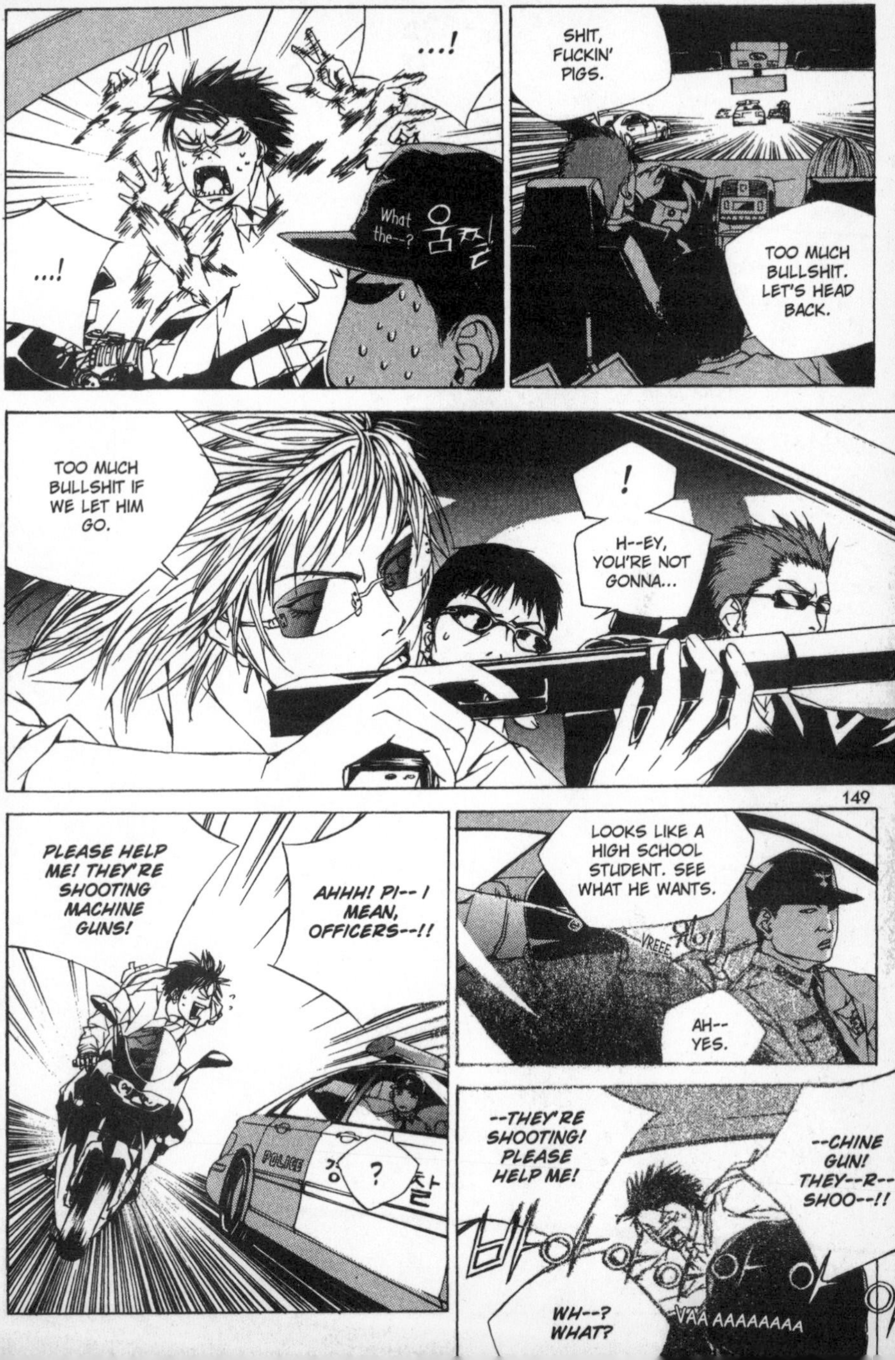
...!
...!
What the--?
움찔!
SHIT, FUCKIN' PIGS.
TOO MUCH BULLSHIT. LET'S HEAD BACK.
TOO MUCH BULLSHIT IF WE LET HIM GO.
!
H--EY, YOU'RE NOT GONNA...
PLEASE HELP ME! THEY'RE SHOOTING MACHINE GUNS!
AHHH! PI-- I MEAN, OFFICERS--!!
POLICE
?
LOOKS LIKE A HIGH SCHOOL STUDENT. SEE WHAT HE WANTS.
VREEE
AH-- YES.
--THEY'RE SHOOTING! PLEASE HELP ME!
--CHINE GUN! THEY--R-- SHOO--!!
WH--? WHAT?
VAA AAAAAAAA

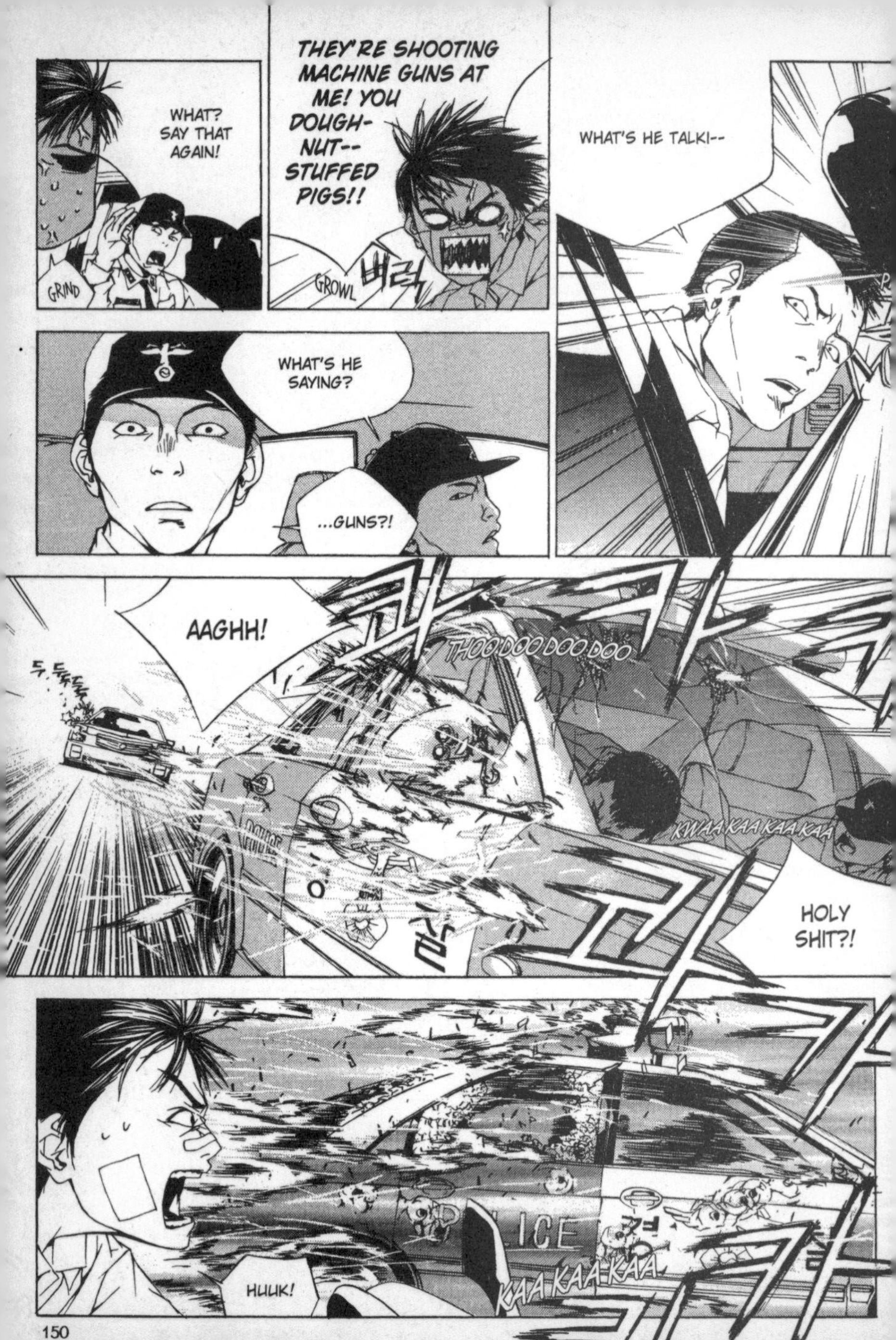
WHAT? SAY THAT AGAIN!
GRIND
THEY'RE SHOOTING MACHINE GUNS AT ME! YOU DOUGH-NUT-- STUFFED PIGS!!
GROWL
WHAT'S HE SAYING?
...GUNS?!
WHAT'S HE TALKI--
AAGHH!
THOO DOO DOO DOO
KWAA KAA KAA KAA
HOLY SHIT?!
ICE
HUUK!
KAA KAA KAA

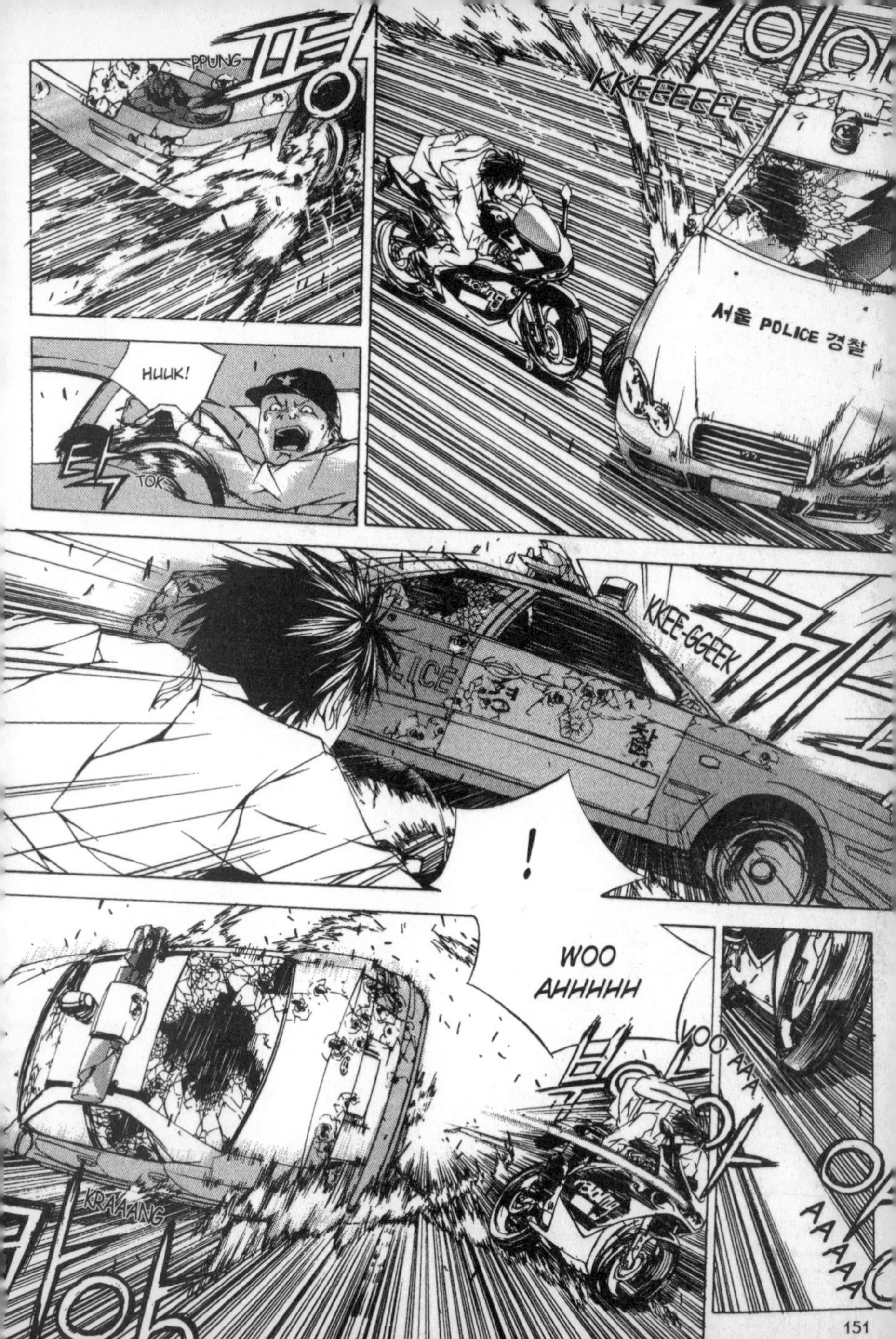
PPUNG
HUUK!
TOK
KKEEEEEEE
서울 POLICE 경찰
KKEE-GGEEK
!
WOO AHHHHH
KRAAAANG
VOO AAA
AAAAA

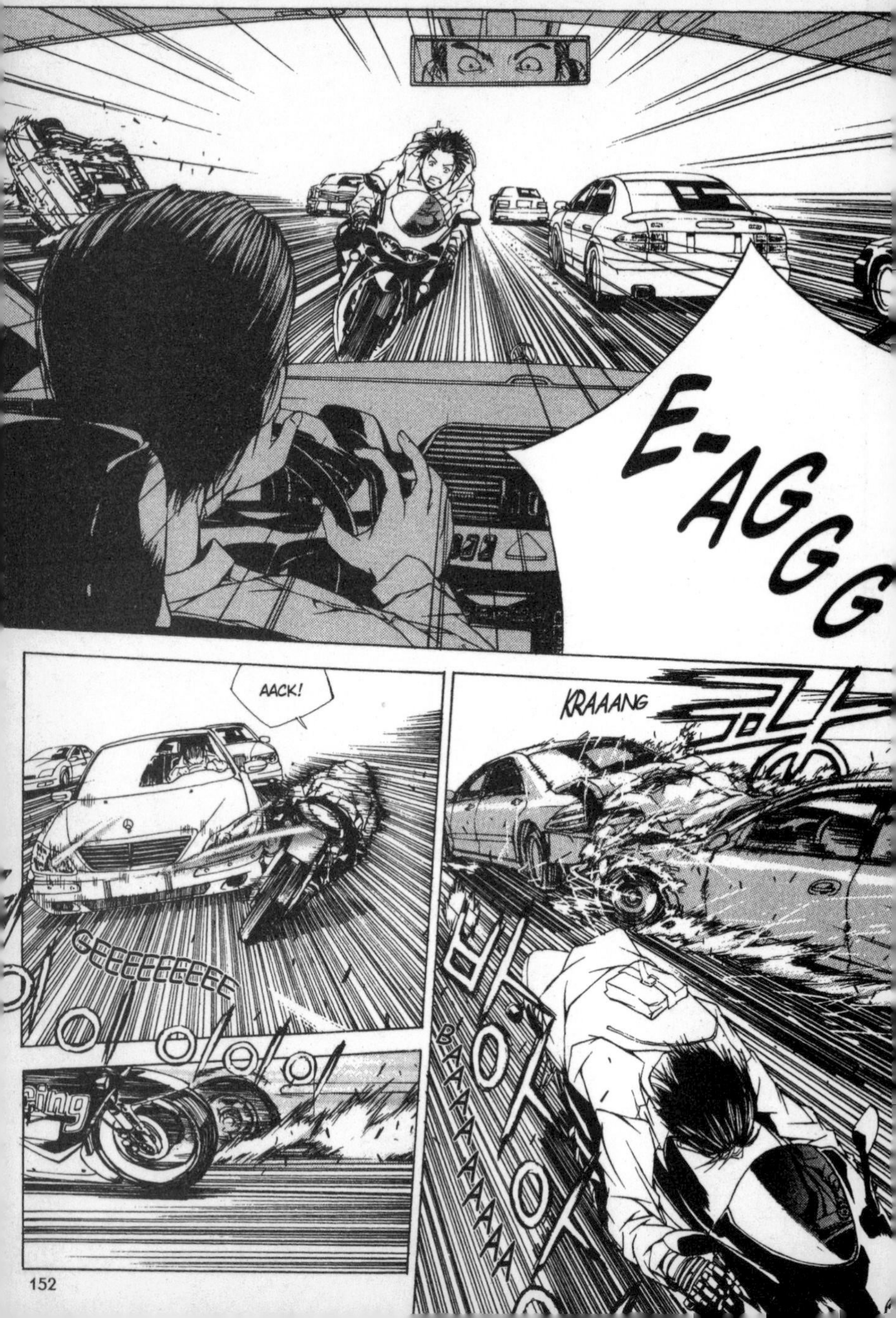
E-AGGG
AACK!
GEEEEEEEEEE
KRAAANG
BAAAAAAAAAA

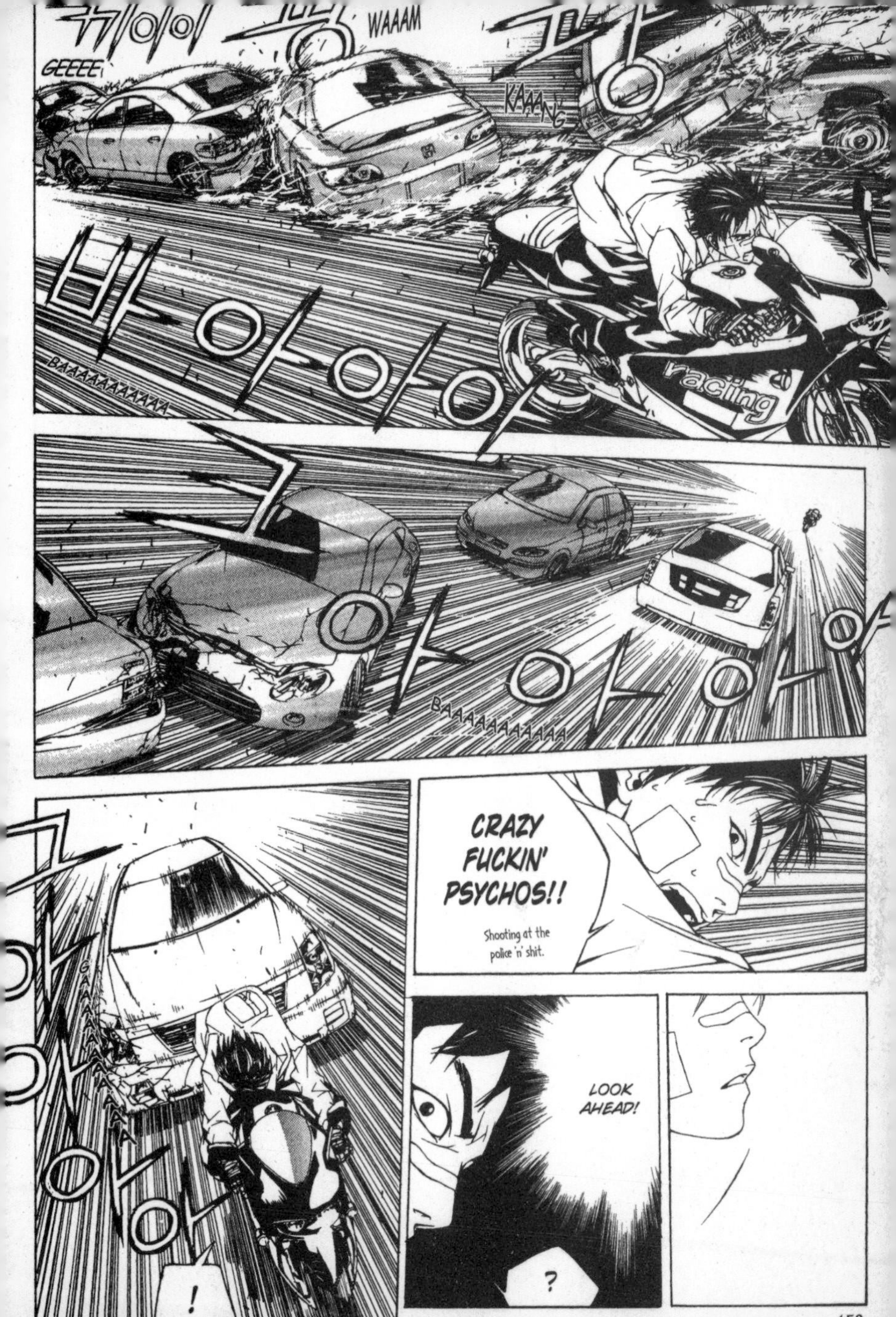
GEEEE
WAAAM
KAAANG
BAAAAAAAAAAA
BAAAAAAAAAAA
GAAAAAAAAAA
!
CRAZY FUCKIN' PSYCHOS!!
Shooting at the police 'n' shit.
?
LOOK AHEAD!

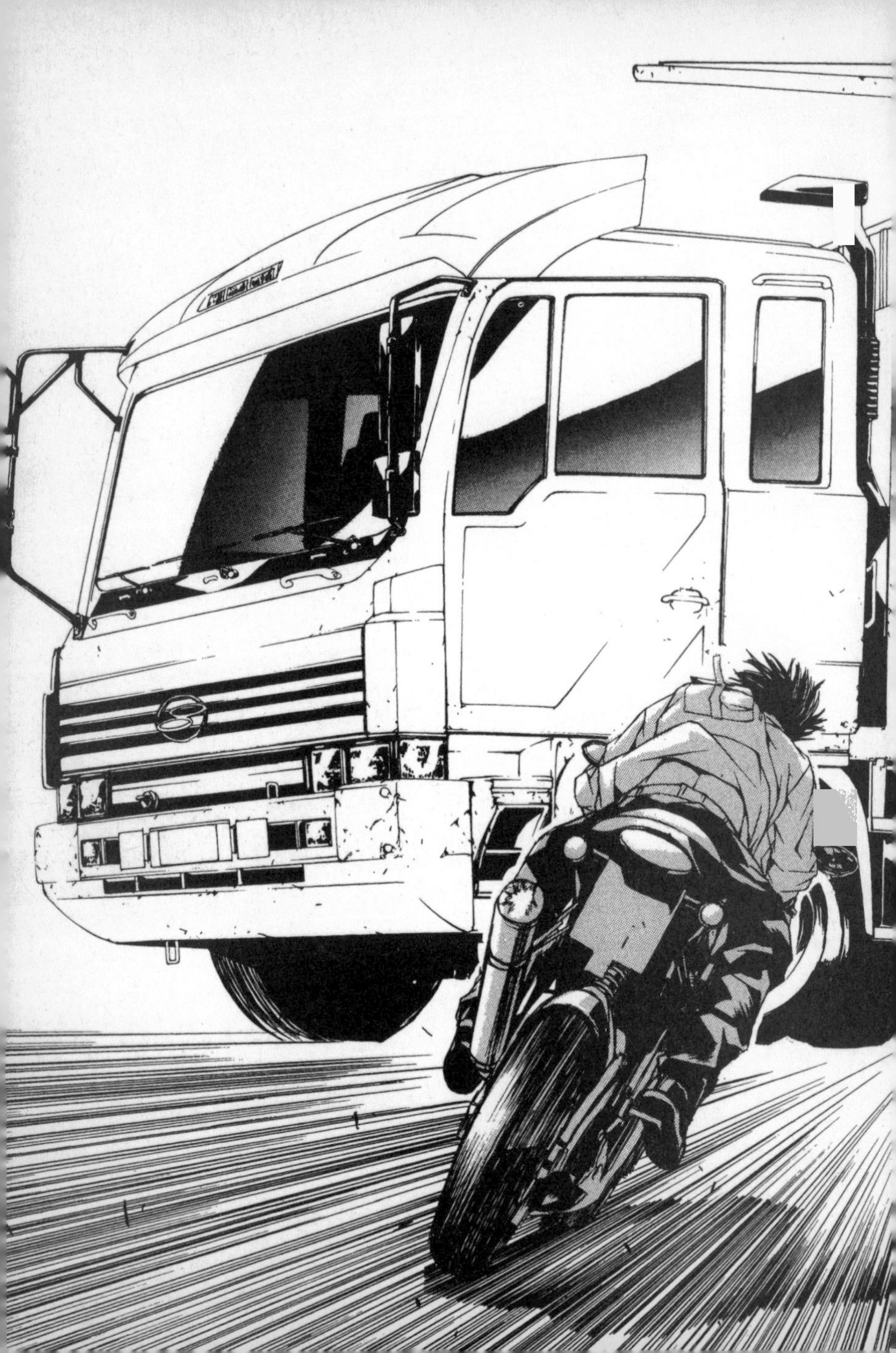

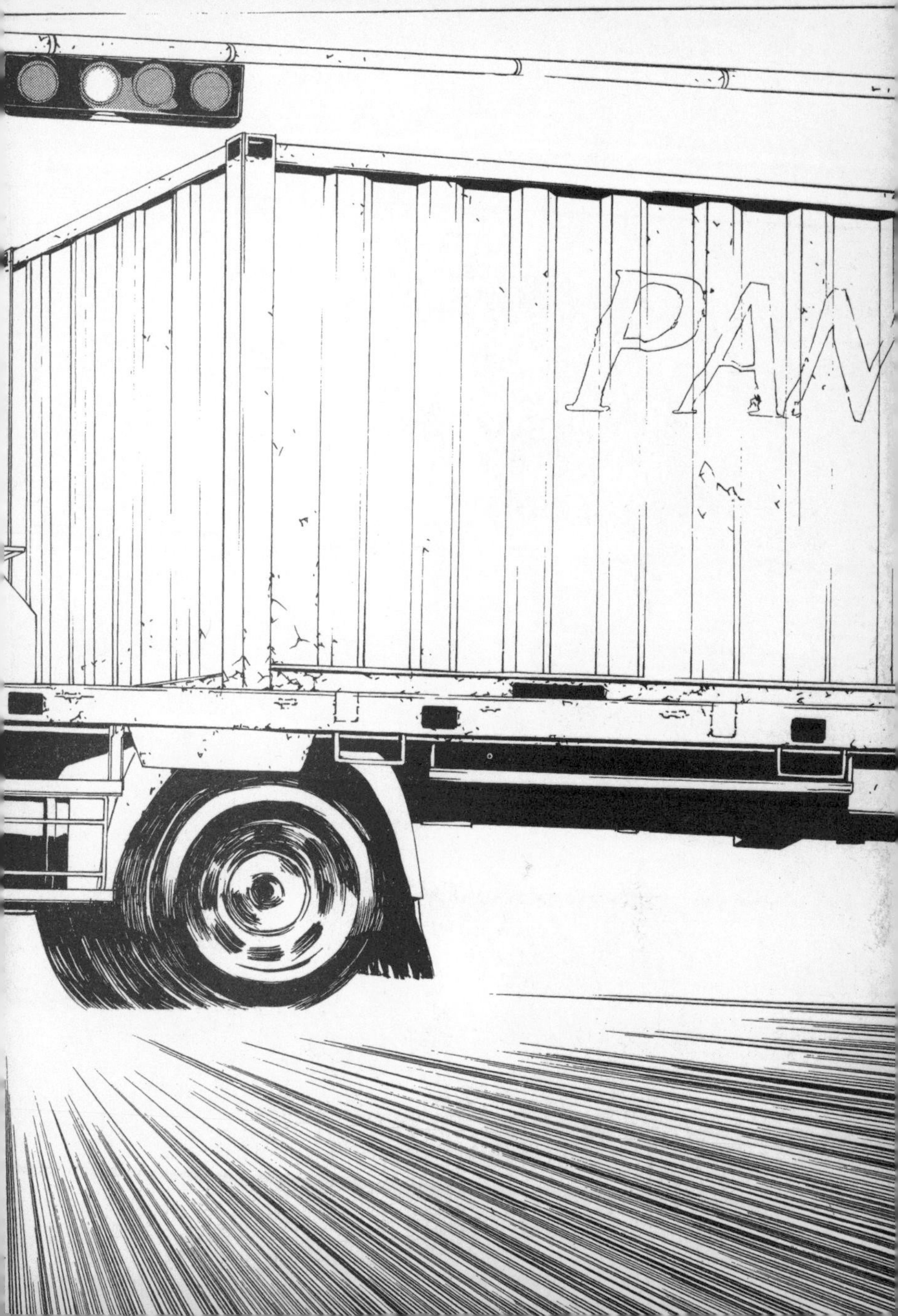
PAN

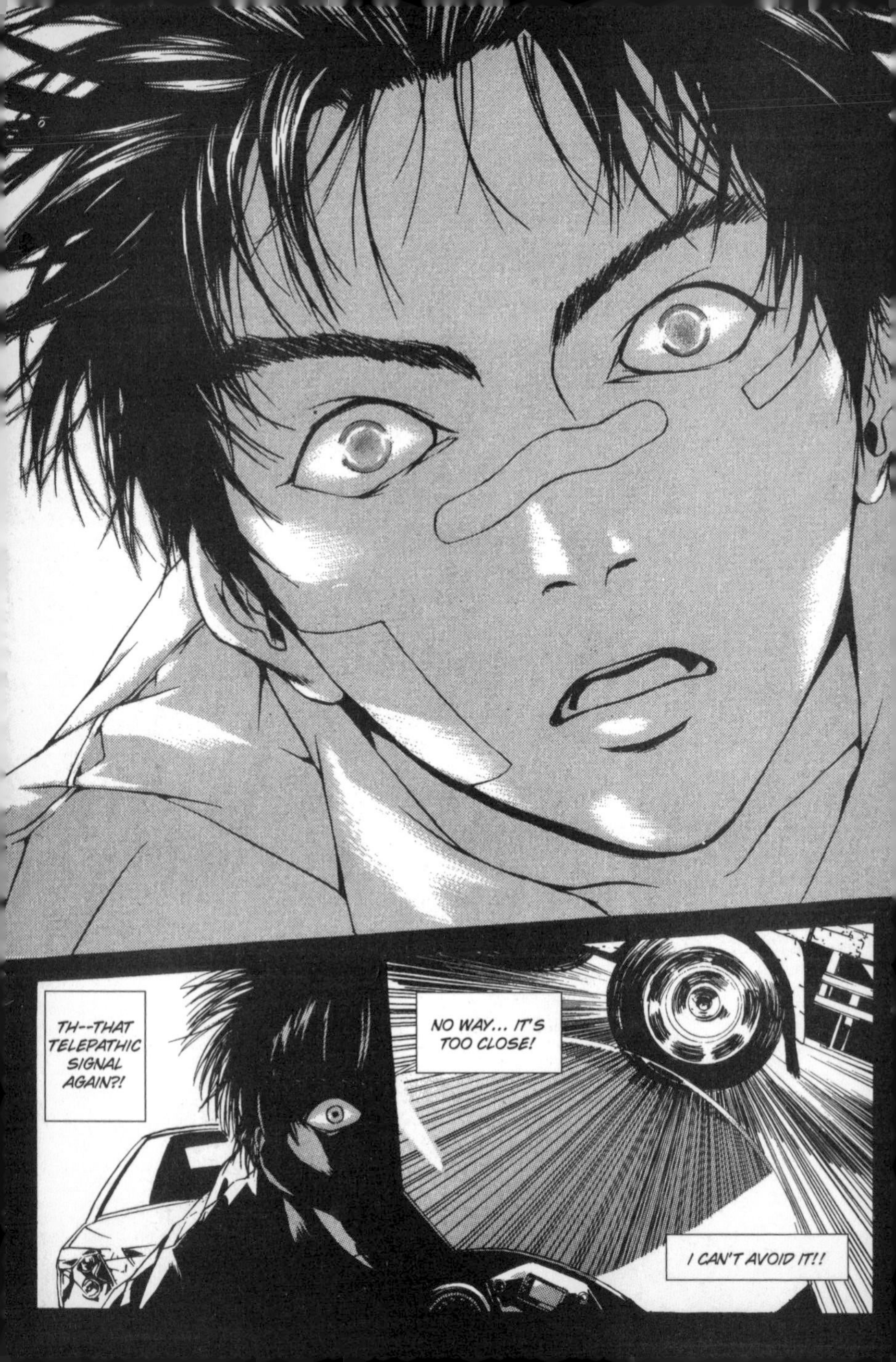
TH--THAT TELEPATHIC SIGNAL AGAIN?!
NO WAY... IT'S TOO CLOSE!
I CAN'T AVOID IT!!

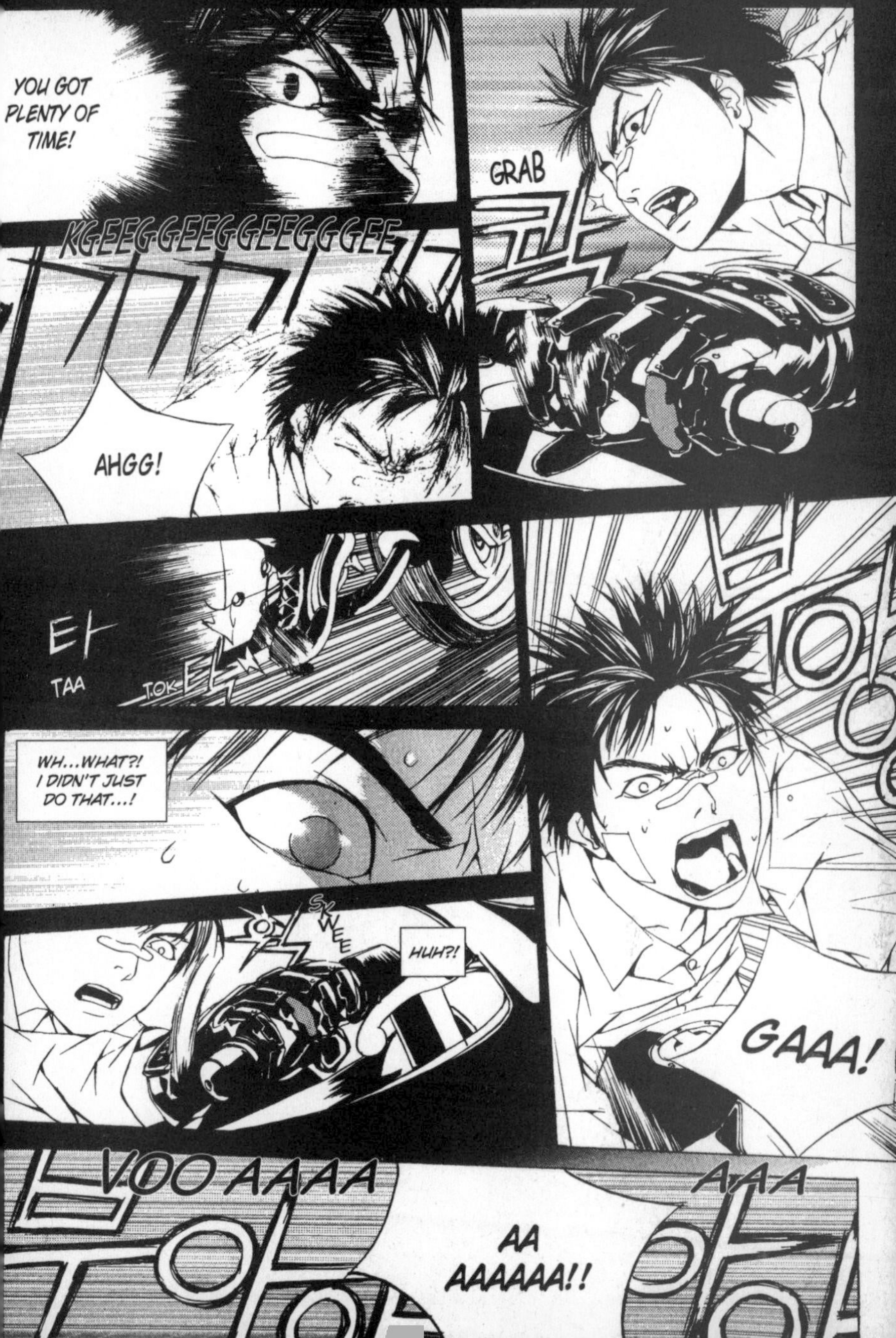

YOU GOT PLENTY OF TIME!
KGEEG GEEG GEEG GGEE
AHGG!
GRAB
타
TAA
TOK
WH...WHAT?! I DIDN'T JUST DO THAT...!
SKWEE
HUH?!
GAAA!
VOO AAAA
AA AAAAAA!!
A A A

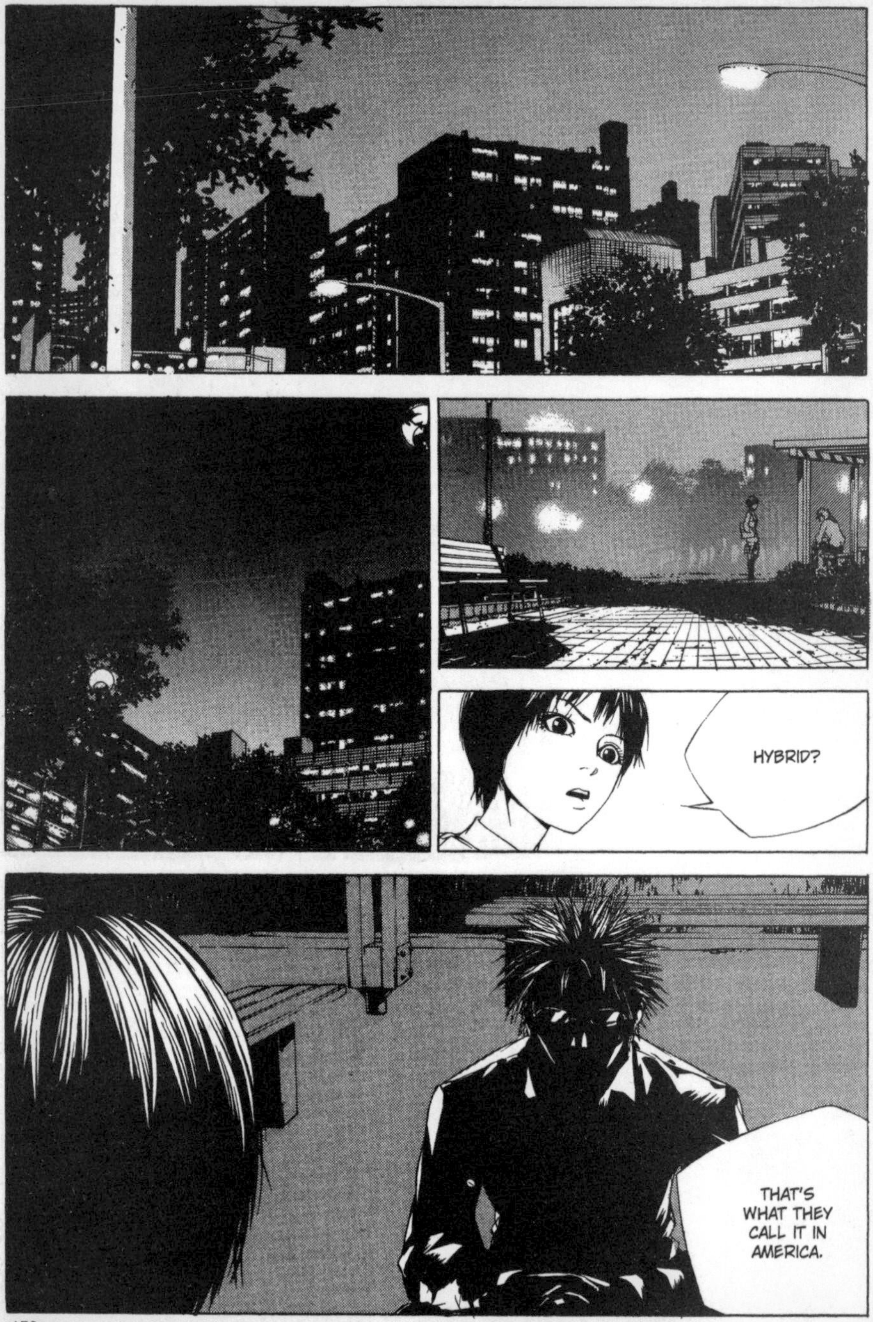
HYBRID?
THAT'S WHAT THEY CALL IT IN AMERICA.

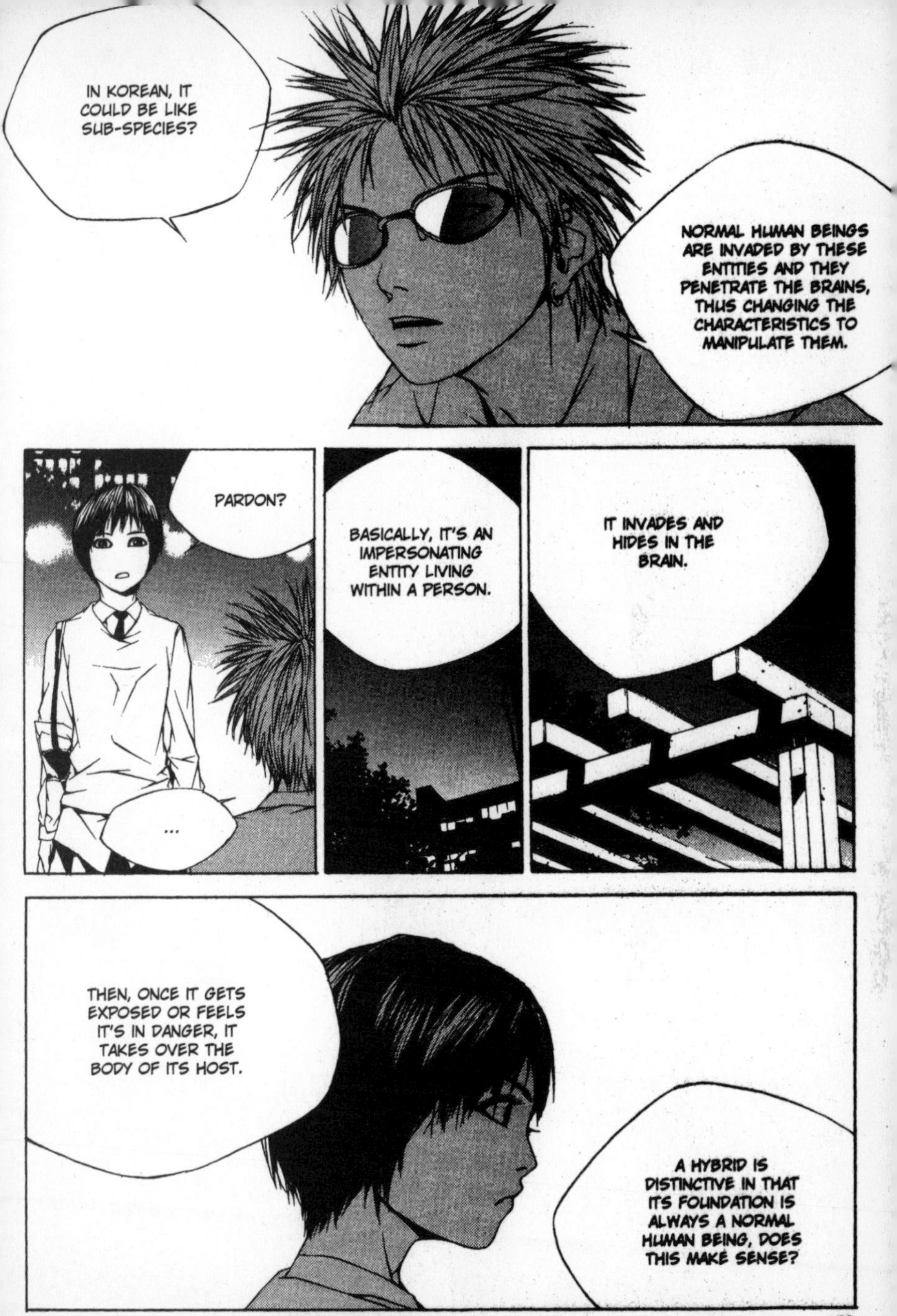
IN KOREAN, IT COULD BE LIKE SUB-SPECIES?
NORMAL HUMAN BEINGS ARE INVADED BY THESE ENTITIES AND THEY PENETRATE THE BRAINS, THUS CHANGING THE CHARACTERISTICS TO MANIPULATE THEM.
PARDON?
...
BASICALLY, IT'S AN IMPERSONATING ENTITY LIVING WITHIN A PERSON.
IT INVADES AND HIDES IN THE BRAIN.
THEN, ONCE IT GETS EXPOSED OR FEELS IT'S IN DANGER, IT TAKES OVER THE BODY OF ITS HOST.
A HYBRID IS DISTINCTIVE IN THAT ITS FOUNDATION IS ALWAYS A NORMAL HUMAN BEING, DOES THIS MAKE SENSE?

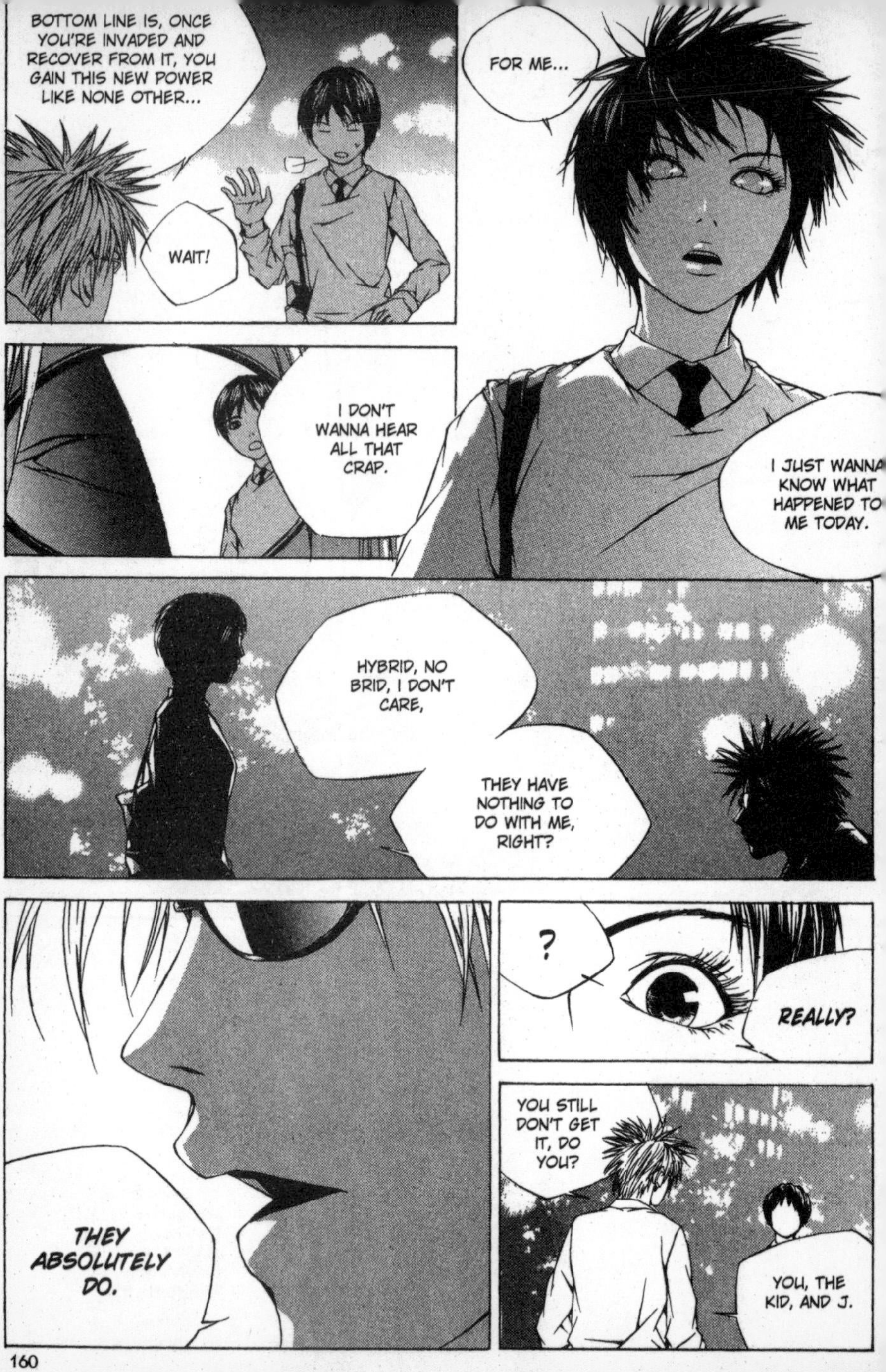
BOTTOM LINE IS, ONCE YOU'RE INVADED AND RECOVER FROM IT, YOU GAIN THIS NEW POWER LIKE NONE OTHER...
WAIT!
I DON'T WANNA HEAR ALL THAT CRAP.
FOR ME...
I JUST WANNA KNOW WHAT HAPPENED TO ME TODAY.
HYBRID, NO BRID, I DON'T CARE,
THEY HAVE NOTHING TO DO WITH ME, RIGHT?
THEY ABSOLUTELY DO.
?
REALLY?
YOU STILL DON'T GET IT, DO YOU?
YOU, THE KID, AND J.

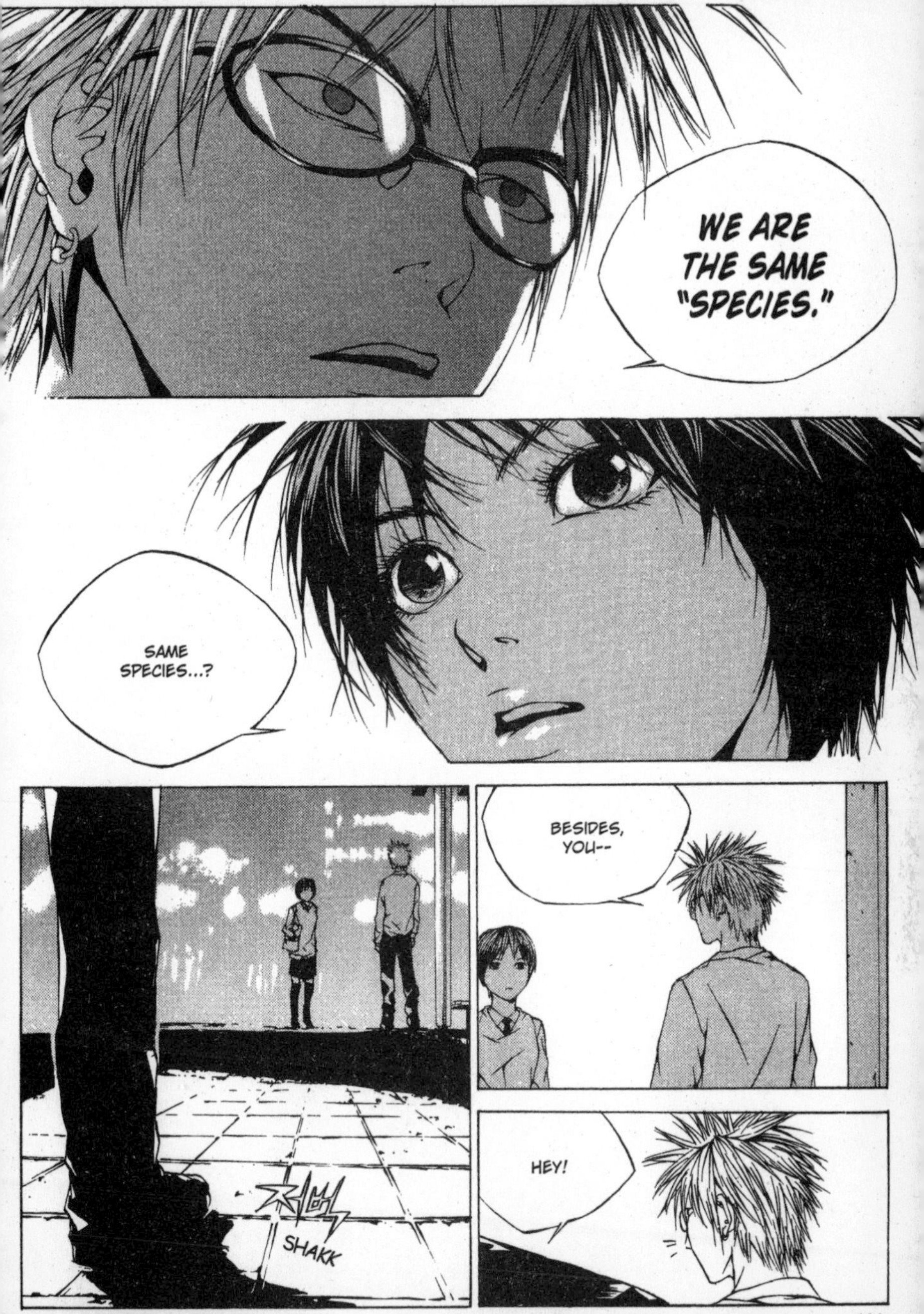
WE ARE THE SAME "SPECIES."
SAME SPECIES...?
SHAKK
BESIDES, YOU--
HEY!

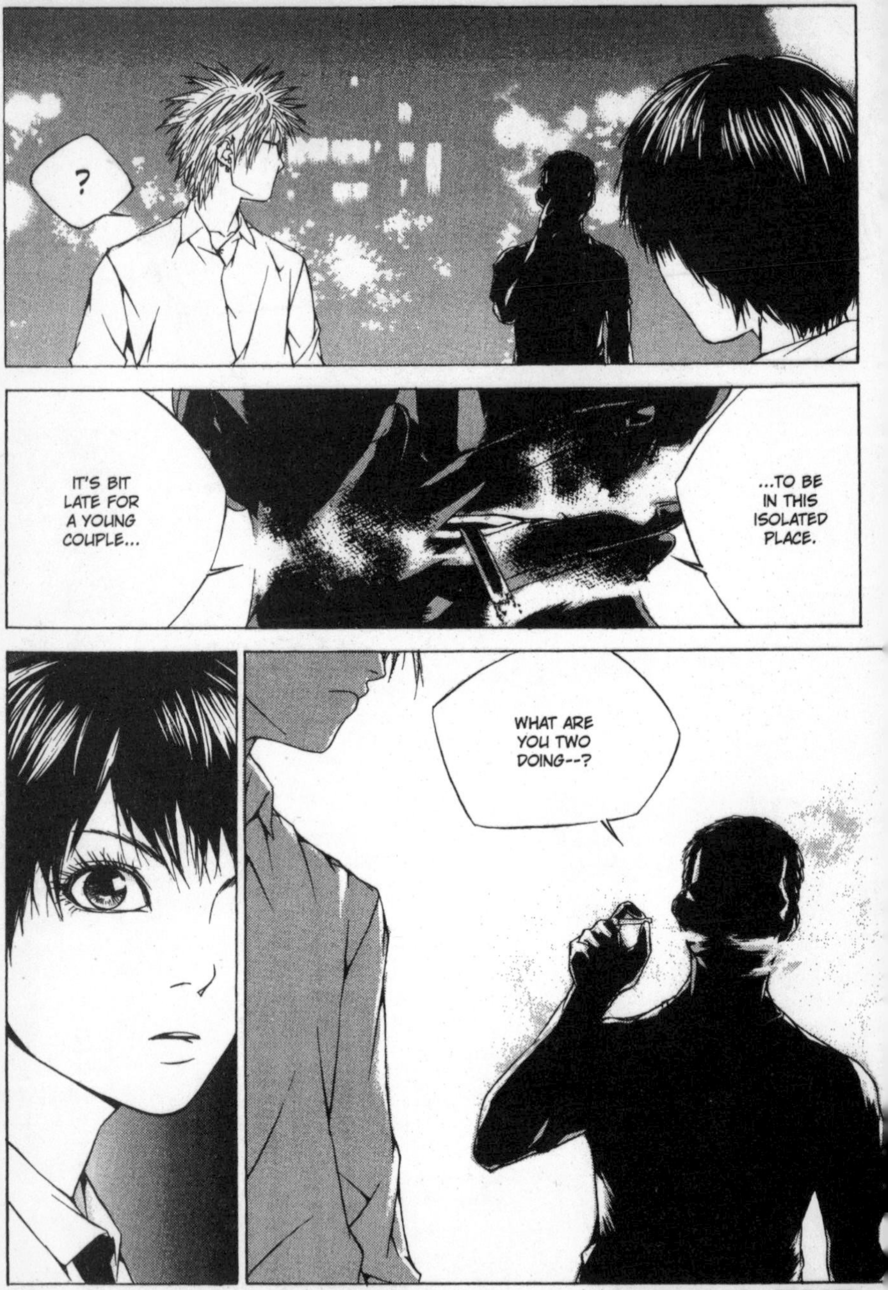
?
IT'S BIT LATE FOR A YOUNG COUPLE...
...TO BE IN THIS ISOLATED PLACE.
WHAT ARE YOU TWO DOING--?

Log-6 END

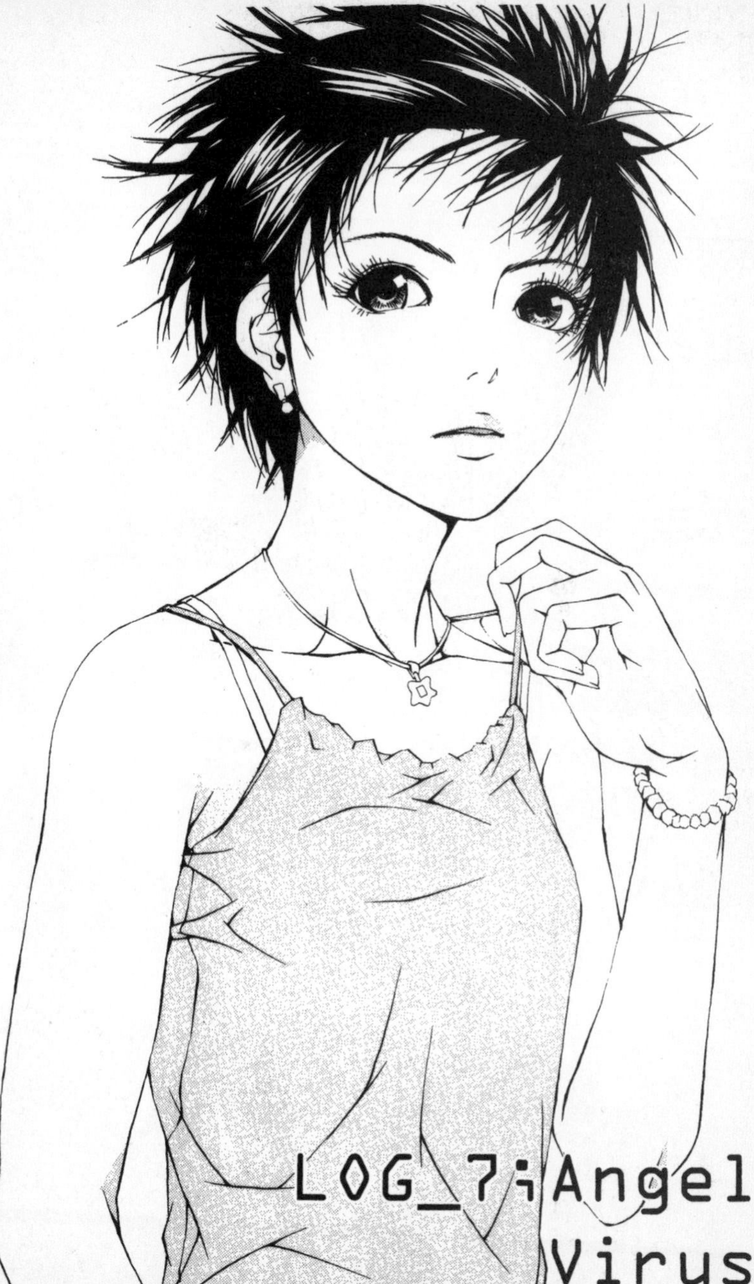

LOG_7: Angel Virus

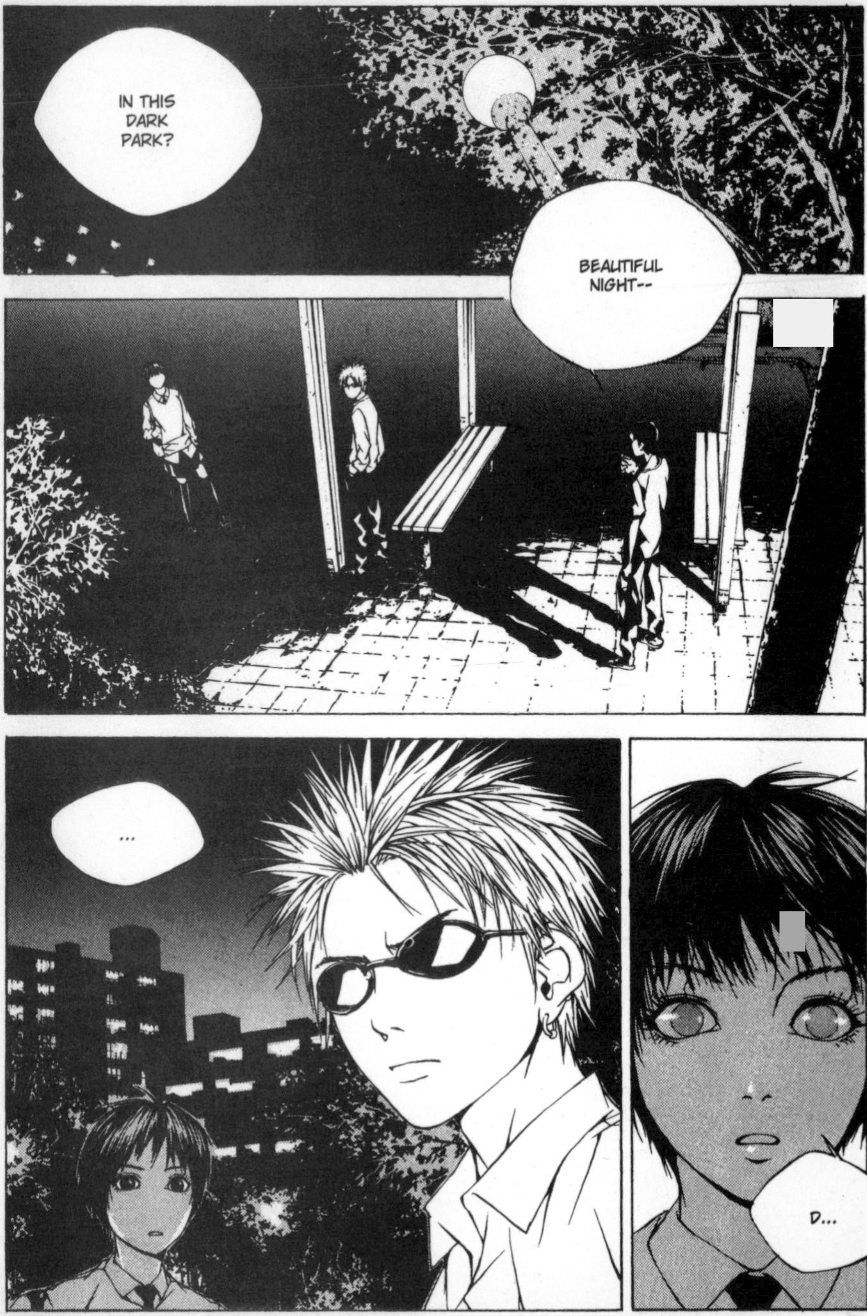
IN THIS DARK PARK?
BEAUTIFUL NIGHT--
...
D...

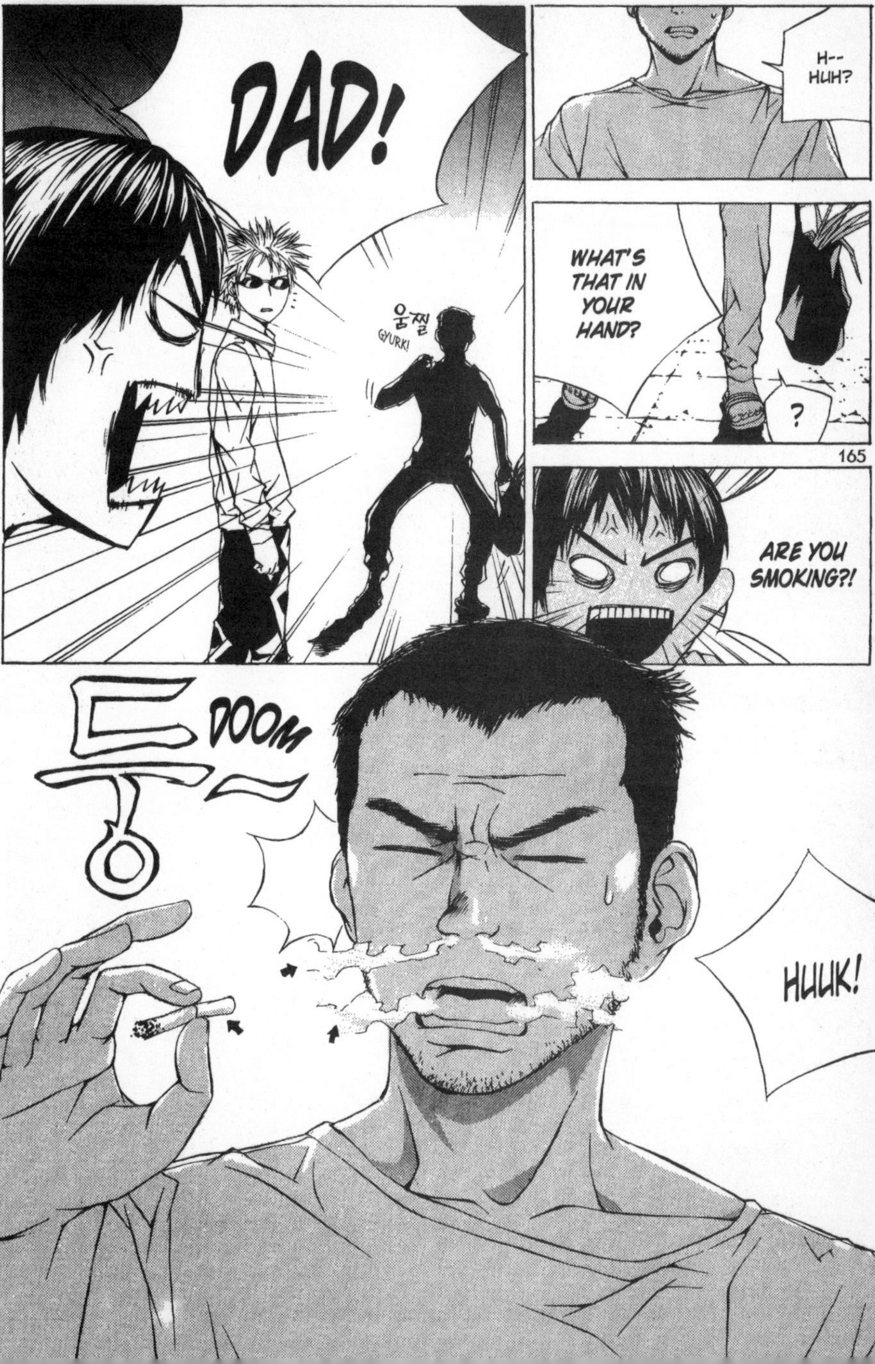
DAD!
움찔
GYURK!
H-- HUH?
WHAT'S THAT IN YOUR HAND?
?
ARE YOU SMOKING?!
DOOM
HUUK!

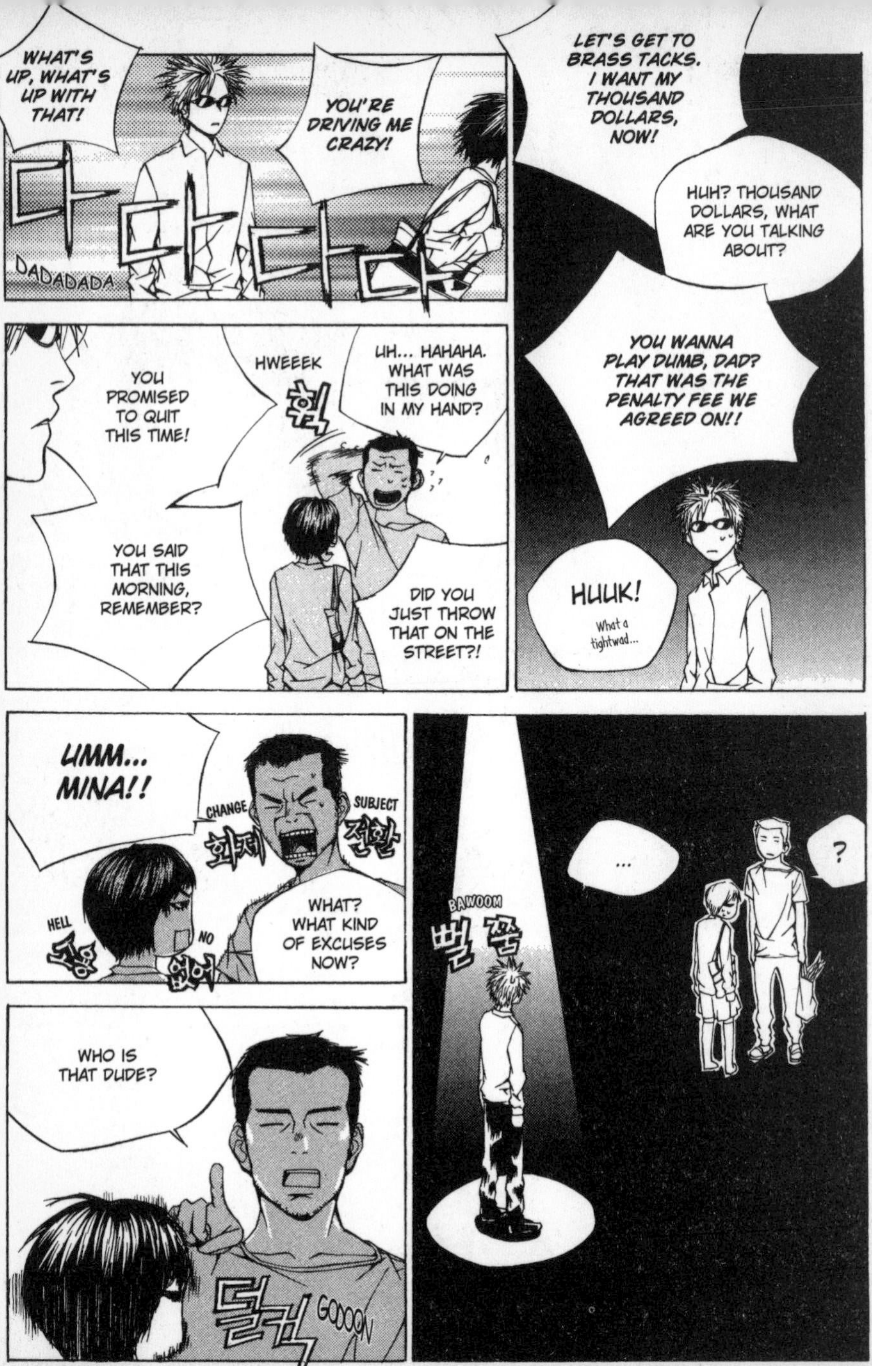

WHAT'S UP, WHAT'S UP WITH THAT!
YOU'RE DRIVING ME CRAZY!
다다다다
DADADADA
YOU PROMISED TO QUIT THIS TIME!
HWEEEK
휙
UH... HAHAHA. WHAT WAS THIS DOING IN MY HAND?
YOU SAID THAT THIS MORNING, REMEMBER?
DID YOU JUST THROW THAT ON THE STREET?!
LET'S GET TO BRASS TACKS. I WANT MY THOUSAND DOLLARS, NOW!
HUH? THOUSAND DOLLARS, WHAT ARE YOU TALKING ABOUT?
YOU WANNA PLAY DUMB, DAD? THAT WAS THE PENALTY FEE WE AGREED ON!!
HUUK!
What a tightwad...
UMM... MINA!!
CHANGE
SUBJECT
화제 전환
HELL
NO
WHAT? WHAT KIND OF EXCUSES NOW?
WHO IS THAT DUDE?
덜컥
GODOON
...
?
BAWOOM

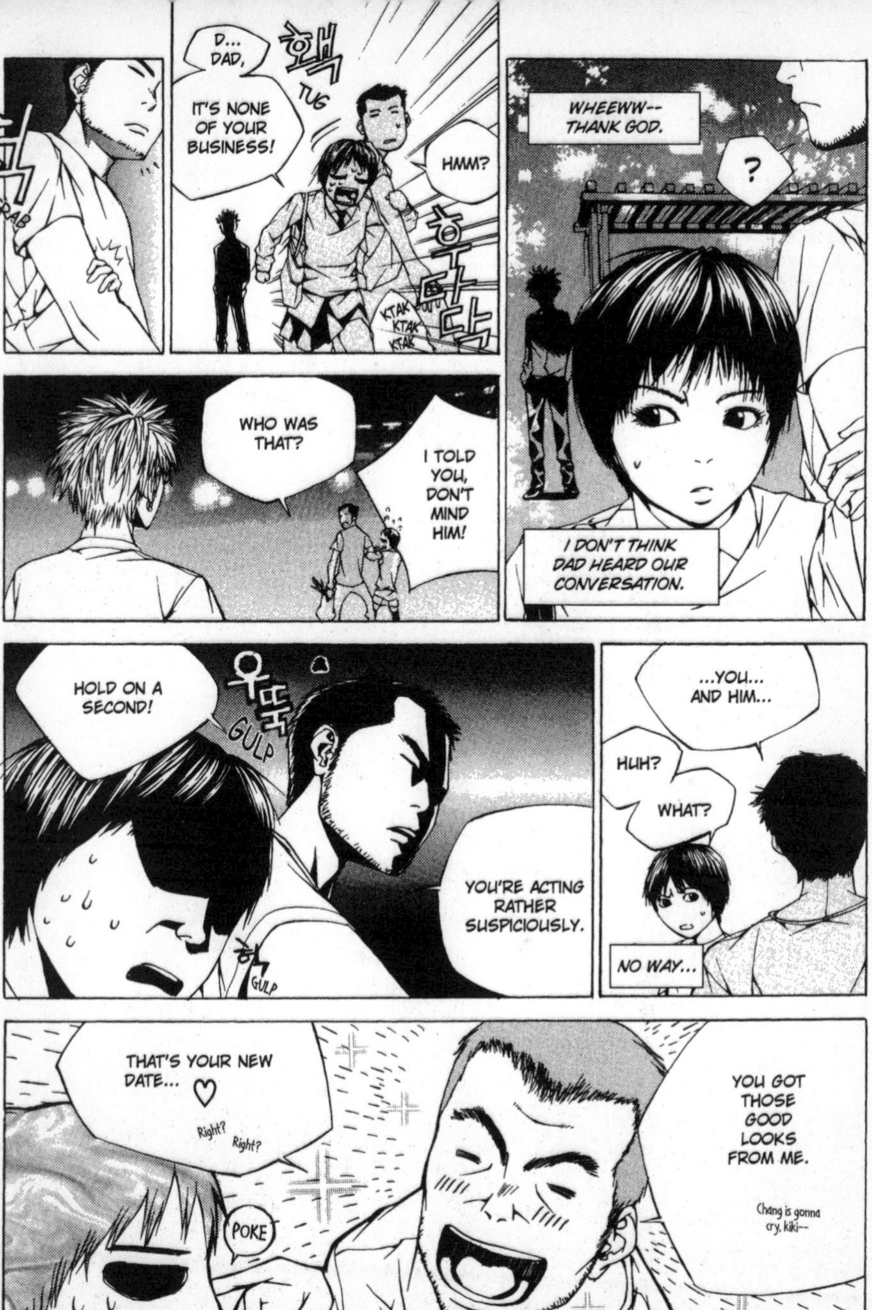
GRAB
D... DAD,
IT'S NONE OF YOUR BUSINESS!
홱
TUG
HMM?
후다닥
KTAK KTAK KTAK
WHO WAS THAT?
I TOLD YOU, DON'T MIND HIM!
WHEEWW-- THANK GOD.
?
I DON'T THINK DAD HEARD OUR CONVERSATION.
HOLD ON A SECOND!
GULP
YOU'RE ACTING RATHER SUSPICIOUSLY.
GULP
...YOU... AND HIM...
HUH?
WHAT?
NO WAY...
THAT'S YOUR NEW DATE... ♡
Right? Right?
POKE
YOU GOT THOSE GOOD LOOKS FROM ME.
Chang is gonna cry, kiki--

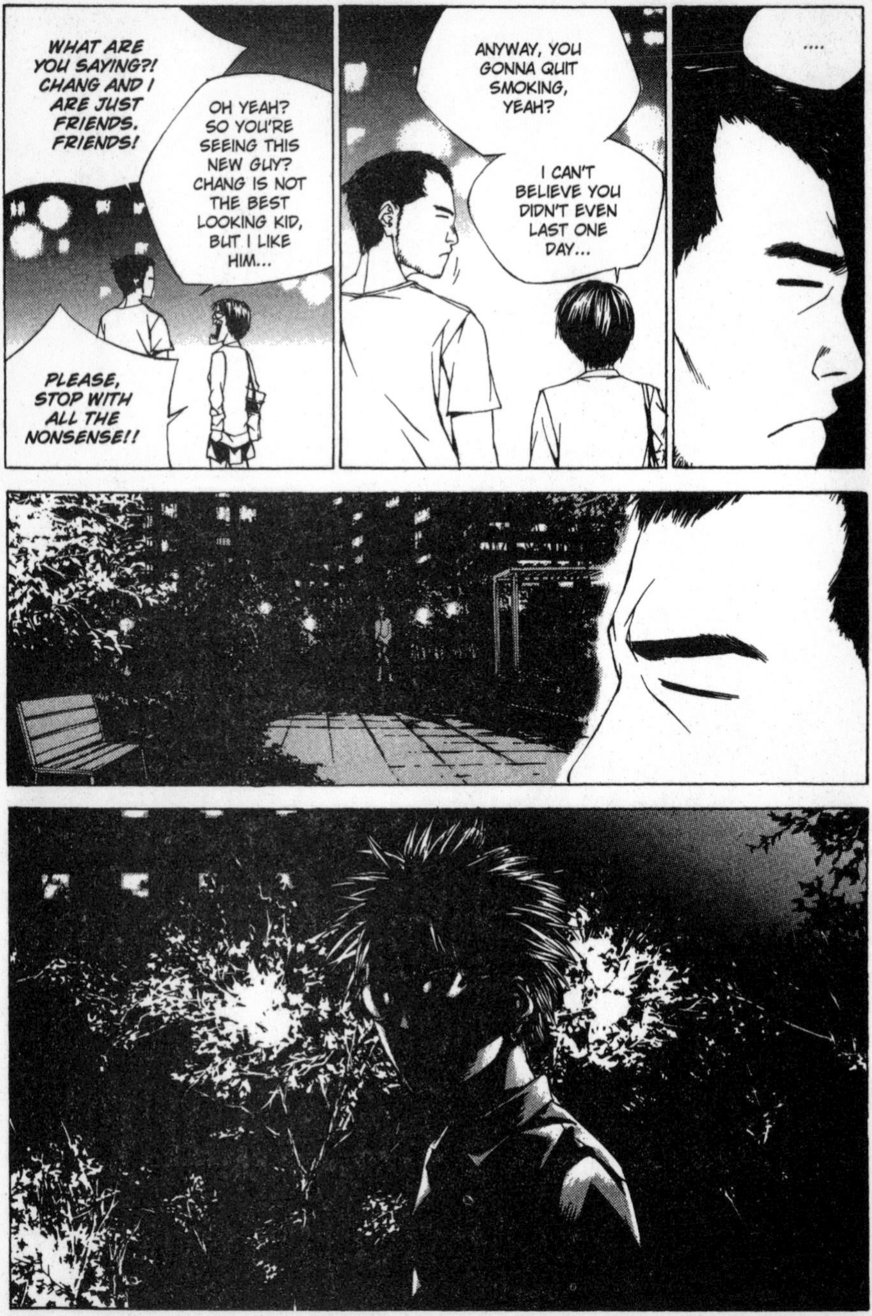
WHAT ARE YOU SAYING?! CHANG AND I ARE JUST FRIENDS. FRIENDS!
OH YEAH? SO YOU'RE SEEING THIS NEW GUY? CHANG IS NOT THE BEST LOOKING KID, BUT I LIKE HIM...
PLEASE, STOP WITH ALL THE NONSENSE!!
ANYWAY, YOU GONNA QUIT SMOKING, YEAH?
I CAN'T BELIEVE YOU DIDN'T EVEN LAST ONE DAY...
....

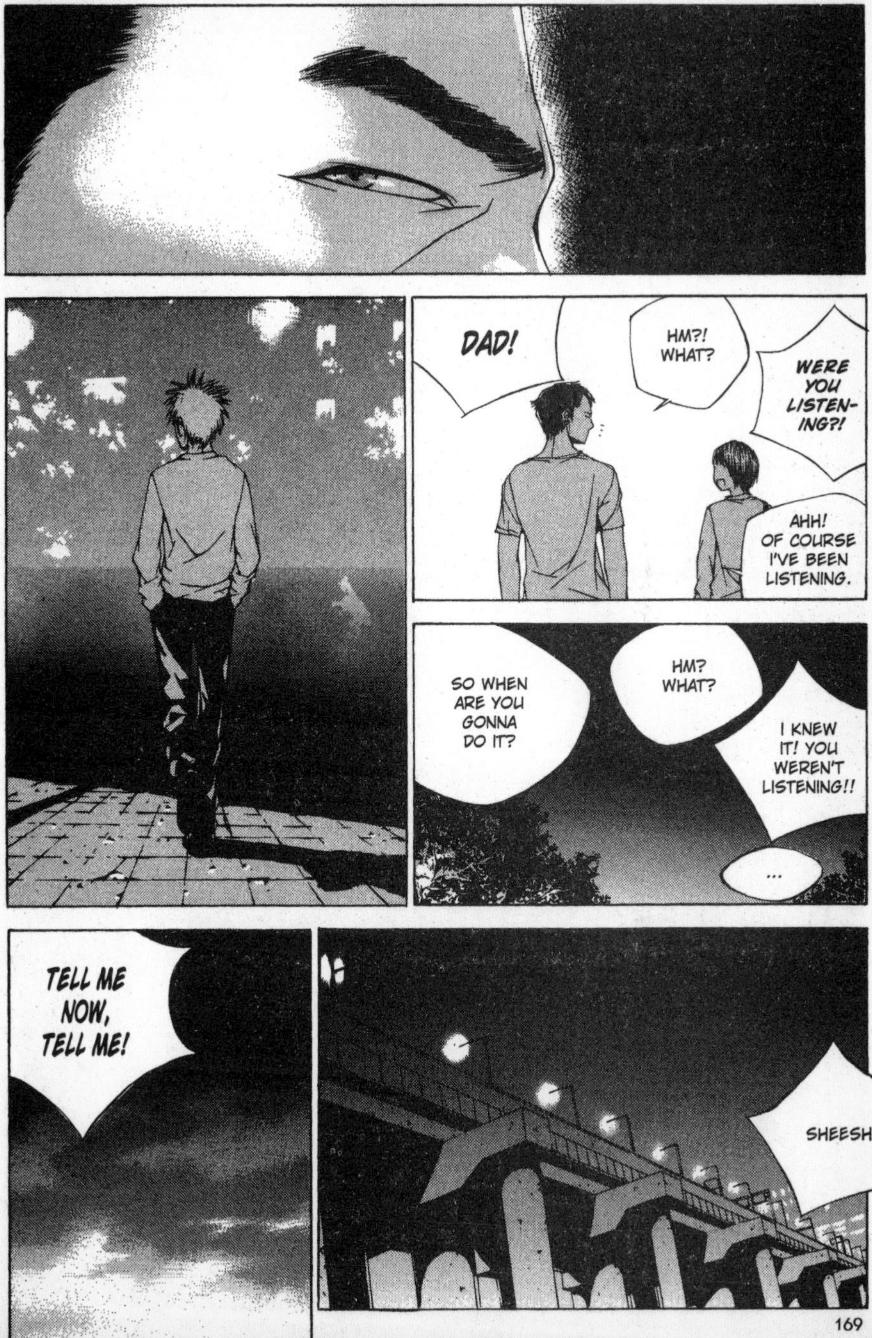
DAD!
HM?! WHAT?
WERE YOU LISTEN-ING?!
AHH! OF COURSE I'VE BEEN LISTENING.
SO WHEN ARE YOU GONNA DO IT?
HM? WHAT?
I KNEW IT! YOU WEREN'T LISTENING!!
...
TELL ME NOW, TELL ME!
SHEESH!

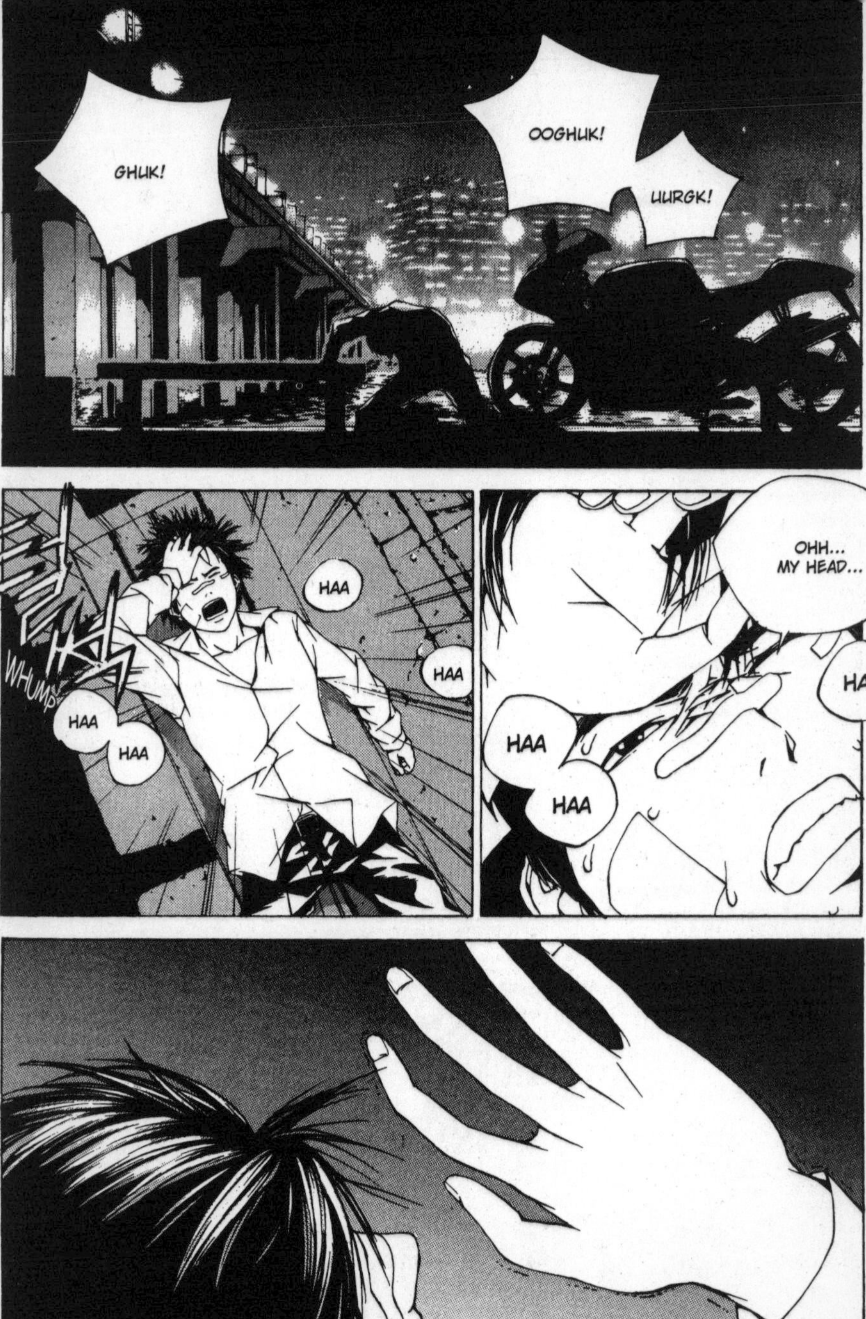
GHUK!
OOGHUK!
UURGK!
HAA
WHUMP
HAA
HAA
HAA
OHH... MY HEAD...
HAA
HAA
HAA

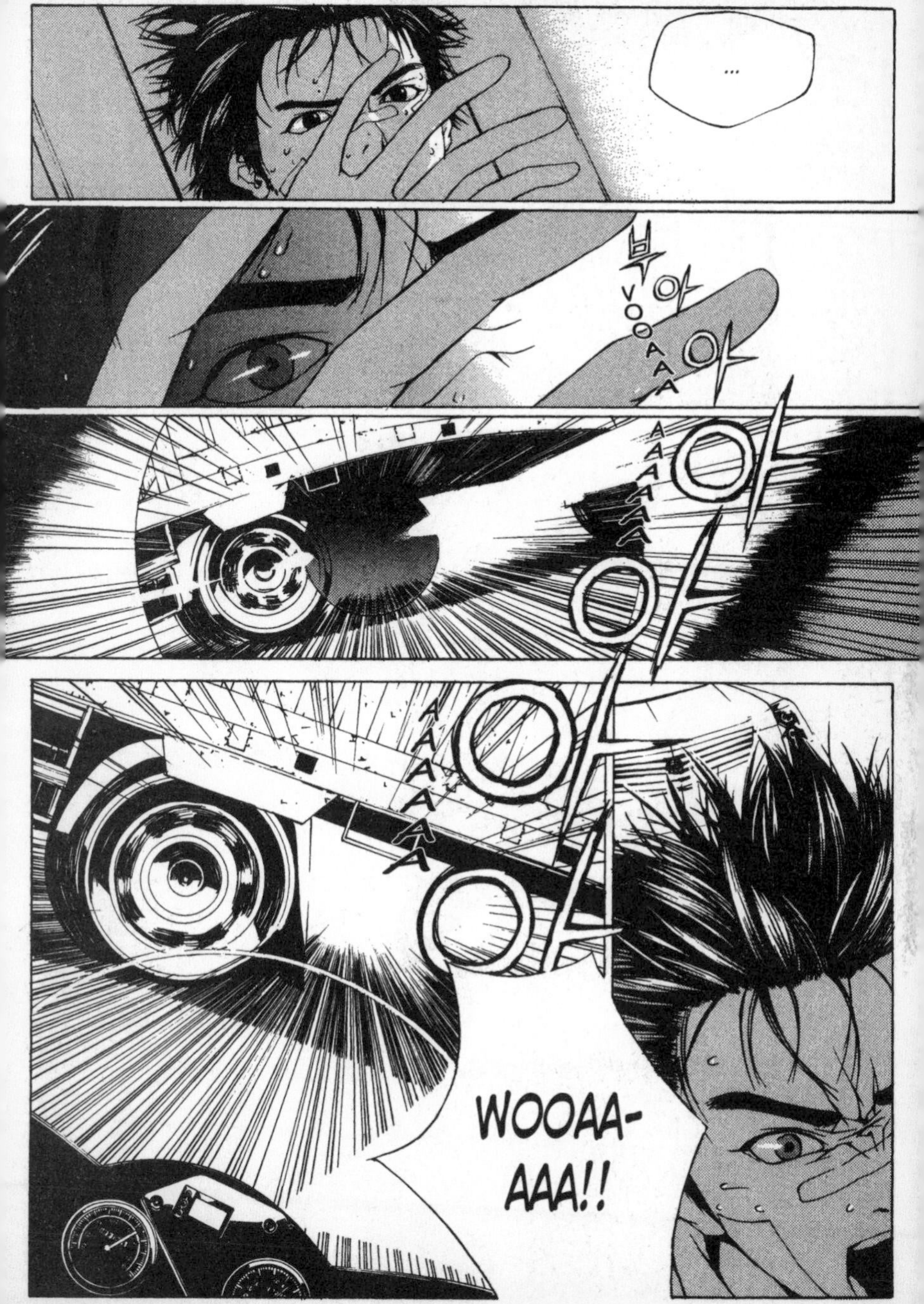
...
부아아
VOOAAA
아아
AAAAAAA
아아
AAAAAAAA
WOOAA-
AAA!!

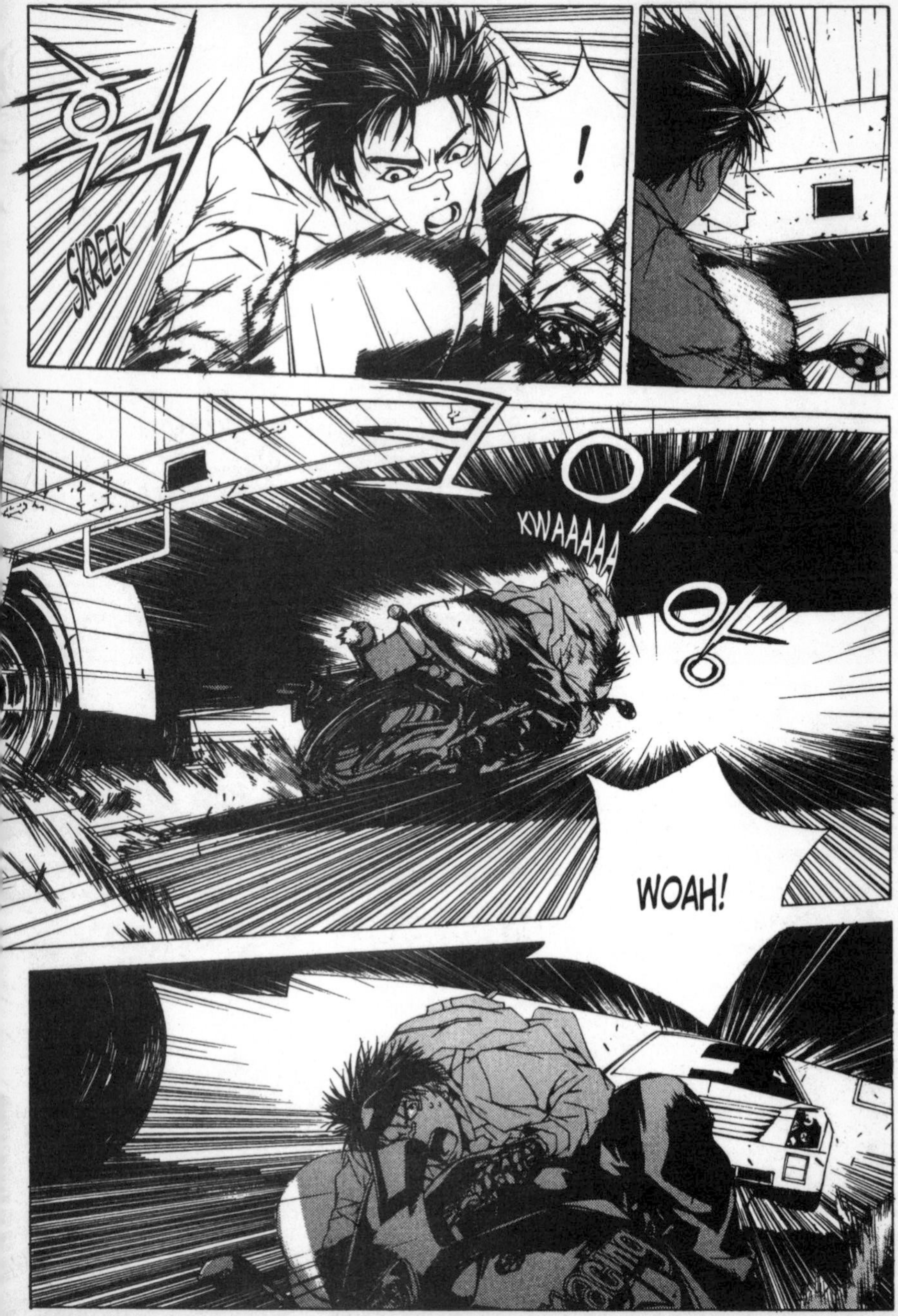
SKREEK
!
KWAAAAA
WOAH!

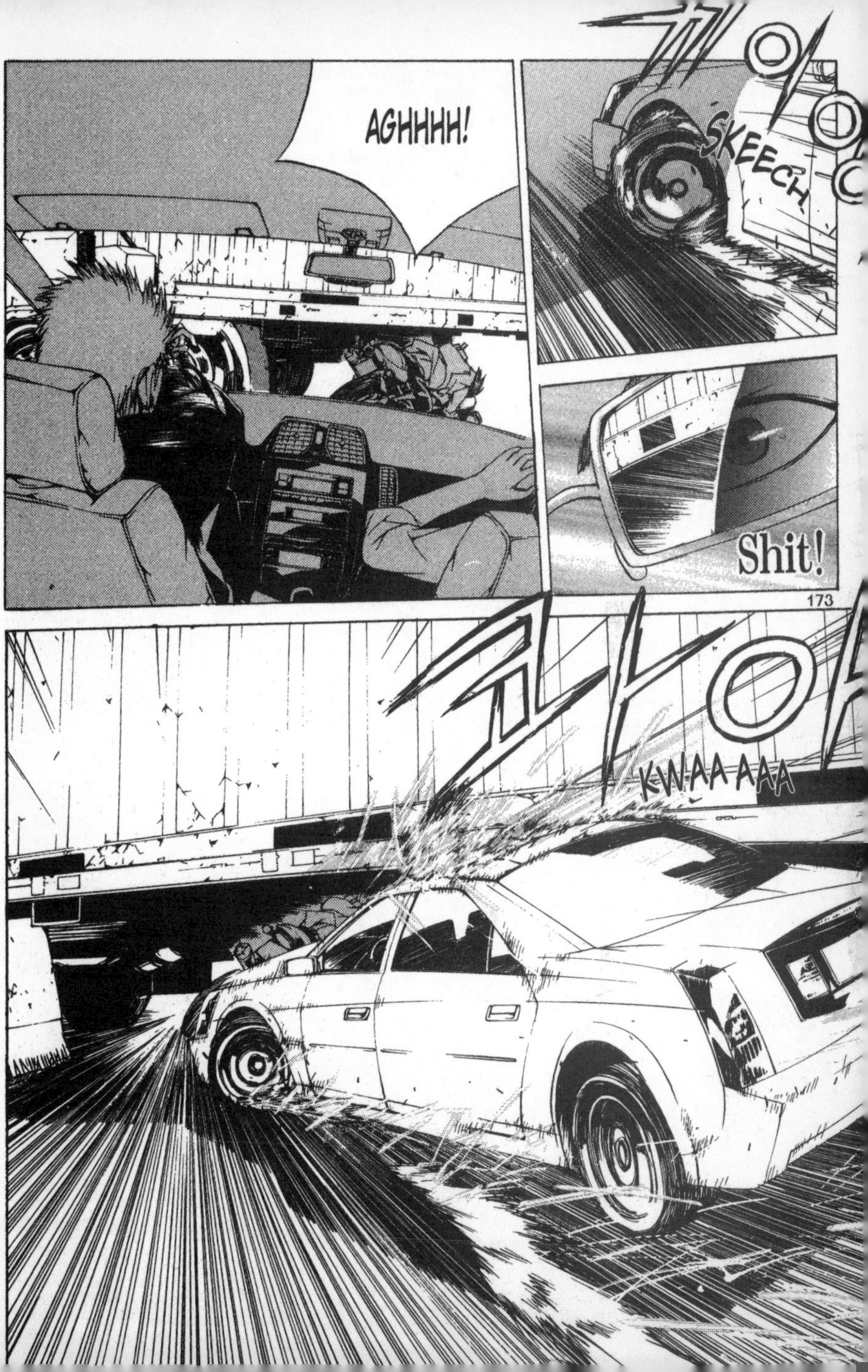
AGHHHH!
SKEECH
Shit!
KWAA AAA

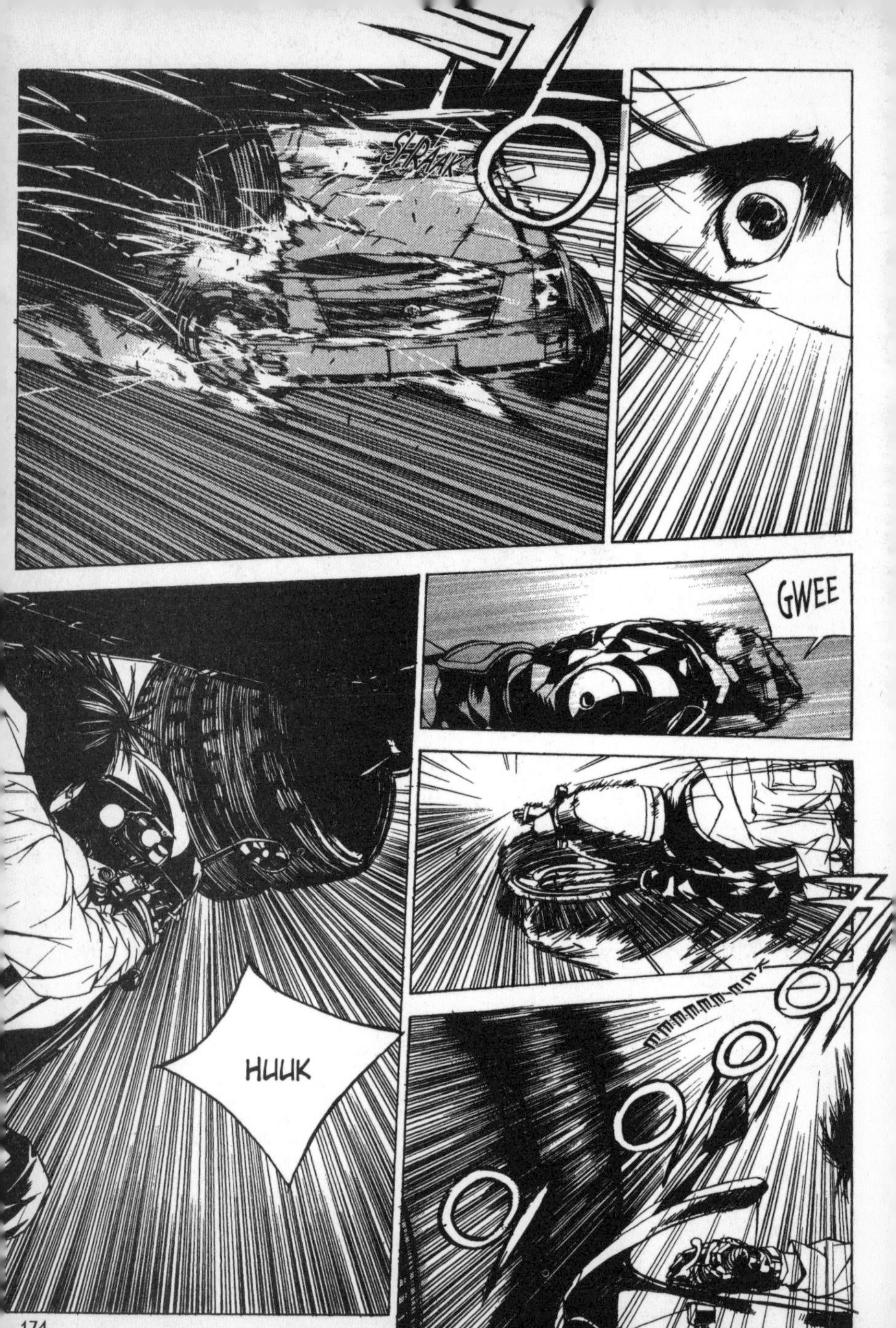
SHRAAK
GWEE
HUUK

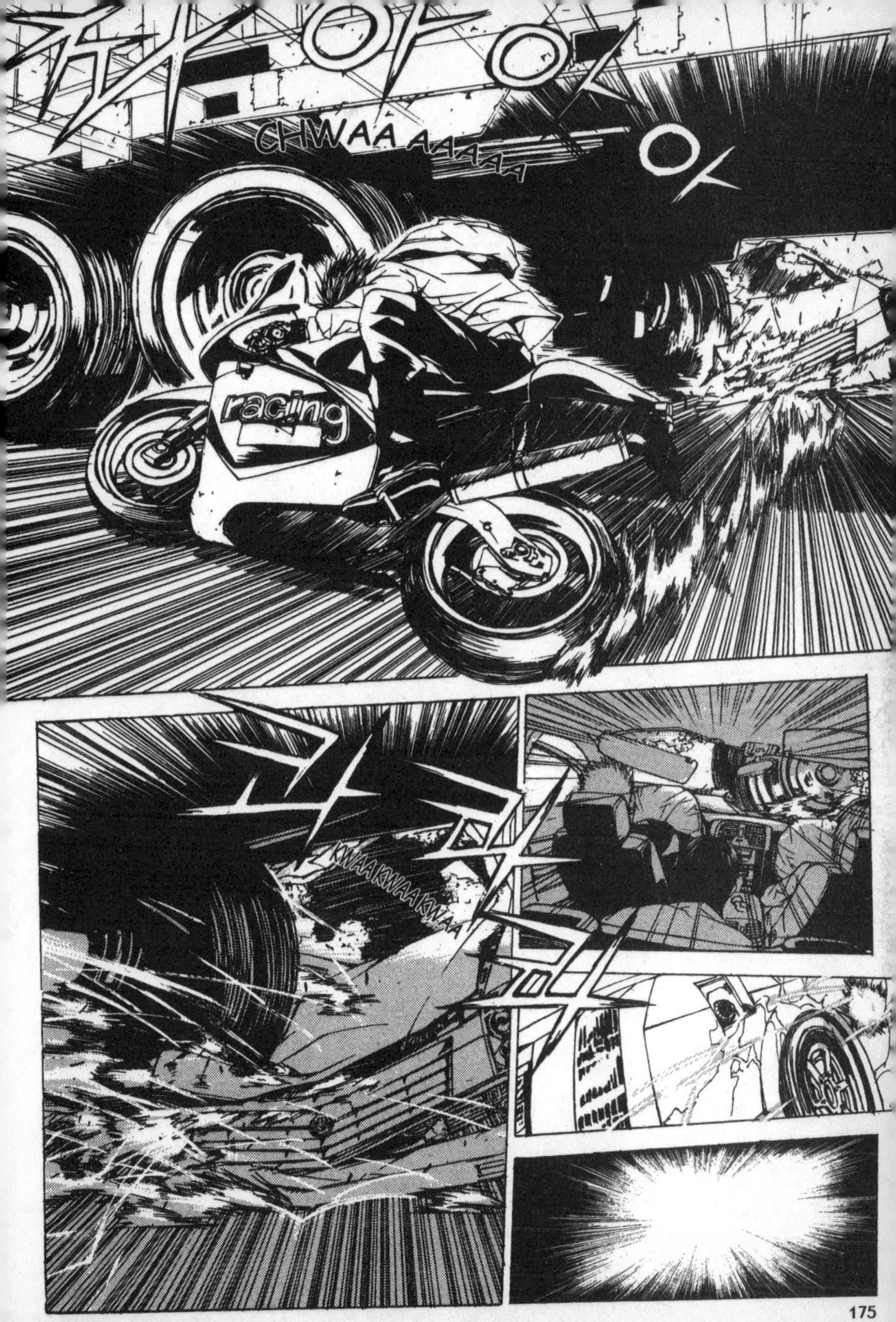
CHWAA AAAAAA
racing
KWAAKWAAKWAA

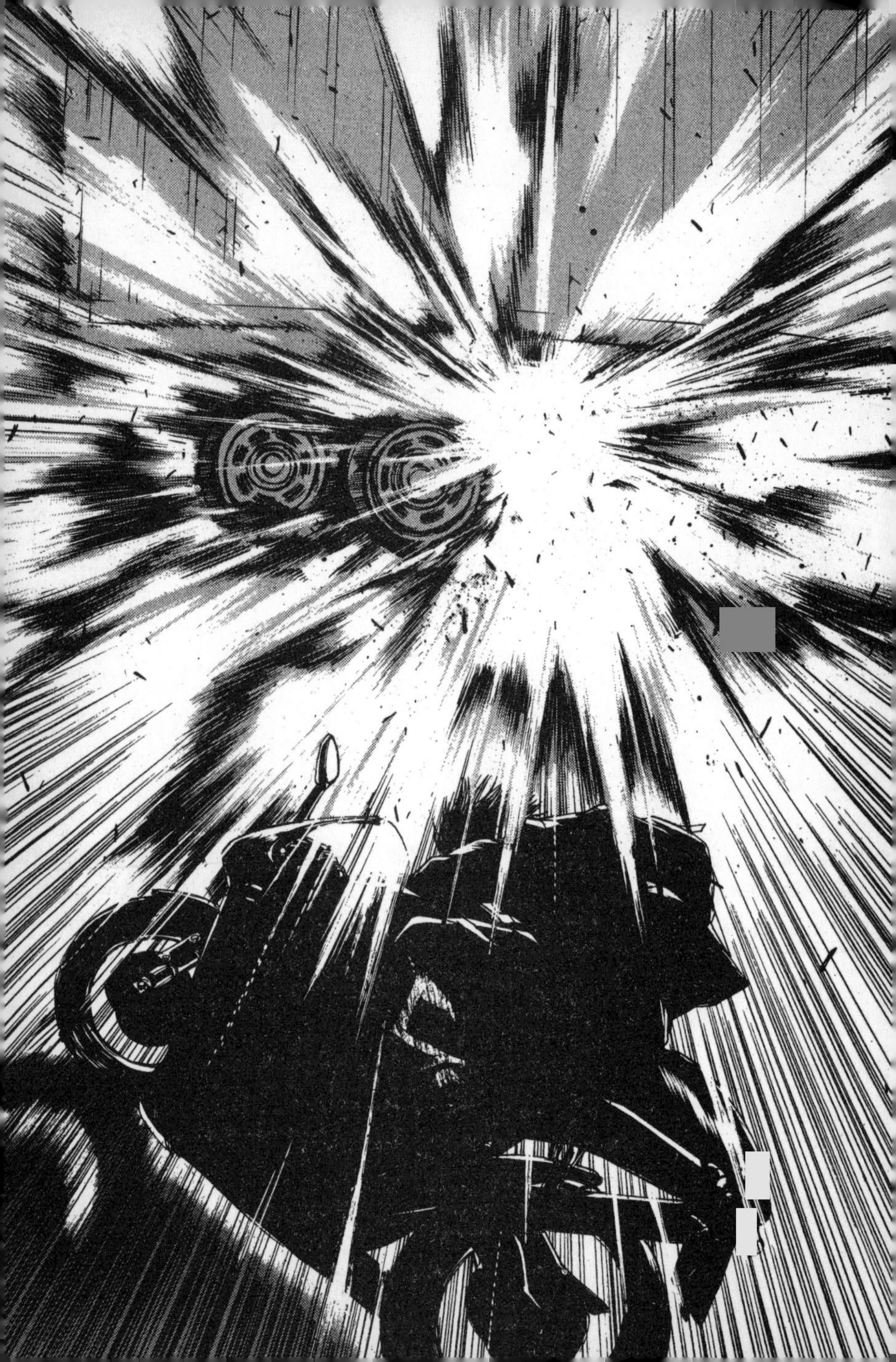

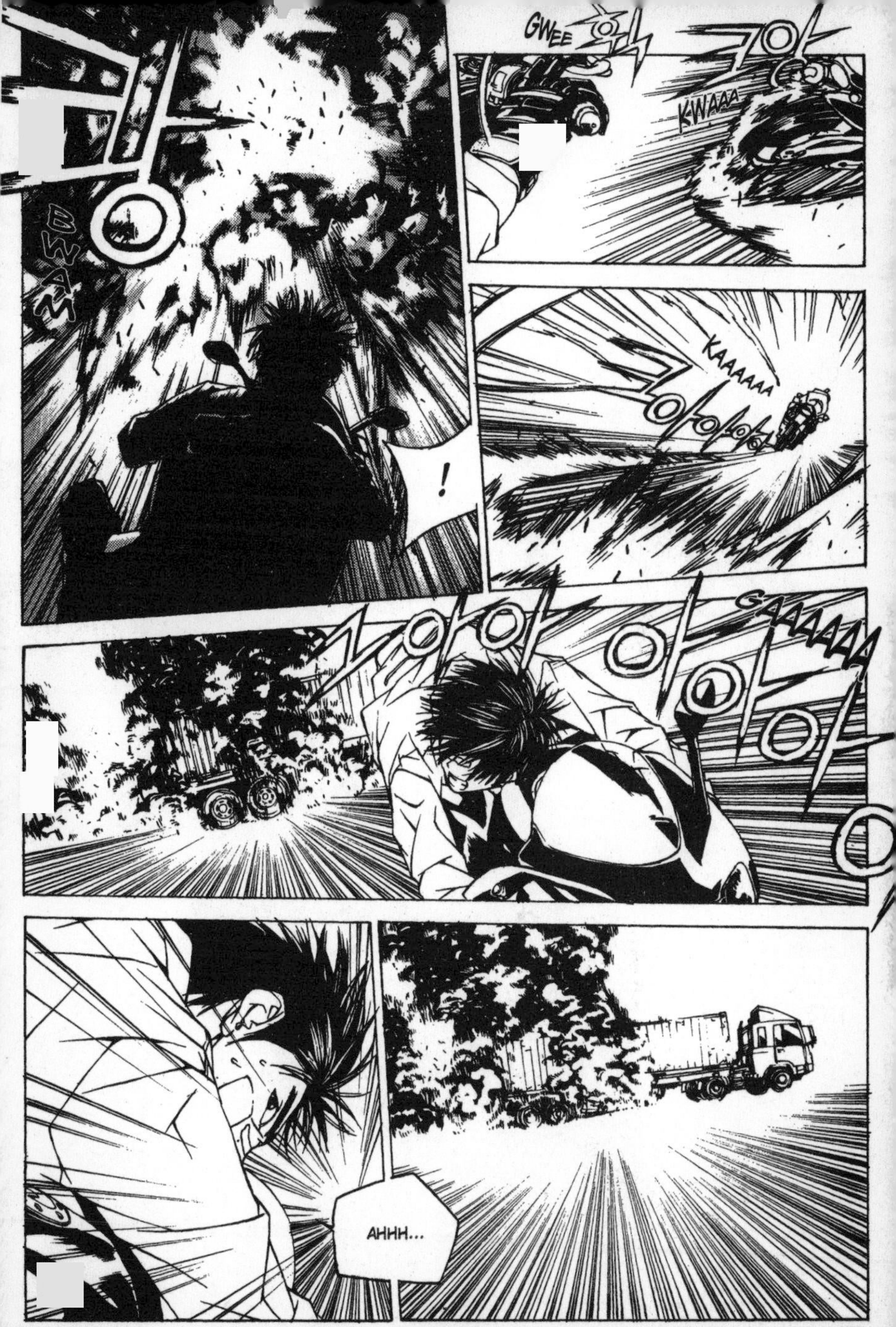
BWAM
!
GWEE
KWAAA
KAAAAAA
GAAAAAA
AHHH...

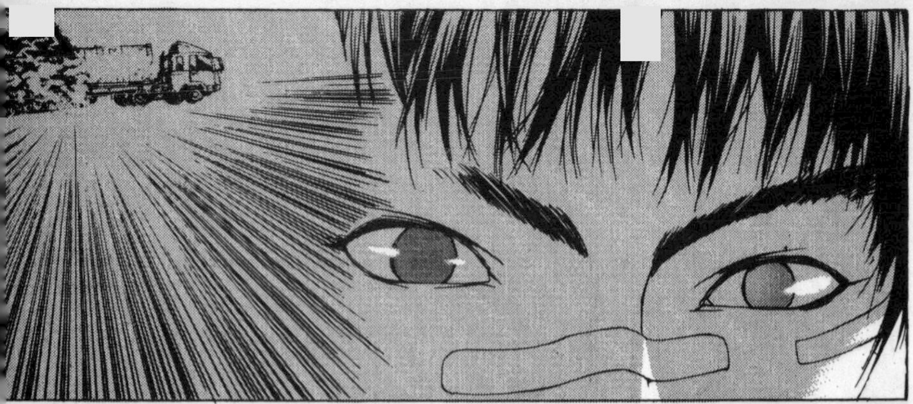

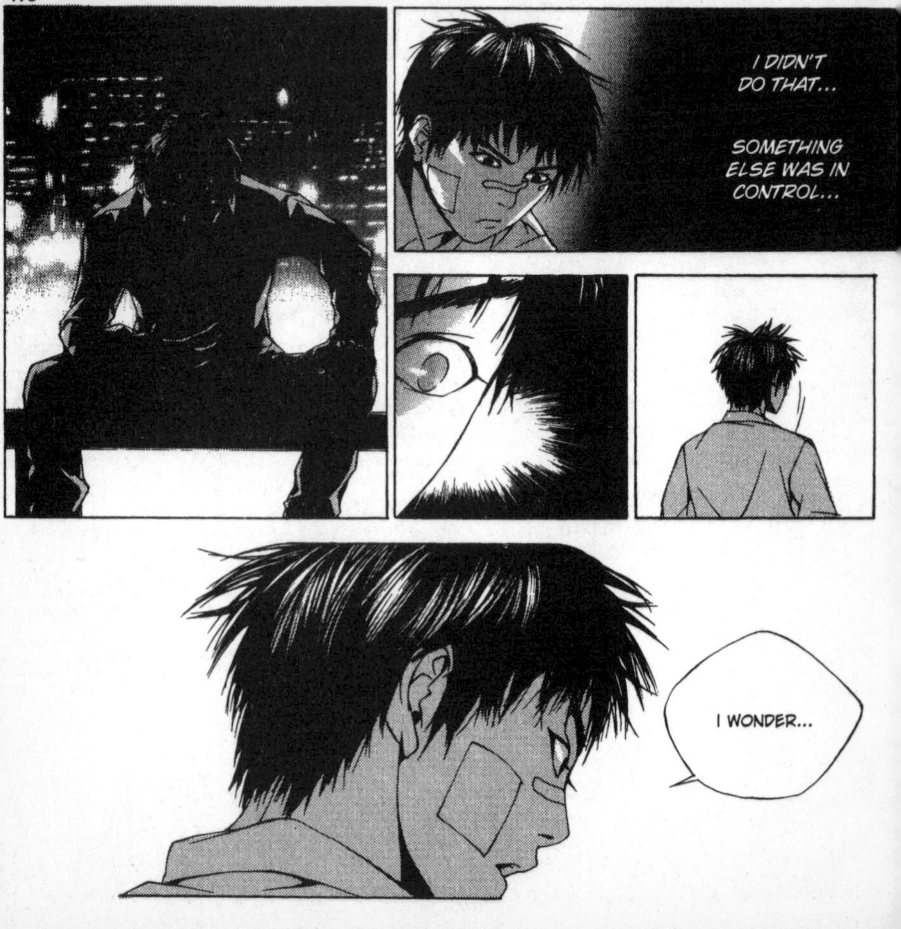
I DIDN'T DO THAT...
SOMETHING ELSE WAS IN CONTROL...
I WONDER...

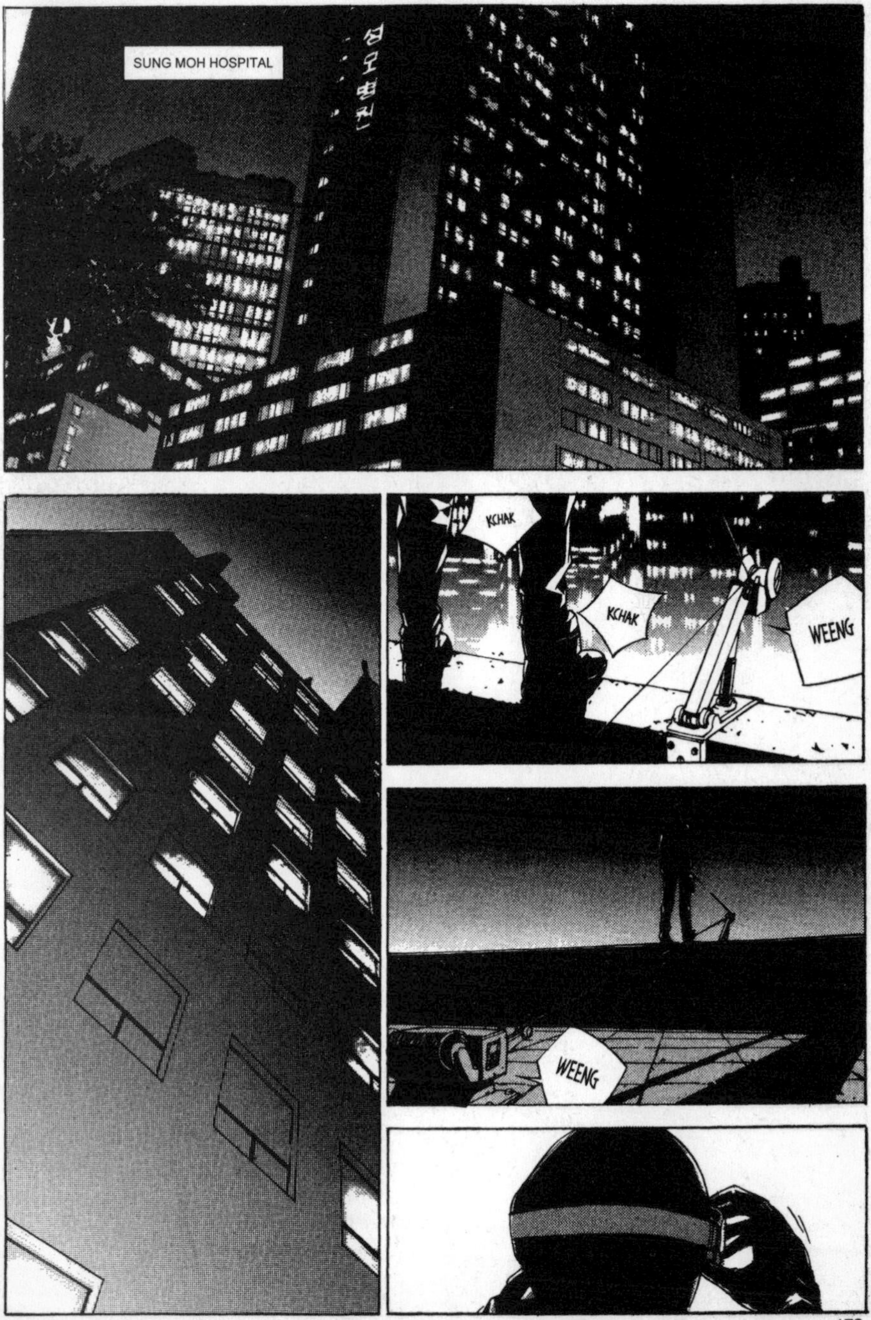
SUNG MOH HOSPITAL
KCHAK
KCHAK
WEENG
WEENG

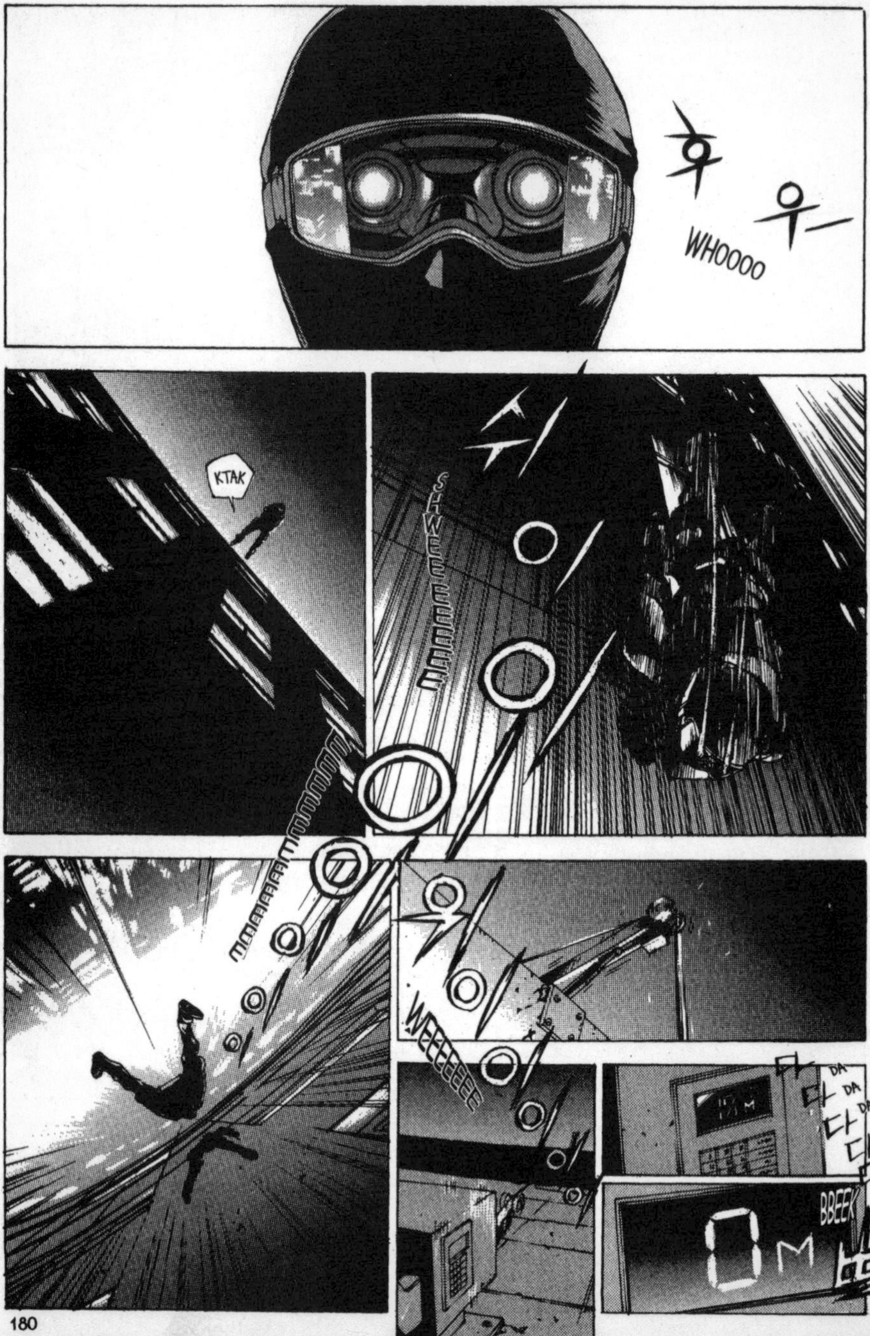
후우ー
WHOOOO
KTAK
SHWEEEEEEEE
WEEEEEEEE
DA
DA
DA
BBEEK

S-LURR
CHAAK

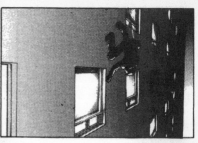

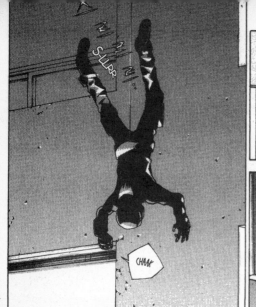

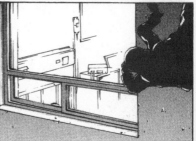

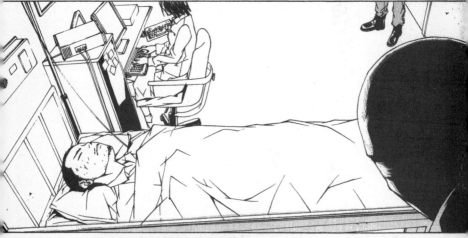

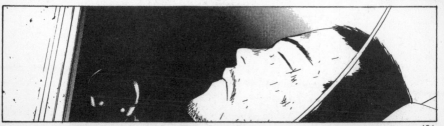

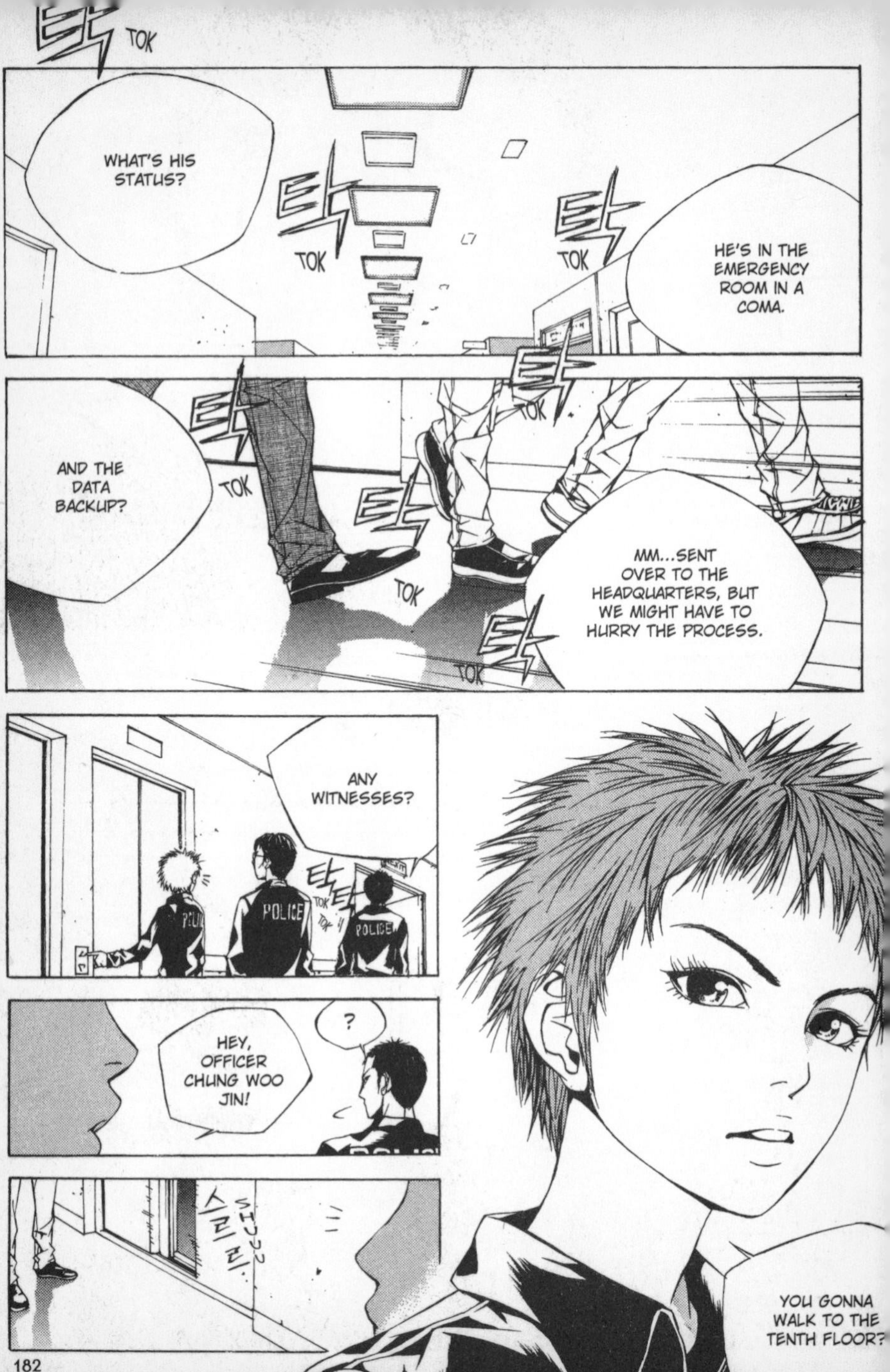
TOK
WHAT'S HIS STATUS?
TOK
TOK
HE'S IN THE EMERGENCY ROOM IN A COMA.
AND THE DATA BACKUP?
TOK
TOK
TOK
TOK
MM...SENT OVER TO THE HEADQUARTERS, BUT WE MIGHT HAVE TO HURRY THE PROCESS.
ANY WITNESSES?
POLICE
TOK
TOK
POLICE
?
HEY, OFFICER CHUNG WOO JIN!
SHUUU
YOU GONNA WALK TO THE TENTH FLOOR?

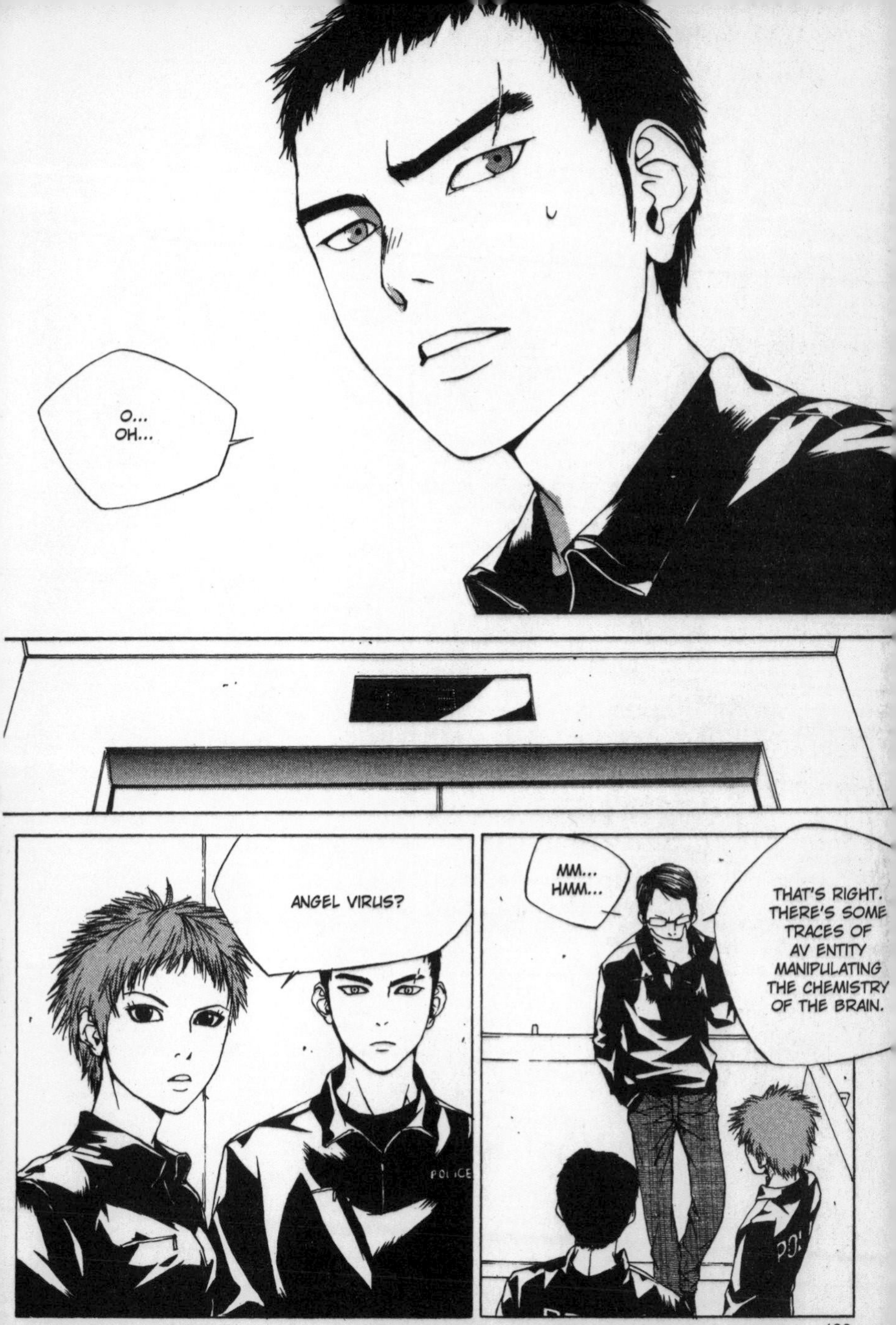
O... OH...
ANGEL VIRUS?
MM... HMM...
THAT'S RIGHT. THERE'S SOME TRACES OF AV ENTITY MANIPULATING THE CHEMISTRY OF THE BRAIN.

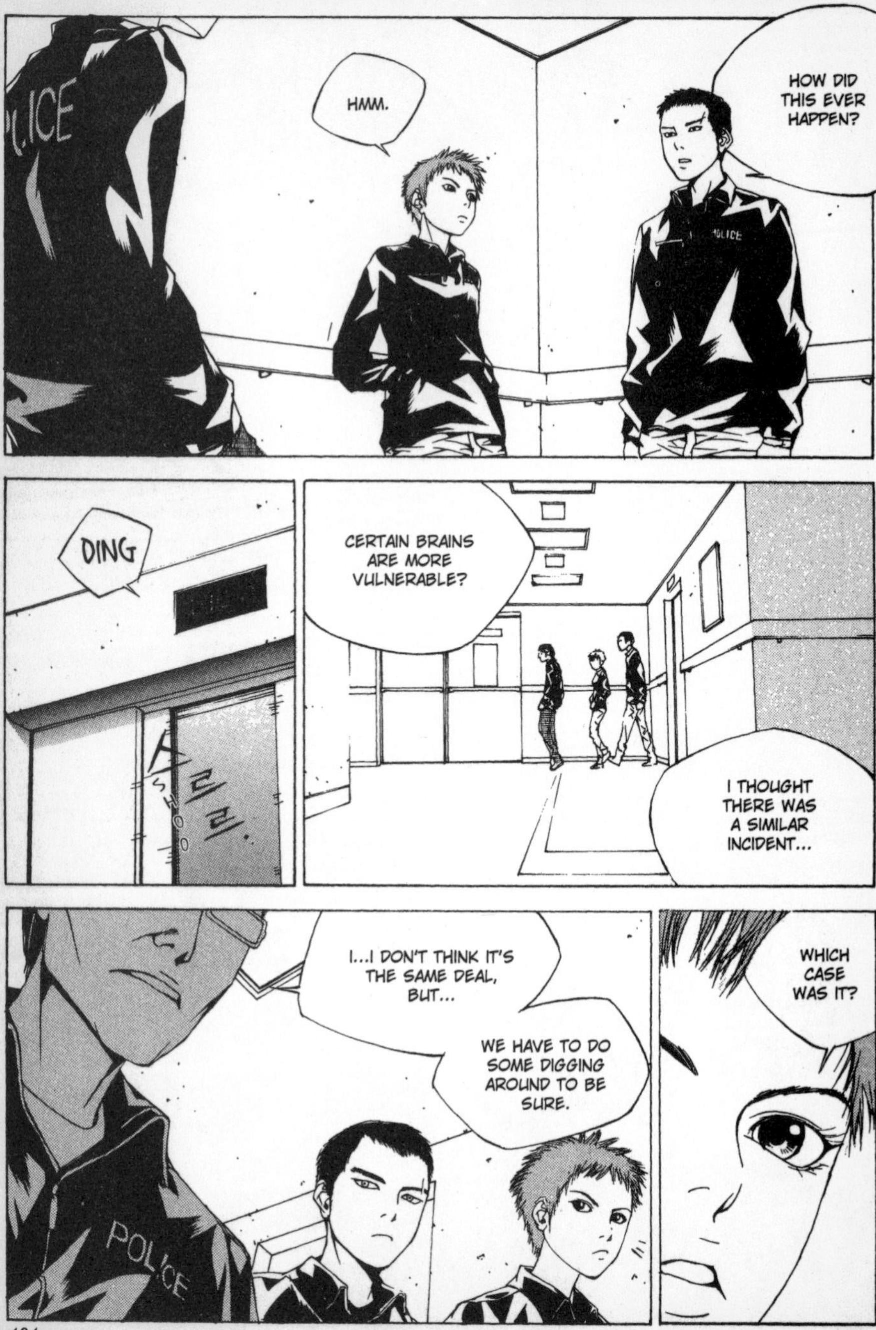
HMM.
HOW DID THIS EVER HAPPEN?
DING
SHOO
CERTAIN BRAINS ARE MORE VULNERABLE?
I THOUGHT THERE WAS A SIMILAR INCIDENT...
I...I DON'T THINK IT'S THE SAME DEAL, BUT...
WE HAVE TO DO SOME DIGGING AROUND TO BE SURE.
WHICH CASE WAS IT?

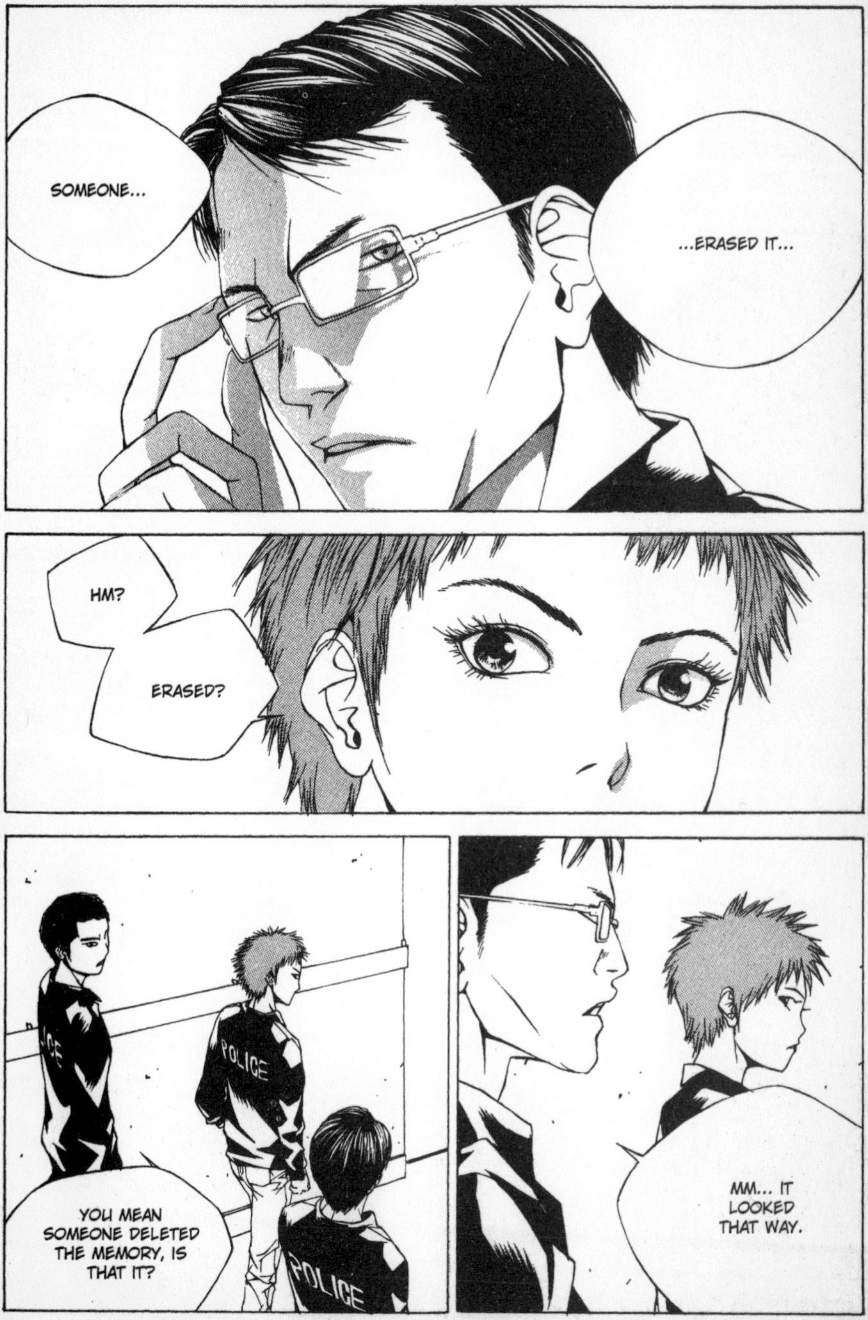
SOMEONE...
...ERASED IT...
HM?
ERASED?
POLICE
POLICE
YOU MEAN SOMEONE DELETED THE MEMORY, IS THAT IT?
MM... IT LOOKED THAT WAY.

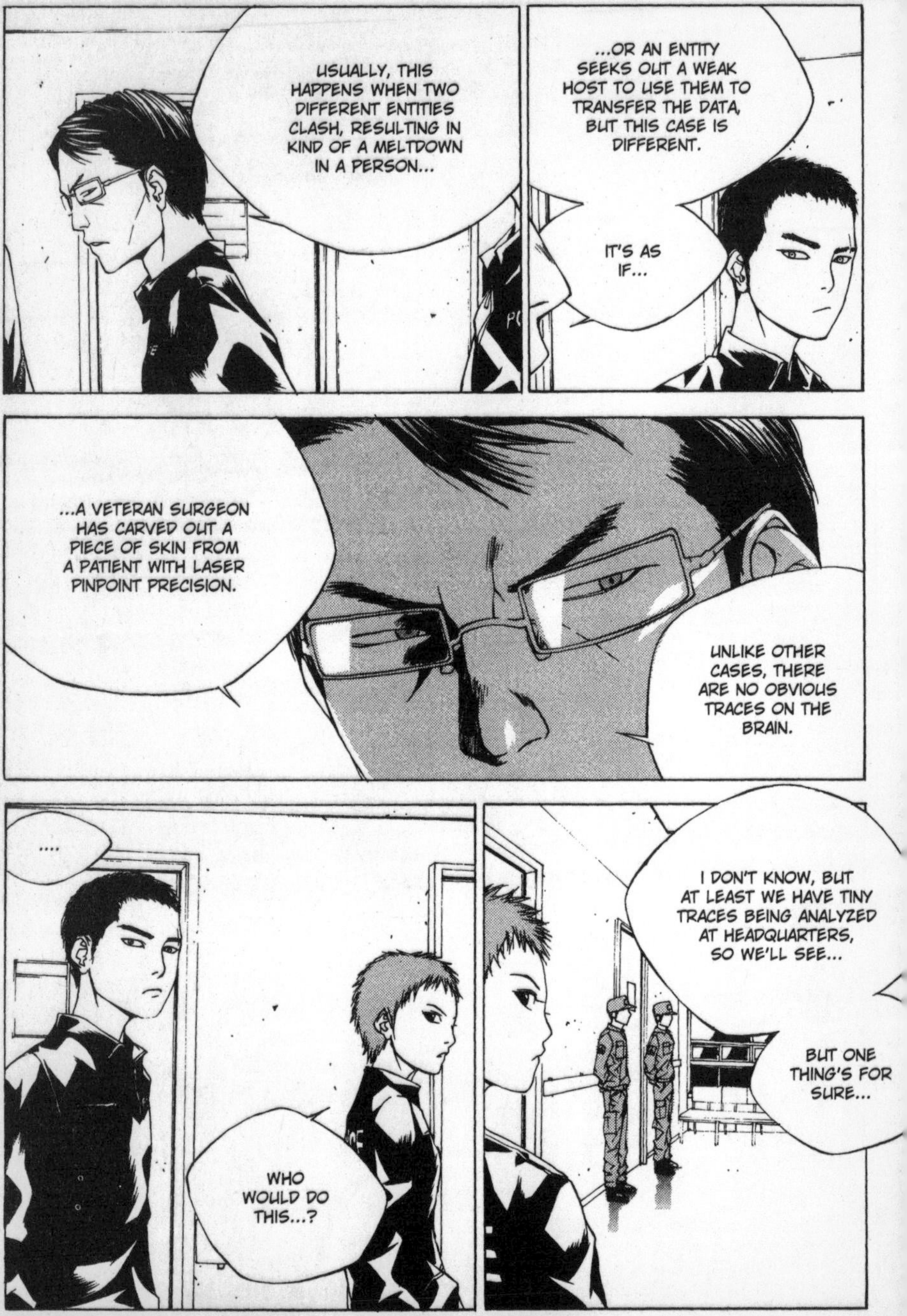
USUALLY, THIS HAPPENS WHEN TWO DIFFERENT ENTITIES CLASH, RESULTING IN KIND OF A MELTDOWN IN A PERSON...
...OR AN ENTITY SEEKS OUT A WEAK HOST TO USE THEM TO TRANSFER THE DATA, BUT THIS CASE IS DIFFERENT.
IT'S AS IF...
...A VETERAN SURGEON HAS CARVED OUT A PIECE OF SKIN FROM A PATIENT WITH LASER PINPOINT PRECISION.
UNLIKE OTHER CASES, THERE ARE NO OBVIOUS TRACES ON THE BRAIN.
....
WHO WOULD DO THIS...?
I DON'T KNOW, BUT AT LEAST WE HAVE TINY TRACES BEING ANALYZED AT HEADQUARTERS, SO WE'LL SEE...
BUT ONE THING'S FOR SURE...

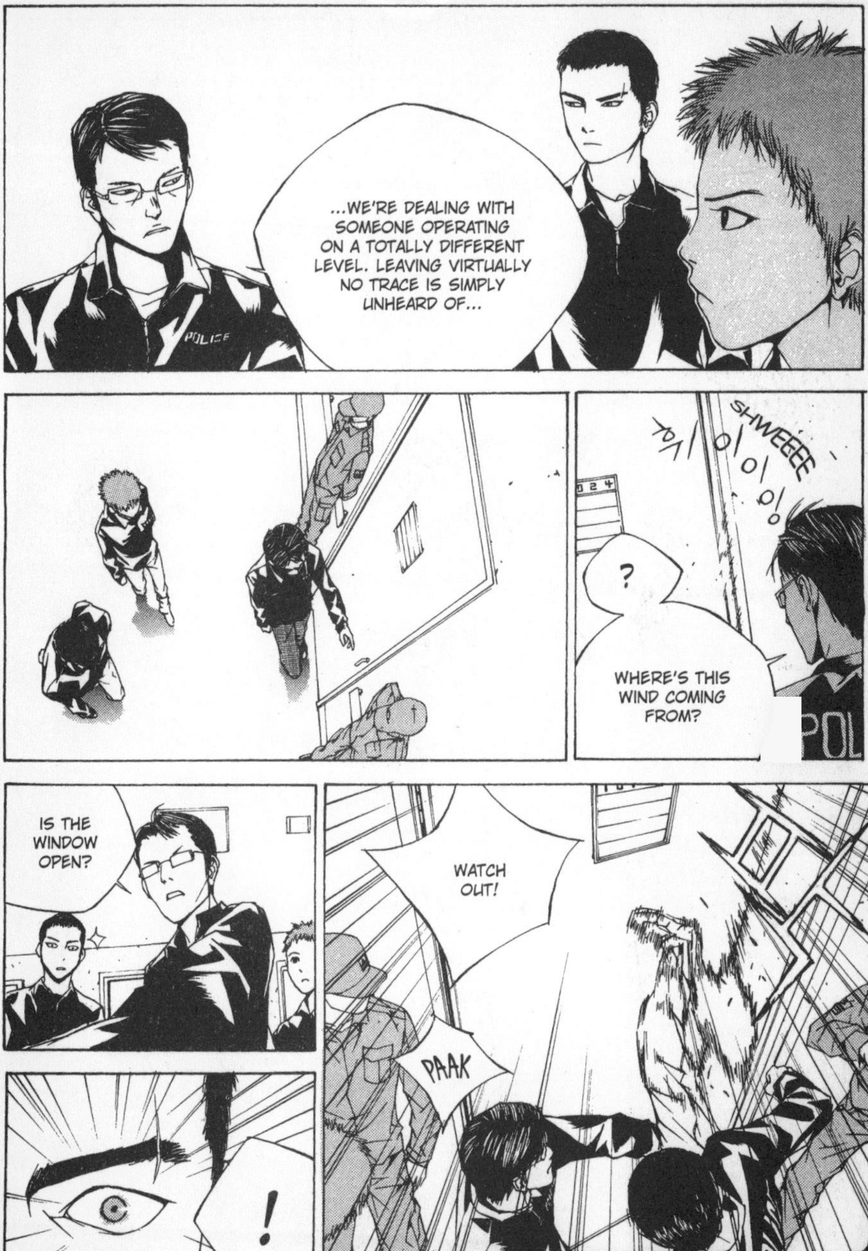
...WE'RE DEALING WITH SOMEONE OPERATING ON A TOTALLY DIFFERENT LEVEL. LEAVING VIRTUALLY NO TRACE IS SIMPLY UNHEARD OF...
가시이이잉
SHWEEEEE
?
WHERE'S THIS WIND COMING FROM?
IS THE WINDOW OPEN?
!
WATCH OUT!
PAAK

SHIT!

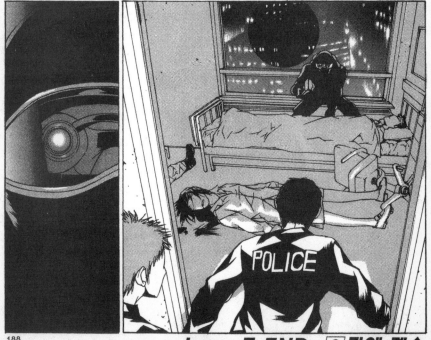

POLICE

Loa-7 END_ 2 권에 계속

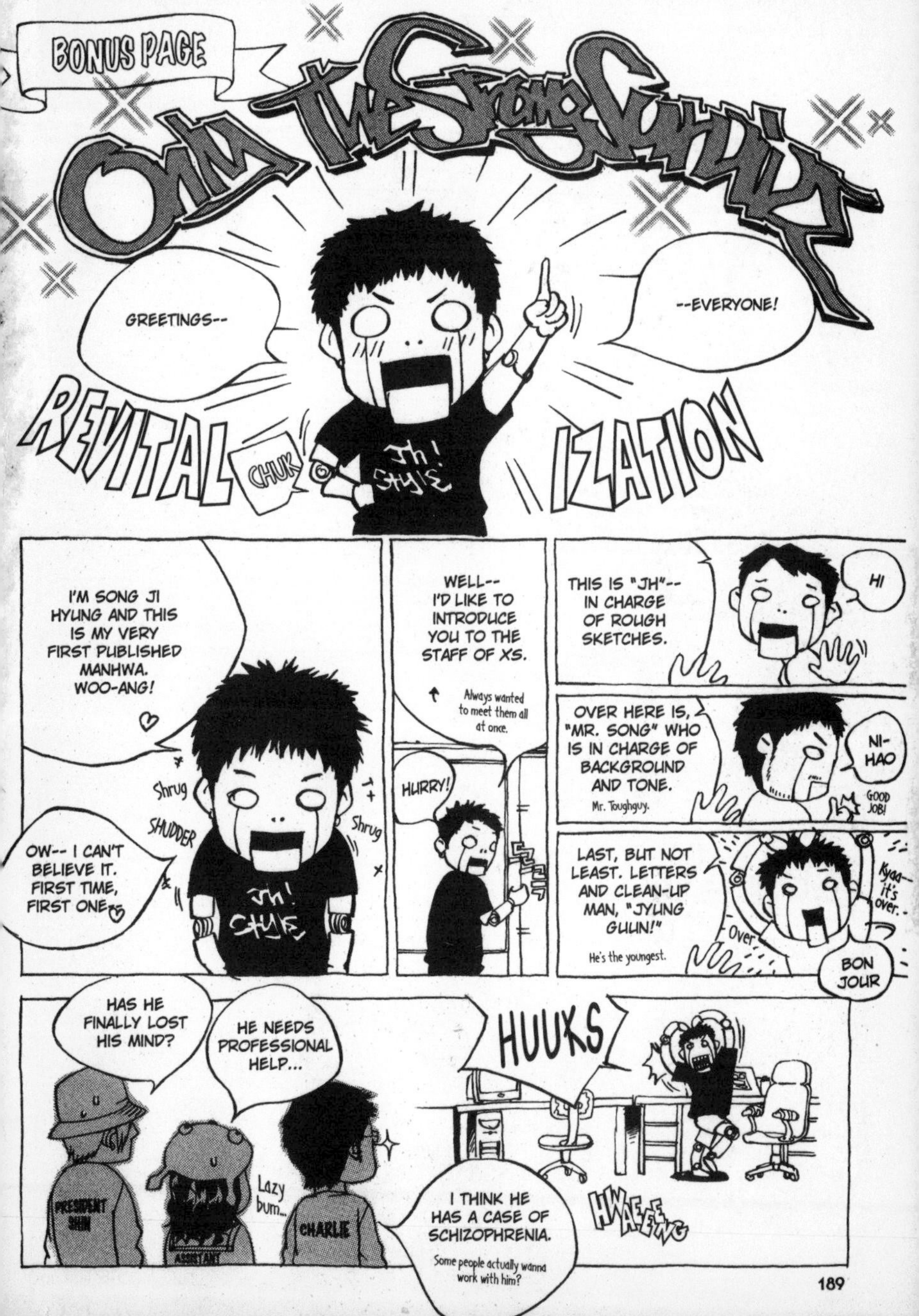

BONUS PAGE
Only the Strong Survive
GREETINGS--
--EVERYONE!
REVITAL
CHUK
IZATION
I'M SONG JI HYUNG AND THIS IS MY VERY FIRST PUBLISHED MANHWA. WOO-ANG!
Shrug
SHUDDER
Shrug
OW-- I CAN'T BELIEVE IT. FIRST TIME, FIRST ONE
WELL-- I'D LIKE TO INTRODUCE YOU TO THE STAFF OF XS.
Always wanted to meet them all at once.
HURRY!
THIS IS "JH"-- IN CHARGE OF ROUGH SKETCHES.
HI
OVER HERE IS, "MR. SONG" WHO IS IN CHARGE OF BACKGROUND AND TONE.
Mr. Toughguy.
NI-HAO
GOOD JOB!
LAST, BUT NOT LEAST. LETTERS AND CLEAN-UP MAN, "JYUNG GUUN!"
He's the youngest.
Over
Kyaa-it's over.
BON JOUR
HAS HE FINALLY LOST HIS MIND?
HE NEEDS PROFESSIONAL HELP...
HUUKS
PRESIDENT SHIN
Lazy bum...
CHARLIE
I THINK HE HAS A CASE OF SCHIZOPHRENIA.
Some people actually wanna work with him?
HWAEENG

RIGHT. AND MR. KIM SEUNG HWAN IS REVIEWING THE STORY, AS YOU CAN SEE.

QUIVER

GRRR.

COUGH COUGHS

VIVA VACUUM

I WAS ALWAYS THANKFUL TO HIM. IN MY MIND...

SO, NOW YOU KNOW OUR TEAM MEMBERS' EVERLASTING DEVOTION TO THE PROJECT...

...AND WITH THAT I CONCLUDE THE INTRODUCTION.

ACK!

WH-- HEY.

VIVA VACUUM
http://www.thevacuum.org

WH-- AT?

THAT'S IT?

PA P

THE TITLE XS CAME FROM ONE OF MY FAVORITE SONGS XS DENIED BY UMC. IT WAS AN ATTEMPT TO MAKE IT SOUND LIKE "ACCESS."

THE PROTAGONIST'S NAME HU-IN CHANG IS ALSO A NAME OF AN EMCEE. BUT XS IS NOT ACCESS.

You know what I'm saying--?

I LV HIP HOP

THE REASON I DIDN'T WANT TO CALL IT "ACCESS" WAS BECAUSE I DIDN'T WANT IT TO SOUND LIKE IT'S JUST ONE THING. IT ALSO HAS ELEMENT OF "EXTREME" IN IT.

ROLL!
QUIVER
QUIVER

I DON'T KNOW HOW YOU READ IT, BUT A LITTLE BIT OF CYBER PUNK, X-FILES EPISODIC TONE, AND SOME EXTREME SPORTS THEME WAS KIND OF MY INTENTION FOR THIS MANHWA.

GYAA!

WHBAM

He love skating, i an't ri at all

FINALLY, I ADDED THE DEFINITIONS OF INITIALS AND WORDS FROM THE STORY. HOPEFULLY, THIS WILL CLEAR UP SOME OF YOUR QUESTIONS.

It's no fun if you know it all.

NEXT PAGE...

XS VOLUME 1--DEFINITIONS

Hybrid: Sub-species. Originally a human, but has been invaded by a foreign entity that uses the body as a host and eventually takes it over.

SET (Special Espionage Team): An American unit that specializes in information technology and analysis of hybrid's movement.

Zombi: SET's strike-force unit.

Thoth: Code name derived from ancient Egypt's mythical god of knowledge. SET's supercomputer.

NSA (National Security Agency): Legendary department of American security system. They use the biggest and most comprehensive system that can monitor every phone call, e-mail, faxes, or other communication system anywhere in the world.

Kali: Originated from Hindu religion, a goddess of mortality.

Angel Virus: a computer virus that can transfer vast amounts of information and is currently not deletable by today's technology. Sub-virus of Queen Virus.

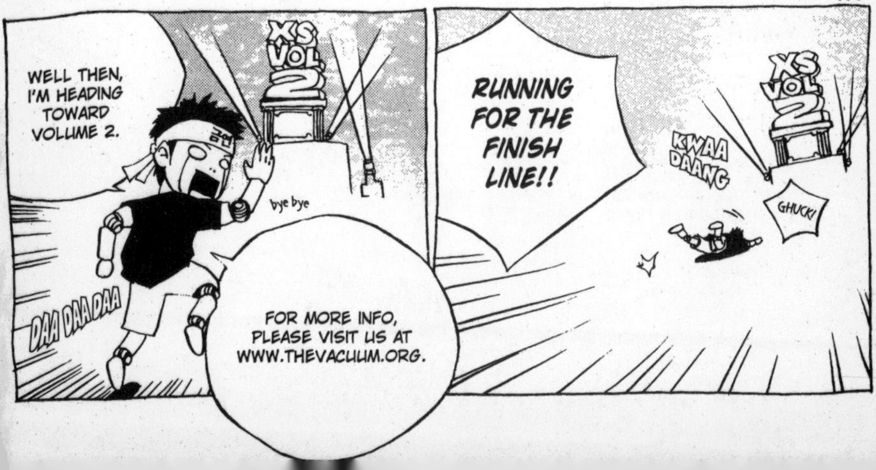
WELL THEN, I'M HEADING TOWARD VOLUME 2.
XS VOL 2
bye bye
DAA DAA DAA
FOR MORE INFO, PLEASE VISIT US AT WWW.THEVACUUM.ORG.
RUNNING FOR THE FINISH LINE!!
XS VOL 2
KWAA DAANG
GHUCK!

publisher
MIKE RICHARDSON

editor
TIM ERVIN

book design
TONY ONG

art director
LIA RIBACCHI

English-language version produced by DARK HORSE COMICS.

XS Hybrid vol. 1

Dark Horse Manhwa
A division of Dark Horse Comics, Inc.
10956 SE Main Street
Milwaukie, OR 97222

darkhorse.com

First edition: June 2007
ISBN-10: 1-59307-628-2
ISBN-13: 978-1-59307-628-3

10 9 8 7 6 5 4 3 2 1
Printed in Canada

To find a comics shop in your area, call the Comic Shop Locator Service
toll-free at 1-888-266-4226.